Color-Blind Justice

Albion W. Tourgée, ca. 1882. Courtesy of the Chautauqua County Historical Society, Westfield, NY.

Color-Blind Justice

Albion Tourgée and the Quest for Racial Equality
from the Civil War to *Plessy v. Ferguson*

MARK ELLIOTT

OXFORD
UNIVERSITY PRESS
2006

OXFORD
UNIVERSITY PRESS

Oxford University Press, Inc., publishes works that further
Oxford University's objective of excellence
in research, scholarship, and education.

Oxford   New York
Auckland   Cape Town   Dar es Salaam   Hong Kong   Karachi
Kuala Lumpur   Madrid   Melbourne   Mexico City   Nairobi
New Delhi   Shanghai   Taipei   Toronto

With offices in
Argentina   Austria   Brazil   Chile   Czech Republic   France   Greece
Guatemala   Hungary   Italy   Japan   Poland   Portugal   Singapore
South Korea   Switzerland   Thailand   Turkey   Ukraine   Vietnam

Copyright © 2006 by Mark Elliott

Published by Oxford University Press, Inc.
198 Madison Avenue, New York, NY 10016
www.oup.com

Oxford is a registered trademark of Oxford University Press

Library of Congress Cataloging-in-Publication Data
Elliott, Mark, 1969–
Color-blind justice : Albion Tourgée and the quest for racial equality :
from the Civil War to Plessy v. Ferguson / Mark Elliott.
p. cm.   Includes bibliographical references and index.
ISBN-13: 978-0-19-518139-5
ISBN-10: 0-19-518139-5
1. Tourgée, Albion Winegar, 1838–1905.
2. African Americans—Civil rights—History—19th century.
3. United States—Race relations—History.
4. Abolitionists—United States—History.
5. Reconstruction (U.S. history, 1865–1877)
I. Title.
PS3088.E55 2006
813'.4—dc22   [B]   2006011311

1 3 5 7 9 8 6 4 2
Printed in the United States of America
on acid-free paper

For Kimberly, Zachary, and Nicholas

Contents

Note on Usage

In 1882, after he became a nationally recognized novelist, Albion Tourgée added an accent mark over the first *e* in his last name to assist the public in its correct pronunciation (he preferred Toor-zhay). For the sake of consistency, I have applied the accent mark to his name throughout the text in discussing the events of his life both before and after 1882. I have retained the original spelling, however, as it appears in quotations from others.

Color-Blind Justice

Introduction:
Albion Tourgée and Color-Blind Citizenship

The Negro finds a friend indeed in the person of the gallant and noble hero Albion W. Tourgée . . . he has sacrificed himself for the Negro's rights as a loyal citizen. The general mass of the white papers denounce him as a crank, fool, lunatic, and etc. But, however, he bears the burden that is heaped on him by his own race and continues to speak for a race that has been oppressed and is yet oppressed. Surely indeed the heart that beats within him is of the purest and loftiest kind.

—*Indianapolis World*, January 30, 1893

Civilization will not permit the permanent subjugation of a race. . . . The wrong is moral, legal, and political. The colored man is wronged as a man, having a right to equal liberty with other men. He is wronged as a laborer, being deprived of free opportunity. He is wronged as a citizen, being stripped of lawful political power and civil privilege. He is wronged as a Christian, being denied by his white brethren the just and equal application of the Golden Rule.

—Albion W. Tourgée, *Is Liberty Worth Preserving?* 1892

I N HIS 1879 AUTOBIOGRAPHICAL NOVEL, *A Fool's Errand. By One of the Fools*, Albion Tourgée cast himself as the "Fool." Set in the Reconstruction South, *A Fool's Errand* was based upon the Northerner Tourgée's own fifteen-year struggle to revolutionize race and class relations as a carpetbagger in the war-torn state of North Carolina. A fool in the Shakespearean mold, Tourgée's fictional alter ego perceived reality better than the congressional "Wise Men" in Washington, and his warnings of the catastrophic moral and social ills that would result if they abandoned the project of Reconstruction too soon went unheeded. The popularity of this best-selling novel during 1879 and 1880 suggests that a reservoir of sympathy still existed in the North for the higher aims of Reconstruction and for idealists like the Fool who fought bravely for equal citizenship in the South until thwarted by the white conservative campaign of terrorism, lies, and propaganda. Tourgée had argued that the only safe policy for the nation would be to protect citizens' rights with federal power and to promote equal opportunity with massive federal aid to education that especially targeted the former slaves—that would prevent future civil wars and social strife.[1]

Yet, only a little more than a decade later, Tourgée found himself again in the role of the Fool. This time the storm of abuse and scorn came not only from his conservative Southern foes, but from his former supporters in the North as well. Tourgée's error was that he had remained an outspoken proponent of the "color-blind" ideal—that all Americans must enjoy equality in the law, regardless of race or color. His support of this proposition may sound hardly radical today, but in the 1890s it made him a troublemaker. At a time when the nation had begun to put the bitter political conflicts of the Civil War era behind it, he seemed determined to revive them. Tourgée antagonized white Southerners in his efforts to mobilize public opinion against lynching, disenfranchisement, and segregation. He irked Northern intellectuals and social scientists who scoffed at his unscientific "foolish utterances" in refuting doctrines of racial inequality.[2] He exasperated Republican Party leadership when he denounced them as traitors and hypocrites for failing to live up to long-standing promises to protect minority rights and promote equal citizenship. Finally, he even displeased a few black leaders who had adopted a more conciliatory tone toward racist whites and objected to his uncompromising and confrontational politics.

One of the most striking aspects of the outcry against Tourgée in the 1890s in the Northern press was its echo of the anti-abolitionist mobs of the previous generation, whose spirit had been revived perhaps by the practice of lynching that recently had spread from Southern states into the Midwest. Denouncing him as a "demagogue" and an "educated villain" who "has succeeded in exciting ignorant imitators among the colored race," one Indianapolis newspaper called upon all "decent people" to oppose "the curse of Tourgeeism" and "manifest their disgust in such manner as to impress upon [his followers] that *a danger line still exists beyond which it is improper to venture.*"[3] The *Chicago Times* openly suggested that Tourgée deserved to be lynched after he spoke in Chicago in support of a black boycott of the national anthem using "words for which others have been hanged in this city. . . . Let this disturber beware how he thus incites his protégés," it warned, "some day there may be a reckoning that will make [Tourgée] realize the meaning of the term 'A Fool's Errand.' "[4] Tourgée's critics were at a loss to explain his undiminished zeal for a cause that seemed hopeless and that so many other whites in the North had disowned. Southern author Joel Chandler Harris, in a review of his 1890 novel *Pactolus Prime*, was surprised that Tourgée remained unchanged since his carpetbagger days. "Twenty years of reflection have not softened Tourgée's heart," he wrote. "He counts each year as lost that does not see another book from his pen, designed to disorganize the whites of the south, and pave the way for black supremacy." Musing upon his apparent "burning hatred of his own race," Harris questioned Tourgée's sanity. "What shall we say of such a writer?" he wondered. "Is he a monomaniac, or simply a refugee from his race?"[5]

Despite the overblown rhetoric of his detractors, Tourgée was neither an obsessed attention-seeker nor a perverse rabble-rouser. He had been an extremely capable lawyer and an accomplished jurist in the state of North Carolina during his Reconstruction years. As a political commentator, he wrote fifteen political novels, eight books of historical and social criticism, and several hundred newspaper and magazine articles that constitute an impressive monument of dissent against the prevailing tide of racial oppression. His works have been acknowledged by leading authorities in his time and our own as some of the most illuminating, even profound, analyses of race and democratic citizenship in the post–Civil War era.[6] Joel Chandler Harris may have been correct in one thing, however. Tourgée was a refugee from his "race" in the sense that he denied the utility of the concept of race as a meaningful category of social distinction. "Race is a scientific and legal question of great difficulty," he insisted, whose very definition "science is totally unable to solve."[7] On the other hand, "some things are self-evident, among these is that every argument and demonstration [of] the inherent inferiority of the African of the United States . . . has been shown by irrefragable evidence of experience to be false."[8] But, by the 1890s, public tolerance for this viewpoint was waning.

Still, the greatest legacies of his struggle for racial equality may have been achieved in this decade. A pioneer of civil rights activism for the next century, he founded the National Citizen's Rights Association (NCRA) in 1891, a short-lived national organization that foreshadowed the National Association of the Advancement of Colored People (NAACP); he framed the nation's first comprehensive anti-lynching law that drastically reduced the crime of lynching in the state of Ohio; and he served as lead attorney in the first direct constitutional challenge to state-mandated segregation to make it as far as the United States Supreme

Court. Tourgée's clients lost the infamous 1896 case of *Plessy v. Ferguson* that established the constitutionality of the "separate-but-equal" doctrine used to justify racial segregation within the strictures of the Fourteenth Amendment. Yet, his arguments on Homer Plessy's behalf have cast a long shadow across the winding terrain of civil rights discourse from the end of the nineteenth century to our own time.

In his brief to the Supreme Court in *Plessy*, Tourgée summed up one line of argument by reminding the justices that the Greek goddess of justice, Themis, was normally represented wearing a blindfold. "Justice is pictured blind," he observed, "and her daughter, the Law, ought at least to be color-blind."[9] This arresting turn of phrase caught the attention of Justice John Marshall Harlan who borrowed it for his powerful lone dissent. "Our Constitution is color-blind," Harlan memorably asserted, "and neither knows nor tolerates classes among citizens."[10] Harlan's declaration has been quoted innumerable times since and the metaphor *racial color-blindness* has endured as one of the most powerful rhetorical expressions of the ideal of racial equality in America. But what are the implications of a color-blind citizenship? How does this phrase capture the relation between race and civic identity? What are the intellectual and social origins of this concept?

Interestingly, Justice Harlan never elaborated on his color-blind doctrine outside of his *Plessy* dissent; he never used this phrase either before or after it. His unusual political and judicial record has proven a poor guide to the intellectual history of the concept of a color-blind constitution.[11] On the other hand, Tourgée used this phrase repeatedly over his long career, and he fully elaborated on his views regarding race and citizenship. More than a favorite figure of speech, color-blind citizenship constituted one of Tourgée's most deeply held principles. In fact, his entire career can be viewed as a consistent, unfulfilled quest to establish this principle. Thus, he is a particularly relevant figure in the study of the historical roots of this important principle.

At the present time, the meaning and implication of constitutional color-blindness has become the subject of deep disagreement and heated debate. What once had excited alarm among white supremacists as an extreme and dangerously radical viewpoint in the 1890s, one hundred years later had become a rhetorical weapon of social conservatives. New Right conservatives who deny the continuing influence of racism on society have adopted the mantra of color-blindness as a powerful rationale to oppose much of the civil rights legislation from the late 1960s and 1970s. Turning a blind eye, so to speak, to the effects of racism, they propose to end all "race-conscious" governmental policies in the name of equal citizenship. By severely limiting economic and educational opportunities for nonwhites, this approach, its opponents fear, would quickly return the United States to the veritable racial caste system that existed before the 1960s. A few critics have dubbed the conservative strategy "color-blind racism."[12] This unhappy oxymoron serves to illustrate the rhetorical power of the color-blind metaphor and the difficulty of countering its logic of impartiality—after all, how can one who is blind to racial characteristics be racist? While a detailed analysis of the present-day color-blind controversy falls beyond the scope of this book, the historical perspective offered here may shed light on the origin and political evolution of the color-blind principle and thereby deepen our understanding of its past, and its potential, uses.

One might conclude that it is a measure of how far America has traveled on the road to racial justice that the principles of yesterday's radicals have become those of today's conservatives. But this presumes that white radicals of the past, such as Tourgée, would agree with recent conservative uses of the color-blind principle. Would they? Total agreement on the meaning of a legal or political principle, of course, no more existed in the past than it does in the present. As this book will demonstrate, disagreement about how best to guarantee equal citizenship through legislation and constitutional law even among radicals precludes any single "original meaning" of civic color-blindness. But taken on the individual level, the question might be answered simply. In Tourgée's case, the answer is almost certainly no.

One thing that makes Tourgée a notable civil rights strategist was his pragmatic belief that racial justice must be achieved in the results of the law, not merely in the abstract principles behind it. As a radical leader during Reconstruction, Tourgée proposed a variety of interventionist policies by the federal government to protect citizens and to promote equal opportunity, including "color-conscious" legislation in the realm of public education. In fact, when conducting research for his arguments in the *Plessy* case, Tourgée expressed surprise to discover what he felt was the "curious dread" of the "old abolitionists" regarding "any legislation respecting color or race." He concluded that: "The struggle for the expurgation of 'white' as a restrictive term in our law had given them a strange horror of 'colored' as an enabling description."[13] He himself, as we shall see, had not been afraid to propose racial distinctions in the law where they served as "enabling descriptions."

Even more remarkable in light of current debates over the color-blind principle, Tourgée argued to the Supreme Court in *Plessy* that *whiteness* should be considered a special form of property that inherently advantaged some citizens, while disadvantaging others. Tourgée asked the Supreme Court to consider:

How much would it be *worth* to a young man entering upon the practice of law, to be regarded as a *white* man rather than a colored one? Six-sevenths of the population are white. Nineteen-twentieths of the property of the country is owned by white people. Ninety-nine hundredths of the business opportunities are in the control of white people. These propositions are rendered even more startling by the intensity of feeling which excludes the colored man from the friendship and companionship of the white man . . . under these conditions, is it possible to conclude that the *reputation of being white* is not property? Indeed, is it not the most valuable sort of property, being the master-key that unlocks the golden door of opportunity?[14]

One implication here is that the social advantages of whiteness must be taken into account when judging the discriminatory or stigmatizing effect—not merely the intent—of laws that make public distinctions based on race. This "cutting edge" argument has been made in recent years by a group of law professors, the Critical Race Theorists, who are among the most outspoken opponents of racial color-blindness. They contend that laws that advantage nonwhites cannot be viewed as equivalent to those that advantage whites because of the unequal social power given to "whiteness." Tourgée's legal strategy in this passage (to be discussed in a later chapter), though somewhat different in purpose, does not contradict this argument. Indeed, he deserves credit as the originator of the assertion that "whiteness" functions as property.[15]

For a fruitful analysis of Tourgée's arguments beyond his legal rhetorical strategies and political rhetoric, one first must understand his underlying worldview. His ideas, writings, and subsequent actions must be understood in their historical context and in his lived experiences.

Like nearly all Americans of his time, white and black, Tourgée believed in race as an objective, biological reality, though he thought it inadequately understood. He did not claim that race was a social invention, but only that assertions of human hierarchies based upon race were demonstratably false and contrary to the teachings of Jesus in the New Testament. Though he pressed the logic of this viewpoint further than most, it was not a remarkably uncommon view for one of his social background and upbringing. But Tourgée was an unusually articulate and insightful social critic, and he left behind a remarkably full record of his observations, interpretations, and actions. Equally important is the fascinating variety of responses that Tourgée elicited—from both blacks and whites, Northerners and Southerners. Through this dialogue—Tourgée's perspective and that of those around him—we can learn with greater precision the worldview he represented.[16]

Tourgée was deeply influenced by the political culture of the abolitionist movement. Often deemed a latter-day abolitionist, he, in fact, had absorbed the individualistic ethos of the movement as a youth growing up in a notorious hotbed of abolitionism, the Western Reserve region of Ohio. Abolitionists of every stripe emphasized the unity of mankind, quoting the Bible's dictum that "God hath created of one blood all nations of men upon the earth." The late historian Paul Goodman asserted that "a total abandonment of prejudice against color" superseded even the abolition of slavery as the primary message of the abolitionists of the 1830s.[17] William Lloyd Garrison, for one, extolled the variety of human races in Whitmanesque tones as the "gorgeous multifarious productions of Nature," and he dismissed theories of racial inequality by saying, "I would as soon deny the existence of my Creator as quarrel with the workmanship of his hands."[18] The abolitionists, to be sure, were no multiculturalists. They had a single, Protestant-based standard of moral behavior, but they insisted that every human being had the capacity to be moral and enlightened.

What made the abolitionists believe in racial equality? While racism calls out for explanation, the belief in racial equality is often accepted without analysis by historians, who from their perspective view the position as correct and therefore requiring no explanation.[19] But as the scorned viewpoint of a relative minority of radicals who risked ostracism and even bodily harm for espousing it, this belief should require more historical analysis. Derived from religious doctrines of perfectionism that flourished during the Second Great Awakening, the racial egalitarianism of the abolitionists reflected a particular notion of the self that I have termed *radical individualism*. Radical individualism was not an ideology or a political creed, but an ontological notion of the self. It was a foundation for many egalitarian creeds because it presumed that every individual was divinely endowed with a conscience, a soul, and a capacity for moral understanding. Because Africans and other "races" possessed a divine conscience and a soul, they had the same capacity for moral improvement as whites. Along with this capacity came an imperative, however, to discover and obey the "moral law," also referred to as "God's law" or "the higher law." Knowledge of this universal moral law came not from earthly or human authorities but ultimately through consultation of one's own conscience through which moral truth was revealed to each individual.[20]

Not all abolitionists agreed with one another—their individualism itself made them notoriously disputatious, fostering intense disagreements and fractious divisions among their ranks. Still, most agreed that one's physical biology, including racial and gender characteristics, was utterly irrelevant to one's moral substance and worth. Radical individualism made abolitionists receptive to Christian doctrines of universal brotherhood and

equality before God as well as to natural rights theory and to the rational-
ism of the Enlightenment. It was no coincidence that women joined
the ranks of the abolitionists in large numbers, nor was it that the first
organized women's rights movement emerged from abolitionism. "I have
a will! and tastes, and habits, and propensities! and loves and hates! yes, and
conscience!" exclaimed the liberated heroine of one 1850 proto-feminist
novel, "all go to make of the sum total of my separate individuality, a
distinct life! for which I alone am accountable, and only to God!"[21] The
logic of this radical and nonmaterialist understanding of the self thus had
explosively liberating potential.

Despite their insistence on a singular standard of morality, radical
individualists implicitly recognized a principle of tolerance.[22] Those
whose opinions differed were entitled to the same absolute respect for
their obedience to conscience as one would require for oneself—provided,
that is, that they were not enslaving or otherwise infringing upon the
equivalent rights of others. To emphasize this point, radical individualists
liked to cite the Golden Rule, which implicitly recognized human
equality by endowing others with a moral value equal to oneself. In his
later career, Tourgée developed a theory of democratic citizenship in
which he advocated civic ethics based on the Golden Rule. " 'Whatsoever
ye would that men should do to you, do ye even so to them.' This is the
measure of the citizen's duty to his country and fellow-citizens," he wrote
in 1892, "As I, a citizen of the United States, would desire you, another
citizen of the great republic, to act, were our positions reversed, so must
I act in the discharge of my duties as a citizen."[23] It was Tourgée's belief
that democracy itself had evolved as much from Christian humanitarian
precepts as it had from classical political theory. This emphasis on tolerance and freedom of conscience, despite its Christian foundation, helped
to resolve some of the tension between individualism and moral absolutism within abolitionist thought.

Though his worldview was rooted in the radical individualism of the
abolitionists, Tourgée had to confront a different set of social problems
than had the abolitionists, within a changed historical context. By the time
he reached political maturity in the 1860s, slavery had been abolished, but
the establishment of a government that respected freedom of conscience
and the absolute worth of the individual had yet to be realized. As a Union
officer in the Civil War, Tourgée had been infused with nationalism and
awed by the military power of the United States government. After the
war, he imagined that the state would become the ultimate protector and
enforcer of individual rights. And he had good reason to believe so. The
Reconstruction Amendments indeed would inscribe antislavery principles
—the moral law—into the Constitution, including the guarantee of

equal citizenship. But Tourgée's challenge was to remain true to the ethic of radical individualism while staying within the bounds of constitutionalism and respecting the authority of the state.

While it fostered doctrines of racial and gender equality, radical individualism also encouraged a distinct mode of participation in political life. To speed the progress of humanity toward moral perfection, one's knowledge of the moral law came with an imperative to persuade others of its truth. A moral conscience could not be silent in the face of injustice. Reflecting their absolute faith in humankind's innate rationality and morality, abolitionists sought to make, as Wendell Phillips put it, "every single home, press, pulpit and senate a debating society" on the issue of slavery.[24] Tourgée, too, relied primarily on what abolitionists called "moral suasion" to galvanize the public against racial injustice. This often meant injecting sharp and sometimes shocking language into the public dialogue about race to startle citizens out of their complacency. Garrison sought to awaken Northerners to their complicity in slavery by burning copies of the Constitution and calling it a "compact with hell." Tourgée tried to shock his audiences into action by repeatedly prophesizing a race war of "inconceivable horror," in which "cities may be burned, railroads destroyed, and civilization in all its forms [will] be forced to do penance for injustice and oppression" if their tolerance of racial oppression did not immediately cease.[25]

Radical individualists like Garrison and Tourgée who disturbed public complacency with matters of moral conscience did so at great personal cost to themselves. It was psychologically and emotionally taxing work that normally brought little remuneration despite immense effort. Such work required peculiar personalities and temperaments. While often overbearing and self-righteous in presentation, Tourgée was simultaneously deeply empathetic to others and self-sacrificing in his actions. He felt compelled to ally himself with the downtrodden and to tirelessly oppose what he perceived as tyranny with relentless argumentation and accusations. Though he often denied it, he secretly hoped to be rewarded for his efforts with public approval and elevation to a position of prestige and power. Yet, in addition to public agitation, he wrote dozens of harshly critical and accusatory personal letters to Republican Party leaders, including President Benjamin Harrison, that almost certainly cost him any chance of achieving some of his grandiose aspirations. Four times he sought a Republican nomination to run for U.S. Congress, and twice an appointment to the Federal bench, but to no avail. His unwillingness to sacrifice conscience to ambition and his inability to subordinate himself within an organizational structure vastly limited his success. These disappointments gnawed at his self-esteem and fed his periodic depressions.

Nearly every white person who spoke out publicly for racial equality in the nineteenth century had his motives disparaged, her character slandered, or his sanity questioned. Abolitionists were threatened, beaten, mobbed, and sometimes murdered right up until the outbreak of the Civil War. Moreover, they were viciously criticized in the press. Americans have always been discomfited by their political style, blending a fierce urgency with an unshakable moral certainty, and have tended to discredit their arguments by labeling them impractical or fanatical. The suggestion that these radical individualists were incapable of rational discourse is grossly inaccurate. Most abolitionist leaders were, like Tourgée, skillful lawyers and highly educated men and women whose convictions were grounded in the most rigorous logic. But devotion to principle when it comes at the cost of one's own reputation and self-interest seems strangely abnormal in a nation that has normalized the pursuit of economic self-interest as rational behavior. Despite its oppositional—and therefore marginal—position, the political style originated by the abolitionists has had a far-reaching impact on the protest tradition in America and has become an enduring, even integral, element of our political culture.

The radical individualists' style of public engagement, it should be clear, differed in substantial ways from the kind of politics that is usually associated with American individualism.[26] Ever since Alexis de Tocqueville used the novel term *individualism* to describe what he perceived as a predominant American trait in the 1830s, the meaning of it has followed his definition. Tocqueville described it as a centrifugal force in American culture that led each citizen away from public life and into the pursuit of individual gain and private enjoyment of material comforts. "Individualism," he observed, "is a calm and considered feeling which disposes each citizen to isolate himself from the mass of his fellows and withdraw into the circle of family and friends." "With this little society formed to his taste," he wrote, the American "gladly leaves the greater society to look after itself."[27] This anti-public spirit, Tocqueville feared, presented a danger to the future of democracy in America and he regarded it as a force that needed to be held in check in order for democracy to survive. By contrast, the public-spirited ethos that flowed out of radical individualism was ultra-democratic in the sense that it virtually required engagement in public culture on matters of conscience.

One reason that Tocqueville's definition has dominated our understanding of individualism is that it accurately describes the dominant mode of conduct that triumphed in the late nineteenth century. When first he described it in the 1830s, Tocqueville felt that atomistic individualism had been successfully checked by the moral restraints of America's

Puritan inheritance and by a vibrant culture of political participation derived from the New England town meeting. But a major cultural shift occurred after the Civil War. Deterministic theories of the self challenged older morality-based ones in intellectual culture as part of a much-studied philosophical shift that characterized Tourgée's generation in both Europe and America. Whether controlled by the iron law of supply and demand, Marxian class conflict, human evolution, or the behavioral traits of racial inheritance, individuals were said by the most respected social authorities to be lacking moral agency and at the mercy of forces beyond their control. Natural laws could never be overcome by human intervention—all attempts to alter them, as William Graham Sumner argued, would be disastrous. These notions fit well with the kind of laissez-faire individualism whose growth Tocqueville had warned against.[28] Rather than the rule of moral conscience, the unsentimental pursuit of economic self-interest was lauded by late-nineteenth-century social scientists as the best means of serving the public good.

For those inclined toward determinism, the failure of Reconstruction was a case in point. No subject more often elicited a deterministic explanation than the failure of Reconstruction. Governments whose policies violated the laws of nature, the argument ran, would only experience failure and social disorder. The lesson of Reconstruction was that only natural laws should be allowed to resolve matters of racial conflict. "It is irrational to attribute these race antipathies and aversions to the laws of this country," Alabama senator John T. Morgan wrote in 1890 in response to the Reconstruction era's attempt to eradicate racial distinctions from the statute books:

> They rest upon a foundation that men have not built and are supported by ordinances that human power can neither enact nor amend nor repeal. After we have done all that we can to abolish or to neutralize these race distinctions and the feelings that grow out of them—attempting to set aside the eternal laws of nature—we shall find that we have only marked more plainly the differences between the races.[29]

Reconstruction, therefore, which had attempted to make equal ineradicably different beings that nature had made unequal, was destined to fail. It was an abomination to be eternally denounced and ridiculed. "A black skin means membership in a race of men which has never . . . created a civilization of any kind," Columbia University history professor John Burgess wrote of Reconstruction in 1902. "To put such a race of men in possession of a 'state' government . . . is simply to establish barbarism in power over civilization."[30] This deterministic argument served multiple ideological interests in the nineteenth century, underscoring the folly of governmental interference with so-called natural laws of all kinds, while at the same time affirming the abandonment of the egalitarian reforms of Reconstruction.

Tourgée's great challenge was not merely to counter racism and to challenge deterministic theories of the self but to keep alive the public's memory of the Civil War and Reconstruction as a radical, indeed revolutionary, era.[31] The debate over the role of race in American citizenship has been inextricably linked to the public memory and interpretation of emancipation and Reconstruction. Tourgée advanced what might be termed a "radical" interpretation of these events. His writings placed the causes and consequences of emancipation at the center of the Civil War that, for him, had produced a revolution of citizens' rights and national power to protect them. The Union victory in the Civil War meant not merely the elimination of the Southern "slaveocracy" in economic and political life but the utter destruction of class and race privilege in American law and politics—the "new birth of freedom" that Abraham Lincoln hoped for at Gettysburg.

He was not alone in his interpretation of the Civil War. Although racist mythologies about Reconstruction would later become entrenched in American popular and academic culture, they were not accepted entirely uncritically in the late nineteenth century. When he launched the N.C.R.A. in the 1890s, hundreds of letters of support arrived, especially from white Civil War veterans, that praised his "true and genuine republicanism of the original stamp," applauded his efforts "towards securing to the colored people . . . the rights guaranteed by the Constitution," and lamented that "if the general government cannot stretch forth its strong arm and protect its citizens where the state refused, then as well had Calhoun's doctrine triumphed" in the Civil War.[32] Though his was a minority viewpoint at that time, Tourgée's historical interpretation resonated with others who recalled the transformative hopes of the Civil War and who once supported the visionary reforms of Reconstruction. Indeed, W.E.B. Du Bois's historical classic, *Black Reconstruction in America*, which began the process of dismantling the racist mythologies about the era, not only vindicated much of Tourgée's position, but drew inspiration directly from his writings and the suppressed public memory from which they sprang.[33]

This book is structured in three parts. Part I discusses the ideological elements of the "Radical Civil War" as Tourgée understood and experienced it. It is important to grasp both the possibilities and limitations within Tourgée's worldview at the outset and to examine the concept of *color-blind citizenship* as he conceived it. Part II examines Tourgée's experiences during the Civil War and Reconstruction. In this section, his views are moving in concert with the fast-paced political developments of his time. He is both an important participant in, indeed a shaper of, these events and a careful observer who himself is being transformed by the historical change taking place around him. In Part III, Tourgée's worldview is no longer taking shape, it has become fully developed and rather rigidly fixed. Yet, the society around him continues to change, and often in unexpected ways. In this section, the divergence between Tourgée and the views of his contemporaries provides the centerpiece of my analysis. This divergence reveals much about the cultural transformations that took place in the late nineteenth century and how they served to undermine older notions of the self.

When Du Bois and other radicals launched the modern civil rights movement with the Niagara Movement in 1905, they prominently honored Tourgée along with William Lloyd Garrison and Frederick Douglass as three "Friends of Freedom" whose radical tradition they intended to carry forward.[34] All three men viewed American citizenship as rooted in the principle of equality before the law and as respecting the individual's moral worth regardless of race or gender. While Garrison's and Douglass's contributions to the tradition of civil rights protest in America are well known, Tourgée's is not. Unlike their efforts, Tourgée's crusade did not experience the crowning triumph that the antislavery movement did with the final abolition of slavery in 1865. Reconstruction was to be remembered as a failure and much of its work would be undone in the counterrevolution exemplified by the Supreme Court decision in *Plessy v. Ferguson*. Tourgée's important contributions to the public discourse on race and citizenship were obscured and forgotten as the triumph of opposing viewpoints heaped discredit on all of the participants in Reconstruction and the principles they stood for. This book seeks to recover Tourgée's perspective and to examine its place in the critical dialogue about race and citizenship from the 1850s to the end of the nineteenth century. In so doing, it will reassess the origins of the concept of color-blind citizenship that continues to influence the public discourse on civil rights in our own time.

PART I

The Color-Blind Crusade

1

Judge Tourgée and the Radical Civil War

There was a minority of the North who hated slavery with a perfect hatred; who wanted no union with slaveholders; who fought for freedom and treated Negroes as men. As the Abolition-democracy gained in prestige and in power, they appeared as prophets, and led by statesmen, they began to guide the nation out of the morass into which it had fallen. They and their black friends and the new freedmen gradually became the leaders of a Reconstruction of Democracy in the United States, while marching millions sang the noblest war song of the ages to the tune of "John Brown's Body."

— W.E.B. Du Bois, *Black Reconstruction in America*, 1935

IN THE SPRING OF 1902, a package arrived at the U.S. Consulate in Bordeaux, France, containing a complimentary volume of *The Leopard's Spots: A Romance of the White Man's Burden*, by Thomas Dixon, Jr. Walter Hines Page, the prominent publisher who had personally arranged for the publication of *The Leopard's Spots* at Doubleday, Page, and Company, probably sent the volume believing that the American consul in Bordeaux would find the subject matter of great interest. If so, Page was not alone in this assumption. More copies of Dixon's first novel were sent to Albion Tourgée by friends and foes alike.[1]

White-haired, overweight, and suffering from diabetes, the sixty-four-year-old Tourgée read *The Leopard's Spots* from his quiet post in the Bordeaux Consulate with a mixture of disgust and perverse bemusement. The book's prefatory note declared that all of the historical incidents described within were selected from "authentic records," or came within Dixon's "personal knowledge." An amazed Tourgée, however, found an historical portrait within that was, in his words, "entirely worthless as a narration of events or an analysis of causes" and that bore "not the remotest similitude to anything that ever happened."[2] Though he dismissed the book's historical claims as simply ludicrous, it concerned him that others seemed to take them seriously. As copies of Dixon's novel continued to arrive at his doorstep, an increasingly irritated Tourgée picked them up with tongs and deposited them directly into the fireplace.

It is not surprising that Dixon's book caused so many to think of the once-popular author Tourgée. The literary strategies and historical arguments of *The Leopard's Spots* were conceived in direct response to Tourgée and the historical viewpoint he represented. As an ambitious young man growing up in post–Civil War North Carolina, Dixon, in fact, had known and even admired Tourgée. At that time, Judge Tourgée had been the most prominent Republican carpetbagger judge in the state, as well as a noted author. Dixon in the 1880s even sought out and received the prominent author's "kindly" encouragement of his literary aspirations.[3] "I liked Judge Tourgee," Dixon would protest in defense to his widow, Emma Tourgée, years later when she wrote a scathing letter accusing him of having " 'defamed' his memory" by spreading falsehoods.[4] It is likely no coincidence, then, that *The Leopard's Spots*, set in Reconstruction North Carolina, seemed to be a rewriting of Tourgée's *A Fool's Errand*. One friend of Tourgée's, E.H. Johnson, was so struck by its evocation of *A Fool's Errand* that he published a short review in the *Watchman* comparing and contrasting the two works. Johnson sent his review, along with another copy of Dixon's book, to Tourgée, warning him, "[*The Leopard's Spots*] traverses the ground of your 'A Fool's Errand,' with practically the opposite motive, and opposite effect." Echoing the others who alerted Tourgée to Dixon's book, Johnson said, "It seemed to me too remarkable a contrast to go unnoticed."[5]

If Dixon was indeed responding to *A Fool's Errand*, it is highly significant that twenty-three years elapsed before Dixon's fictional response appeared. The central theme of *The Leopard's Spots* espouses the necessity for whites to control black male sexuality and to protect the Anglo-Saxon race against the dangers of racial intermixture—"The future American must be [either] an Anglo-Saxon or a Mulatto," the narrator repeatedly insists.[6] So extreme were its historical fabrications that, in one scene, a mulatto Republican was depicted proposing a bill to the North Carolina Legislature to annul all marriages between white women and former Confederates so as to pave the way for racial amalgamation. Cultivating an impression that this incident was part of a "secret" history of Reconstruction, Dixon explained in an authorial aside that the white carpetbaggers privately censured this overeager mulatto ally and brought "the entire power of Congress" to bear on news agencies to keep word of this outrageous measure from "being circulated throughout the country."[7]

Its excesses notwithstanding, *The Leopard's Spots* was the culmination of a propaganda campaign that traced its origins to white Southern newspapers and journals of the 1860s and '70s. Even before the Reconstruction Act of 1867 went into effect, a desperate smear campaign was launched against Southern Republicans. The Southern conservative press during the Reconstruction era had been dominated by rumors of African American violence and conspiracies against whites and by unrelenting accusations of corruption, opportunism, and cynical manipulation of blacks by white Republicans. Too young to take part in politics, Dixon's formative years were spent in this political atmosphere. The overblown rhetoric of the Southern press had long since hardened in his imagination into historical fact by the time he sat down to write *The Leopard's Spots* at the age of thirty-seven.

Though disgusted by falsifications of history in *The Leopard's Spots*, Tourgée nevertheless felt almost glad that Dixon had presented his case in such stark and unambiguous terms. Tourgée thought it "most remarkable" the degree to which Dixon's book "unconsciously revealed" the nightmarish fantasies of white extremists. He was even glad, "after a fashion," that someone had written such a book. Dixon stated in plain language the false presumptions underlying the sexual hysteria so evident in the actions of Southern lynch mobs. "As a delineation of the dominant thought of the southern white man of yesterday and to-day," Tourgée concluded, "it is of inestimable value."[8] But if he hoped that the book might alert sympathetic Northerners to the depths of race-hatred of unreconstructed Southerners, he would be bitterly disappointed.

Even his friend E.H. Johnson, a self-described *mugwump*, or liberal reformer, failed to express either alarm or outrage at Dixon's audacious historical claims.* In his comparison of Tourgée's and Dixon's novels, Johnson placed their contributions to historical understanding on the same level. Each author, he suggested, had merely told the truth from his own perspective: "Neither writer can be called a whit more honest than the other . . . neither means to be less humane than the other, or less patriotic." The difference was merely that "the sympathy awakened by the one story all goes to the colored race, that aroused by the other story all

---

*Originally a term of derision, the word *mugwump* was coined by stalwart Republicans to ridicule a group of patrician reformers who, in the 1880s, broke with the Republican Party because of their disgust with its corruption and machine politics. Most mugwumps were inclined toward laissez-faire economic policies in accordance with classical liberal thought and regarded Reconstruction as a mistake.

goes to the white race."[9] In a generous spirit of reconciliation, Johnson implied that a reading of *both* books would provide the most accurate picture of the times. Deeming both authors patriotic Americans, he implicitly legitimized Dixon's perspective as historically credible. Johnson's tolerance of *The Leopard's Spots* was enough to arouse Tourgée's ire. Responding to him in a thirty-eight-page typewritten letter, composed in short stints over several weeks, he gave full expression to his feelings. This extraordinary letter reveals the depths of Tourgée's ideological distance both from Dixon, the Southern extremist, and Johnson, the Northern liberal.

Tourgée began by refuting Dixon's litany of falsehoods and misrepresentations of history. He explained that he not only knew Dixon personally, he also knew "his type and the influences by which he and those like him had been shaped." Dixon had been shaped by a generation of hate and malice, and he exemplified the "murderous tendencies" of those white Southerners "whose mouth is full of cursing and heart is bent on murder." *The Leopard's Spots* could not be taken lightly, because it signaled a rising tide of genocidal rage among Southern whites. "Lynchings and burnings are sure seedlings of slaughter," Tourgée warned, and based upon his own experience, he hypothesized that "if it was left to a secret ballot whether the Negro should be deported . . . or 'exterminated' by the Southern whites, there would be a big majority in favor of 'extermination.'" Yet, considering Johnson's own complacency, Tourgée had to wonder if even he would be offended by such a prospect. "Or do you perhaps believe," Tourgée queried him sharply, "that the killing of a colored man for 'impudence' to a white person . . . [or] failing to give the whole sidewalk to a lady and stand cap in hand while she passed by, is not a crime?"[10]

This long letter gave Tourgée an opportunity to reflect upon the crusade for social justice to which he had devoted his career. By 1902, he had become a voice from the political wilderness, and no one knew it better than himself. He had once believed that the Civil War had set his country upon a course of humanitarian enlightenment and moral progress. Recalling the idealism of his war days, he remembered his joy at "the Miracle of the overthrow of slavery," which had removed that "stain" of "injustice and oppression" on his country. Emancipation, he had believed, had made the United States truly "the flower of liberty, security, and equal right for all." But somehow the true spirit of the crusade against slavery had been afterwards forgotten. "We have made the *name* of Slavery anathema," he told Johnson, "but [we] have sanctified its most degrading and debasing element, the subjection of one race to the will of another."[11]

Dixon's claims to historical accuracy were almost laughable. "It is enough to make a cast-iron dog laugh to read the tales of atrocities committed by the 'Union League,'" Tourgée scoffed at Dixon's assertion that outrages against whites by this organization made the Ku Klux Klan necessary. The Union League was, in fact, nothing more than a fraternal organization with an interracial membership that mobilized support for the Republican Party. "No such thing as a crime was ever charged against such organization or an indictment found for any offense traceable to it," he explained to Johnson. "I know as much of its workings as any man ever did. It was the most harmless of voluntary associations." In reality, the greatest offenses committed by Republican rule in North Carolina were of much more benign character. "The mere fact that the Negro was allowed to testify [in a courtroom] against any one of the superior race was the most grievous fact of reconstruction," Tourgée suggested, "unless it was that, as judge I would not allow a witness or defendant to be called 'Nigger.'" This policy was regarded, he recalled, "as an absolute denial of a vested divine right" by white Southern lawyers.[12]

Tourgée held no illusions about the dire conditions Southern blacks faced in the present. "Lynch law and the stake" had been substituted for the physical terrorism of slavery, while "the control of wages and general immunity from punishment of the master's right to kill" had ensured a permanent black laboring caste. Sadly, he had seen his country increasingly disavow the goals of equality and freedom while "twist[ing] with enthusiasm" its own ideals "to excuse wrong to the colored man individually and collectively."[13] A transparently self-serving, laissez-faire rationale had undermined the Reconstruction Amendments in the courts and served to justify a continued racial caste system in society at large.

None of these sentiments should have surprised Johnson. Tourgée had been repeating this message for decades. What might have surprised Johnson, however, was that Tourgée marked each page of his letter "Personal and Confidential" and warned Johnson that "if this letter should get into print," it would risk his position at the consulate. Owing his job to the personal support of the recently deceased President McKinley, Tourgée felt it necessary to keep the contents of his letter private under the new Republican administration. He had received the Bordeaux consulship as a reward for his strenuous support of McKinley in the 1896 presidential campaign, but McKinley may also have hoped to quiet his intemperate pen. Indeed, for the first time in his career, Tourgée, upon accepting the appointment from McKinley, had promised to hold his tongue on public controversies.[14]

Since accepting his consulate position in 1897, Tourgée's public voice had been effectively silenced. He told Johnson that he would no longer publicly agitate on the "race problem" because Northern editors had stopped publishing his work and because his viewpoint had lost the support of the Republican Party. As a consequence, he decided that his life's work was finished. As he brought his long epistle to a close, Tourgée's anger began to exhaust itself. "I never wrote such a letter before and am never likely to do so again," he apologetically explained:

> [but] I cannot help thinking or writing upon these things because it was burned into my soul in that wonderful epoch to which we were exposed, that the chief aim of what we call Christian civilization, was to create conditions favorable to the uplifting and development of the weak—to lead humanity upwards not downwards.

He told Johnson that he was happily situated in Bordeaux and intended "never to return to the United States." Bordeaux, he had decided, was "an excellent place in which to pass the last days of an ill-spent life."[15]

WHEN TOURGÉE DIED IN MAY OF 1905, it was at another inauspicious moment for the cause to which he had devoted his career. Emboldened by the success of *The Leopard's Spots*, Thomas Dixon had just published *The Clansmen*—a sequel that would surpass the original in notoriety. This novel painted the era of Reconstruction in even starker shades of good and evil, incorporating such national figures as Abraham Lincoln, Charles Sumner, and Thaddeus Stevens (as "Austin Stoneman") into its plot. So symbolic and stylized were its themes and characters that Dixon easily adapted it to the stage, where it captured the imagination of film director D.W. Griffith. Ten years later, Griffith would collaborate closely with Dixon to bring these stark and aggressively racist images vividly to life in the first long-running feature film ever produced, *The Birth of a Nation* (1915).[16] Both on the stage and the silver screen, Dixon's historical message would live on for decades, reaching a wider and more diverse public than he could have ever imagined or hoped for when he sat down to write his first novel.

Conversely, the works of Tourgée slipped into a long period of oblivion. After his death, the numerous obituaries carried in the American press spoke volumes of his fading place in historical memory. Most American newspapers remembered "Judge Tourgée" as an author of great promise, once hailed as the next Dickens or Thackeray, but whose "bitter partisanship" overshadowed the artistic value of his works. "It is a fashion now to refer to 'A Fool's Errand' as the work of a partisan who wrote only with a political purpose," admitted the *Chicago Inter Ocean*, still one of Tourgée's staunchest defenders. Indeed, most obituaries called the historical accuracy of his novels into question. According to the *Rochester*

Herald, Tourgée had "contrived to color history as to make the worse appear the better cause, and to disguise a reign of injustice and sordid oppression as a mission of mercy and righteousness." The influence of his works, it claimed, "did more to prolong the period of mutual misunderstanding and enmity between the North and the South than any other literary production since the Civil War." With almost an audible sigh of relief, the *Herald* declared that Tourgée's "false conception" of the "race problem is *only now* disappearing" from the political scene.[17]

With Thomas Dixon's *The Clansmen* running serially on another page of its newspaper, the *Brooklyn Daily Eagle* took the opportunity offered by Tourgée's obituary to proclaim: "The death of the author of 'A Fool's Errand' is merely a sign post showing how far the country has gone in the quarter century since that book was published." Applauding the absence of controversy occasioned by Dixon's latest work, it observed: "To-day Mr. Dixon's powerful 'Clansmen' has merely a literary and historical interest." "No book dealing with the negro or the future of the South could by any possibility now arouse the ferment which Tourgée's books created in their day." The writer for the *Eagle* went on to explain why the "Race Problem" could no longer trouble the nation. "The future of the negro is settling itself along industrial lines and in accordance with natural laws," the writer concluded, "it is a happy progress toward peace and light and order." This attitude was indicative of widely held sentiment about the changed political culture in the North since Reconstruction. The goal of "peace" and "order" for many Americans, including even some pragmatic black leaders, had taken the place of "freedom" and "democracy," at least when it came to the equality of blacks.[18]

Interestingly, former political opponents from Tourgée's old adopted state of North Carolina struck a different, and far more appreciative, tone in remembering him. The *Raleigh Daily Observer* ran its obituary on the front page, honoring him in a banner headline as a "BRAVE AND TRUE MAN" whose name would have been "written high" in the state's history had it not been for his "blind adhesion to the Negro Suffrage Idea."[19] "Open, bold, determined, fearless and self-reliant," wrote Andrew Joyner, an old Greensboro acquaintance, "he had convictions, and with them, the courage and resources to proclaim and maintain them. He was clean-handed and clean of life . . . his supreme effort to make northerners out of southerners was well-meant, but it was more than a human task." This article went on to describe him as "the ablest Judge in the State" during Reconstruction and the main architect of the 1868 constitutional and civil code reforms. A great jurist, whose "mind was a marvel in its capacity to grasp, absorb, digest and retain," his tragic flaw was an inexplicable devotion to the principle of racial equality. Joyner seemed to think that

Tourgée's legal accomplishments might finally be appreciated now that "peace, order, law and quiet" had been "restored to North Carolina."[20]

Another political foe reached similar conclusions in the *Biographical History of North Carolina* published the following year, 1906. Frank Nash, author of the short entry on Tourgée, praised him as "a man of real culture and ability, having a definite and clear policy, and determined to pursue that policy regardless of the consequences," but he struggled to explain Tourgée's insistence on racial equality. "He seemed to have the Latin's toleration for miscegenation," Nash observed, and he speculated that "perhaps this was an inheritance from French-Canadian ancestry, perhaps a theory." But, because of this defect of character—itself a racial inheritance he imagined, though he misidentified Tourgée's French ancestry as also Canadian—Nash concluded, "he could never be an impartial judge for the whites." As a judge he had been "a partisan on the bench" on the account that:

> On all party questions affecting the relations of the races he without scruple voted with these people. He was willing to put a negro officer over a white militia company. He was willing to regiment white and negro companies together. He was willing to have mixed schools. In short, as between the negro and the white man the scales would stand equally balanced.[21]

So strong was the Southern taboo against racial equality that this otherwise fair-minded assessment did not recognize a contradiction in deeming Tourgée a "partisan" "without scruple" for his scrupulous adherence to the equal balance of the scales between black and white.

For Southerners, Tourgée's career was a tragic one, marred by his zealous adherence to a false theory. Now that the theory itself seemed universally repudiated, and the conservative account of Reconstruction universally vindicated, it seemed safe to indulge in some long-overdue praise for his other worthy accomplishments. For Northerners, Tourgée's career was a bad memory. The *Brooklyn Daily Eagle* made this point most bluntly when it wrote in Tourgée's obituary: "Happy are the people who have no history."[22] Tourgée seemed to personify history, or at least a particular historical memory. In his absence, the *Eagle* seemed to say, the nation would no longer be called on to remember its past failures or the embarrassing ideals of Reconstruction.

The unrepressed desire of these Northern papers to forget the divisive issues of Reconstruction—to have no history of racial egalitarianism— were reaching a crescendo at the time of Tourgée's death. This attitude marked the ascendancy of a particular liberal tradition at the turn of the century, a new era in which race issues seemed ready to disappear from the agenda of progressive reform. Even some prominent African

Americans, led by Booker T. Washington, declared that the solution to the so-called race problem was beyond legislation and dismissed the crusade to eradicate civil inequalities based on "race, color or previous condition of servitude" of the previous generation as misguided folly.[23] At bottom of all discussions of racial injustice was the "failed" experiment of Reconstruction and the lessons to be learned from its troubled history.

Although the history of Reconstruction has been exonerated from the slanders of Thomas Dixon and other conservative mythologists, historians still differ in explaining its downfall. Some historians argue that the Republican Congress that framed the policies of Reconstruction hardly meant for it to do more than it accomplished, ultimately leaving blacks with only the slightest improvement from the conditions of slavery. But the dominant view of historians at present agrees with W.E.B. Du Bois's interpretation of Reconstruction as a genuine experiment in interracial democracy that was overthrown only after a protracted and difficult struggle. In his acclaimed history of the period, Eric Foner, who prominently cites the work of Du Bois as an antecedent to his own, dubbed Reconstruction "America's Unfinished Revolution."[24] Yet, one might ask, whose revolution was it and what happened to its principles?

Historians have found it difficult to explain the utter repudiation of Reconstruction, even by some of its most devoted supporters, in its aftermath—a fact leading some to question the depth of commitment to Reconstruction in the first place. Du Bois, though offering slight explanation, gave an intriguing description of this wholesale renunciation. Of Northern public opinion during Reconstruction, he wrote:

> For a brief period—for the seven mystic years that stretched between Johnson's "Swing round the Circle" [1866] to the Panic of 1873, the majority of thinking Americans of the North believed in the equal manhood of Negroes. They acted accordingly with a thoroughness and clean-cut decision that no age which does not share that faith can in the slightest comprehend. They did not free draft animals, nor enfranchise gorillas, nor welcome morons to Congress. They simply recognized black folk as men.

But the retreat from this "faith" was astonishingly rapid. Marking 1873 as the turning point, Du Bois pointed out that the retreat from the principles of Reconstruction were only part of a much larger cultural transformation. "Then came in 1873–1876 sudden and complete disillusion not at Negroes but at the world—at business, at work, at religion, at art" in the midst of which, he observed, the "bitter protest of Southern property [i.e., the planter class] reinforced Northern reaction" against Reconstruction. After discarding their commitment to black equality, along with many other former beliefs, Americans looked back on the history of

Reconstruction and "never yet quite understood why it could ever have thought that black men were altogether human."[25]

Albion Tourgée experienced the history of Reconstruction much as Du Bois described it. He believed that a healthy majority of the North had shared in the egalitarian goals of Reconstruction and he was mystified by the sudden shift of public opinion away from those goals in the 1870s. In many ways, Tourgée's career tells the story of the remarkable cultural "about-face" that Du Bois described, though the deeper disillusionment sunk in more slowly and took place over a longer period of time. Historians such as George Fredrickson and Louis Menand have illuminated many dimensions of this transformation, but not the principle of racial equality as such. In order to understand exactly what happened to the principles behind Reconstruction and what had been repudiated along with them, it is essential to begin with a brief introduction to the Radical Republican worldview.

As with the principles of any revolution, the principles of Reconstruction were hotly contested. At the cutting edge of the revolution were those like Tourgée who styled themselves Radical Republicans. The Radical leaders in Congress who led the revolution were few in number, but their message drew upon moral and political values widely held in Northern middle classes. A glimpse into the Radical worldview can be found in Horatio Bateman's ambitious 1867 illustration, simply titled *Reconstruction*. Though somewhat overcrowded with imagery, Bateman's allegorical interpretation evoked all of the elements of the radical meaning of the Civil War that Tourgée would come to personify in a later era, and thus it offers a useful introduction to his ideological roots. A New York artist, Bateman created this work with the hope that it would prove "useful and instructive" in promoting the congressional Reconstruction program by capturing the meaning of these policies in a single, stirring illustration. But he also felt it necessary to include a sixteen-page pamphlet, sold along with the illustration, in which all the figures and scenes represented were fully explained.[26]

At the centerpiece of the illustration stands a large pavilion representing the national government, under which new foundations are being laid. The old foundation of slavery, upon which the Confederate states had rested, has been destroyed. Pillars representing each of the eleven states that had left the Union by secession are now being restored at the left of the picture, as Bateman explains, "with the help of the FREED-MEN who had been made *Citizens*, giving them Civil and Political rights, and [who] plant [the pillars] firmly upon the *new Foundations* placed there for them, when they become *RECONSTRUCTED*."[27] Alternating figures of black and white men carry the Southern states'

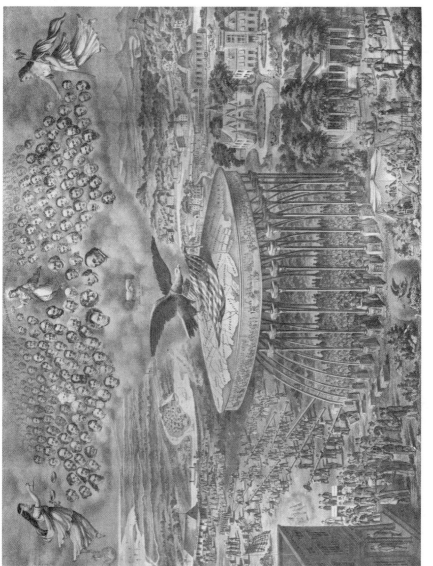

Reconstruction, illustrated by Horatio Bateman, 1867. Collection of the New-York Historical Society (#12611).

pillars back into the Union, under the helpful direction of the Union army, emerging from a building labeled "Freedmen's Bureau." Bateman explains that the new foundations on which they are placed represent "Liberty, Justice, and Education," which signify "the True Idea of Reconstruction" and which replace the old Confederate foundations of "Liberty and Slavery."[28] These three principles—Liberty, Justice, and Education—he notes, had been the foundation of the free states from the beginning, and with "the happy results of Reconstruction" the nation will finally be "United on the *true basis of a Free and Independent Republic*— ONE COUNTRY AND ONE PEOPLE."[29] National reconciliation is accomplished therefore through a political and cultural revolution in the South that introduces equal rights (i.e., Liberty), citizenship (i.e., Justice) and equal opportunity (i.e., Education).

What is most remarkable about the illustration is the depiction of an interracial and integrated citizenry that permeates nearly every corner of Bateman's allegory. On the lower right side of the pavilion, at least sixteen pairs of black and white children can be seen holding hands, locking arms, and playing games in interracial groups in front of a schoolhouse where a white woman and black man greet children at the doors (see detail A, opposite). On the lower left side of the pavilion, a political gathering that represents the body politic takes place in which small, integrated groups of white and black men interact in genteel conversation with each other (see detail B, opposite). According to Bateman, these two scenes represent "Universal Education" and "Universal Suffrage" respectively. At the bottom center of the illustration a black infant and a white infant lie beneath a banner reading "All men are born free and equal," a scene that represents the "Original Equality of the Races" at birth (see detail C, opposite), while near the top of the illustration is shown "the Spirits of a Black, and White man as they leave the GRAVE showing the souls of both alike" in the afterlife.[30] By showing the equality of all men at birth and after death, Bateman suggests that the Christian doctrine of the equality of all souls before God had been brought into harmony with the democratic principle of equal citizenship before the law.

Bateman's image depicts Reconstruction as bringing harmony between the material and spiritual worlds, the secular and the sacred. The upper portion of his illustration shows the spirit world, where the faces of "departed spirits of prominent men" look down "with satisfaction upon Reconstruction." At the center of the crowd of spirits is Jesus himself, positioned between Lincoln and Washington, proclaiming peace and heralding the restoration of the moral law with the words, "Do to others as you would have others do to you." It is significant that the words of the Golden Rule occupy the top center of the illustration, above the head of

A

B

C

Jesus. Flanked by representations of Liberty and Justice, the Golden Rule
is thereby positioned as a kind of "higher law" holding dominion over the
entire scene (see details D and E, below).[31] Chapter 2 addresses in some
depth how appeals to a law higher than the Constitution became common in the 1850s as Northerners sought to justify their civil disobedience
to the Fugitive Slave Law.[32] The blending of nationalist and religious
imagery in Bateman's illustration reflects the antislavery viewpoint typical
of the time. Constitutional law had been finally aligned with God's moral
law as a result of Reconstruction.

D

E

Another example of the infusion of religion into radical ideology comes from the most comprehensive constitutional argument against segregation made before the Civil War. Charles Sumner, who became the leading Radical Republican senator during Reconstruction, made a ground-breaking case against school segregation before the Massachusetts Supreme Judicial Court in 1849. "The Christian spirit, then, I again invoke," Sumner declared near the conclusion of his brief in *Roberts v. City of Boston*, "from this, we derive new and solemn assurance of the Equality of Men, as an ordinance of God. Human bodies may be unequal in beauty or strength; these mortal cloaks of flesh may differ, as do these worldly garments . . . but amid all unessential differences there is essential agreement and equality." Bolstering his constitutional arguments with religious doctrine, Sumner insisted that racial differences were as inconsequential as clothing, being mere outward apparel, while the essence of the self was the eternal soul. Sumner, like Bateman, urged that earthly law must be made to agree with the divine law, as he concluded: "[All] are equal in the sight of God; they must be equal in the sight of all human institutions."[33] After the war, Sumner came to believe that his argument in *Roberts* offered the best rationale for Reconstruction, and he consequently ordered it published in pamphlet form and distributed throughout the South.[34]

In the radical atmosphere of 1867, it was possible to believe that the utter obliteration of the color-line would be the logical consequence of emancipation and the desired goal of Reconstruction. Though, in truth, it would necessitate a social revolution on both sides of the Mason and Dixon line to bring to fruition Bateman's and Sumner's vision, it nevertheless followed the logic that had been growing in the antislavery movement for decades. Though the religious influence has often been overlooked in the study of Radical Republican thought, it served as the most important foundation of the radicals' belief in racial equality. The secular principles of the Declaration of Independence, the full text of which was included in Bateman's pamphlet, had merged with Christian precepts even in the antislavery arguments of such moderates as Abraham Lincoln.[35]

In Bateman's allegorical illustration *Reconstruction* one can detect in the background, and on the margins, some of the seeds of the Radicals' downfall. Railroad trains and navigable waterways are clearly visible in the backdrop of the illustration, connecting the South and West to the rest of the nation and symbolizing the promise of economic progress that would come from the opening of new markets to Northern investment and industry. Northern confidence in the railroads as the engine of progress and prosperity would turn out to be the source of much turmoil during Reconstruction. Instead of bearing the promised economic miracle to the South, they bore scandals of political and financial corruption that would be severely damaging to Reconstruction at both the state and federal levels. Even worse, they transported the nation into a crushing economic depression that began when railroad construction unexpectedly hit stagnation in 1873 after decades of expansion. These setbacks sprang from conditions endemic to the construction of the railroads everywhere, but they had far-reaching ill-consequences for the proponents of Reconstruction. Scandal and economic deprivation led to the political reversals of the mid-1870s that defeated the Republicans and delivered the Southern state governments back into the hands of the old ruling class.[36]

But all of this remained in the future in 1867. It would be wrong to presume that the eventual overthrow and repudiation of Reconstruction was indicative of a lack of sincere commitment to the principle of racial equality at the outset. The overriding goal that united Radical Republicans was to establish an interracial, color-blind citizenry throughout the nation. This is indeed what made the Radicals "radical." For a few "mystical years," as Du Bois put it, this vision seemed to gain acceptance in the North as the inevitable outcome of emancipation and the only justice for the freedpeople. Bateman placed his allegorical Justice and Education at the heart of the Reconstruction program, and in the hands of radicals like Tourgée these remedies were truly revolutionary. Justice, for Tourgée, meant simply "equality before the law" and "no discrimination on account of race," both of which were put forward by Radicals as the constitutional basis for Reconstruction. Education meant self-improvement and upward social mobility for all regardless of race. Though some scholars have viewed education as a vehicle of moral indoctrination and white social control, Radicals, as we will see, saw it quite differently.

Critics of congressional Reconstruction, including President Andrew Johnson himself, accused the Radicals of favoritism toward blacks, claiming that their policies provided "safeguards" for black citizens that went "infinitely beyond any that the General Government have ever provided for the white race."[37] In response to such accusations, Republicans in Congress took pains to defuse the outcry of "black supremacy" by wisely adopting a language of race-neutrality in its legislation. Ohio Congressman Robert C. Schenk made this point when he insisted that the Freedmen's Bureau Bill of 1866 made "no distinction on account of color," and remarked that for Republicans this had become "a favorite phrase, as is well understood, in these times among us all."[38] Abolitionist Wendell Phillips exemplified this strategy too when he campaigned for a version of the Fourteenth Amendment, eventually introduced on the floor of Congress by Thaddeus Stevens, that would have prohibited any state from making "any distinction in civil rights" based on "race, color, or descent." The final version of the Fourteenth Amendment employed race neutrality by avoiding any direct reference to race at all, discarding Phillips's phrasing in favor of the more ambiguous "equal protection" clause that lent itself to greater interpretation.[39] Impartial justice, in all of these formulations, was the emphasis.

An enormous challenge for Reconstruction was that, for most Southern whites, accepting blacks as equal citizens meant accepting a policy formulated by Republicans that would result in the electoral dominance of the Republican Party in the South. Few believed such a self-serving policy could be based on principle. When he first took the bench in North Carolina, Tourgée was accused of being "a partisan judge" because he intended on "administering laws made by partisans for partisan party purposes."[40] From the conservative perspective, justices elected by an interracial, Republican majority were inherently "corrupt." "I do not understand the word *corruption* to mean simply the receiving of money for official acts," one North Carolina conservative testified before a Congressional Committee in 1870, assenting that "If a judge allows his decisions to be governed by political bias, that is one species of corruption." This witnesses specified, "[In fact] I have heard Judge Tourgee charged with corruption simply on that account."[41] As an outspoken Republican, Tourgée was regarded as inherently biased and partisan by many white Southerners.

When Tourgée accepted the nomination in 1868 to be a Superior Court Judge for North Carolina's 7th District, he felt pressure to demonstrate his impartiality by withdrawing from politics. Yet, he refused to do so. His pledge in accepting the nomination, which would become an oft-repeated philosophy, was to be an outspoken Republican outside the courtroom, but to administer the laws impartially within it. "It has been said that a judge should not be a partizan [*sic*] and so far as the performance of his judicial duties is concerned, nothing should be truer," Tourgée acknowledged but insisted, "I cannot accede to the proposition that it is the duty of a judge to so far forget his citizenship" as to maintain a public silence on matters of political importance. "Within the penetralia of Justice, all the exterior relations of life should be forgotten," he explained, "and like the goddess who represents [justice], the judge should be blind to friend or foe."[42]

Remarkably, by practicing impartial justice, Judge Tourgée earned the grudging respect of many conservatives and slowly overcame fierce opposition to enjoy considerable popular approval by the end of his six-year term in 1874. He accomplished this, in part, by running an efficient and competent courtroom that rapidly dispensed with a massive backlog of cases he inherited. But no less important, he administered equal justice regardless of race or party politics. In a review of his courtroom entitled

"Can Any Good Thing Come Out of Radicalism?" a conservative commentator observed in 1873: "As a judge he, seemingly, presides with becoming dignity, commendable firmness and acknowledged impartiality." "We don't know what Judge Tourgee is at home," the reviewer concluded, "but, as a judge, he certainly made a most favorable impression here, upon jurors, clients, court house loiterers and attorneys. If it is treason to say this of a political adversary it is treason to speak the truth."[43] Such sentiments were typical by the end of his term. Other conservatives paid him compliments for being "faithful to his trust," "unbiased by party prejudice" and "an excellent court disciplinarian."[44] Though not all joined in his praise, the extent to which Tourgée vindicated his claim to impartial justice was impressive.

How did Tourgée overcome such intense conservative skepticism? The turning point in his judicial term came perhaps in 1870 during the height of the Ku Klux Klan's campaign of terror in North Carolina. In January of that year, Tourgée's jurisprudence had come under attack on the floor of the state legislature where State Senator John W. Graham had accused him of acting as a "partisan judge" who used his position merely to favor blacks and punish conservatives. Citing his decision to set aside two separate guilty verdicts for "a colored man found guilty of larceny," Graham insisted that Tourgée's partisanship had forced the white men of Orange County to undertake their own "species of wild justice" in a series of lynchings to instill law and order among blacks. Graham reported being told this directly by "the men themselves" who committed the lynchings that his rulings had prompted their spree.[45]

With the very legitimacy of his court in question, Tourgée wrote a letter to the editor of the North Carolina *Standard* to explain his actions. Believing there was insufficient evidence to convict the man, he concluded that the all-white jury had disregarded his instructions out of racial prejudice and that, in the words of the defense attorney, no "white man would have been convicted upon the evidence in the case and under the same charge from the Court." After admonishing the senator for his admitted association with "the men themselves," he concluded his letter by pledging:

> In the future, as in the past, I shall continue to act upon my own sense of justice, my own apprehension of the law, and my own conviction of duty, entirely unmindful of whether the same pleases friend or foe, or ascents with the wishes and ideas of the administrators of "wild justice" in the county of Orange or elsewhere or not. I prize my own self-respect too highly to do otherwise believing as I do that justice should be at least "color-blind," I shall know no man by the hue of his skin.[46]

This was his first recorded use of the metaphor of "color-blind" justice.

There is little doubt of Tourgée's sincere belief in the "color-blind" principle. At the time of his letter to the *Standard*, he was receiving death threats from the Klan, and with this statement he, in essence, staked his life on this principle. By taking such a public stand in the face of these threats, he made himself a conspicuous target for the Klan, but he also demonstrated to white Southerners the sincerity of his convictions. A few months later, in June 1870, Tourgée would hold court in Alamance County—the heart of the Klan uprising—against the advice of the local authorities and Governor Holden himself, who had proclaimed the county in a state of rebellion and told Tourgée to suspend his scheduled circuit court session until state troops arrived. His decision to hold his scheduled court at Alamance despite the great risk to his own life (discussed in Chapter Five) added further credibility for his devotion to the rule of law over personal self-interest. It is surely not a coincidence that admiration for Tourgée began to grow in the aftermath of this crisis in which he fulfilled his judicial duties without appearing to yield or compromise his principles.

For Tourgée, the metaphor *color-blind justice* referred to a transcendent goal of equality before the law, regardless of race. It did not blind him to the multifarious influence of racism in his courtroom nor prevent him from taking active measures to combat it. When Tourgée threw out the convictions in the larceny case in the name of color-blind justice, he did so because he felt the jury's verdict had been based on racial prejudice rather than a reasonable assessment of the evidence. "The juries are all Ku Klux, or at least a controlling element of them are so," he had complained to his wife soon before the incident.[47] To achieve equality before the law, therefore, he found it necessary to take the realities of racism into account. In another effort to do so, he fought back against all-white juries by tearing up old jury lists in his districts and using his influence to ensure that jurors were not excluded on account of their race. His policy of including on juries "enough negroes to satisfy his own sense of justice," as one opponent put it, elicited much criticism at first, but when mixed juries proved capable of reaching verdicts without regard to the defendant's race and political affiliation, opposition to them quieted.[48]

At the 1870 trial of Nelson Marrow, a black man accused of barnburning, the white mob backed down when the court proceedings proved themselves fair and unbiased. Marrow's white lawyer, Ike Strayhorn, recalled years later, "every ruling, every question, every utterance [was] watched & weighted [sic] by an enraged crowd thirsting for blood and for the blood of any who would shield him." When Judge Tourgée suggested that the trial be moved to another, safer district, Strayhorn refused, fearing that such an attempt would unleash immediate mob action against not only Marrow, but himself and perhaps the judge as well. "You who presided and I who defended went before the public with our lives in our hands," Strayhorn reminded Tourgée; one misstep and "the Fool's Errand might have ended right there." When a racially mixed jury exonerated Marrow, amazingly, the local mob accepted the verdict—a fact that Strayhorn attributed to the authoritative persuasion of Tourgée's courtroom. "You, by your fairness, firmness, and decision, justly saved that poor Negro," he reminisced with Tourgée in 1887. "I heard from him lately: he is living in Wilson and doing well."[49]

Evidence indicates that, despite his political sympathies, Tourgée kept to his pledge to be blind to "friend or foe" in his administration of the law. His rulings left Republicans as often discomfited as conservatives. While he regularly received anonymous threats from conservative opponents, in at least two instances he received threatening mail from persons claiming to be Republicans. Apparently reacting to the dismissal of charges against suspected Klan members, one note, signed by "Many Persons," accused him of accepting bribes. "We never thought you would have sold your selfe [sic] to a damed [sic] a party as the Ku-clucks," the note stated, "you have went back on us and you will be rewarded." A subsequent note a few weeks later in the same style indicated that Tourgée had ignored the threat and made no effort to reassure his Republican supporters.[50] Nothing came of these misguided threats and, in truth, no one was more disappointed at the escape of the Klan members from indictment than the judge himself.

On another occasion, Tourgée sentenced three black men to harsh prison terms for committing acts of terror and intimidation in disguise against another black man, which ironically violated the Enforcement (or Ku Klux Klan) Act of 1871. The conservative press used this case, as it did all of his rulings that went against Republican interests, to discredit Tourgée among his followers. "Freedmen remember!" the *Greensboro Patriot* entreated: "Judge Tourgee ascertained, at his last court in Alamance, that all the murders, whippings and barn-burnings had been done by the Loyal Leagues [sic] under the garb of the Ku Klux! Remember fellow citizens, that the only men convicted of Ku Kluxing in this State, were the three negroes sentenced to the penitentiary by Judge Tourgee!"[51] Despite the super-charged atmosphere and the shameless manipulation of his rulings for political purposes, Tourgée's jurisprudence remained unmoved by partisan pressures. In the interests of fairness, however, he later fought insistently, but unsuccessfully, for the release of the three convicted black men after the dozens of Klan members subsequently convicted under this law were pardoned in 1873.[52]

Nor did he let his own religious beliefs interfere with his duty to administer the law as he interpreted it. Tourgée personally objected to the death penalty as a sin, and he actively sought to abolish it, but that did not prevent him from applying it when he felt that the facts of the case required it. After sentencing two black men to death when a racially mixed jury convicted them of a gruesome murder, his distress was evident as he reported to his wife that the sentence had prompted him to break his personal boycott of the local churches: "It was a horrid affair, but it was a terrible task for me to sentence them. I have been to church—Episcopal—today."[53] His stern administration of the law did not soften even when presented with a show of penitence or religious conversion by the convicted. "I have *sworn* to administer the law, and I were a poor officer, a false man, if I failed to do it," he replied to one lawyer's plea for clemency for his client. "His *conversion,* or even his *sanctification,* would have no more effect upon the judgment which I am called to give than the color of his skin or the name of his father."[54]

Tourgée believed that, in time, white Southerners would become used to the principle of equal justice and embrace the moral law of human equality. Therefore, education was central to his Reconstruction agenda, and it was as necessary for poor whites as it was for blacks. Reason, logic, and knowledge were essential for the apprehension of moral truth. Public schools were practically nonexistent for poor whites and blacks alike throughout the antebellum South—which he regarded as the source of their subordination to the planter class. With the establishment of schools, he believed both the class and caste systems would be broken. Race prejudice would weaken as poor whites learned to base their judgments on reason and as blacks proved their equality by demonstrating the capacity for intellectual advancement.

Though some scholars have denigrated Northern efforts to educate freedpeople as driven by a desire to culturally homogenize and economically control them, this was not the goal as Tourgée saw it.[55] Recalling the advantages gained from his own education in rural Ohio, he viewed it as the only means of advancement for those who, like himself, lacked family wealth or connections. Academic achievement led to individual empowerment and autonomy, not cultural or economic dependency. "The first result of knowledge is to teach the individual his rights; the next, to inspire him to assert and maintain them," he insisted. It also provided the intellectual skills necessary for social advancement: "Knowledge is power, whether for good or ill," he wrote in another instance. "Every colored man or woman who has learned to read and write makes the race just so much harder to control—so much the more dangerous to oppress."[56]

This is not to say that Tourgée disavowed a culturally imperialistic agenda. But, the cultural "uplift" he proposed for the South was rooted in a deep respect for human equality and individual rights. The moral and religious underpinnings of Tourgée's creed were made clear in a lecture that he delivered regularly on the North Carolina lecture circuit in 1876–77. Entitled "The Ben Adhemite Era," after one of his favorite childhood poems, this speech advanced Christian ethics as the basis for democratic society.[57] He asserted that the first true principles of democracy and humanitarianism had their origins in the Christian religion and had been progressively unfolding throughout the globe since the time of Jesus of Nazareth. "The idea of human oneness and correlative duty [toward others] was absolutely new," when first preached by Jesus, Tourgée argued. Greek democracy had restricted citizenship to property owners and coexisted with human slavery. "In all the ancient languages there was no word at all corresponding to our present use of the word 'Humanity'" until introduced in the teachings of Jesus. The concept of human oneness was "at the heart and core, the keystone of the Nazarene religion," he explained:

> "Do unto others as ye would that they should do to you." "Love thy neighbor as thyself." "What God hath cleansed call not thou common." "Of one blood hath He made all nations of the Earth." These are some of the pearls of wisdom that fell from his lips.

Tourgée urged his Southern audience to adopt these values, not out of religious faith, but out of fidelity to the democratic tradition on which the American republic was founded. "It matters not . . . whether he of Galilee was an inspired being . . . or whether he was a philosopher of such depths of discernment as first to fathom human nature and declare its hidden oneness," he insisted. "Whether he was the Messiah . . . is immaterial so far as the relation of these ideas is concerned."[58] What mattered was that the rise of democratic governments, the expansion of individual liberty, and the downfall of slavery had proved the moral truth of this philosophy and its connection to human progress.

A final example from Tourgée's Reconstruction career demonstrates the liberating individualism embedded within his worldview. In 1878, after his judicial term expired, he represented the first woman to petition for admittance to the State Bar of North Carolina as her legal counsel. The twenty-five-year-old Tabitha A. Holton applied for an attorney's license at the same time as her younger brother Samuel, but her application was questioned on account of her sex. Tabitha probably received legal training from Tourgée, who was a practicing attorney in Raleigh and accompanied her and her brother to their application for examination. Previously, Tourgée had trained their older brother, Alfred E. Holton, who went on to have a long, distinguished legal career in the state. When the younger Holtons' applications were presented, the Supreme Court agreed to hold a formal hearing on Tabitha's case, no doubt at Tourgée's request. The very next morning, he presented a meticulously prepared, lengthy argument on her behalf to the Court. A women's rights journal that later reported on the case would praise "the excellent charge of Judge Tourgee" and commend it "to all thinking women."[59]

Arguing broadly for the rights of women, Tourgée linked the liberation of women to the abolition of slavery and the destruction of caste systems everywhere. The hearing attracted extensive press coverage, especially because her application provoked the opposition of William H. Battle, a distinguished ex–Supreme Court justice who still had influence on the Court. Tourgée refuted the argument that women were not intended to be included in the term *person* when the antebellum North Carolina Legislature's statute was originally framed. Although the statute's language stated merely that "any persons who may apply for admission to practice as attorneys in any court shall undergo an examination," other contemporary legislation was shown to explicitly exclude women from other professions and strictly limit their sphere of activity. Acknowledging this, Tourgée replied that the legislature's original intent was irrelevant, as a revolution had occurred in the years since the statute had been passed. "The Court has already held that the term 'person' in this state includes colored males which was certainly as far from the intent of the Legislature at the time of its adoption as the construction now contended for could *possibly* be," he told the Court. "The same reason which induced the Court to extend the law to the colored men, applies with equal force to women. The circumstances surrounding the former had been changed by revolution. The circumstances which surround the latter are constantly changing by the progress of enlightened thought."[60] Enlightened "progress," he believed, tended toward the widening of individual rights and opportunities. Why should women be excluded from this trend?

Declaring himself "in favor of enlarging the sphere of women's activity," Tourgée described the prejudice against women's advancement in a manner that resonated with parallels to the history of racial prejudice and slavery: "A quarter century ago public sentiment was shocked at the idea of a woman engaging in business. She could not do so without losing caste. A brand like a spot of leprosy was put upon her, however great her necessity." Yet, in the wake of the Civil War "this is changed," and the stigma of caste had begun to fade away for women in the workforce. "Now, women are presidents of banks," he observed, "they are physicians, cashiers, employers and employees in almost all branches of business." He directly challenged Justice Battle's objection that it would be improper for women to work in professions that exposed them to indelicate matters. Though it "clothes itself in the guise of chivalric concern for women,"

Tourgée dismissed this objection because women had proven themselves able to handle all manner of indelicacy during the Civil War. The work of the "noble Christian women who attended the wayside hospitals of the South" exposed the fallacy of "rag tag chivalry" that vanished in a time of crisis. Describing Holton as a "simple, earnest country girl, who desired to elevate herself and her family," he concluded, she "only asks of the court the privilege of using the brain which God has given her . . . she asks no favors, but a fair chance." Tourgée's argument prevailed and the Court administered her examination. Holton promptly passed, and soon afterwards opened a law practice with Samuel in Dobson. North Carolina became the first Southern state, and only the sixth state in the Union, to admit women to the bar.[61]

For Tourgée, individual empowerment was the key to a democratic society. Democracy would achieve its purpose only when every individual was valued according to his or her own merit and given an equal chance for success. If radicalism is measured by an idea's potential to effect social change, then his individualism—which fueled his concept of color-blind justice, his educational agenda, and his humanitarian ethics—was truly radical. The fervor with which Tourgée advanced this secularized gospel during Reconstruction reflected his absolute confidence in its eventual triumph. The failure of its realization, and the turn away from these ideals in the retreat from Reconstruction, left him perplexed and ultimately disillusioned and shattered. In his long letter from Bordeaux, he lamented of his Reconstruction efforts: "I was never more a Fool than when I thought knowledge and Christian civilization would peacefully reconcile the new barbarism [i.e., white supremacist violence] with the Christ-idea of justice between man and man, and race and race, or our national ideal of equal right, security, justice and opportunity for all."[62] That had been the essence of his Reconstruction crusade. We now turn to the origin of his radicalism to discover why he believed such "foolishness."

PART II

The Radical Advance

2

The Making of a Radical Individualist in Ohio's Western Reserve

Must the citizen ever for a moment, or in the least degree resign his conscience to the legislator? Why has every man a *conscience*, then? . . . I say, break the law. Let your life be a counter-friction to stop the machine.

—Henry David Thoreau, "Resistance to Civil Government," 1849

Whoso would be a man must be a nonconformist . . . nothing is at last sacred but the integrity of your own mind.

—Ralph Waldo Emerson, "Self-Reliance," 1841

WHEN FREDERICK DOUGLASS DIED IN FEBRUARY OF 1895, the people of Boston called for a memorial service to honor him. Proud of its abolitionist heritage, Boston's city council chose to hold a ceremony for the great black abolitionist at Faneuil Hall, once the favored site for rallies in the heyday of the movement. Members of Douglass's family and former abolitionist colleagues spoke at the ceremony, but the task of delivering the main eulogy was given to Albion W. Tourgée. His two-hour address, delivered on December 20, 1895, was later published at the city's expense.[1]

Tourgée had been neither a close friend of Douglass's nor a former abolitionist. "We met occasionally as our paths crossed, here and there," Tourgée said of Douglass. "Our acquaintance was always candid, earnest, thoughtful—never continuous or intimate."[2] Tourgée was not chosen to eulogize Douglass because of his personal knowledge of the man. Rather, he was chosen because he had carried on the crusading spirit of the abolitionist movement more faithfully than any other white American. Indeed, the torrent of abuse that had been recently directed at Tourgée in the press was so reminiscent of the early public reception to the abolitionists that to many he had become the "new Garrison."[3]

Hoping to rekindle the spirit of the early abolitionist movement, Tourgée reminded his audience of the courage it took for antislavery speakers such as Douglass to face down hostile audiences and brave public scorn and ridicule. He dramatically illustrated this theme by telling the story of his own first encounter with Douglass "some forty years" earlier. Tourgée's youth had been spent in the Western Reserve section of Ohio, a notorious hotbed of abolitionism, where boisterous public debates were regular events and Tourgée witnessed Douglass's dramatic confrontation with a heckling audience. At the time, many people held abolitionists — and African Americans in general — responsible for the rapidly escalating sectional crisis over slavery. Despite the prominence of local abolitionists, Frederick Douglass could not expect a warm welcome in the Western Reserve. Indeed Sojourner Truth's famous "Aren't I A Woman?" speech was said to be delivered before a taunting Western Reserve crowd in 1851.[4]

Tourgée recalled how, with great anticipation at the youthful age of "a dozen years" or so, he went to hear Douglass speak. He described vividly how Douglass's "eyes flashed" and his "lithe but powerful frame swayed with the force of his emotion" while he testified against the "sins" of slavery in loud and "impassioned tones." The frankness of his remarks stunned some members of the audience and "murmurs of disapproval" became increasingly audible as his talk progressed. When "one of the shafts of his denunciation struck deeper than the others," Tourgée recalled, it provoked "a storm of groans and hisses" as well as a few projectiles. One of these struck Douglass; he was hit on the shoulder by an egg that splashed onto the side of his face, leaving "yellow streaks on his black beard and mustache" and yellow traces across his "long wavy hair." The scene prompted the young Tourgée to laugh — and laugh loudly — at Douglass's humiliation. He quickly regretted it, for a nervous hush had fallen over the room the moment the egg hit its mark and Tourgée's laugh rang out. Douglass, as well as several audience members, cast accusing glares in the young lad's direction, which happened to be the same direction from which the egg had been hurled. Then, as Tourgée described it, the orator unleashed "an overwhelming tide of denunciatory eloquence" that had "rarely [been] equalled in any age or by any orator." When he was finished, the audience dispersed, while praising the courage of Douglass and believing Tourgée guilty of hurling the egg.[5]

The next day, Albion decided that he must somehow exonerate himself from suspicion. So he went to Douglass to humble himself in apology, "not for the egg for which [I] was guiltless, but for the laugh, which [I] regretted." But he found this self-congratulatory act of humbling himself to a "Negro" was not received with the anticipated gratitude. Tourgée recalled, "It was not a pleasant call. The orator was still sore over the indignity that had been offered him. The affront was one apologies could not cure." The young Albion found himself listening "wonderingly" to "a furious tale of insults [Douglass] had suffered because he was a colored man pleading for justice to his people." Tourgée's attentiveness, or stunned silence, eventually prevailed on Douglass to relent and grant the boy the benefit of the doubt. Satisfied that his point had been made, Douglass let the young man go. "The interview ended peacefully," Tourgée recalled, "as if in apology for its rough beginning."[6]

This anecdote, told forty years after the fact, undoubtedly contains some dramatic embellishment and distortion of memory. But its fundamental elements ring true. Though abolitionists were no longer being mobbed in the 1850s, their reception on the lecture circuit continued to be punctuated by hecklers.[7] Though Tourgée characterized himself as approximately twelve years old, the incident probably occurred when he was somewhat older and less innocent, at sixteen. The date cannot be verified, but it likely occurred in July 1854, the only documented instance of Douglass visiting the Western Reserve while Tourgée was still a youth. His speaking tour of northeast Ohio began that month with a celebrated speech, "The Claims of the Negro Ethnologically Considered," delivered as the commencement address at Western Reserve College (now Case Western) in Hudson. Hailed by abolitionist papers as a "triumph for humanity," this speech marked Douglass's first systematic critique of "scientific" racism and the first time a black man, and former slave, had been given the honor of delivering a college commencement address in America.[8] This event brought a great deal of publicity to Douglass's subsequent speaking tour, during which he no doubt continued to address the controversial theme of racial equality.

Moreover, indirect evidence supports Tourgée's account of the tongue-lashing he received at Douglass's door. Douglass, reflecting on his Ohio tour immediately afterwards, vented his irritation with patronizing whites in his newspaper column. Referring to himself in the first-person plural, he wrote: "Sometimes we think that the public has an entirely too extravagant notion of our amiability . . . which allows anybody and everybody to claim a portion of our time and attention, apparently without the slightest apprehension that their advances will be construed as intrusiveness." Though Douglass gave no specific examples of these intrusive "advances," he went on to express his exasperation with actions precisely such as the apology offered by young Tourgée:

> [These advances] would be tolerable . . . but for the patronizing and favor-extending air with which these advances are performed—Almost everybody appears to think that our negroship will be highly delighted by remarks of their consideration—that they will be pouring balm into a

wounded soul by allowing themselves to be seen giving us the most condescending recognition. It is really amazing (within certain limits) to observe
the self-satisfied air with which we are thus condescendingly approached.[9]

If nothing else, this passage shows the accuracy of Tourgée's depiction
of Douglass's personality and his feelings about apologies such as the one
he attempted.

More important than the accuracy of this incident, however, is the lesson
that Tourgée hoped to impart to his 1895 Boston audience. This archetypical
scene echoed the prevailing hagiography of the abolitionist movement that
celebrated the men and women who had the courage of their convictions.
William Lloyd Garrison had frequently likened himself and his followers
to the early Christian martyrs, and this tradition was continued in memoirs and histories like Parker Pillsbury's *Acts of the Anti-Slavery Apostles*
(1883).[10] The hallowed image of the Christian martyr resonated deeply for
Tourgée, who had himself confronted relentless public ridicule and threats
of violence since his days as a North Carolina carpetbagger. Tourgée's
dramatic retelling of his encounter with Douglass drove home this mythico-
historical interpretation by emphasizing these elements of the story.

The lesson of his anecdote is found not only in its familiar icono-
graphic elements, but also in Tourgée's surprising account of his personal
meeting with Douglass afterwards. Having been rebuffed in his attempt to
apologize to him in a self-congratulatory way enabled Tourgée to see
Douglass not as a symbol or as an object to be pitied but as a unique individual. He saw an obstinately proud man who struggled painfully for
social acceptance and a simple recognition of his human dignity. Vividly
relating this encounter, Tourgée tried to bring his white Northern audience to contemplate their own failure to treat Douglass as a true social
equal.[11] Despite his extraordinary political abilities, Tourgée lamented,
Frederick Douglass had been deprived of the kind of reward and social
status that would have come to him in a truly meritocratic society. "Given
a white skin," Tourgée told his Boston audience, "there is no limit to be
placed on the political success he might have achieved." Remarking
about America's meritocratic creed, he ruely observed: "A white skin is
the greatest blessing that has been enjoyed on American soil."[12]

Tourgée's eulogy offers several clues to his political worldview and the
nature of his commitment to racial equality. The eulogy casts the evils of
racial prejudice in strikingly individualistic terms: it blocks upward mobility;
it fails to recognize and reward talent; and it undermines a truly partici-
patory democratic culture. Empowered by the right of free speech and motivated by individual self-improvement, Douglass achieved the ultimate
expression of the promise of democracy, though even he could not fully
overcome the barrier of racial prejudice and enjoy his just deserts.

Douglass's hardest lesson, Tourgée said, was when he learned that "the long struggle for the abolition of slavery was not the end of the conflict for the establishment and perfection of the liberty of the individual. The destruction of slavery had only unmasked the other and more difficult problem of caste." But, Tourgée insisted that American democracy would one day fulfill its egalitarian promises by eliminating the final barrier to fully realized individuality. He concluded: "We are destined some time to be as ashamed of caste based on color, as we are now ashamed of slavery based on caste. Whether it will require two centuries and a half to overthrow this monster, as it did to destroy its fellow, Heaven only knows."[13]

The success of the abolitionist movement convinced Tourgée that public opinion, no matter how hostile, could be transformed by an uncompromising assertion of the truth. For him, the truth was that race is a superficial characteristic utterly irrelevant to an individual's worth. He believed that democracy meant giving all individuals, regardless of race or heredity, the same opportunity to succeed because great contributions to society could be only made when individuals of great talent were given sufficient opportunity and encouragement to accomplish great things. Moral and material progress resulted when individuals were given the widest possible room for thought and self-improvement. But, what made Tourgée so confident in the unleashed capacity of the individual? Why was it that he could believe that race was not a fundamental determinant of one's abilities as a human being? To understand the source of his political principles, it is important to understand the wider culture from which Tourgée, the individual, had sprung.

AN ORPHAN IN SPIRIT

Tourgée's value system was the product of a particular place and time. He spent his youth in the Western Reserve of Ohio at a time when this region of the country was a veritable cauldron of radicalism on political, religious, and social issues. The Western Reserve, a label not much used today, consisted of twelve counties in northeast Ohio, covering about 5,000 miles of land on the southern border of Lake Erie. Originally granted to the state of Connecticut by the Northwest Ordinance of 1787, this territory was known alternatively as New Connecticut, the Connecticut Reserve, or Connecticut's Western Reserve, until 1800. In that year, Congress belatedly incorporated the Western Reserve into the Ohio Territory, although the deeds for much of the land already had been collected in the hands of Connecticut speculators. The Western Reserve has been called the "last footprint of Puritanism" in the West because it marked the terminal point of a solid line of New England migration that stretched from Massachusetts, through Connecticut, across upstate New York, and through western Pennsylvania, to northeastern Ohio. Its small towns and farming villages bore a striking material resemblance to the towns and villages of New England.[14]

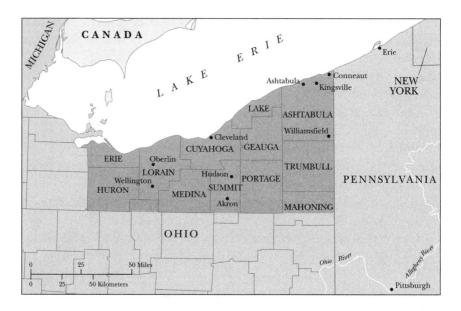

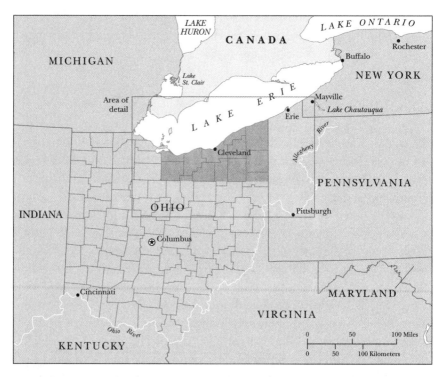

The disinherited sons and daughters of Connecticut and Massachusetts who settled there, however, felt a strong sense of independence from the staid New England social hierarchy they left behind. Spiritually orphaned from New England's institutional establishment, the western migrants transformed their cultural heritage to fit their new circumstances. As a frontier region in the 1810s and 1820s, the Western Reserve lacked the institutional hierarchies of New England, especially an established local church structure. Itinerant Methodist and Baptist preachers who traveled through the Ohio frontier left behind scores of believers who continued their work in informal gatherings of followers, often without the assistance of a minister. Methodism, in particular, dominated the Western Reserve and the West generally, primarily because it provided a powerful unifying force in newly settled frontier communities. Its doctrine of free will and individual responsibility, which rejected the need for learned ministers, fit nicely with the antiauthoritarian spirit of the post-Revolutionary West.[15]

Both western New York and Ohio's Western Reserve developed a distinct egalitarian culture that was fiercely committed to the self-improvement of the individual. In the 1820s and 1830s, these frontier regions became known as "burned-over" districts because of the intense religious revivals that swept through them like a brush fire ignited by still more itinerant preachers. In the process, the cultural landscape of both regions were significantly altered as a multiplicity of reform movements, religious sects, and utopian communities sprang up, giving these regions a reputation for radicalism. The bewildering variety of visionaries shared only the one common belief that society and individuals could be transformed for the better or even perfected. By the 1850s and 1860s, these regions would become Radical Republican strongholds providing the strongest support for the most radical legislation of the Reconstruction era.[16]

Tourgée, for one, believed that the social and economic conditions that followed the frontier stage of development were most responsible for the egalitarian spirit of the Western Reserve. "The Reserve never knew an Aristocracy," Tourgée wrote proudly of his native region in 1868. "The change from New England often reversed the relations of the various families. The 'brahmin blood' of many old families did not give them any preeminence in the Reserve, and so it came that what has formed an aristocracy [in the Northeast] . . . was nipped in the bud."[17] The shake-up of population and social status was most beneficial for Tourgée's generation. Having come too late to experience the rough frontier conditions, they found opportunities abundant in this rapidly developing society and upward mobility mostly unencumbered by an established class of wealth and position. Not even the embryonic formation of an industrial working class existed for most of the antebellum period in the Western Reserve, except in the port city of Cleveland. The population consisted primarily of small farmers who exhibited a proud attachment to the plot of land that had been "reserved" for them and had allowed them to escape the northeastern land shortage that forced many others into a state of economic dependence as wage workers.[18]

Tourgée's father, Valentine Tourgée, Jr., who emigrated to the Western Reserve at the end of its frontier period in the 1830s, was typical of many first-generation settlers. Born on a small farm in Framingham, Massachusetts, in 1813, Valentine was the tenth of eleven children and thus unlikely to inherit land that customarily was passed to the oldest son. Therefore, Valentine and his elder brother, Cyrus, and their nephew, John Brown, left their father's farm as young adults and, after working as migratory farm hands for a short time, found their way into the paper mills of Lee, Massachusetts, in the 1830s.[19] A farmer at heart, Valentine saved whatever capital he could from his job at the mill in hopes of someday purchasing land for himself in the West.

Valentine's experience at the paper mill left him with a lifelong antipathy toward factory work and the conditions of urban poverty. Long afterwards, he continued to rail against "such manufacturing places as Lee," where, he complained, "the mass becomes a sink of corruption and sin."[20] Like many factory workers of the time, Valentine viewed his employment as a degrading dependency that could only be tolerated as a temporary situation. A fortuitous romantic match turned this expectation into a reality. In 1836, he became betrothed to Louisa Emma Winegar, one of seven children of Jacob Winegar, a respected businessman from a prominent Lee family.

Though Louisa belonged to a higher social class than Valentine, the stigma of being a "wage worker" did not present an insuperable barrier toward their marriage. The couple secured the blessing of her parents, it seems, without much trouble. In fact, the couple were married in a dual ceremony in which Valentine's brother Cyrus married one of Louisa's sisters, Ann. As soon as the marriage ceremony was completed, the two couples headed west, thanks no doubt to the Winegars' financial assistance. The Tourgée brothers, their wives, their nephew John Brown, and perhaps other friends and family members, headed westward as part of a large caravan of emigrants seeking better opportunities.[21]

After considering several areas in western New York, the settlers obtained land for themselves near the town of Williamsfield in Ashtabula County, which occupies the extreme northeast corner of the Western Reserve. Though the climate of the Western Reserve could be extremely harsh in winter, the region was dotted by successful small farms and had recently established a growing number of churches, schools, academies, colleges, libraries, literary societies, and reform organizations. Institutional structures had taken hold as the frontier phase of development was coming to a close. But establishing a homestead and raising a successful crop proved to be no easy task. Louisa spent much of the time bedridden with a succession of illnesses, and she gave birth to two children who died in their infancy. Albion, born on May 2, 1838, was the result of her third pregnancy and the only child of the couple to reach adulthood.[22]

Several tragedies struck the Tourgée household during Albion's infancy. First, in 1841, a mysterious "fever" claimed the lives of both John Brown and Cyrus Tourgée and left their town, in Louisa's words, "torn by deaths relentless." The death of Cyrus hit hard because it prompted her sister Ann to return to Lee and ended the sisters' dream of sharing their lives together out West.[23] Then, for the greater part of 1842 Louisa was confined to her bed with tuberculosis. Louisa died on February 13, 1843, at the age of thirty-three.[24]

The death of Louisa transformed the lives of both father and son. Valentine, who had arrived in Ohio surrounded by family and friends, was left to manage a struggling farm alone with a young child. Before long, once again, a lucrative marriage saved him from his financial woes. Within a year his marriage to a woman named Rowena Snow enabled Valentine to sell his farm and move with his family a few miles north to Kingsville, on the shores of Lake Erie. There he acquired a sizable farm of fifty acres and a two-story house of seven rooms, which had been either the property of Rowena or the result of a rich dowry.[25] But Rowena was greatly resented by six-year-old Albion, and their relationship never overcame this hostility. If she made any effort to become a mother to the young boy, it was rebuffed and soon abandoned. In 1846 Rowena gave birth to a daughter named Rosette, on whom, by all accounts, she exclusively focused her maternal affections afterwards.

Despite his economic improvement, Valentine was emotionally drained by the years of struggle and loss. Long after Louisa's death, he continued to correspond with Louisa's family in Lee. These letters belied any guise of happiness in his new marriage and revealed a fatalistic outlook as well as an increasing turn to religion for comfort. Having concluded that "happiness dwells not on earth," he told friends that he longed for "a period when the turbulent passions of life shall be stilled and we enjoy an unfading rest in heaven."[26] Like many others who found life on the frontier to be full of "trial and affliction," he discovered an attractive religious message in Methodism—Ashtabula County was particularly known for its "fanatical Methodist preachers." Valentine himself became an enthusiastic speaker at prayer meetings and earned a reputation for lengthy supplications that could be heard from a long distance off.[27]

Valentine's religious awakening had significant repercussions for his son. When Valentine had first moved to Kingsville, he expressed hope that his son would become a "distinguished Literati" and that Kingsville's "flourishing academy" would prove advantageous to him.[28] But, his determination to dictate his religious beliefs to Albion conflicted with his former desire to see his son achieve a greater education than himself. Some zealous impulse caused him to burn every book in his library that he deemed immoral in nature. Albion recalled that he was strictly forbidden to read any but his father's books and was compelled to memorize lines from either the Puritan favorites *Paradise Lost* and Edward Young's *Night Thoughts* or the Bible.[29]

By the time of Albion's teenage years, Valentine's authoritarian tendencies had become increasingly unbearable to his son. According to family lore, Albion and Valentine would argue so constantly that often "in the midst of tempestuous debate, [they would] seat themselves at the table . . . pause briefly for the saying of grace; and once this task had been performed as speedily as possible, the verbal combat would be renewed with greater violence than ever."[30] Albion also learned to fear his father's "retributory cudgel" enough that he was known to "hie" into the woods, armed with his father's hunting rifle, where he would survive on game until he deemed it safe to return. A hint that Valentine may have been prone to drunken rages is glimpsed in a letter of 1852 in which Louisa's brother warned him, perhaps in jest, to "not keep getting drunk and laying it to me as you did in your last."[31] But whether or not alcohol abuse was involved, the physical confrontations between father and son occurred with enough frequency for Albion, à la Huck Finn, to develop a fondness for escape into the solitude of the wilderness. He would find occasions, throughout his life, to retreat alone into a nearby wilderness for days at a time taking nothing but a gun or a fishing pole for provisions.[32]

One of the most important events of Albion's early life occurred in 1852 when, as a thirteen-year-old, he was allowed to make a journey back to Lee, Massachusetts, to visit his mother's family. For nearly two years, he lived in the home of his maternal uncle, Jacob Winegar, Jr., and was cared for by his maternal aunt Ann (his mother's sister and Cyrus Tourgée's widow).[33] These years turned out to be critical to the development of his literary aspirations. "Very much attached to any book" since the age of five, Albion delighted at the wealth of literature he encountered in the Winegar home and would later wax nostalgic about the small study and library in which he spent so much time.[34] His precocious intellect so impressed one family friend that the man offered to pay for his tuition and expenses to attend Williams College someday, an offer that was, for unknown reasons, apparently declined.[35] Albion made the most of this freedom from his father's household, as the only surviving letter from him attests. "Little did you think when I left you at Ashtabula that on my 14th birthday I would be enjoying the savior's pardoning love," he bragged to his father. "About 2 months ago during the [camp] meetings I went and God was pleased to have mercy on me, I have joined the Baptist sabbat[h] school."[36] One detects an implication that Valentine had prevented Albion from joining a church previously, perhaps considering him too young for conversion. The fact that he joined a Baptist church, while his father was a devout Methodist, suggests some measure of rebellion in his actions at least.

Upon his return to Ohio, Albion immediately enrolled at Kingsville Academy and dreamed of one day attending Harvard University. His new ambitions soon led to a full-scale revolt against his father's authority. In 1856, at the age of eighteen, Albion abruptly escaped from home and traveled all the way back to Lee where he arrived at his uncle's doorstep. It is unknown what prompted this action, except that it involved a serious conflict with his father. In Lee, Albion found work at a dreaded paper mill and defiantly wrote his father specifically to inform him of it—mentioning his adventures with "associates" that Valentine described as being "of the most debasing character." In response, Valentine wrote a furious letter to Jacob Winegar accusing him of providing "evil counsel" and luring Albion to run away. He asserted: "I happen to know that solicitations and enduce-ments [sic] were held out to [Albion] within 10 or 15 days of his leaving home." He demanded that the Winegars cease "instilling his mind" with ideas of his being "a martyr to parental Tyranny." He also accused the Winegars of telling Albion that "he is not bound to submit to [his father's] maltreatment," and that they would "protect him from such fiendish bar-barity." Valentine did not bother to answer whether or not the "barbarity" of which Albion had accused him was true. Rather, he simply warned, "if [Albion] voluntarily and against my will throw[s] himself beyond my authority or control he must rely on his own resources."[37] This threat perhaps convinced Albion to return to Kingsville, realizing that his dream of going to Harvard would not be fulfilled without his father's support.

On its face, Valentine's authoritarian behavior would seem to contra-dict the individualistic culture so characteristic of the Western Reserve, but in fact his actions merely represent a manifestation of its spirit within the family circle. Valentine, like most evangelical converts, considered his own conscience to be the voice of God and therefore the only auth-ority worthy of his obedience. By such actions as his burning of "immoral" books, Valentine sought to impose his will and instill his beliefs on his household—and particularly on his only son. He seemed unwilling to allow that influences outside of himself should shape his son's value system. Moreover, Valentine's inability to live up to his own strict moral codes—especially if he did battle with Methodism's ban on alcohol— probably intensified his dictatorial behavior regarding Albion's moral upbringing. The guilt and self-reproach the father suffered for his own sins may have been visited upon the son in an attempt to keep him from similarly straying off the path of righteousness. What is most notable is the degree to which Albion challenged his father's authority and refused to succumb to his overbearing personality. Setting his own path in life and refusing to be diverted by any outside pressure, Albion probably mirrored Valentine's own submerged personality before the difficult times turned him fatalistic and narrow-minded.

The relationship between father and son would never be a close one. In fact, Valentine would have little contact with his son after he left home for good in 1863 except for infrequent and noticeably impersonal letters that passed between them. In those, Albion typically listed his latest achievements, while Valentine commented extensively on the weather. After Albion became famous, Kingsville residents would often wonder why he never visited his father, a fact that he awkwardly explained as necessary "[because] only annoyance and discomfort [for Valentine] would result from my doing so."[38]

As an adult, Albion acted strangely evasive about his relationship with his father. When Valentine died in 1889, Albion did not attend his father's funeral, attributing his absence to his stepmother's failure to send notification. Even then, however, Albion did not return home to pay his belated respects, but chose instead to publish an explanatory open letter in the local Kingsville paper telling residents not to construe his absence from the funeral as a sign of bad feelings or "coldness" between him and his father. This bizarre public apology oddly—but significantly—contained no words of eulogy or grief for the loss of his father. Whatever his feelings on this matter, Albion chose to keep them to himself.[39]

Albion had to learn self-reliance at an early age. In 1860, he confided to his fiancée that he had always felt himself "an orphan in spirit" and mused that "the ties of the home circle bind me but slightly."[40] The circumstances of his upbringing shaped his character and personality, but to grasp the foundation of his political principles it is necessary to look beyond his family. He lived in a place of great political ferment at a time when fierce public debates raged over the most fundamental moral and constitutional values. Immersed within this culture, Tourgée would begin to formulate the political principles and moral values that would guide him for the rest of his life.

A QUESTION OF CONSCIENCE

Tourgée's dramatic account of his early encounter with Frederick Douglass might lead one to conclude that he experienced an early conversion to the cause of abolitionism and racial equality. This was not so. Although he lived in a region that was considered by some "the most conspicuous and detested piece of abolition territory in the United States," young Albion Tourgée showed few signs of commitment to the immediate abolition of slavery until after he enlisted in the Union Army at the age of twenty-three.[41] Not that he failed to detest what he referred to in 1860 as the "crying sin of Negro slavery."[42] Like others, he found the institution of slavery immoral and barbaric. In the Western Reserve of his youth all political parties—Whigs, Democrats, Free-Soilers, Know-Nothings, and later Republicans—denounced slavery in the abstract while disagreeing amongst themselves about whether to, or how to, oppose it politically. Only the abolitionists called for immediate and total opposition to slavery.

The groundwork was certainly in place for Tourgée's radicalization, but his political development can only be described as erratic in the 1850s. In response to a request for a biographical sketch of himself in 1868, Tourgée described his youthful political outlook in the following manner:

> My political opinions before the rebellion were of a most heterodox and dangerous character. I was an ardent disciple of Josh Giddings and others of that ilk. I believed that "niggers" were men and slavery damnable, but was still such an egregious ass, as to waste my youthful breath in hurrahing for that cowardly and weak-kneed concern known as the old Whig party. I was cured of this youthful malady by my "experience" during the rebellion.[43]

This brief passage offers an intriguing, but somewhat contradictory and incomplete clue to his political views. Though he identifies himself as a Whig and implies that he remained so until the Civil War, he also insists that he was a devoted follower of Joshua Giddings. But it would have been heterodox indeed—in fact logically impossible—for Tourgée to have supported both the Whigs and Giddings at the same time. The Whig Party shattered in the mid-1850s because of its insistence on compromise over slavery, while Joshua Giddings was an uncompromising abolitionist who bitterly broke with the Whig Party in 1842 (when Tourgée was four years old) and became a Republican in 1855. Moreover, we know that Tourgée was *not* a Whig in 1860, not only because the party had ceased to exist, but because he actively campaigned for the Republicans. So why did Tourgée claim that he remained a "cowardly" compromising Whig supporter until the "rebellion" cured him? Perhaps Tourgée's statement can be explained in terms of a divided loyalty between his father's party, the Whigs, and his own inclination toward radicals like Giddings.[44]

A devoted follower of Whig leader Henry Clay, Valentine Tourgée remained a Whig until the party finally dissolved, at which point he appears to have allied himself with Abraham Lincoln and the Republicans. Though Valentine despised the "sinful" institution of slavery, he likely agreed with Clay that the only solution to the slavery problem was the gradual colonization of blacks to another country—a conviction shared by Lincoln, another Clay devotee. The dream of colonization was a popular idea for those northerners opposed to slavery who wished to avoid a political confrontation. There is no evidence Albion ever supported the colonization movement, and he later wrote scathingly of it as an "utterly futile and insignificant" political alternative. "It neither led nor followed public sentiment," he would write of the American Colonization Society, "neither for or against slavery . . . it led a life of queer indecision, apologizing first to one school of fanatics and then to the other." By putting off public action indefinitely, he felt it had only delayed an inevitable day of reckoning and showed "for the millions in bondage it had no regard."[45] Most likely, it was the slavery issue on which Albion deviated from Whig orthodoxy in the 1850s and found himself drawn to the more confrontational and uncompromising politics of men like Giddings.

More clues to Tourgée's antebellum views can be found in Hot Plowshares, his ambitious 1883 historical novel that dramatized the turbulent events that led to the Civil War. Set in western New York, Tourgée explicitly aimed to provide an accurate history of the time by using fiction to "vivif[y] the past of which history only furnishes the record."[46] In it Tourgée credited the abolitionists with having awakened the moral conscience of the North and set in motion the events that destroyed slavery. So radical was their message to the ears of white Americans that, at first, they were treated with scorn, vituperation, and physical threats so that those "who declared . . . adhesion to the odious dogma" of abolition "must need have the courage of [their] convictions." But the "aggressions of slavery" turned them into "prophets" and what had been the strange obsession of a few fanatics mysteriously grew until it absorbed all else, until "every soul, was wrought up to its best and brightest in assault or defense [of slavery]" and there was left "no middle ground." Compromising politicians, like the Whig party leaders, "who stood by and faltered were ground to powder."[47] This is indeed an apt description of how the issues of slavery and sectionalism overtook the political culture of Ohio in Tourgée's youth. One suspects that his valorization of the abolitionist had roots in his own secret sympathies of that time.

The state of Ohio was an especially fierce battleground during the sectional crisis because it contained both political extremes on the issues of slavery and race.[48] While the Western Reserve was settled by transplanted New Englanders, the southern and western portion of the state had been populated by transplanted white Southerners. Had it not been banished by the Northwest Ordinance of 1787, plantation slavery surely would have thrived in the state, with its abundance of fertile soil. Instead, southern Ohio became a refuge for small, white farmers from the south. These early settlers attempted to exclude black migration into the state by legislation in 1804 and 1807 that required blacks, among other things, to post $500 bonds upon entering Ohio. The "black laws" of the 1820s and 1830s excluded resident blacks from juries, public schools, and the militia and denied them public charity. By rule of custom, many local communities also excluded blacks from hotels, restaurants, railroad cars, hospitals, and orphanages.[49] Probably as a result of these discriminatory laws and customs, the black population of Ohio was less than 1 percent of its total in 1850, with those few mostly concentrated in Cincinnati.

Yet, the black laws were not always enforced and had no impact in many places. The scarcity of blacks in northern Ohio made segregated facilities superfluous there, and therefore radical social experimentation met less resistance. In Oberlin, on the Western Reserve, abolitionists founded the first integrated institution of higher education in the United States. Founded in 1832, Oberlin College became a mecca for blacks seeking a higher education after fifty-three students from Lane Seminary in Cincinnati brought national attention to the college in 1834. The "Lane Rebels," as they were known, transferred to Oberlin after Lane's religious leadership refused to admit blacks as equals and commit itself to Garrisonian "immediatism."

In 1835, minister Charles G. Finney added to Oberlin's national reputation by joining the faculty and later becoming college president. His perfectionist doctrine—which became known as Oberlin Perfectionism—called for perfect obedience to the moral law. It was the creed of thousands of Oberlin-trained missionaries who exerted a powerful influence on the Western Reserve and whose message spread across the Midwest.[50] Oberlin eventually attracted a sizable free black population who enjoyed freedom from the state's oppressive laws. By the late 1850s, locals boasted of the large number of fugitive slaves who "had made themselves pleasant homes, accumulated property, improved their minds and educated their children" in Oberlin.[51] In addition, Oberlin extended its tradition of egalitarianism when it opened its doors to women students in 1837, as did Western Reserve College in Hudson.[52]

In 1849, the black laws were repealed throughout the state of Ohio and legislation was passed that encouraged public schools to racially integrate themselves. This led to the rapid establishment of fully integrated schools in some places—most notably in Cleveland, where the largest black population in the Western Reserve resided. Also, the Ohio Supreme Court held that mulattoes more than half-white could vote and attend white schools—thereby effectively drawing a different color-line than most places. At the Ohio Constitutional Convention in 1851, elected delegates from the Western Reserve pushed, almost successfully, for the complete enfranchisement of blacks.[53]

The revolutionary movement to abolish Ohio's racial discriminatory laws was led by two radicals from Tourgée's home county of Ashtabula. Former law partners, the aforementioned Josh Giddings and Benjamin Franklin Wade became national figures in the struggle against slavery and racial discrimination. Giddings and Wade were said to have been converted to the cause of abolitionism at an 1837 revival meeting led by Theodore Dwight Weld, who also inspired the Lane Rebels to take their stand. In 1838, Giddings became the first United States congressman to represent the cause of abolitionism, and he found a powerful ally in John Quincy Adams. In 1839, Ben Wade entered the Ohio State Legislature, where he began his crusade to repeal the black laws in his very first speech, a premature initiative that would cost him re-election. After taking an instrumental role in the Ohio reforms of 1849, Wade was elected to the United States Senate in 1851. During the Civil War, Wade became a Radical Republican leader whose Congressional stature was rivaled only by Thaddeus Stevens and Charles Sumner.[54] Tourgée claimed that Giddings and Wade "spoke the thoughts and sentiments which beat in the breasts of three fourths of the people of" the Reserve by the 1850s.[55]

What Tourgée perceived as moral courage in the acts of such men as Giddings and Wade most captured his admiration. To join the abolitionist movement was widely regarded as a moral choice undertaken by those who simply refused to compromise on what their consciences told them was wrong.[56] As Tourgée recalled, "one end of a street" might be fanatically abolitionist, while the other end "was bitterly hostile to the last."[57] William Dean Howells, whose father's *Ashtabula Sentinel* served as a virtual mouthpiece for Joshua Giddings, observed that "men of conscience" in the Western Reserve commanded the respect and admiration of all—even those who disagreed with their views.[58] Freedom of conscience was perhaps the most jealously guarded right for those descendants of Europe's persecuted Protestant dissenters. Tourgée later explained: "They [the people of the Western Reserve] had been reared to believe that 'resistance to tyrants is a duty to God' and counted any force that deprived a man of his natural rights as tyranny."[59]

The argument against slavery and racial prejudice on the Western Reserve was usually made in terms of the Golden Rule. "Divert yourselves of prejudice, and answer before God," Ben Wade admonished the Ohio State Legislature. "[T]he earliest lesson I was taught, was to respect the rights of others and defend my own . . . to 'do unto others as I would that they should do unto me.'" Consequently, Wade continued, "until the Laws of nature and of nature's God are changed, I will never recognize the right of one man to hold his fellow man a slave."[60] Seamlessly blending the political discourse of individual rights with a widely held religious ethic, this argument was difficult for opponents to answer.

If it had not been for the passage of the Fugitive Slave Act of 1850, the question of conscience in regard to slavery might never have become a pressing one for most Ohioans. But this law, passed as part of the Compromise of 1850, made Northerners directly complicit in the maintenance of the slave system by demanding that all citizens assist in the recapture of runaway slaves upon penalty of prison or a stiff fine. In areas of the North where the moral objection to slavery was strong, the Fugitive Slave Act convinced many that their political leaders had bargained away their ethical purity and tainted them with the "sin" of supporting slavery. It played a key role in transforming passive antipathy toward slavery into active hostility, and nowhere in the United States did the Fugitive Slave Act cause more pain and provoke more political turmoil than in Ohio.

Ohio's geographic location made it a flashpoint in the controversy over the Fugitive Slave Act. The Ohio River—a border between free and slave states—became a veritable sieve through which Southern blacks began to escape from slavery as the sectional conflict grew.[61] The black population of the Reserve doubled between 1850 and 1860, and even more runaways continued on to Canada where they could enjoy comparative safety from recapture.[62] The "Underground Railroad" thrived throughout Ohio, and slave catchers patrolled the border region and conspicuously roamed such cities as Cincinnati searching for fugitives. This brought home the reality of slavery—and the slaves' wish to escape it—to residents like one Harriet Beecher Stowe, whose repulsion toward the slave catchers that she witnessed in Cincinnati inspired her, in part, to write *Uncle Tom's Cabin*. John Brown, too, began his lifelong hatred of slavery as a youth in Hudson, where his abolitionist father worked as an agent of the Underground Railroad.[63]

It was a source of pride for Tourgée that the Western Reserve was a beacon for runaways who knew its reputation for virulent abolitionism. "Throughout the whole country the Western Reserve of Ohio was a synonym for intelligence and freedom of thought," he claimed, causing runaways to seek out this region, "whenever the foot of the slave, fleeing from bondage, struck the white roads that led northward."[64] Local newspapers in Tourgée's hometown made celebratory references to the common fact of runaways attaining the assistance of steamboat operators on Lake Erie. In 1854, a one-line item in the *Ashtabula Weekly Telegraph* casually informed its readers, "Twenty-one negro men, women, and children 'passed over Jordan' through Cleveland last Thursday."[65] Tourgée later recalled the first time he witnessed the escape of a black family from Kingsville. As "a mere lad" traveling with his father on a lakeside road, he spotted a steamer that approached the shoreline and blew its whistle. His father excitedly told Albion that the "boat has come to take off a fugitive slave!" explaining, "The signal [is] flying from the mast. I heard something about there being 'black birds' around, last Sunday, at church. If we hurry, we may see them go aboard." They rushed ahead toward the shore in time to see a man, woman, and child emerge from a small boat and "clamber on board the steamer, which hoisted its boat quickly up [and] went on her way up the lake." The scene prompted Valentine to piously declare, "'Thank God!' . . . another family is rescued from the hell of slavery!"[66] Albion also later said that the only tears he ever witnessed from his father were shed upon his reading in the newspaper of Henry Clay's support for the Fugitive Slave Act. Indeed, the notion that free Northerners would be required to aid, rather than hinder, slave hunters was an unspeakable moral affront.

The attempt to enforce the Fugitive Slave Act in the Western Reserve transformed local politics and sparked a passionate public debate about the relationship between the Constitution and individual conscience.[67] Prior to the Compromise of 1850, local governments had effectively nullified the Fugitive Slave Law of 1793 by refusing to enforce it. But the provisions of the 1850 Act took much of the power of enforcement out of the hands of local communities by appointing federal marshals to assist in the recapture of runaways and by removing the trials of suspected fugitives from state courts and placing them in the hands of a Federal Commission. Reacting to this federal defense of slavery, Northern opponents responded with a chorus of "states-rights" arguments, and many echoed New York senator William Seward's controversial assertion that slavery violated a "higher law" than the Constitution. A group of Oberlin citizens enacted Seward's "higher law" doctrine—which was virtually the same as Finney's perfectionist doctrine—in what became known as the "Oberlin Rescue." On September 13, 1858, a mob of white and black citizens armed with guns and sticks prevented the recapture of a runaway slave, as citizens had done previously in both Boston and Syracuse. When prosecuted by the federal government, the "Oberlin Rescuer" trials in April and May of 1859 captured national attention and dominated the local and national press for weeks.

On the eve of the "Oberlin Rescue" the *Cleveland Leader* remarked that: "It is now ten years since any attempt has been made to get possession of fugitives from service in Oberlin."[68] For this reason, Oberlin became the target of brash slave catchers accompanied by a cooperative federal marshall who arrived in town in September of 1858 boasting of their intention to recapture a runaway slave. In the early morning of the thirteenth, these men seized a suspected runaway, known only as John afterwards, and attempted to remove him from the town without a trial. After pursuing slave catchers several miles to the next town of Wellington, a mob cornered the slave catchers as they attempted to board a train for Kentucky and forced them to relinquish their captive. Upon their return to Oberlin, the rescuers were hailed as heroes, and the runaway John disappeared into the mist. This incident might have been forgotten soon afterward except that news of it provoked a furious response from the proslavery administration in Washington, D.C. Pressuring local authorities to prosecute the "outlaws," President James Buchanan decided to make an example of the Oberlin rescuers, and within weeks a federal grand jury indicted thirty-seven residents from the towns of Oberlin and Wellington for violating the Fugitive Slave Act of 1850.[69]

What followed was less an operation of the judicial system and more a national soapbox on which some of the leading political figures in Ohio displayed their eloquence in defending the rescuers and denouncing the "Slave Power." Ohio governor Salmon P. Chase hand-picked Albert Gallatin Riddle as the lead counsel for the rescuers and served as a behind-the-scenes adviser to him throughout the trial. Chase's long-standing interest in the cause of runaways in Ohio earned him the derisive nickname "Attorney General of Fugitive Slaves" by his opponents. The legal team also included Seneca O. Griswold, who within nine months would become nationally famous as John Brown's lead counsel in the wake of the Harper's Ferry raid. John Brown himself, in fact, was on hand during the Oberlin rescuer trials where he successfully recruited men for his planned raid in Virginia.[70]

When the case came to trial, Riddle's line of defense demonstrated how far the Reserve had become radicalized over the Fugitive Slave Act. Admitting the rescuers "knew they were outraging the law of the land," Riddle proclaimed of the rescuers that "what they did and all they did" was to "obey the laws of God."[71] Rather than present a valid legal defense, Riddle deemed the Fugitive Slave Law immoral and argued that it violated the "Higher Law." Making an instant celebrity of himself, Riddle shockingly pronounced: "I am perfectly frank to declare *that I am a votary of that Higher Law!*"[72]

Almost unanimously defending Riddle, the local press vigorously attacked the federal handling of the case. The press was especially exorcised by the relocation of the case to Cleveland, for fear that no Oberliners would convict the rescuers, and the exclusion from the jury of anyone who admitted to being a "conscientious objector" to the law. Moreover, Judge Hiram V. Wilson also came under attack for his charge to the jury to ignore the "semi-religious . . . sentiment prevalent in the community" that the laws of the state could be ignored with impunity simply out of "a *declared* sense of conscientious duty." Succinctly summing up the higher law doctrine, Judge Wilson told the jury:

> There is, in fact, a sentiment prevalent in [this] community which arrogates to human conduct a standard of right above, and independent of, human laws; and it makes the *conscience* of each individual in society the *test* of his own *accountability* to the laws of the land.[73]

This notion, he insisted, was a "*false*" and hypocritical doctrine that would lead invariably to "intolerance and bigotry."[74] Wilson's opinion provoked outrage in the local press that ran such headlines as "A BURLESQUE OF JUSTICE."[75] When the verdict was rendered in May, two of the rescuers were sentenced to short prison terms and fined $600 and $100 respectively. The government dropped its cases against the other thirty-five indicted rescuers, satisfied that its point had been made.

The weak defense of the Oberlin rescuers put on by Chase and Riddle may have been a political tactic designed to capitalize on antislavery sentiments for upcoming elections. Governor Chase was already a serious contender for the 1860 Republican presidential nomination, while Riddle would run—and be elected—to the United States Congress in the fall of 1860.[76] In the political aftermath, both prominently continued to agitate against the Fugitive Slave Law at numerous rallies and public demonstrations in favor of the rescuers. The largest mass rally was held in Cleveland on May 24, which began with an unindicted rescuer, described as a mulatto, baiting the multiracial crowd with the queries:

> Are you here to-day to obey the Fugitive Slave Law?
> Are you here to sustain the dicta of the Dred Scott decision?
> Are you here to support the decision of the United States Court of the Northern District of Ohio?

To which the crowd replied each time with a thundering: "No! No! No! "[77] The speakers that followed him included Josh Giddings, Governor Chase, and Cassius Clay, who proclaimed himself "ready to fight" a war with slaveholders. If Chase had indeed anticipated the intensity of public fury that would be aroused by the trial, he now presented himself as a voice of reason, moderation, and legality. Chase improbably suggested that the Fugitive Slave Law might be overruled by the constitutional protection of states rights. That is to say, he proposed the state of Ohio could effectively "nullify" the law.

The outcry against the decision prompted a confusing and contentious debate about the nature of the "higher law," revealing a public torn between an allegiance both to the Constitution and to the dictates of individual conscience. Some papers agreed with Governor Chase that the Fugitive Slave Law was "clearly unconstitutional" and that it was necessary to "uphold the sovereignty of the State . . . against the interference of Federal authorities."[78] But others had passed far beyond the need for legal or constitutional consistency. In an article, "The Higher Law Versus The Fugitive Slave Law," the *Ashtabula Weekly Telegraph* attempted to expound on the higher law doctrine: "We know that from the day when Mr. Seward in the Senate publicly affirmed the existence of a 'higher law' down to this," the author triumphantly observed, "slaveholders and their Northern dough-faced allies have thrown up their hands in holy horror at the doctrine. And why? Simply because they well know that chattel slavery and the Fugitive Slave [A]ct can stand the test of no such law." But, the writer admitted that the doctrine had confusing implications: what authority should determine whether or not a law meets its test? Concluding that it was too problematic to leave it to any government to apply the higher law, the author instead placed the final review in the individual's own conscience:

> Who shall decide the question [of] whether a Law conforms to these principles or not? The State or the Courts? Surely neither, for they are not men's conscience keepers, and cannot absolve them from responsibility to God's tribunal. . . . Here then is the "higher law" which Federal minions sneer at. It is simply God's law, guided and applied by an intelligent conscience.[79]

While this author's conclusion was logical enough, he did not state whether such "conscientious objectors" as the Oberlin rescuers should be penalized for breaking the law.

The question of how to reconcile the right of individual conscience with the rule of law befuddled many commentators. On one extreme, editor William C. Howells suggested that the "higher law" was a passive ethic akin to the Golden Rule: "In our relations with our fellows we are never free from the obligations of the higher law, which binds us to do to others as we would have them do to us."[80] On the other extreme, it could be taken as a justification for armed rebellion against the government. In a letter to the *Portage County Democrat*, an irate citizen proposed a more aggressive course: "We must no longer submit to the despotism of the Federal government. Our wrongs must be right, if we can, through the Ballot Box, and if this fail us, then through the Cartridge Box."[81] No South Carolinian "fire-eater" could have put it better. John Brown combined two impulses, defending his violence against slaveholders at Harper's Ferry by citing the Golden Rule and the higher law. In his famous plea to the court before his sentencing, Brown declared:

> This Court acknowledges, too, as I suppose, the validity of the law of God. I see a book kissed, which I suppose to be the Bible, or at least the New Testament, which teaches me that all things whatsoever I would want that men should do to me, I should do even to them. . . . I endeavored to act upon that instruction.[82]

Ultimately, the divided allegiance between the Union, the constitution, and the higher law of individual conscience would be solved by Southern secession and the attack on Fort Sumter. With this turn of events, the ability to defend the sacredness of the Constitution could be held together with the animosity against slavery. This played into the hands of Governor Chase, about to become Lincoln's secretary of the treasury and later Supreme Court chief justice, who had been the most influential advocate of antislavery *and* constitutionalism. Throughout his career, he had dedicated an enormous amount of intellectual energy to demonstrating that the founding fathers intended not to protect slavery in the Constitution but to promote its gradual destruction.[83]

Like others in the region, Tourgée's loyalties were divided. If forced to choose between the Constitution and his conscience, all indications suggest that the youthful Tourgée would have chosen the Constitution—and later, as a judge in North Carolina, he always chose to subordinate his conscience to his duty to administer the law. Yet, this choice was made easier because the Constitution of the postwar era no longer sanctioned slavery. He later recalled the difficulty of Chase's position during the Oberlin Rescue crisis in *Hot Plowshares*. To "hold that instrument [the Constitution] sacred above all things else and yet deny the slaveowner's right to his human chattel," he wrote, was logically impossible. All arguments against slavery "based on the written word of the Constitution," he recalled, had been "incomplete and unsatisfactory." Thus, while it was easy for Tourgée to criticize Chase after the Civil War had settled the dilemma, it was also consistent with his later belief that the Reconstruction Amendments had revolutionized the Constitution and brought it into harmony with the principles of the Declaration of Independence.[84]

Only one piece of evidence indicates what Tourgée's attitude had been at the actual time of the Oberlin Rescue trials. As the two convicted Oberlin Rescuers awaited sentence, he composed a lengthy poem about his having reached the legal minimum age to vote in Ohio, twenty-one. Political turmoil may be glimpsed in several lines of the poem. Tourgée writes: "[W]hen wild excitement rocks / the Nation as with Earthquake shocks / I may approach the *ballot box!*" The thrill of political participation, the young narrator finds, is deflated by bewildering confusion: "But Oh! Ye Gods! That there should be / Such drawbacks unto liberty / Of Speech, of Conscience, and Opinion!" Perhaps the most interesting lines in the poem, however, are those that address the political lesson of the moment. "I just begin my love to see," he writes, "How sweet and glorious 'tis to be / A man, and *white—(by courtesy)* / In this great nation of the free."[85] If written by a typical twenty-one-year-old, it would be tempting to take this as a blunt statement of fact. But against the political backdrop of the Oberlin-Wellington rescue affair, this ironic comment on the privileges of whiteness, and maleness, seems suspiciously deliberate.

The poem is saturated by sarcasm and irony. First, there is the ironic contrast between the modifiers *white* and *man* against the reference of America as being the "nation of the free." The poem, in fact, goes on to lament, "I'm just a sovereign *one* among / This nation of great rogues," having "no estate with rent roll long / No slaves, to cringe beneath my thong." The irony here becomes unmistakable. Life hardly seems "sweet and glorious" after the revelation of his own poverty, the mention of cringing "slaves," and with a "nation of great rogues" having replaced a "nation of the free." The poem closes with an outright complaint of class oppression. He reports that when he finally attempts to vote, he is prevented from doing so by a poll tax that he could not afford to pay. He writes: "I with others was poll-taxed! / And pressed upon the road to work! / Where I'd no refuge, but to shirk!!!"[86] This lighthearted conclusion presents the author comically feeling alienated from, and poorly used by, the political system. In the midst of the political turmoil on the Western Reserve, Tourgée kept a semi-bewildered distance from politics, still referring to himself as a "modest, conservative man" as late as 1859.[87] But soon Tourgée would find his political bearings.

A REVOLUTION LONG, BLOODY, AND RADICAL

As the primary moral and religious authority in society, the family unit took on a heightened cultural importance on the Western Reserve. Despite the glorification of individual conscience, the fundamental social unit on the Reserve was not the individual as much as it was the family.[88] Though Albion's relationship with his own family was a deeply troubled one, he would marry into another family from the Western Reserve whose influence on his life would be enduring.

Abolitionism would enter his life through the Kilbourne family, whose strong moral opposition to slavery encouraged Albion's decisive turn towards radicalism. His engagement and eventual marriage to Emma Kilbourne in 1863, moreover, brought Albion more companionship than he bargained for. He assumed the role of male provider for his wife's family because of her father's poor health, which lapsed into invalidism in 1865. Emma's mother and two of her unmarried sisters would become members of Albion's household for much of their lives, moving with him first to North Carolina and then to western New York. In this female-dominated household, Albion would remain connected to the moral world of the Western Reserve long after leaving the region.

Emma Lodoilska Kilbourne, born in 1840 on her father's farm in Conneaut, Ohio, a few miles from Kingsville, was a studious seventeen-year-old at Kingsville Academy when she met nineteen-year-old Albion Tourgée in 1857. Quietly opinionated, Emma was a good match for the school's brash academic standout. The casual environment of the coed Kingsville Academy where they met fostered an intellectually egalitarian relationship between the sexes. According to the description of Tourgée's nearly exact contemporary, William Dean Howells, Ashtabula County was "a world in which boys and girls . . . valued verbal skills more than they did physical prowess, and in which relationships with other people—young and old alike—seemed to be mainly built upon repartee."[89] The high degree of female participation in reform movements was indicative of their immersion in political life, short of voting.

Albion distinguished himself as one of the top scholars at Kingsville Academy, a boarding school accommodating one hundred and fifty students including many from out of state. Because his father's financial support was inconsistent, Albion worked odd jobs in order to help pay for his schooling, which impressed his instructors, and he walked several miles to school every day because he could not afford boarding costs. Considered handsome, he stood nearly six feet tall, weighed approximately 150 lbs. with blue eyes, dark hair, and a "tough and wiry" frame.[90] Albion was president of the debating club and a favorite of Principal Chester W. Heywood. His debating skills were legendary, and his captivating style enhanced by his glaring right eye—his left eye was blinded in a boyhood accident—that gave him a "bold and piercing stare."[91] Sometimes condescending, Albion's aggressive style was marked by a tendency to want to demolish his opponents in a fury of sarcasm and ridicule.

At the same time, he cultivated a more reflective side in the poetry he read at public gatherings and published in the local papers.

Not surprisingly, Albion's courting of public accolades reflected lurking anxieties and a need for external validation. It seems that he possessed few genuine confidantes at Kingsville before he became friendly with Emma at a school outing. The earliest letters between Emma and Albion make references to his having confided his secret self-doubts to her. Eager to reassure him, Emma responded by promising to always cheer him whenever he had "a desperate attack of 'the blues'" and sardonically advised him not to think of ending his life by "jumping from Kingsville Academy into Lake Erie."[92] Referring to each other endearingly as "sister" and "brother" (terms probably borrowed from the egalitarian language of religious revivalism on the frontier), they vowed to maintain complete candidness in their correspondence. Emma insisted that she would not respond to flattery or other forms of falsehood, and Albion maintained that he would not be false about his ambitions. Emma encouraged his "glorious dreams" of attending Harvard University and achieving literary fame and soon overcame the unexplained "dark pages" in her past that had left her wary of the opposite sex. As their relationship grew more romantic, Emma wondered: "You are so talented and know so much I

Emma Kilborn Tourgée and Albion W. Tourgée, 1865. Courtesy of the Chautauqua County Historical Society, Westfield, NY.

wonder that you should ever have noticed me."[93] Within two years, in 1859, Emma and Albion declared themselves secretly engaged.

Emma's parents did not immediately embrace their engagement. Her parents' transparently unhappy marriage offered a poor model, which her mother reinforced with repeated warnings of the perils and trials of married life.[94] Worse yet, her father objected to Albion's "rude and rough manners" and his lack of deference to them. Though he admitted that Albion possessed "great intellect," he worried that his "never yielding disposition" may make him an undesirable husband. Even Emma's older brother Ned, who lived in Iowa, found reason to criticize their relationship from afar, calling her an "idolator" and mocking her excessive worship of Albion's "divine perfections . . . immaculate excellence, astonishing intellect" and "wonderful genius."[95] However, her father did admit that if "time would remove all that was disagreeable now," Albion could become a "great and honored" man.[96] Emma bluntly confronted Albion with her family's concerns but, ever prideful, he refused to modify his behavior on matter of principle. "I would not sail under false colors," he stubbornly told her. "My motto is not[,] as you know[,] *seem* but *be*. I would not seem great and good but be it so."[97]

Albion's "unyielding" and argumentative personality suggested to Emma's parents that he might tyrannize over his wife. But in truth Emma was far less subservient to Albion, and he was far less dictatorial than it may have appeared to them or others. Accepting his high-minded stubbornness with a shrug, Emma made sure that Albion modified his combative ways around her parents. "Do not always disagree with her," Emma sternly instructed him regarding her mother, "and sometimes yield without many words." Anticipating his reaction, she continued, "now love do not throw the letter away from you . . . you may find it difficult to please her but you can do it[,] and you will try to do so[,] will you not Albion?"[98] Undeterred by their misgivings, Emma successfully brokered her family's acceptance of Albion. Within months, Emma's father reported that he "should be proud to own [Albion] as a son."[99]

Emma also made sure that her needs would be understood and respected by her future husband. In their courtship letters, she spelled out her terms and expectations for married life. She repeatedly made clear to Albion that she expected a marriage much different from that of her parents. Recounting how her mother had worn out her life bearing seven children against her will, she informed him that her aspirations were to be more than simply the mother of many children.[100] Emma confessed that she valued her own education above all else: "I believe that were I allowed to do just as I pleased and could, I would forget home, friend, *love*, everything for my books . . . forty years would be too short a time for me to learn all I wish."[101] She, apparently, hoped that her marriage to Albion would offer an opportunity to pursue a more intellectual path in life. Like other young women of the time, Emma rejected her parents' experience and wished for a marriage based on love and mutual respect that scholars have termed the *companionate ideal* that particularly flourished among antislavery Northerners.[102]

Whenever Emma expressed her sense of individual rights, Albion proved responsive. He quickly informed her, "I do not believe that God *designed and created women merely for childbearing . . . you are never to wear out your life in caring for my children.*" He frankly addressed these concerns. "I know Emma that too many women are in very truth victim of their husband's passions," he gravely admitted. "Many men consider their wives only as *instruments for legally indulging their gross and sensual passions. This is indeed wrong, vile, inhuman.*" Promising that she would never be forced to have more children than she desired, he repeatedly assured her that their marriage would always be based on true love and affection. "Emma have no doubt," he insisted, "I would love my wife very much."[103] Albion's recognition of Emma's right to her own happiness is perhaps another manifestation of the particular individualism of the Western Reserve and radical application of the Golden Rule.

Emma counterbalanced some of Albion's moral rigidity and tendency toward priggishness. As a young man, he often agonized over the moral implications of seemingly small matters. Apparently a teetotaler, he tried to avoid all "degrading vices" and chided himself for indulging in cigars. So powerful was his will to independence that he refused to be enslaved even to the cravings of his own body. "If one submits to appetite in one thing," he philosophized, "he is apt to become its slave in all."[104] But Emma was less concerned over what she saw as trivial moral infractions. She freely admitted to Albion about having become tipsy from drinking wine and once even teased him about her enjoyment of dancing at the Town Fair: "Did I do wrong Albion," she queried, "if I kept time with my feet and moved with the music? . . . I do not know as it is forbidden by the church."[105] Albion's reply offers another example of his individualistic ethos. Smugly, he replied that only *she* could know for sure whether it was wrong, but he told her to consider the following criteria: "Did you love God or your fellow more for having done it?"[106]

Though Emma wished to get married immediately after Albion's graduation from Kingsville Academy in April of 1859, Albion was determined to fulfill his dream of attending Harvard. Overcome with what he called a "restless spirit," the twenty-one-year-old Albion insisted that he first complete his education. He rationalized that their separation would build his character through forced self-denial. "This training is more necessary for me than for you," he told her. "I have . . . to cultivate, to acquire, force steadiness of character, to make me a successful man."[107] More tangibly, Albion had few resources to get married, and those few would be used to pay for his tuition and expenses. To his dismay, his father informed him that he "need expect no assistance from [him] in the prosecution of [his] studies." Unable to see the value of a college degree, Valentine coldly complained that his wealth had "cost him too much toil to be squandered in that manner."[108] Though he had saved up a small fund of his own earnings, Albion needed financial assistance and tried unsuccessfully for three months to change Valentine's mind.

Bitterly disowning his father, Albion resigned to find another means of affording Harvard. "I have only my own strength to rely upon," he concluded, "no one can say that he furnished me with my capital in life."[109] Traveling once more to Massachusetts, Albion attained part of a $400 inheritance from his maternal grandfather but found that Harvard was temporarily impossible because of its "extreme expensiveness." Leaving from Cambridge with a heavy heart, Albion resolved to join a boyhood chum, Seneca Kuhn, for "one or two years" at the University of Rochester at less than half the cost. At Rochester, he soon enlisted Kuhn and a few others in a scheme to transfer to Harvard together once funds were somehow attained. Throughout his time in Rochester, Albion continued to work and save at every opportunity.[110]

The city of Rochester was similar to the Western Reserve in that it was settled by New England migrants and deeply affected by the religious revivals led by Charles Finney in the early 1830s. Rochester buzzed with radicalism and became the home to many leading abolitionists, including Frederick Douglass. There is no evidence that Tourgée had any direct contact with Douglass—or any abolitionist—while at the university, but their presence no doubt influenced the city's reception of the dramatic events of 1859–61. The city was deeply divided along ethnic and class lines, however, with a rapidly growing working class made up of many Irish Catholics who detested abolitionism. The university, meanwhile, was dominated by its conservative president, Martin B. Anderson, a devoted Hamiltonian nationalist who distrusted all forms of popular politics.[111]

Tourgée tried to remain happily oblivious to the explosive political situation outside when he began his course of study at the university, "safely cloistered beyond the noise and turmoil of the fight," as he put it.[112] In mid-October of 1859, when John Brown and his band of revolutionaries launched their attack on Harper's Ferry, Tourgée paid little attention and later joked, "[the] Union might go to smash without my knowing anything about it."[113] Reveling in the freedom of college life, and the many opportunities to "do just about as [he] pleased," he did not excel in his studies.[114]

Instead of concentrating on "hated" subjects like mathematics, he indulged his love of Sir Walter Scott's novels and ambitiously continued his "first attempt at prose fiction," a novel about the conquest of America written in the romantic vain, which he had been composing since 1859.[115] Though he eventually abandoned the novel, he made a name for himself among the students, who voted him Class Poet.[116] Despite his oppositional ways and average marks, Albion did capture the respect of some of his professors, such as one whom he said was secretly "very much pleased with the perfect boldness and audacity which I exhibit in criticizing either himself, the authors, or the productions of my classmates."[117] Even President Anderson took an especial interest in his rebellious student, and eventually he would become a new father figure for Albion.

While Albion enjoyed his cloistered life in Rochester, Emma remained in the Western Reserve and became increasingly interested in the problem of slavery. While studying piano at a female music school, she reported to Albion that she had become "quite a rabid little petticoated Black Republican" and endeavored with her friends to boycott the consumption of cotton as a moral stand against slave labor.[118] By the election season of 1860, Emma had become a committed "Lincoln Girl" and enjoyed the endless demonstrations and torch-lit processions of the local Wide Awake Club—a controversial antislavery group that used quasi-military spectacle to mobilize support for the Republican Party.[119] Her brother Ned also seems to have converted to abolitionism around 1860. His unexplained visit to New Orleans in fact caused Emma to fear that he might meet the same fate as "Old Brown."[120]

At first, Albion reacted with some confusion and disapproval to Emma's interest in abolitionism and the Republican Party. Incredulous over her decision to boycott cotton, he asked whether her principles would require her to "discard crinoline" for the wearing of "cowhides." Then, echoing a conservative viewpoint, he mockingly asked whether she had become a female abolitionist: "Will you . . . endeavor to kick your northern brethren into compliance with your particular tenets, and beliefs, as some of your amiable sisters have done?" Pointing out to Emma that she could not vote, he mockingly asked her also if she would like him to pledge in writing to vote the Republican ticket as a prerequisite of marriage. Finally, adopting a more serious and less sarcastic tone, he wrote, "you may dabble in politics as much as you please for I know you will never carry it so far as to make yourself unwomanly."[121] However, as the 1860 Presidential election approached, Albion began to feel himself uncomfortably on the sidelines.

When President Anderson informed the student body that no political clubs could be established on campus and expressed concern over the

Wide Awakes, to whom he was "violently opposed" in principle, Albion sprang into action. Probably for no other reason but to assert his right of assembly and conscience, Albion immediately took it upon himself to found the University of Rochester Wide Awake Club. After discovering this, a furious President Anderson brought a policeman to campus and threatened the club leaders with arrest. Only after a heated meeting with Anderson did Tourgée convince him to tolerate their group—in exchange for dropping all reference to the university in their official name.[122]

In November, Emma rejoiced at Abraham Lincoln's victory as he swept every county within the Western Reserve.[123] For his part, Albion expressed no satisfaction at the election of the first antislavery president. He was "heartily sick of Campaign excitements" and glad that the demands of Wide Awaking were finally over. "I have written, sung, cheered and speechified enough," he declared.[124] Despite all of his work, his only brush with a serious political meeting outside of the university came when his roommate, Seneca Kuhn, dragged him to hear Democratic candidate Stephen A. Douglas speak at a large rally in Rochester. Ironically, Albion, who would later become an accomplished stump speaker, was horrified at the "great disorderly crowd of drunken border ruffians" who "pushed and crowded, stamped and yelled like Paddies at a Wake." After this meeting, he swore off such "immoral" political gatherings and warned his roommate of his "growing dissipation" in regard to attending them.[125]

Only when the Confederate States of America ratified its constitution in February of 1861 did Albion finally acknowledge the gravity of the political situation. By the time of Lincoln's inauguration in March, a Civil War was at hand. Albion gloomily predicted "this will be the last inauguration of a President of the U.S." Though the shape of things to come was unclear, he imagined an upheaval of untold proportions through which a democratic government would not survive. "I believe," he predicted, "that a *Monarchy* of limited *powers* will be erected on the *ruins of this Republic*." Moreover, he reported a "strong impression that the convulsion will be long, bloody and the Revolution radical." Whatever the result, Albion was sure of one thing: "I shall share in it."[126]

3

Citizen-Soldier: Manhood and the Meaning of Liberty

Their slaveholding Sodom . . . must be razed and got out of the way, like any other obstacle to the progress of humanity. It must make room for something more consonant with the railroad, electric-telegraph, printing press, inductive philosophy, and practical Christianity.

—John William De Forest, *Miss Ravenel's Conversion From Secession to Loyalty*, 1867

I dont care a rag for *"the Union as it was."* I want and fight for the *Union "better than it was."* Before this is accomplished we must have . . . a thorough and complete revolution and renovation. This I expect and hope. For this I am willing to die—for this I expect to *die.*

—Lieutenant Albion W. Tourgée, January 1863

T HE TWO AND A HALF YEARS THAT CONSTITUTED TOURGÉE'S CAREER as a Union soldier in the Civil War would become the touchstone of his politics for the rest of his life. When he enlisted into the army soon after Lincoln's first call for troops in 1861, Tourgée showed little evidence of political idealism. A detailed analysis of his experience shows that Tourgée's political understanding of the war slowly began to emerge from concerns about manliness and moral duty that played a greater role in motivating him to enlist. Also, the nationalizing impetus of the war to preserve the Union had a profound influence on his democratic ideals. Though he had been committed to the absolute moral worth of the individual, Tourgée had strong misgivings about the anarchistic rhetoric of the higher law adherents on the Western Reserve. During the war, he would begin to reconcile and synthesize the abolitionists' radical individualism with his desire for a stronger federal government. It became possible for him to believe that the government, by abolishing slavery, had committed itself fully to the absolute value of individual rights. As a result, he would emerge from the war as an avid Radical Republican whose extreme individualism had been merged with, but no means submerged by, a commitment to the national ideal.

THE CALL TO DUTY

The outbreak of the Civil War found Tourgée at a crossroads. Having used up his inheritance from his Lee relatives, he had been forced to drop out of the University of Rochester in December 1860 after a difficult fall semester in which his studies suffered because of the excessive time he had spent working at odd jobs.[1] Reluctantly accepting the fact that he could not continue his studies, he abruptly left school to accept a teaching position at the Wilson Collegiate Institute near Niagara Falls, New York. Yet, the month of April 1861 found him back in Rochester staying with friends at the university and having decided to abandon his "experiment in real life."[2] It is not clear whether Albion had accumulated enough savings to reenroll at the university; nevertheless he had come to discuss his situation with President Anderson. But Albion would never return to college life. On Saturday morning, April 13, 1861, the city of Rochester woke up to the first reports of the bombardment of Fort Sumter by Confederate rebels in South Carolina.

The news of Sumter's fall to Confederates precipitated an outburst of militarism and patriotism that shook cities and towns all over the North. President Lincoln's call for the raising of 75,000 militiamen on April 15 was met with unbridled enthusiasm. As Tourgée described the scene, the call for soldiers rung out everywhere he went. "Every pulpit in the city was almost a recruiting aid[e]. Every minister preached War—as a duty to ourselves and to God." Tourgée reacted to the call for recruits with a nervous excitement that bordered on intoxication. On April 14, he and his former roommate Seneca Kuhn stayed up all night trying unsuccessfully to compose a poem for the morning press. "I have amused myself by pounding him [Seneca] with the pillows," a giddy Albion reported. "I have laughed until I have hardly strength enough to hold my pen."[3] As able-bodied young men, they realized with a strange exhilaration that their country was calling upon *them* to rescue it.

Pressure to enlist was intense and it came from unexpected sources. His father, who had not contacted Albion in more than a year, wrote to him asking that he return to Kingsville to enlist in a company that he was raising. President Anderson, the male authority figure whose opinions

Albion most respected, made an impassioned plea to support the war to the Rochester students in the congregation of the First Baptist Church, with Tourgée in attendance. As Anderson would proclaim to the Rochester student body a few days later: "Your education, your capacity, your all, belong to the service of *God* and *your country*." Anderson's emotional call to arms both surprised and deeply affected Tourgée, who knew him to be a conservative on the issue of slavery.[4] "Many went from the Church to the recruiting station and volunteered immediately," Albion reported, and he began to feel an irresistible urge to do so as well. "The war spirit has been very high in my heart but I have [thus far] resisted," he warned Emma, adding: "there is no knowing how soon I may [enlist.]"[5]

The grandiose, nationalistic rhetoric that pervaded the North in spring 1861 temporarily assuaged the deep divisions over the Union's war objectives. The Lincoln administration predicted a rapid victory over the rebels that would preserve the Union and restore the Southern states to their prior condition. Yet many abolitionists expected a protracted war that would result in the destruction of slavery. "It matters little, comparatively, that the rallying cry is 'the Union and the Constitution,'" wrote abolitionist Oliver Johnson on April 20. "We all know that, in spite of every effort to control or qualify it, the war must be, essentially, a war of freedom against slavery."[6] So confident were the Garrisonians in this regard that they initially chose to keep an uncharacteristically low profile after the attack on Fort Sumter, even canceling a planned convention so as not to disrupt the unity of purpose in the North.[7]

While Tourgée's various predictions and offhand remarks indicate that he agreed with the abolitionists from the outset, he also found himself influenced by more conservative viewpoints. Although there is no record of what President Anderson said in his sermon at the First Baptist Church, no doubt his commencement address to the Rochester Class of 1861 only a few days later echoed the same message.[8] In this speech, Anderson offered a nationalistic interpretation of the meaning and purpose of the conflict. He viewed the war against secession as a chance to destroy the centrifugal dynamics of the antebellum political structure. He suggested that the "antagonisms of slave labor and free labor" had been the true cause of the war. Furthermore, he argued that "local sovereignty and intense individualism" would become pernicious unless "incorporated into the life of a nation [and] brought within the influence of a centripetal force which can hold it to a regular orbit."[9] The United States, he said, now must fight a war of unification—a "baptism of fire and blood"—to eliminate the anarchistic doctrines of state rights and nullification. In a forceful, jingoistic conclusion, he declared:

We are fighting the battle of the ages. Shall the disgraceful history of Mexico be reproduced on our soil? Shall a score of petty States overtaxed to support standing armies, vexed by passports, border-police and *Zollverein* treaties . . . replace on this continent the name and power and fame of our mighty republic? No! Never![10]

Secession would inhibit free-market operation, raise trade barriers, and require each small state to support "standing armies" of self-defense. An ardent Hamiltonian, Anderson insisted that "national unity" was the key to both civil liberty and economic success.

Tourgée would later remark that he only "but half-comprehended" Anderson's views at the time, and he described his mentor with mild criticism as a "worshiper of success" and "power" whose nationalism caused him to think "less of the relation of the State to the individual than of the duty of the individual to the State."[11] But the crisis of secession brought radical-minded men like Tourgée together with conservative-minded ones like Anderson in common need to establish federal supremacy once and for all. For both, slavery was an obstacle—whether to establish national power and prosperity or the equal protection of individual rights. The young Tourgée absorbed Anderson's desire for a greater national unification, but his fierce individualism steeled him against the undercurrent of authoritarianism of Anderson's antislavery viewpoint. In the war cries of April 1861, the differences between the two seemed inconsequential.[12]

Yet, it would be misleading to grant too much weight to political ideologies in Albion's decision to enlist. Probably more influential than Anderson's appeal to nationalism was his appeal to manhood. Everywhere he turned, Albion was reminded that "manly courage" and "patriotic duty" demanded he serve his country in its time of need. He recalled that President Anderson, in general, "was not [e]specially promotive [*sic*] of the views of any party," but rather molded his students with "an Andersonian ideal of manhood, of public duty, and of patriotic purpose."[13] Albion was deeply susceptible to such appeals. The faithful performance of one's duty to others was, in fact, a central element of the middle-class ideology of manhood.[14]

Fear of having his manhood questioned would be the deciding factor in his decision to enlist. On April 22, he wrote a letter to Emma that confessed feeling "almost crazy" with thoughts about enlisting, but he informed her that he had made up his mind *not* to fight. Having asked God on his knees for guidance, Albion related, he concluded that he had "still dearer duties to perform" than enlisting. Although risking social ostracism for cowardliness, he explained to Emma that the thoughts of their future marriage and happiness would enable him to "suffer the name of coward." His duty to his country, he decided, could not outweigh the "sweet caresses of a virgin's love" and the devotion of one, whom he called, "an impassioned love, of a maiden angel who has often kept [me] from evil and whom [my] heart calls *wife*."[15] In other words, despite the powerful appeal of his father, President Anderson, and others, he chose to follow his duty as a husband (to be) rather than his duty to his country.

Emma too felt great social pressure to "do her duty" and demonstrate her support for the war effort. The Western Reserve, still simmering over the Oberlin-Wellington Rescuer trials, displayed an extraordinary degree of militancy. The *Conneaut Reporter* reported that the war fever on the Reserve "pervades all parties, all classes, old and young, male and female." It proudly announced: "We glory in recording the fact that the tocsin of war is sounding all over the North . . . never, since the days of the Revolution, has there been such a determined spirit exhibited to resist aggression, as at the present time."[16] In Ashtabula County alone, more than three times the number of men signed up for the war than could be outfitted—five of the seven companies that reported for duty were turned away in the spring of 1861. Not only had Albion's father helped recruit a regiment for which he desired his son to join, but Emma boasted to her friends and family that her beau had already enlisted.

Unfortunately for Albion and Emma, many of her friends and family began to write to Albion to congratulate on his decision to enlist. One letter he received from a classmate of Emma's declared, "I honor you—I love you for your decision." Even Emma herself had written to him elliptically about her confidence that he would enlist if "allowed to do as he pleases."[17] Thus when Emma received Albion's letter of April 22 proclaiming his determination not to enlist, she replied in panic: "Oh! Albion—I did not mean what I wrote," she begged, fearful that she would cause him to enlist: "I *would not*[,] *could not send you away* by my seeming indifference." She insisted that she had only written what she thought he wanted to hear.[18] Her retraction would arrive too late. The mail soon brought Emma news that Albion had enlisted for two years' service in a company of Dragoons that had been formed in Rochester. It is likely that the letters Albion received from Emma's friends and family had prompted him to reconsider his decision to remain at home.[19]

This important episode of miscommunication reveals something about the motivation of young men and women caught up in the "war fever." Though he resisted the appeals from his father and from President Anderson, Albion could not withstand the thought that Emma and her friends might deem him a coward. For her part, Emma conformed to the supportive role expected of her, going apparently against her true desires. When Emma learned of Albion's enlistment, she greeted it with resignation. "Your letter of Tuesday came but . . . I knew its contents before I opened it." Emma sighed, "Go, go and Heaven help my soldier love and keep him safe."[20] Albion and Emma had both revealed a half-repressed desire to reject social pressure and avoid the call of duty. But afterwards, both would overcompensate for their early expression of "weakness" by exhibiting an unflinching devotion to the war effort.

Emma soon after even took pains to reassure Albion that his previous doubts were nothing of which to be ashamed. "Albion love[,] I know you are *no coward*," she told him. Instructing him to fight bravely, she declared: "I should not have the thought of *Emma* make you a coward [and] much rather should I have them tell me my love fell on the battlefield than that he *fled from danger*."[21] Albion never again expressed to Emma any fears or doubts about fighting in the war. On the contrary, his actions suggest that he took her admonitions to heart and responded with vigilance against any expression that might cast doubt on his conformity to masculine ideals.

HONOR AND MANHOOD

When the Union troops marched from Washington, D.C., for the first great clash between the Confederate and Union armies, crowds of cheering men and women waved them on. On July 21 the Battle of Bull Run (or "Manassas" to Confederates) ended in a humiliating defeat for the Union Army. It was as much a disaster for Albion Tourgée as it was for the Union cause. He came away from the battle with an injury so severe that, for a time, it seemed he would be partially paralyzed for the rest of his life.

The road to disaster began with the woefully deficient and chaotic training camp at Elmira, New York. Though originally planned as mounted cavalry, his regiment was transformed into the 27th New York Infantry at Elmira. Coupled with this loss of prestige, Albion suffered the further disappointment of failing to be elected an officer by his comrades, earning instead the humble rank of third sergeant.[22] Tourgée's regiment drew its ranks from all over New York State and was commanded by Colonel Henry W. Slocum (later, General Slocum of Gettysburg fame). In early July, the 27th Regiment was abruptly rushed to Washington, D.C., to help defend the city from the Confederate troops massing across the Virginia border along the south bank of Bull Run, a creek near the strategically important Manassas rail junction. After receiving their first arms on July 16, the troops had a single day of target practice in a vacant lot outside the city of Washington and then received marching orders the next day toward the front.[23]

Albion was awoken at 2 a.m. on July 21 to begin a long and difficult march to the battlefield at Manassas junction. After marching for eight hours straight, the 27th proceeded onto the battlefield at about 10 a.m., as Albion put it, "without a moment's rest, a drink of water, or a mouthful of breakfast, right into battle."[24] The sound of artillery flying overhead induced a "horrible sickness in my heart," Albion reported, prompting him to seek out a companion's hand: "Webster and I shook hands as the first cannon shot began to fly over our heads with small hopes of our doing it again."[25] When their first charge was repulsed, the 27th fell back leaving many of their men dead on the field. An "intimate friend" standing directly next to him was killed by an artillery shot that struck him in the back as he reloaded, while Albion himself had a close call when "a spent grape paid respects to my head," violently knocking him to the ground but not inflicting serious harm.[26]

The battle itself lasted until the late afternoon. The 27th New York remained on the battlefield through several confusing cycles of advances and retreats. At one point, the 27th was overrun by a Confederate regiment that had marched nearly into them unhindered because they had been mistaken for the 8th New York volunteers, a Union regiment outfitted in similar gray uniforms. By 4 p.m. the Union army appeared to be on the verge of winning the day, when Albion and his comrades received orders to retreat. After eight hours of marching and six hours of battle, the men of the 27th were nearly too fatigued to leave the field. As Albion complained, "How could such men retreat in that condition! They could only drag themselves along as fast as possible. It was [a] physical impossibility for us to retreat."[27] But the rumor quickly spread down the line that General Johnson had arrived with forty thousand reinforcements for the Confederacy that would arrive presently to overwhelm them—in fact the newly arriving troops numbered about four thousand.[28]

So retreat they did. The march back toward Washington began in an orderly fashion but soon deteriorated. The narrow roads and bridges on the way toward Centreville quickly became jammed with fleeing artillery vehicles, soldiers, and frightened civilians who had come to witness the great battle. All order broke down as fear of capture or death incited panic among those delayed in the rear. "It seemed as if the flood-gates of Pandemonium had been flown open" as people pushed, trampled, yelled, screamed, and fled in terror toward Washington.[29] His regiment, trapped near the rear of the evacuating army, was among the last to leave the battlefield. Albion's self-possession was noticed by his superior officer, who later singled him out for praise: "Had it not been for the energy displayed by him [Tourgée] the men could not have kept together."[30] But soon after, a terrible misfortune befell him.

The congested roads became extremely dangerous at nightfall as horse-drawn wagons carrying equipment attempted to force their way through the crowds to escape capture. In the confusion, an artillery vehicle speeding through the crowd ran Tourgée down. The official report stated: "Where the road is very narrow, a retreating Battery passed through our ranks at full speed, and before Sergt. Tourgée could get out of the way one of the wheels of a gun carriage struck him a severe blow in the back from the effect of which his spine was injured."[31] Tourgée was fortunate to escape capture. At some point, he was lifted onto a retreating wagon and taken the rest of the way to Washington. Years later, in his novel *Figs and Thistles*, Tourgée's vivid description of his wounded protagonist's escape from Bull Run likely matched his own experience:

> The fear of capture took hold of me. I could not walk. That was out of the question. But I crawled to the edge of the wood . . . and kept on—God only knows how—through the long hours of the night, crawling, clambering, hobbling, on toward Centreville—not by the way we had come, but by some sort of blind instinct, taking the right direction. It was morning when . . . somebody put me into an ambulance—they said it was the last one—and I was brought to Washington. The doctor said the night's trip did me more harm than the wound itself.[32]

Sixty men from his regiment who were injured or collapsed from exhaustion were captured by the Confederates, and some of them spent the next four years inside Libby military prison in Richmond. He was lucky to escape.[33]

Unconscious for thirty hours after returning to Washington, Tourgée awoke at Camp Anderson hospital and discovered that he had no mobility in his legs. But either the seriousness of Albion's injuries was not apparent to him or he was simply not ready to acknowledge them. Though "scarcely awake," his first act was to write two letters: one to Emma and one to his father. He did not reveal the extent of his injuries, mentioning only swollen feet, bruises, stiff joints, and feeling thoroughly beaten up. "Ah! Emma," he wrote in a visibly labored, slanted script, "that was a terrible day, a horrible battle, a more terrible retreat, and a more horrible night. . . . You cannot imagine the horrors of that day . . . it was so awful sickening that I have not yet recovered myself."[34]

Both of his letters demonstrated a greater concern for defending his honor and that of his comrades than for explaining his state of health. "The men won the day, the officers lost it!!" he told Emma. "Web. [Webster] did bravely and I hope I did not disgrace myself." To his father, he explained, "I must hold my tongue for I am a soldier [but] . . . you can have no idea what we suffered through the mere incompetency [*sic*] of those who led us."[35] Thus, Albion left the impression that he had come through the battle with his health—and honor—firmly intact.

After two weeks of attempting to, in his own words, "play well," he finally had to confront the doctor's grim prognosis. On August 12 an army surgeon examined him, pronounced him "wholly unfit for military duty," and officially declared his opinion that he would be "permanently disabled" and "not again be able to resume duties."[36] Alone, and undoubtedly frightened, Tourgée insisted, against medical advice, that he be transported home to Kingsville. His friend Webster, who would be killed a year later, reluctantly laid him on a mattress on the floor of a passenger train, which took him west. Friends who met him at Elmira "begged him not to try and travel further," but Albion persuaded them to load him aboard another train to Ohio. "I had my face set homewards," he explained later.[37]

It is unknown how much further damage this journey inflicted on his spine, but when Albion arrived in Kingsville, he had completely lost feeling and mobility in his lower body. His return home was a remarkable event in the town, since he was surely the first eyewitness to return from the warfront. After his train arrived at the city of Ashtabula on August 15, he was transported to Kingsville by an "easy carriage" equipped with a bed. Albion memorably described the scene soon afterward: "My arrival nearly set the sober little town wild with excitement. Everybody seemed to think I was going to die at once and the village doctor said I would never walk again. I called him a fool, upon which father remarked that he guessed I would get well as I could tell the truth yet."[38] Still refusing to accept the opinion of doctors, Albion would spend the next seven months in his father's home trying to recuperate by force of will.

Albion's return from the war was, in his mind, less than heroic. In the weeks after Bull Run, the Northern press had bemoaned the "disgraceful" panic that followed the battle and cast doubt on the courage of the Union soldiers who broke ranks and fled from the battlefield. To appease public outrage, Congress went so far as to open an investigation of the conduct of the officers who led the battle. On top of this psychological burden, Albion must have felt humiliated to return to his father's home as an invalid to be cared for—although he was not unwelcome. When he had left for Rochester in 1859, Albion bitterly declared that he would never return to his father's house and for a time refused to even speak of his father. But he had nowhere else to turn. Valentine, for his part, appeared to be genuinely proud of his son's service, as he had both of Albion's letters following Bull Run published in the *Conneaut Reporter* (to Albion's annoyance, as he was not consulted first). Later, after Albion returned to the war, Valentine would continue to publish his letters whenever he received one, however infrequently they arrived.[39]

Before Albion had left for war, Emma had strongly wished for them to marry immediately, but Albion, prophetically, resisted on the grounds that if he were to return from the war "maimed" he would not want Emma saddled with "such a husband."[40] Under those circumstances, he believed, the honorable thing to do would be for him to release her from their engagement. Emma, who lived a few miles away in Conneaut, was forbidden to visit the injured Albion—by both himself and her father—and she was left in the dark as to the nature of his injury. Too upset to write, Emma had her older sister, Angie, beg him for information. "*All* the rumors we heard *can not* be true," Angie wrote him, "we can only conclude that something *terrible* has happened to you and you are fearful of letting us know because of the pain and sorrow it will cause us."[41] Although he did not want to see Emma until he could walk again, Albion finally relented and allowed her one brief visit. He wrote to a friend in Washington of the pleasure he experienced in seeing her again: "My own Emma stepped into the room with the old quiet smile upon her face, and the same warm lovelight in her eyes. . . . Your Washington beauty lacks one thing far more essential to a man of sense than every other charm— character."[42] Despite the uplifting effect of seeing her, however, Albion would not allow her to visit again until nine months later.

Concepts of honor and manhood were integral to Albion's sense of identity, as they were for most nineteenth-century American men. His standards of manliness were set extremely high, and Albion anguished when he failed to meet them. The dual burden of his physical disability and the "disgraceful" defeat at Bull Run consumed Albion with over-whelming feelings of failure. "I am completely discouraged," he con-fessed to Emma, "I cannot live here, I cannot work, I cannot go to war, and what I shall do I don't know."[43] Albion maintained a miserable and isolated existence as an invalid in his father's home. When Emma tried to boost his spirits, he sharply replied, "Please Emma do not ever again call me 'noble' or 'glorious'; do not speak of 'fame' or 'honor' in connection with me . . . it pains me to read the words, they are so undeserved by me."[44] He could not imagine life without his physical faculties intact.

Although it is unknown whether his injury had affected his sexual functions—or if that was even at issue—Albion became convinced that he could no longer perform the role of husband for Emma. "You know that it would be unjust and unmanly for me to permit you to share my misfortune," he told her. "If I ever get to be a *man* again it will be differ-ent, but . . . for your sake I am *sorry you are my betrothed*."[45] Furthermore, he told her that it would be "a sin of no slight magnitude" for him to "marry any woman in [his] current condition."[46] Emma had little patience for such talk. Again and again, she assured him that his condition posed no obstacle to their relationship: "It has been my life, my joy, my happiness to [love you] and if I could have foreseen all that has come upon us I would have loved you *just the same.*"[47] Though Emma was prepared to accept their misfortune, Albion was not. Driven on by his overwhelming sense of honor, Albion finally broke off his engagement to Emma after several months of indecision. He entreated her, "Let me beg you to look calmly and reasonably at our position, to think that you have a duty to perform toward yourself and the future." He explained that he could never allow himself to be a "burden to [her] life." Though Emma still refused to acquiesce to his logic, she finally agreed to "put aside" their promises to each other for the immediate future, unable to argue against something so meaningful to his sense of "duty" and "honor."[48]

In *Patriotic Gore*, Edmund Wilson suggested that Tourgée's romantic and "chivalrous view of the world" made him somehow more akin to Southerners than Northerners in his temperament.[49] But a desire to embody "manly courage" and "honor" was just as prevalent in the North as in the South at this time, though perhaps somewhat differently defined. In the Northern middle class, courage was an essential ingredient of the man of character, and a man of self-possession and self-control could control his fear, and his impulse to flee danger, along with all other bodily impulses. Courage under fire bespoke of a morally upstanding nature. In the advice literature of the North, the ideal Union soldier was expected to be a man of character—to control all of his impulses and to shun such habits as drinking, smoking, gambling, cursing, and extramarital sex.[50] Tourgée undoubtedly would have been guided by these principles. To have been injured in a retreat and now to have to live as a helpless dependent, unable to fulfill the duties of a husband, grated harshly against his idealized self-image. Tourgée believed that he could only reclaim his honor and demonstrate his manhood on the battlefield. At times when this possibility seemed remote, he would become almost suicidal. "That I should be stricken in my youth, should lose the hope of manhood," he wrote in self-pitying tones, "methinks I could rest sweetly in the grave [where] there is no pain, no sorrow, no blasted hope, no regret, no shame!"[51] After one such morbid letter, Emma admonished him: "My Allie, would you have the light of my life *all go out do not* oh! *ever*[,] if you love me[,] *pray for that.*"[52]

To anyone who would listen, Albion insisted that he would return to the war as soon as he could walk. Over long months of rehabilitation he enlisted the support of a close friend, Joe R. Warner, to attend to him nearly every day and to assist with a variety of treatments to his back. He described his condition at that time: "Much of the time [my legs] were numb and nearly without sensation; at intervals there was a prickly sensation, and at all times a sense of heaviness."[53] As the swelling in his spine receded, Albion regained limited mobility in his legs—although he could not stand on them—as well as intermittent sensation. According to Warner years later, only Tourgée's "invincible pluck and obstinate courage" enabled him to get around a little on two crutches that raised his hopes of a full recovery. "I could only move my legs by swinging the body," Tourgée later recalled. "It was dragging with staff and crutch rather than walking with them."[54]

Feeling that his life was growing worthless to the war effort, he compensated for his disability by becoming a recruiter for the Union Army. In early 1862, after having received an A.B. degree from the University of Rochester on the strength of his military service—courtesy of President Anderson—he began to travel throughout the Western Reserve delivering speeches and reading poetry at enlistment rallies. Albion spoke "sitting in a chair" and, with the help of Joe Warner, was carried to and from the stage. During this time, he even succeeded in getting a book of patriotic poetry published, at his own expense, which included an epic poem of eight hundred lines. When Albion showed the poem to his father "in hope of winning some paternal praise," he was instead convinced of its utter inferiority—and perhaps immorality. Albion reportedly destroyed the only copies of his first book by shoving them into the kitchen stove.[55]

Soon after, Albion left his father's home and began to study law as a clerk in the town of Ashtabula. During the summer months, he and Joe Warner became involved in the raising of a company for the 105th Ohio Volunteers regiment. Albion received an appointment as a lieutenant, although it was given to him with the understanding that he would serve only as a recruiter. However, miraculously, a prescription he obtained in Cleveland that contained "strychnine in large quantities" provided sudden relief to his intermittent paralysis. Within weeks after starting the medicine, he found himself able to walk without the aid of his crutches and with merely "a little drag" in the movement of his right leg. On July 14, 1862, he wrote to Emma for the first time in months with the good news: "I think you may dismiss *all your fears!* . . . I can *walk!*"[56] Yet this miracle did not lead to marriage; it led to reenlistment. On August 20, he walked into a recruiting office, leaving his crutches outside, and managed to pass a physical exam.[57] Even Emma seemed to understand his course of action. She told him:

> Oh I am *so glad* you can be yourself again and do what you so long wished to again. . . . I do not feel one bit as I did a year and half ago, when you enlisted. You know I was *willing* then but it was more the romance and the novelty of the thing than the patriotism . . . a year has brought wondrous changes and what we dimly saw might be[,] has become *real*.[58]

A year and one month after the Battle of Bull Run, he returned to the war. By that time, Albion's predictions of a long and bloody revolution had become, indeed, terribly real.

CONFRONTING SLAVERY

Tourgée would always insist, long after the war, that his radicalism on race issues resulted from his "'experience' during the rebellion."[59] Though the groundwork had been prepared in his youth, the emergence of his Radical Republicanism was brought on by the circumstances of the war. His second tour of duty with the 105th Ohio Infantry brought him into direct contact with slavery for the first time. Not only was he confronted with the reality of men and women held in bondage, he found himself in situations that forced him to choose whether to actively support the institution of slavery or to actively oppose it. Along with others of his regiment, he consistently chose the latter and allied himself with the slaves who sought to escape it.

Unlike his New York regiment, the Ohio 105th Volunteer Infantry was a tight-knit and homogenous group, made up of 1,013 men drawn almost exclusively from the Western Reserve. Albion personally recruited forty men, many of whom had attended the Kingsville Academy.[60] More than two-thirds of the regiment were composed of farmers—or farmer's sons—while the rest was largely made up of clerks, teachers, and students. A highly literate group, the members of the 105th wrote letters and memoirs prolifically, leaving behind a wealth of documentation. In 1895, Tourgée himself published a 350-page regimental history, *The Story of a Thousand*, based upon the extensive letters and diaries provided to him by his comrades. Unlike "ordinary regimental histories" which, he felt, "seem to have no object but to record insignificant and often discreditable personal incidents," he agreed to write their history as a kind of social history.[61] His book "subordinated" personal incidents and focused on larger issues, such as "why these men took the oath of office, what manner of men they were, and what controlling impulse they typified."[62] His depiction of them, overall, suggested that the young men of the 105th carried the anti-slavery fervor of the Western Reserve with them to the warfront.

Even before Fort Sumter fell, Senator Ben Wade had set the tone for the Western Reserve by making fierce and inflammatory speeches in the Senate against compromise during the winter of 1860–61. In fact, when Texas senator Louis T. Wigfall resigned his seat on March 4, after failing in his efforts to broker a compromise, he laid full responsibility for the coming war on "the Gentleman from Ohio" and his "abolitionist"

Lieutenant Tourgée (left) with Lieutenants Wallace and
Morgaridge of the 105th Ohio Infantry, taken near Deerherd,
Tennessee, after a "dusty march." Courtesy of the Chautauqua
County Historical Society, Westfield, NY.

constituents.[63] Likewise, the *Cincinnati Daily Times* denounced the
population of "our own half-crazed Reserve" who would "rather see the
country shattered to a thousand fragments than submit to a pro-slavery
triumph." The extremist "harangues" of Senator Wade, the newspaper
insisted, "represents the Reserve, and not the State of Ohio."[64] Thus,
Tourgée may not have greatly exaggerated when he wrote of his regiment's
antislavery idealism: "We counted our cause supremely noble because success could add little to our own honor, prosperity, or ease, but offered all its
rich harvest of blessing to other ages and an alien and oppressed people."[65]

Even if the members of the 105th Ohio did not view themselves as
liberators when they enlisted to fight, they did soon afterwards. After their

deployment from Cleveland on August 22, the regiment headed for Kentucky to join what was about to become the Army of the Cumberland. During their first, long march from Lexington to Louisville they were promptly met by "colored men" who appeared on the roadside offering to carry equipment, knapsacks, and water for the exhausted soldiers. Weighted down by excessive equipment, and lacking the endurance of seasoned soldiers, the 105th gratefully embraced their offer of assistance. By the time the army camped at Frankfort, they had collected a large number of black "assistants."[66]

The soldiers were appalled when local authorities rounded up their black followers, who were presumed to be runaway slaves. The 105th and several other regiments refused to surrender them, naively demanding to see warrants before allowing slave patrollers to enter their ranks—according to state law, warrants were not required to recapture runaways. Just as the Fugitive Slave Law had prompted civil disobedience among outraged Northerners, now the 105th felt morally obliged to protect their suspected runaways from recapture. Commanding General James S. Jackson had to be personally called to force the soldiers to submit to this legal "search and seizure." Still, an outraged officer of the 105th, Captain Charles G. Edwards, managed to save one man from bondage by claiming him as a longtime personal servant from Ohio and challenged the slave patrol to prove otherwise when his story was questioned. Furious by this transparently false alibi, General Jackson shouted in disgust at Edwards and his soldiers, "You are all Abolition nigger-stealers!" They would often repeat this epithet with pride afterwards. As Tourgée observed later, this incident demonstrated "how far apart in moral sentiment were between the gallant general and the troops he led—the one fighting for the Union to save slavery, the other inspired by hope for its destruction."[67]

The 105th found themselves in a peculiar position in Kentucky as "an 'abolition regiment' in a loyal slave state," in Tourgée's words.[68] The Congressional "confiscation" acts that prohibited the return of fugitive slaves from Union lines did not apply in Kentucky, where slave owners were not waging armed rebellion against the government. This meant that it was the duty of the Union Army to maintain the institution of slavery and protect the property of slaveowners. Some officers of the 105th, however, took significant risks by harboring fugitive slaves anyway. Over the next few months, numerous conflicts between local authorities and Union soldiers broke out over the issue of returning runaways. The officers, according to Tourgée, cleverly construed orders that were intended to keep fugitives out of their camps in a manner that protected their fugitives by keeping slave masters and law enforcement agents from entering. On one occasion, Colonel Tolles of the 105th risked arrest for refusing to allow a slave owner to enter his ranks without sufficient proof to identify his slave. The offended slave owner, who felt his word should be enough, returned with an order from the commanding General demanding that the Colonel relinquish the man in question. When the Colonel disobeyed the order, Albion recalled, "The general threatened arrest for disobedience; [but] the colonel threatened to report the general to the President for conspiring to kidnap a free man."[69] The arrest order never came.

In November of 1862, Tourgée himself was temporarily quartered at a Kentucky plantation, where he observed the daily life of slavery up close for several weeks. He had been wounded at the Battle of Perryville, his first serious engagement with the enemy since Bull Run, and accepted the hospitality of a local Unionist family for his convalescence. Many Kentucky slaveholders, attempting to ingratiate themselves to Union generals, offered to house wounded officers and nurse them back to health in the comfort of their luxurious manor houses. Despite his opposition to slavery, Tourgée was glad to escape military hospital conditions and readily accepted this opportunity. He found Southern culture very strange and complained of being forced to take part in formal parties. But on November 23, he witnessed one of those cruel acts that were endemic to slavery. With unconcealed horror, he scrawled a frantic and cryptic note to Emma:

> Oh! I am sick today—so sick! Not bodily sick—but so sick at heart! I have seen what would make a cynic heart-sore! My brain throbs—my blood boils! I cannot tell you what I think or *feel* and God grant that you may never know its awfulness, which I could never tell! If it ever become necessary for you to enter a Slave State I shall wish you to come blindfolded and with shut ears. I cannot write any more . . . I cannot forget what has occurred.[70]

What occurred can only be imagined, but his reaction suggests that it was traumatic for him to witness. It may have been an ordinary cruel act, such as whipping, or perhaps it was a more extreme abuse that he was not meant to see. Whatever the case, it evidently confirmed his worst fears about the institution of slavery.

While no single incident converted Tourgée to radicalism, it seems that the most critical period in his political maturation took place during the fall and winter of 1862. On September 22, President Lincoln had announced the Emancipation Proclamation and, as the deadline for its implementation drew near, the inhumanity of slavery had never been more evident to Albion. On January 1, 1863, a mere five weeks after the disturbing encounter on the Kentucky plantation, the Emancipation

Proclamation officially went into effect. Though it affected none of the slaves in the vicinity of the 105th—as with the Confiscation Acts, Kentucky was exempt from its scope—it was a moment of great relief and inspiration to the men of the regiment. It prompted Albion to write a long, revealing letter to his Psi Upsilon fraternity brothers at the University of Rochester.

Addressed to the "Brothers of the Union," this letter conveys the impression that Albion had reached a deeper understanding of the conflict in which he was engaged. Written for both new fraternity brothers and old, it told of the events of his military career from his enlistment in Rochester in 1861 to the present moment. He fondly recalled his fraternity brothers' "incredulous sneers" at his prediction that the war would be long and bloody and that it would result in the abolition of slavery. Now, he exalted, "two bloody years have proved their truth in every particular except *one, that one* is yet partially demonstrated, the idea of a national revolution."[71] Though he firmly believed the Union would prevail, Tourgée was certain that a sweeping political revolution would occur to bind the states together more firmly and fundamentally alter Federal-State powers. "The Revolution has but just begun," he declared.

He left the exact nature of this "national revolution" unexplained, but the implications were clear. He suggested that Northern society had proven itself in possession of "a higher notion of freedom" than its Southern counterpart and that it was this notion of "freedom" that must prevail. He scoffed at the "oft-repeated maxim" "we are fighting for the Union as it was." This slogan, he gloated, had been "a sublime hoax" perpetuated by the Lincoln administration, which now had taken an irrevocable step forward by abolishing Southern slavery—paving the way for the establishment of the Union upon a new and better foundation. Tourgée concluded:

> I dont [sic] care a rag for *"the Union as it was."* I want and fight for the Union *"better than it was."* Before this is accomplished we must have . . . a thorough and complete revolution and renovation. This I expect and hope. For this I am willing to die—for this I expect to *die.*[72]

Thus having proclaimed his commitment to radicalism, he hoped his fraternity brothers would follow his example. It was not too late for them to enlist; much more still remained to be accomplished.

Evidence suggests that the men of the 105th in general began to see themselves as liberators in the months after their arrival in the South. A few of the soldiers attempted to more fully explain the meaning of the war in verse. Captain Ephraim Kee, once Albion's fellow student at Kingsville Academy, left two of his poems in Tourgée's possession before he was killed. One, entitled "A Vision," explicitly described the war's object as the freeing and "uplifting" of the African slaves. Kee wrote, "Then there came the kindly feeling/ Dwelling every patriot-breast/ That to lift these trodden children/ from the dust was God's behest." Kee's poem also describes the gratitude of slaves toward their "liberators," whom they tell: "We have prayed and we have waited/ Watching anxiously the strand/ for the hour . . . each bondman should go free/ the birth-hour of our Jubilee."[73] One of Tourgée's poems describes the war from the perspective of a young slave. Calling John Brown the "High Priest of our deliverance," the slave is depicted as expecting to be liberated by the North even before the war broke out: "and so we looked toward the North and prayed/ for that way were we taught by dim and vague/ tradition that our help must come."[74] As these poems suggest, the slaves' own embrace of Union soldiers as a liberating army may have encouraged the soldiers to view themselves in this way.

By 1863, though contrary to orders, the 105th had acquired a permanent contingent of black volunteers whom the regiment employed in a variety of tasks. Many officers, including Tourgée, acquired personal servants who became intimate companions. Albion mentioned the daily ritual of his being awoken by "Big John our faithful Negro man calling me to" breakfast.[75] Their increasing contact with blacks elicited a growing respect for the "colored population" among them. Albion later would write admiringly of the slaves' contributions to the Union war effort. Even those who did not become fugitives or join the Union lines, he recalled, would often act as informants. "Black figures stole softly down from the 'quarters,' crept up to the sentinels" after dark, he recalled, to exchange critical information. He commended "their capacity for secret, effective, and concerted action" and "their marvelous power of obtaining and transmitting intelligence in regard to military operations."[76]

Such interactions encouraged Albion's already evident curiosity about black life in the South. He reported in his diary one day of having attended a "meeting of the 'Cullud population' of the Brigade" that impressed him. "No uninteresting thing," he wrote of the experience. "I have heard worse things than I have listened to there today."[77] A subtle illustration of his changing habits of mind can be briefly glimpsed in a diary entry of October 24, 1863: Albion first describes a newly arriving fugitive as a "colored man" but then crossed these two words out and replaced them with the unusual, more respectful designation "an American citizen of African descent."[78] This growing interest and respect for blacks prompted him to apply for an appointment as a commander of one of the newly formed colored regiments. These positions were advertised by the Bureau of Colored Troops as prestigious appointments designed only for "intelligent white men with high morals who were willing to make a commitment to uplifting the black race." Indeed Captain R.D. Mussey, who was given the task of appointing the officers from the army of the Cumberland, let it be known that he would accept no man merely looking for "higher rank and pay," and each candidate had to pass a rigorous examination before a board of commissioners.[79]

To his great disappointment, Tourgée never received a commission as the captain of a colored regiment; in fact, he never even received a hearing—his file appears to have been lost. Surprisingly, the Bureau of Colored Troops received nearly nine thousand applicants of which less than one-fourth were ultimately appointed.[80] In Tourgée's estimate, leading a colored regiment "is certainly the place for men who would serve the country best."[81] Although it carried high prestige and responsibility, such a position also carried additional risks. Confederate President Jefferson Davis let it be known early in 1863 that any white officer commanding black troops would be tried and executed for "inciting insurrection" if captured. This threat was taken seriously by the 105th. One of their own captains, Byron W. Canfield, was threatened with a public execution after being captured by the Confederates in January of 1863 because of their regiment's well-known reputation as "nigger-stealer[s]."[82] In the privacy of his diary, Tourgée weighed the risks and moral duties involved in submitting his application:

> I know there is little hope of any mercy being shown any one who may be in any way connected with the colored troops but why not play with large stakes as well as small ones? I know I owe a duty to Emma but a little more danger cannot make much of [a] difference.[83]

This step might be seen as an extension of that declaration to his Rochester fraternity brothers a few months earlier that he was ready and willing to die for his cause. The *cause*, moreover, was increasingly tied to the freeing and "uplifting" of the enslaved.

INDIVIDUALISM AND NATIONALISM; ONE AND INSEPARABLE?

The Civil War gave birth to a more powerful national government and also to a stronger sense of national identity among the people—at least for those who supported the Union. Some scholars have viewed the harsh and prolonged sacrifices demanded by the war as a cultural watershed through which the individualistic and anti-institutional tendencies of the antebellum era gave way to the hierarchal, organizational society of the Gilded Age.[84] In this view, the regimented life of the military and collective hardships of the home front instilled a new respect for authority and deference to national institutions. While this may have been true for many, Tourgée's experience suggests that other ideological consequences were possible as well.[85] He relinquished very little of his prewar individualist sensitivities to the blind "worship of force" or respect for authority that historians have described. Nor did the horrors and inhumanities of the war cause an existential crisis or create doubt in Tourgée's mind regarding the antislavery principles for which he fought. Despite the psychological burden of waging an increasingly brutal and total war, he and his comrades tried to maintain a balance between the execution of war and the personal integrity and freedom of conscience they held dear.

One scholar has written of Tourgée: "He left the Army as much a civilian as when he entered it and [his] history of the Ohio 105th . . . is really a celebration of civilians in uniform, the farm boys who nobly submitted to the war's indignities."[86] Indeed, Tourgée insisted in his regimental history that the young men of the 105th believed in nationalism only in so far as a strong government was the best means of protecting individual liberties. "They always spoke of 'Liberty and Union,'" Tourgée wrote of his comrades, "invariably putting the most important word first, showing conclusively that union was regarded by them as a means of establishing and securing liberty."[87] In other words, they did not allow nationalist sentiments to overwhelm their concern for individual rights.

Tourgée remained highly sensitive to any issue that impinged upon his personal sense of honor and he showed a willingness to defy commands that struck him as violating his individual concept of moral duty. Within weeks of his first enlistment, Albion organized a protest movement against the poor quality of food at his training camp in Elmira. The challenge of supplying so many soldiers at the very outset of the war caused army suppliers to cut corners and provide highly adulterated or spoiled food, a source of "great dissatisfaction" among the soldiers. In protest, his company staged a mock funeral for their dinner beef at which Albion himself preached a sermon that infuriated the commander. However, Colonel Slocum later recalled that he was so taken by Tourgée's oratory that he allowed him to finish his speech over the food situation, though it was "contrary to all military discipline."[88] The entire regiment later joined in a demonstration by kicking over their dinner tables in unison and marching out of the mess hall.[89]

Albion's defiance of military protocol went beyond mere adolescent pranks and juvenile rebellion and began to manifest itself in an explicit desire to democratize army life. He continually bristled at the sharp contrast between the ingrained discipline of career soldiers and the relaxed attitude of volunteers like himself. "The theory of discipline which prevails in our regular army is purely monarchical and aristocratic," Tourgée complained, "it is in theory and in practice a disgrace to the republic."[90] As a Lieutenant in the 105th, he took pride in "directing rather than ordering" the men under his charge. Tourgée explained:

> The enlisted men sought his officer's tent for counsel as freely almost as his comrade's. On the march, they chatted as familiarly as they had done at home . . . in education, wealth, and all that society counts essential to gentility, save the accident of temporary rank, he was often their equal; sometimes their superior. . . . No wall of exclusion separated them; rank made little difference in their relations.[91]

Tourgée's approachable and sympathetic demeanor earned him the gratitude of his men, such as one who wrote to thank him years later for his "many act of kindness and consideration . . . which I shall retain as long as life."[92] But on occasion, this democratic sensibility led to an open confrontation with the regiment's commanders.

The most dramatic incident of this type of conflict in Tourgée's regiment came in June 1863. A great many men of the 105th became outraged with their commanding officer, Colonel Albert S. Hall, when he dismissed Captain Canfield from the service as punishment for causing the capture of more than one hundred men of their regiment after they fell into a Confederate trap, a mistake they believed was the fault of Colonel Hall's own incompetence.[93] To voice their sympathy with Canfield, the officers of the 105th held a meeting and drafted a collective letter expressing their regrets for his dismissal. Colonel Hall, having learned of the meeting, furiously ordered the seizure of the letter and arrested two lieutenants who refused to surrender it. Tourgée reported in his diary: Colonel Hall "has demanded the letter, has heard it read and [threatened] . . . to dismiss everyone who signed it in disgrace." He defiantly added: "Let him try it. I am ready." The following day, all of the 105th's officers except one demanded the release of their comrades and tendered their resignations when Hall replied "he would see us all in Hell first." One lieutenant explained in his diary that the men could not respect Hall's violation of their individual rights as that amounted to an "improper order." "The paper [is] a private one containing nothing treasonable," he insisted. Albion, likewise, stated in his resignation letter, "Our rights cannot be respected [and] our most private affairs are unlawfully pried into." Faced with the humiliation of a full-scale mutiny, Hall ultimately backed down. After the release of the lieutenants, Tourgée exalted, "By concerted action we have conquered our tyrant."[94]

In July 1863, a mere month later, Tourgée's defiant attitude led him to be court-martialed for "conduct to the prejudice of good order and military discipline." Though the incident itself appears to have been a minor infraction blown out of proportion—perhaps as retribution for Tourgée's role in the Canfield affair or for his general laxity of discipline—the charge reflected his poor relationship with the commanding officers of the 105th. The case turned on the issue of whether Albion "thrust his sword" at a Sergeant in anger or whether the man merely "walked into" the point of his drawn sword, as Tourgée claimed. In his spirited self-defense, however, Albion also took especial pains to defend himself against the charge of having used profanity, calling on several character witnesses, because it touched upon his character. In the end, Albion received the incongruous verdict of "not guilty," while being sentenced to reprimand before the other commissioned officers. Albion quipped, "I suppose the court was of opinion that if I did not need a reprimand for what was charged, I did for something else."[95]

While Albion and the men of the 105th were extremely vigilant over their own individual rights, they often showed a frightening lack of concern for the rights of Southern civilians. The regiment brought with them a predilection to view everything Southern as morally suspect. Lieutenant Henry H. Cummings, formerly a student at Oberlin College, exemplified this attitude when he concluded: "The entire society here is coarse, brutalized, degraded. . . . Slavery in various ways has destroyed . . . virtue, has corrupted the minds of the people, and made them coarse and sensual."[96] His abhorrence of Southern mores reflected a preexisting Northern chauvinism heightened by wartime animosity. They felt a moral sanction for the destruction of the fruits of slavery, as Ephraim Kee suggested when he wrote, "And roll on the tide of conquest/ O'er the cursed Sodom-land/ To bring low the proud oppressor/ And to smite the [oppressive] hand/ And incline the hearts of freemen/ Unto Justice and Truth/ That they may slay the Gorgon Slavery/ And its children, Lust and Ruth."[97]

Their fury was not only the angry passions raised by a terrible war, but also a belief that they were instruments of God's vengeance. By repudiating the Constitution, pro-Confederate Southerners had broken a national compact that was to the men of the 105th a sacred inheritance from the founding generation. After the 105th crossed over into secession territory in Tennessee, the men began to lay waste to the cities and towns that they encountered and helped themselves to anything they could carry. At Tullhoma, according to Cummings, the "street resounded with noise of demolition. The houses were torn down, every conceivable article of furniture was carried off to the camps . . . the soldiers seemed wild with the idea of emptying the town."[98] "You cannot imagine what a sorry place it was," Albion wrote of Tullahoma. "Buildings were first 'gutted' and then 'peeled.'"[99] Soldiers filled their camps with all kinds of property—including expensive, antique furniture that they could not possibly carry with them when they left. Much of this ended up as firewood. Despite an order by the commanding general that strictly forbade the pillaging, houses and barns continued to go up in flames wherever the army marched. Though Albion described the scenes to Emma, he never explained the failure of the 105ths officers—including himself—to enforce the general's orders. He became so used to scenes of destruction that he mentioned them merely in passing, such as when he wrote, "a burning house gives me light to write by."[100]

It would be wrong to suppose, however, that the soldiers had absolutely no conscience about these actions. Officers, like Tourgée and Cummings, often expressed regret and even sympathy for the victims. "In my heart I pitied them," Tourgée wrote of the terrified Southerners in 1863. "What sorry faces the women had. I saw many a one fleeing with a few treasures in her hands—and tears in her eyes [due to] the rudeness of our soldiers." But Albion ultimately rationalized the destruction. "Yet whom had they to blame for all their misery?" he asked rhetorically. "As a poor farmer said . . . 'If we had staid in the Union you would not have dared do this.'"[101] As far as the soldiers were concerned, secession had severed Southerners' right to the protection of the laws of the United States. The destruction served as almost divine punishment upon those who had taken up arms against the country and forfeited their allegiance to the Constitution. Lieutenant Cummings explained coldly, "While I regretted such a performance, I could feel no pity for the people. They have sown to the wind, let them reap the whirlwind."[102]

But there were limits to what men like Tourgée and Cummings could accept as appropriate retribution. The retribution enacted by the 105th during the Tennessee campaign was only a prelude to the much greater rampage they would witness and help accomplish. After Tourgée had left the service, the 105th joined Sherman's army in Georgia and took part in the destruction of Atlanta. Tourgée later expressed indignation over Sherman's March, calling it the only "really regrettable" and "shameful" action of the Union army. He placed the responsibility squarely on General Sherman and his staff, whom he felt had not only refused to discourage lawless activity, but encouraged the "bad, rough spirits" in the Army to run rampant. Tourgée strongly insisted that it was the purpose and duty of the officers to keep the "rougher elements" among the ranks in check.[103] This is an ironic indictment, of course, considering Tourgée's own inability to control his soldiers' pillaging as an officer at Tullahoma.

The diary of Lieutenant Cummings, who continued to serve in the 105th during the Atlanta campaign, also expressed regret over the destruction. During the Atlanta campaign, Cummings's previous cool attitude about the destruction gave way to discomfort. He agonized over the excessive cruelties that were allowed to go unpunished. On November 16, 1864, he wrote:

> Last night a considerable portion of Atlanta was burned . . . I confess I rarely have witnessed sights that caused me more pain. Whatever destruction of property or life or whatever suffering the necessities of war may impose let it be so, as it must be so, but wanton destruction of life or property or needless inhumanity is unchristian, and unworthy of a brave or . . . honorable man.[104]

In the midst of war's worst acts of "total war," this ex-student from Oberlin had not completely forgotten the Northern ideal of manhood and Christian charity.

Tourgée neither experienced the terrible grind of the last six months of the war nor was present for the excesses of Sherman's march. This may help explain why his abolitionist fervor remained intact even after he left the military. During the last days of the war, Lieutenant Cummings, whose political outlook closely resembled Tourgée's, found his commitment to the war effort wearing thin. "I was [once] full of enthusiasm, burning for military success and honor," Cummings wrote in August of 1864, "as far as the love of it goes, soldiering is 'played out.'" Moreover, he saw this as a general trend among the 105th: "The change in the spirit of the army [is] striking. No military ambition, no enthusiasm, no high chivalric spirit. Officers and men alike speak of the service as something to be endured."[105]

Unlike Cummings, Tourgée did not remain long enough to feel his enthusiasm wane or diminish his fervor for the "higher notion of freedom" for which he fought. If anything, these convictions grew stronger during his years of service. One suspects that Tourgée's enthusiasm for the cause would not have been completely extinguished even had he remained with the 105th until Lee's surrender. The maddeningly abbreviated conclusion to his service, however, clearly left him feeling unfulfilled. The origin of his postwar restlessness can be glimpsed in his frustration with his military career.

MANLINESS AND MEMORY

Albion was disappointed in his military career because, to his mind, he had never accomplished anything heroic. "Not many of us did," he later remarked.[106] He had been once captured, once court-martialed, and never decorated or promoted. In the three major battlefield engagements in which he participated—Bull Run, Perryville, and Chickamauga—the Union failed. His finest hour came when he took part in a bayonet charge that delayed a Confederate advance long enough to help earn General George Thomas his nickname as "the Rock of Chickamauga." But Albion was confined to camp because of his injured back when the 105th finally tasted victory. He watched from camp below as his comrades routed the Confederates from their superior positions at Lookout Mountain and Missionary Ridge in late 1863.

His lack of military glory left him feeling personally unsatisfied. Yet friends and family repeatedly expressed amazement at his single-minded devotion to the cause. "None can say that you have not done *your* duty," one Rochester fraternity brother consoled him in 1864. "When you went into the service the second time, I was astonished. No such repeated evidence of your patriotism could have been asked or expected—you seemed, to me, almost reckless. And I must honor you for a devotion which I fear would fail *me*, if I were called to pass through all that darkened your path."[107] Tourgée's devotion to the war was extraordinary indeed. He remained a steadfast soldier as long as possible, despite many opportunities to honorably resign from the service.

In January 1863, he was captured and spent most of four months in the miserable conditions of Richmond's Libby prison. Despite returning malnourished and weakened after a prisoners exchange, he insisted on returning to his regiment after a mere two weeks of recuperation. Tourgée's prison experience only seemed to deepen his fierce commitment to the war and the cause of freedom. "Freedom! The word means more to me than it ever did before," he explained to Emma, upon release from Libby. "It means life, manhood, volition—being—existence and all its pleasures. . . . And prison—bondage! Oh! I know and [can] tell what *they* mean . . . it is chagrin, humiliation—insult and fused in fierce flash of misery." He emphatically concluded his letter, "Damn the Confederacy!"[108] *Life, manhood, volition*: the three synonyms for freedom that Tourgée selected illustrate his 1860s worldview remarkably well. His equation of *bondage* with freedom's opposite, involving personal degradation, insult, and humiliation—i.e., unmanliness—likewise illustrate his deepening commitment to the cause of Emancipation.

Only Tourgée's lingering back injury prevented him from serving for the length of the war. After he was released from prison, Emma did not challenge his unwavering devotion to the war effort and supported his return to his post after a hasty marriage ceremony in May of 1863. Sergeant Joe Warner witnessed Albion's painful endurance of the back injury that plagued him during long marches and taxing physical labor. "During service [Albion] used to complain to me of the pain in his back and whenever we halted he would always instantly sit down," Warner recalled.[109] But, Albion was too proud to inform anyone other than Joe Warner about his frailty. Then, in October 1863, he severely reinjured his back when he stumbled in the dark and fell several feet into a trench, incapacitating him for weeks.[110]

This setback came at a most inopportune time. Albion had assumed the command of his company after Captain Spalding, his immediate superior, was killed in the Battle of Chickamauga. Thus he hoped he was on the verge of promotion to captain. But despite taking over the duties of captain, the high command failed to promote him to the appropriate rank, to Albion's increasing frustration. Concluding that some superior officers in the 105th had some "undefined pique or prejudice" against him, he placed all of his hopes for promotion on his application for a command of Colored Troops.[111]

When Albion's health did not rebound rapidly enough, he was pressed by his commanders to either resign or face transfer to the "Invalid corps." He refused, regarding this possible assignment "as a sort of disgrace." Albion resolved, "If I could not remain in the active service I would not remain at all." Once Emma learned of his predicament, she scolded him: "Now I am going to give you a command which if you do not obey *instantly* I shall be very apt to make an appearance down in Dixie to claim my husband who had lost his senses. *You are to come home*, certainly, *resign.*"[112] Giving up "all hope of ever hearing from my [Colored Regiments] application," Albion finally resigned on December 6, 1863. In his resignation letter, he could not resist a final, parting jibe at his superiors. Among the reasons given, he included "the spirit manifested towards me by" certain "suspicious officers" whose treatment, he said, had made it impossible for him to serve with "honor." This document was angrily returned to him, and a revised one was gratefully accepted the same day.[113] This unceremonious ending to his military career ensured that he would leave the military without achieving distinction.

Tourgée's dissatisfaction with his military record is evident in the fact that, afterwards, he would sometimes distort or exaggerate it to enhance his accomplishments. In his fiction, his main characters usually rose to the rank of general, and never ranked less than colonel by the end of the war. When discussing his own history, he was prone to compensate for his undistinguished record with distortions of the truth. These distortions never had to do with battlefield prowess. Tourgée never discussed whether he had killed any Confederates, nor could ever be found in public or private spinning a veteran's yarn of daring and bravery under fire. Rather, his distortions focused on issues of rank, the nature of his injuries, and his devotion to black freedom.

Most egregiously, Tourgée would sometimes claim that he had been "court-martialed for refusing to surrender a fugitive slave," though it was Colonel Tolles who refused to surrender the fugitive slave and Tourgée was court-martialed for other reasons.[114] Likewise, he would consistently claim in later years to have been appointed to the rank of "Captain," or sometimes "Major," of a black regiment in the spring of 1865 only to have the Confederate surrender prevent him from assuming his post. There is no evidence to support this claim.[115] Both of these stories have the distinct ring of wishful thinking. It must be noted that they also served political ends for him too. When his sincerity was questioned regarding his support of black civil rights during Reconstruction, these stories provided "evidence" of a longstanding devotion to black freedom dating back to a time when great risk and little political advantage might be gained by such a stance.

Regarding injuries, more than once he claimed to have lost his left eye at Bull Run when in fact his blind eye was the result of a childhood accident.[116] In addition, he may or may not have carried shrapnel in his hip from a wound received at Perryville—he made conflicting statements about this.[117] Both tales, if the second one is an invention, improve upon the actual injuries he suffered in these battles. When Emma complained after Perryville that he had not described the battle to her, Albion explained: "Only once—to Coon [Seneca Kuhn]—have I mustered sufficient 'grit' to detail the affair, and it sickened me then . . . you must be content to wait and hear it from my lips."[118] Psychologically, Tourgée was deeply scarred by his experiences in these battles and perhaps he felt a need for his emotional scars to be better illustrated by his physical ones. His glass eye offered a far more demonstrable "badge of courage" than his sore back. At Perryville, too, his actual injury may have been little more than an aggravation of his bad back, which again did not indicate the ferocity of the battle as well as a piece of enemy shell in his hip did. Whatever the psychological basis for his distortions, however, he regarded his actual injuries as somehow insufficient.

Despite these lingering concerns over his injuries, the ideals of courage and manhood that had pulled Albion into the war would become less significant to him afterwards. His formal writings on the war expressed disdain for those who laid claim to individual heroism, and he tended toward an ironic and self-effacing portrayal of the soldier's experience. The protagonist of *A Fool's Errand* learns to be a true soldier only after "an incredible amount of boasting at the outset, a marvelous amount of running soon after, and a reasonable amount of fighting still later in the

Civil War."[119] Rather than detailing the horrors of war in his fiction, he spent the rest of his life insisting that the war meant something more than individual suffering and heroism.

By contrast, politicians who sought the reconciliation of white Northerners and Southerners in the decades that followed the Civil War would dismiss the political issues that led to the war, particularly the memory of antislavery zeal, and instead venerate the courage and manliness of the Blue and the Grey alike. Woodrow Wilson's fiftieth anniversary address at Gettysburg in 1913 epitomized this tactic when he proclaimed, "the quarrel [is] forgotten—*except* that we shall not forget the splendid valour, the manly devotion of the men . . . the blood and sacrifice of unknown men lifted to great stature in the view of all generations by knowing no limit to their manly willingness to serve."[120] The celebration of manliness was the accepted, dominant meaning of the war in the North by the time Wilson spoke.[121] But, for Tourgée, this aspect of the war would remain subordinate in meaning to the antislavery ideals for which he fought. "The great war of yesterday is *not* the battles, the marches, the conflicts," Tourgée would later write, "not the courage, the suffering, the blood, but only the causes that underlay the struggle and the results that followed from it."[122] The war may have exhausted his anxiety about fulfilling the gendered ideal of masculine heroism, but it awakened his personal interest in the political "revolution" against slavery. And that revolution was far from over.

4

A Radical Yankee in
the Reconstruction South

We are . . . transplanting the whole South with the higher
civilization of the North. The New England Schoolhouse is
bound to take the place of the Southern whipping post.

    —Frederick Douglass, "The Mission of the War," 1864

Poor men of Guilford! Laboring men of Guilford, now is our
golden moment! . . . Will you be free men or Serfs? Will the
"new people" have a "new" state, or the old one patched up,
with its whips and stocks, its oppressive system of taxation and
its tyrannic landed aristocracy?

    —A.W. Tourgée, *To the Voters of Guilford*, October 21, 1867

WHILE MUCH OF THE NATION GAVE LITTLE THOUGHT to what
might occur in the post-emancipation South, those who had
championed abolitionism acted swiftly upon their own idea of
the direction the new South must take. A veritable army of missionaries
and schoolteachers followed in the wake of the Union army bringing
with them a vision of "civilization" that distinctly smacked of the culture
of New England. As early as 1862, the abolitionist-founded American
Missionary Association had taken the lead in dispatching Northern teachers to the South to staff newly established freedmen's schools. In St.
Louis, in 1864, one observer was struck by the host of the energetic New
England schoolteachers who suddenly descended upon the occupied city
to establish "colored" schools and begin the work of making citizens out
of slaves. One astonished St. Louis Democrat was heard to exclaim, "This
war is the conquest of America by the state of Massachusetts!" "He was
right," the observer remarked, "but it was not a conquest by the sword."[1]

With their ambitious program, these reformers would play a critical,
and much-maligned, role in the turbulent era ahead. Among the ranks of

this cultural army, Tourgée would become a distinguished leader. As Tourgée would later point out, their task was not so much work of "reconstruction" as it was an act of *construction*, laying new foundations for a new society. "The word [Reconstruction] itself was one of ill-omen," he observed, "by its very force, it accustomed the people to the idea that the work which was to be done was but the patching up of an old garment; that it was an act of restoration rather than one of creation."[2] Though many in the North, including President Andrew Johnson, would have disagreed with Tourgée's approach, those missionaries would have undoubtedly understood.

History has not always been kind to the men and women who, like Tourgée, presumed to transplant their Northern-grown values into Southern soil. Despite scholars' repudiation of the most egregious myths about the "carpetbaggers," few would paint them as selfless heroes and heroines, risking their lives to spread the democratic creed of equal citizenship and racial equality even though many of them risked, and some gave, their lives for just that purpose. Their egalitarian principles were embedded within an arrogant sense of cultural superiority and an unquestioning commitment to free market capitalism that leaves modern critics uneasy. Hoping to instill their middle-class values of free markets and contracts, thrift and hard work, marriage and domesticity, these self-proclaimed "liberators," in the view of some recent historians, merely brought new shackles to replace the old ones.[3] But, this criticism fails to give due consideration to the democratic vision of carpetbaggers such as Albion Tourgée.

Reconstruction brought political empowerment and economic upward mobility to the downtrodden of the South, both black and white. Even Tourgée had shared "the Northern man's unfailing faith in the healing efficacy of trade" when he embarked to the South and expected that "the whole region [would] be transformed by the power of commerce, manufactures, and the incursion of Northern life, capital, industry and enterprise."[4] But his experience convinced him otherwise. Rejecting the miracle cure of market operations, he favored instead the causes of free speech, equal citizenship, the politicization of the masses through voluntary associations, a government-supported public education system, and the value of an active, informed citizenry. While Tourgée believed wholeheartedly in "the higher civilization of the North," that superiority derived, in his view, from the democratic social traits that empowered the individual and promoted self-rule. A closer analysis of Tourgée's actions and ideas demonstrate that his radicalism, though contained within the "free labor ideology," had political ramifications quite different from those who put blind faith in free markets and labor contracts.

A SOUTHERN SCHEME

Tourgée was haunted by his unsought retirement from the army and spent the next sixteen months restlessly trying to adapt to civilian life. His physical ailments had left him, in his own estimation, "unfit" for manual labor. After quickly completing his legal training and gaining acceptance to the Ohio bar, he joined a law firm based in Painesville, Ohio, but found the legal field overcrowded. He blamed this on those of his peers who got a "head start" in their careers while staying home from the war. Adding to his concerns, the failing health of Emma's father prompted him to assume responsibility as head of the Kilbourne family. After taking on some reporting assignments for the *Erie Dispatch*, he abruptly gave up the law and moved to Erie, Pennsylvania, where he continued to do freelance journalism and eventually took a new position as principal of the Erie Academy. The Kilbournes sold their family farm in Conneaut, and Emma and her sisters joined Tourgée as teachers at the school.

Albion continued to imagine a grander future for himself and remained unfulfilled in his new position. "I don't believe I was ever intended for a teacher," as he had once told Emma, "I don't think this business harmonizes with my mental constitution."[5] Emma, too, felt that her husband was meant for something greater. "I have often asked myself would I be willing to give up all my ambitious views for you for some quiet[,] unobtrusive sphere for which God may have designed you," but, she confessed, "My heart rebels and the thought is hateful to me."[6] As the Civil War ground to a close in the spring of 1865, they began to consider the possible economic opportunities in the devastated South. Though later claiming that his primary reason for relocating to the South was the belief that "a milder climate" would prove beneficial to his health, which had been "somewhat shattered by the shocks of war," his correspondence of the time suggests that he saw relocation of the South as a means to finish what he began in the war.[7] Tourgée viewed a move to the South as a new opportunity to serve his country, to assist the former slaves, and perhaps to achieve social standing and financial security in the bargain.

One indication of his underlying civic purposes was that he turned to his mentor President Anderson for advice and approval. Ever the nationalist, Anderson strongly encouraged Tourgée's idea of relocation. Though their original correspondence has been lost, a version of it appears in *A Fool's Errand* that may well have been taken verbatim. The Fool's mentor and former college president tells him that the reconstruction of the South is an important national project: "It is only by such intermingling of the people of the two sections that they can ever become one."

Imagining a future in which the Southern economy could be shaped in the image of the Northern free labor market, the mentor continues:

> I think men who have been acquainted with free labor will be able to give valuable aid . . . the old economies of the plantation and the negro-quarters will have to give way [and] the labor of that section must be organized, or rather taught to manage itself, to become automatic in its operations.[8]

Just as the conservative Anderson and his radical ex-student had previously, for different reasons, found a common cause in the abolition of slavery, now they agreed upon the direction Southern reconstruction must take.

Seeking what he thought to be the path of least resistance, Tourgée chose North Carolina as the most suitable place to scout for opportunities. The state's reputation for antislavery Unionism piqued his interest. During the war, a significant number of its non-slaveholders remained loyal to the Union and even mounted a peace movement that openly resisted the Confederate government. Even before the war, he had been deeply impressed by the North Carolinian author Hinton Helper, who passionately denounced slavery and called upon poor whites to reject the institution in *The Impending Crisis of the South*. As a Rochester student, Tourgée wrote an essay lamenting the public burnings of Helper's book in North Carolina and the arrest of several disobedient citizens of Guilford County for illegal possession of it. Perhaps not coincidentally, Guilford would become Tourgée's new home in 1865.[9] Tourgée wrote to the provisional governor of North Carolina, William W. Holden, a few weeks after Lincoln's assassination to inquire about economic opportunities for a group of families who were interested in emigrating. He received an encouraging reply.

A North Carolina native, Holden earned his appointment as provisional governor by leading the state's powerful wartime peace movement. "I would be most happy to welcome you into our state, and to show you the fraternal feeling the loyal people of the state entertain for their northern brethren," Holden responded on June 16, 1865. Like many Southern Unionists, he encouraged Northern investment and the immigration of white Northern labor into the state. Promising excellent opportunities for Tourgée and his associates, he emphasized the cheapness of the land, the depreciated local currency, and the state's desperate need for skilled labor. Revealing his own anti-black prejudices, Holden confessed his fear about the reliability of "unskilled and uncertain negro" as a free laborer and suggested that an influx of white workers might lessen dependence on black labor.[10] On July 22, emboldened by Holden's response, Tourgée set out alone for Raleigh to assess the situation for himself.

Tourgée made several crucial decisions in choosing Greensboro, North Carolina, as the place to begin his new life. Soon after his arrival in Raleigh, he was introduced by Governor Holden to the leaders of a Quaker community in Guilford County with whom he shared political sympathies. Though the greatest opportunities for profit existed in North Carolina's coastal regions, where vast rice and cotton plantations could be had at bargain prices, he chose to settle in the Quaker belt of the central Piedmont instead. The region had been openly antagonistic to slavery before the war and a stronghold of the wartime peace movement during it. Now the Quakers of this region were taking the lead in establishing freedmen's schools across the state. A year later, Tourgée would explain that the Piedmont attracted him because it "ha[d] more good will toward the government" than any other place in the South.[11]

A region dominated by farms of a humbler size, devoted to fruit, corn, and tobacco farming, the Piedmont offered fewer opportunities for turning commercial profits and far more for missionary work where Quakers needed teachers to staff freedmen's schools.[12] In his letters to Emma, it was clear that his purposes in North Carolina went beyond a desire for worldly success. He felt that he had achieved "a new view of myself" in contriving what he now referred to as his "southern scheme." "I know I wish to do right. I know I wish to do good," he declared, but wondered, "Am I ready to be and to do all and everything that God may assign to me to be done?"[13] "My aim is as good as poor man's may be," he cryptically told Emma: "I have faith that God will open a way for its accomplishment [—] or if not that some other as good or better."[14] Whatever challenges awaited him in the South, Albion was convinced that he would "do good" for society by undertaking this venture—and he hoped that he would be duly rewarded by God for his benevolent intentions.

Armed with President Anderson's endorsement of his "southern scheme," Tourgée had persuaded two of his Rochester fraternity brothers, Seneca Kuhn and Rueben T. Pettengill, to join him and become his business partners.[15] After returning to consult with his business associates, A.W. Tourgée & Co., as the partnership was christened, leased a 750-acre nursery farm outside of Greensboro in Guilford County from the leading citizen and former Quaker Cyrus P. Mendenhall. Tourgée and his two partners took possession of the farm on October 15, 1865, agreeing to a yearly rent of one thousand dollars for a term of fifteen years. Their business firm would own and operate the West Green Nursery while practicing law and investing capital in other local ventures. In addition to bringing Emma's parents and her younger sister, Sarah Emilia ("Millie"), Tourgée may have recruited several other families to join their caravan to Greensboro.[16] Tourgée and Pettengill took responsibility for the legal practice and their initial clients mostly consisted of Southern Unionists who hoped to recover damages from the government for property destroyed by Sherman's Army. By taking on these cases, Tourgée began to forge a close alliance with the loyal Southerners who had suffered loss or retribution despite their defiance of the Confederacy. Meanwhile, the West Green Nursery hired dozens of black laborers to raise a diverse crop of apples, peaches, pears, apricots, nectarines, plums, and cherries, as well as a variety of shrubs and ornamental trees, for the market. Relations between the carpetbagger employers and their black labor force appear to have been harmonious throughout the winter and spring of 1865.[17] In *A Fool's Errand*, Metta, the Fool's wife, gives an account that was probably true for the Tourgées: "The colored people flock around us as if they thought 'de Yankee Kunnel' could do every thing and hire them all. I think I could have a hundred housemaids if I would take all that come to me."[18]

Elsewhere turbulent labor relations began to ravage the state. As the freed people of North Carolina attempted to improve the quality of their working and living conditions from what they had experienced in slavery, they faced planter resistance that quickly escalated into violence. Faced with black labor demands, angry whites openly threatened to "exterminate the whole race" and showed contempt for the authority of the Freedmen's Bureau, the Federal institution created to smooth the transition to wage labor by mediating labor disputes. By January of 1866, the bureau's agents were so overwhelmed with cases of "robberies, frauds, assaults, and even murders" committed against blacks that one reported hearing "as many as a hundred and eighty complaints in one day" and lamented that "no records of them could be kept." A total of fifteen murders of blacks by white men were recorded by the North Carolina Freedmen's Bureau in 1865 and 1866, though many more crimes probably went unreported.[19]

The degenerating state of race and labor relations shocked both Albion and Emma, who had taken a keen interest in promoting black advancement. From their first days in Greensboro in October 1865, they busied themselves by organized the city's first "colored" school on their West Green property (later to become the Bennett Seminary in 1873).[20] Albion, Emma, and her family members alternated teaching duties at the school until June 1867 when the school moved location, and Emma made a daily habit of reading the newspaper aloud to "the boys" who worked at the West Green Nursery.[21] Albion had become involved in an interracial fraternal organization that called itself the Loyal Reconstruction League, which later became an official chapter of the Union League of America, a national Republican Party fraternal order founded in Philadelphia during the war. Though later credited, or rather blamed, for creating the league, Tourgée was probably invited to join by his black allies who founded it on their own volition.[22] Nevertheless, he had begun to establish a reputation for being "nearer to the Negro than any white man in the state."[23]

In the November 1865 elections, W.W. Holden lost the governorship to Jonathan Worth, the leader of the newly formed Conservative Party. Worth's ascendance made Tourgée's entry into politics inevitable. Under Worth's direction, the Conservative-dominated State Assembly passed a series of Black Codes that restricted black civil rights, controlled their movement, and legalized "apprenticeships" and other forms of coerced labor.[24] Brotherhoods, such as the Loyal League, quickly became political organizations mobilized to prevent the reenslavement of blacks under these new racial laws. The charter of the Wilmington-based Equal Rights League, for instance, announced that its mission was "to secure, by political and moral means . . . the repeal of all laws and parts of laws, State and National, that make distinctions on account of color."[25] In this political showdown, Tourgée would be given a new opportunity to take part in a crusade against slavery and inequality. His emergence as a Radical Republican leader would destroy his business partnership and reveal the priority of principle over profit in his mission to the South.

A RADICAL REVEALED

As a Union veteran with radical convictions and excellent oratorical skills, Tourgée was destined to become a leader in the state Republican party. He leapt to prominence among Guilford County's Radicals in August of 1866 when he delivered a rousing speech at the Quaker Deep River Meeting House at a meeting called to choose delegates to the upcoming Southern Loyalist Convention. Declaring his support for the proposed Howard (Fourteenth) Amendment, he suggested that Southern Conservatives should accept it as a moderate measure or be prepared to submit to martial law and unrestricted black suffrage. Tourgée himself advocated impartial but restricted suffrage that would give the vote to everyone who was literate regardless of race. Overconfidently, he predicted that, "if the men, institutions, or traditions of the South stand in the way of this inevitable destiny it will be the worse for them, for they will be ground to powder."[26] He also denounced the *Greensboro Patriot*, the city's only newspaper that had been a constant source of anti-Radical demagogic rumors, and offered to establish a Radical newspaper to counter its influence. Following the speech, the interracial audience promptly nominated him, along with Quaker Unionist Jonathan Harris, to represent Guilford County at the convention in Philadelphia.[27]

The Southern Loyalist Convention, called by Radical Republican leaders, was an attempt to rally Southern Republicans against President Johnson's Southern policies that had allowed secessionists and ex-Confederates back into power. Outrage swept through the North as the scope of anti-black violence became known and the Black Codes proliferated after the 1865 elections. Despite its intent to attract loyal Southerners, Northerners dominated the convention. Only one-third of the four hundred delegates who attended came from the "unreconstructed" South, and most of these were transplanted Northerners. Especially dominated by carpetbaggers was the North Carolina delegation, of which Tourgée was the chairman. William W. Holden's Union Party, North Carolina's main anti-Conservative umbrella party, ignored the call for delegates for fear of too close identification with the still-distrusted party of Lincoln.[28]

After talking with "almost all of the prominent delegates here," Tourgée found a "remarkable unanimity of sentiment" among them. "You would never have dreamed that such enthusiasm could grow up over anything less Godly than religion itself," he wrote Emma of the radical convictions of the delegates: "I know I am doing good for the great cause."[29] With Frederick Douglass and Benjamin F. Butler on hand as delegates, there was certainly enough radicalism in Philadelphia to warrant Tourgée's assessment. But, while the convention fully endorsed the Howard Amendment that would nullify the Black Codes and exclude ex-Confederates from the political system, the delegates remained divided over the issue of black suffrage. Opposition to the amendment came mostly from the large contingent of border state delegates who represented the former slave states—Missouri, Kentucky, Maryland, West Virginia, and Delaware—that had not been part of the Confederacy.[30] Though the Radicals' attempt to send the border state delegates home failed, their vociferous support for impartial suffrage appeared to be winning converts as the convention wore on.

When Tourgée addressed the convention, he went beyond his previous support for impartial suffrage and came out in favor of universal male suffrage. He told the crowded hall that two thousand North Carolinians had sent him to Philadelphia to support both "the disenfranchisement of all traitors" and "the enfranchisement of all loyal men." The second point was greeted with wild cheers, which were matched in enthusiasm only by the spontaneous applause that met Frederick Douglass when he entered the hall in the midst of the speech.[31] Black suffrage was ultimately left off the final list of resolutions adopted by the assembly, but Tourgée, who served on the committee that drafted the resolutions, nevertheless felt extremely optimistic about the growing support for the measure. He conveyed his optimism to Emma, and told her to encourage his black associates in North Carolina: "Tell Clark that he will have a chance to vote and all other rights in less than two years. All is bright here."[32]

In Philadelphia, Tourgée found a group of kindred spirits who shared his optimism for the total reformation of the South. Moreover, the convention opened a new path for success as he received affirmation and praise from powerful political figures from across the nation. The experience would solidify his radicalism and steady him for the difficult road ahead. Tourgée and Henry Clay Warmouth of Louisiana distinguished themselves, in historian Richard Current's estimation, as "the two most influential men in the entire convention." In jointly drafting the vital "Report on the Condition of the Non-Reconstructed States," these two men presented a damning indictment of President Johnson's policies that charged Johnson with facilitating the reestablishment of planter class hegemony over the South by encouraging the proliferation of Black Codes and political violence.[33]

As a result of their influential work, both Tourgée and Warmouth were chosen by Republican leaders to take part in a "great electioneering" campaign to bring their message to the Northern public. Following in the footsteps of President Johnson's disastrous "swing around the circle," through which he attempted to quiet the growing criticism of his Reconstruction policies, they undertook a speaking tour to personally vouch for the deplorable conditions in the South that had so shocked and outraged the Northern public when first publicized. This included a stop at Lincoln's tomb in Illinois, laying claim to his legacy by urging Northerners to finish the work Lincoln began during the war when he issued the Emancipation Proclamation.[34] "I come here tonight as one of the pickets of the grand Army of American Liberty to report to you what I have seen," began Tourgée's typical speech, warning his Northern audience, "the enemy who we thought we had routed has merely executed a flank movement."[35] With the help of speakers such as Tourgée, Radical Republicans exposed Johnson's bankrupt claim to have settled the labor turmoil in the South. In the November congressional elections, the electorate gave an overwhelming mandate to the Radicals—bolstering their congressional majority to the point that any further congressional initiatives would be safe from presidential veto.[36]

While Tourgée and his friends were scoring a critical success in the North, conservatives in North Carolina were reacting to press coverage of the Philadelphia convention with a growing fury. After reading the *New York Herald*'s account of Tourgée's Philadelphia speech, Governor Worth indignantly declared it "a tissue of lies from beginning to end." Denying the veracity of some of the alleged facts regarding the white supremacist violence and attempts to drive off carpetbaggers, Worth demanded proof of Tourgée's statements. His attack focused especially on Tourgée's claim that "I was told by a Quaker in North Carolina as I was coming here, that he had seen the bodies of fifteen murdered negroes taken from one pond."[37] Greatly concerned "lest the Quakers have made this Tourgee their leader," Worth wrote a series of intimidating letters to Greensboro's Quakers inquiring about the man he referred to as a "vile wretch" and a "lying villain" and demanding to know "the name of his informant." Reminding Quaker leaders of his past tolerance of their work, Worth warned that they should "hold themselves aloof from the bitterness of wicked partisans of all sorts," particularly "such men as Tourgee [who merely intend] to make the North hate the South."[38]

At the same time, he instructed the Conservative editor of the *Patriot* to print Tourgée's speech and "call a mass meeting of the County and invite [Tourgée] and his followers to be present and to vindicate his facts."[39] Despite the pressure, Tourgée's supporters refused to contradict the claims made at Philadelphia. Although his assertion regarding the fifteen murdered blacks was never substantiated, it was later defended by Tourgée and never disclaimed by his followers. The man who made the statement had asked that his name not be revealed in connection with it, but Tourgée later recorded that he was "in the office of Jesse Wheeler . . . and in the presence of David Hodgin and perhaps another gentleman" when the statement was made and that all the witnesses attested to the good character of the Quaker who made it. (Quakers, for whom lying is a mortal sin, were renowned for their honesty—hence the reason for Tourgée's claim, "I was told by a Quaker.")[40] After weeks of private and public pressure, Worth finally gave up his attempt to extort a repudiation of Tourgée's speech, privately concluding that "the Radicals of Randolph, Guilford, Chatham . . . by appointing Tourgee their representative [have] made him their mouth-piece. By their silence since the publication of his speech they endorse it."[41]

Governor Worth may have failed in his attempt to discredit Tourgée to his Radical cohorts, but he succeeded in stirring up the wrath of Greensboro's white Conservatives. Emma began to receive anonymous threats against her husband soon after Worth had begun his orchestrated attack through the pages of the *Greensboro Patriot*. One unsigned note read: "It is about time that your lying tong [sic] was stopped—and if you ever show your face in Guilford County again I will take care with some of my friends that you find the bottom of that *niger* [sic] *pond* you have been talking so much about."[42] One, written to Emma by a woman claiming to possess "the best of motives," advised her not to let Albion return from the North because she had heard ominous talk among the ladies in town, and "we who have always lived in the South know what such hints mean."[43]

Of course, the outburst of public contempt for his speech and the threatening letters he received merely confirmed the atmosphere of hostility that Tourgée had described at Philadelphia. The question regarding the existence or whereabouts of the alleged mass grave was pumped up by Conservatives to obfuscate the larger truth that the widespread use of deadly violence against both Radicals and freedpeople was undeniable. The remarks of one of Tourgée's "outraged" assailants underscored the reality beneath the Conservative denials. "You have traduced and vilified us at Philadelphia. You *knew* that what you said in that convention was false," the anonymous writer stated. "Negroes are safe here provided that they behave themselves." What was ironically implied here, and passed over silently by the conservative press, was that negroes who *did not* "behave themselves" were *not safe*. Neither were their Radical allies, as the conclusion of the letter made clear: "Your stay in North Carolina had better be short if you expect to breathe the vital air. It is settled that you cannot live here. You must either go North and stay there or roll on."[44]

While Tourgée continued to tour the North, he remained unaware of the peril his activities had created for his friends and family in Greensboro. The social and financial pressure upon Tourgée's business partners, Kuhn and Pettengill, prompted them to drop his name from the West Green Nursery advertisements and their stationary. Moreover, the political divide between them widened as they falsely told their customers that "such an obnoxious individual as [Tourgée]" was no longer "connected with them." Despite having been threatened to be "put out of doors by my Lord Kuhn or Lady P[ettengill]," Emma and her family bravely continued to teach at the Greensboro's "colored" school, and they even fought for decent terms for West Green's black workers in the face of the firm's dwindling business profits. Conditions for the workers at West Green appear to have worsened quite suddenly. Emma detailed the dire situation of their workers in a desperate letter to Albion on October 7, 1866:

> The boys . . . look upon me as the only protector of their rights while you are away. They have had but half rations for sometime and not a cent of money and some of them are getting barefoot and the cold weather coming on they need their winter clothing and no money nor promise of any. I have distributed over ten dollars among them and fed them time and again when they had no rations. . . . When the workers were given breakfast by "Wm. Hardy and Abram" . . . the firm were so mad that they threatened to [throw?] them off the place. . . . There is not a colored man on the place who will stay another year if you sell out.

One of the workers told Emma that "if Mr. Tourgee had not gone away" and allowed the other two partners to reveal their indifference toward their worker's welfare, "we never would have known who was our friend here." Concluding her letter, Emma rejected the advice of her "well-meaning" neighbor and pleaded with Albion to return immediately.[45]

Emma's letters and the news of the happenings in Greensboro finally caught up with Tourgée in mid-October while he campaigned in Western Pennsylvania. Though he first entertained thoughts of selling out to his partners and returning north, he realized that this was not an honorable solution. Greensboro's Radicals, who had stood by him, were now ready to carry their political movement forward by launching a Radical newspaper with Tourgée as its editor. In addition to these obligations, he undoubtedly was moved by Emma's revelation that the black workers of West Green Nursery would not get their due compensation without his continued presence. As Emma advised him, "Dealing justly and honestly by these negroes who have toiled faithfully for you will be a great thing for you in counteracting the vile falsehoods of the rebels of this place."[46] Emma for one was determined to demonstrate that "free labor" was distinguishable from slavery. Albion therefore chose to remain in Greensboro, but he applied for Federal permission to carry sidearms for protection.[47]

The Quaker community, upon his return to Greensboro, enthusiastically welcomed him. "Tourgee has returned from the North and reports favorably," one of his supporters wrote to a friend, commenting:

> He is a radical I know, but we are going to have to become so here as a general thing, before we get straight. . . . Great changes are taking place here in regard to public sentiment—it is astonishing. People are getting tired of suspense and will eventually rise in their might and accept any reasonable measure that will settle the matter.[48]

His former friends Kuhn and Pettengill, however, were not as supportive. They insisted that he purchase their legal interest in the West Green Nursery and A.W. Tourgée & Co. although it would mean that he would assume full responsibility for the firm's significant debts. Tourgée bought Kuhn's interest for eighty dollars and a promise to assume his debts and not to sue. His arrangement with Pettengill cost him $850, but Tourgée refused to assume all of his obligations. It was later discovered that Pettengill had taken a secret loan of $438 in the firm's name and apparently embezzled one client's settlement money. After an attempt to revive the business with a new partner, Tourgée finally terminated the nursery several months later—owing thousands of dollars to creditors.[49]

Though Pettengill had always been more Kuhn's friend than his, Tourgée had been chums with Seneca Kuhn since the Kingsville Academy.

The ending of this friendship must have been particularly painful. A year ahead of Albion in school, Seneca always held a certain influence over him. It was Seneca whom he had followed to the University of Rochester and into the Psi Upsilon fraternity. Once, before the war, Seneca had boasted to Emma that he had the power to make Albion "obey" him. But no longer. Their split was not amicable, and the two never spoke again. A few months after Seneca returned North, Albion received a letter from Seneca Kuhn's father, who apparently took Albion's side in the feud. Profusely apologizing for what he considered wrongful behavior by his son, he even offered to take over Seneca's stake in the partnership and relocate to North Carolina. "I am certain that Seneca could not misuse you worse than he has me since his return, but let that pass," Mr. Kuhn remarked cryptically. Tourgée apparently declined his offer.[50]

From a larger perspective, the parting of ways between Tourgée and his associates unmasked the degree to which their political outlooks and individual motives in moving to the South differed from one another. Unlike Tourgée, neither Kuhn nor Pettengill had fought in the war nor shown an interest in the abolition of slavery. Kuhn was a Democrat who had always dissented from his friend's political views, and he perhaps did not perceive or take seriously the extent to which Tourgée's army experiences had radicalized him on racial issues. This only became clear when Tourgée's political views began to endanger the partners' livelihood and, indeed, their lives. Kuhn and Pettengill clearly could not relate to the concern of Emma and Albion for the rights of the former slaves. They were a type of Northern immigrant that tended to rapidly assimilate to Southern racial customs, especially when it was in their financial interest to do so.[51]

Northern immigrants who went South solely to "get rich quick" often began to sound and act more like Southerners as time passed, especially in their treatment of black laborers. Ironically, few of such men were branded with the label *carpetbagger*. That term was reserved for "troublemakers" like Tourgée. The conservative *Greensboro Patriot*, for instance, declared in 1869 that the term " 'Carpetbagger' is known throughout the South, in fact, by this time, all over the United States, as the synonym of an *impudent, mean adventurer* from the North who comes to thrive" on the conditions of the South. But, it suggested that "honest" Northern men should be exempt from this term:

> Such men bring more and better things than could be crammed into a dozen carpet bags: they bring money; they bring skill; they bring habits of economy and industry; they bring character; they bring willing hands and big hearts, to join our people in a long pull and a strong pull for the prosperity of our war-wasted land . . . we join [the Republican press] in the declaration that "all such are truly welcome!"[52]

Even Conservatives recognized the desperate economic need for Northern capital and industry, but they made sure that Northern newcomers either conform to Southern ways or suffer vilification—or worse.

Tourgée left himself little time to worry about Conservative criticism or dwell upon the disastrous failure of his original "Southern scheme." Undaunted by death threats and debts totaling more than four thousand dollars, he continued to campaign on behalf of the Republicans and counterattack the conservative press with blistering editorials in his new weekly newspaper, *Union Register*. "I have made upwards of forty public speeches and traveled probably seven or eight hundred miles in the State . . . and have yet to receive the first cent for expenses," he wrote exhaustedly to Quaker Nathan Hill in June 1867, "I have been working for the good cause, and paying my own way [for so long] that I am played out intirely [*sic*]."[53] A letter home to Emma's parents confirmed that the Tourgées were indeed "penniless," provoking Angie, Emma's older sister, to suggest that perhaps Albion had "too many irons in the fire."[54]

On December 1, 1866, the first issue of Tourgée's *Union Register* denounced the North Carolina Assembly's overwhelming vote against the ratification of the Fourteenth Amendment. Their vote was not unexpected as the amendment's third article would have excluded a majority of the assembly's members from holding office. Their action, however, portended a showdown with the newly elected U.S. Congress, which now contained a large majority of anti-Johnson Republicans. Tourgée predicted harsh congressional measures to follow. The Radicals of Guilford and Randolph Counties afterward sent a petition to Congress, which bore Tourgée's signature among others, suggesting the division of the South into new territories and the creation of territorial governments in which former slaves and loyalists would be enfranchised and former Confederate office holders would be disenfranchised.[55] Tourgée hoped that the federal government would take control of the South for an extended "territorial" period, until proper economic and cultural changes could be introduced that would begin the process of making the region "de-Southernized and thoroughly nationalized."[56] It was a bold proposal that Tourgée would always look back on as the wiser course, one that congressional leaders shrunk from, opting for less aggressive measures.

The Reconstruction Act of March 1867 was the congressional response to the crisis and its answer to the plight of North Carolina's Radicals. It was only a partial fulfillment of Tourgée's hopes, but it marked the beginning of the so-called Radical Reconstruction period in North Carolina— a period that would last roughly two years.

THE DIVIDED SOUTH

The period of Radical ascendance in North Carolina would be marked by surprising success in Republican party-building among native whites, by the achievement of vast democratic reforms, and by the escalation of shrill and divisive rhetoric between Radicals and Conservatives that made rational public discourse about the needs of the state nearly impossible. Tourgée's own effectiveness as a leader of the Radicals was mixed. On one hand, he would play a leading role in the State Constitutional Convention and help institute some far-reaching reforms in the legal and educational system that would endure long after Reconstruction. But whereas his humanitarian reform policies were often sensible and even visionary, his confrontational rhetoric and impulse to taunt and belittle the opposition did little to calm the volatile atmosphere that stood in the way of Reconstruction's success.

The fate of Reconstruction in North Carolina rested upon the ability of either the Radicals or the Conservatives to woo a sufficient number of poor white voters into their party to maintain an electoral majority. The Reconstruction Acts of 1867 that temporarily enfranchised blacks and disenfranchised many planters created a new electorate that included 106,721 whites and 72,932 blacks.[57] Native, white Republicans (branded "scalawags") typically had not held slaves and thus, in one historian's words, "for generations had been shut out of political decision making."[58] These men and women harbored deep resentments toward the elite planters whose families monopolized political and economic power in the state. As such, they tended to enthusiastically embrace egalitarian reforms where they promised to abolish class distinctions among whites; however, they became uneasy when this social leveling was applied too scrupulously to matters of the color line.[59]

To the surprise of the planter class, the Republicans grabbed the initiative and demonstrated their ability to rally these disaffected whites to their banner. In an 1867 campaign broadside entitled "To the Voters of Guilford," Tourgée cast the Republican platform in class terms. "The aristocracy of slavery is dead. Shall we now build up an aristocracy of land?" he challenged the electorate. "Shall we have a government of a few, by a few and for a few?" Calling on poor white voters to end planter monopoly of political office, he asked, "shall the honest and capable, though landless voter, be allowed to hold offices of trust . . . or shall that privilege be granted only to the 'lord of barren acres?' "[60] These words struck home for many whites, who voted Republican and joined inter-racial fraternal societies in large numbers. In the fall elections of 1867, an estimated thirty thousand white voters joined with nearly sixty thousand black voters to restore Holden, now a Republican, to the governorship. This same electorate swept nearly every district in the state and sent 107 Republicans out of 120 total delegates, including Tourgée, to the 1868 State Constitutional Convention.[61]

The Republican program, though distasteful to some for its racial egalitarianism, offered opportunity for advancement for native whites for the first time. Some joined for practical reasons, aspiring for office or land. Some simply wished to end the turmoil and return to peacetime activities. "Let us try and make the best of a bad bargain," wrote one former Democrat who admitted to casting a vote for the Republican ticket: "the civil war nearly ruined us—another will finish the job."[62] Others, however, became true believers in radicalism, including the principle of racial equality. "I never had much prejudice against the negro and what I had I have laid aside," a new Republican voter confided to a Quaker missionary:

> I visited several of their schools last winter and I heard several of them speak in the Convention and my opinion is that there is but little if any difference in the talents of the two races and I am willing to give them all an even start in life. I am for Liberty, Union, and political equality.[63]

Indeed the Union League and other fraternal organizations created a biracial alliance that, however fragile, produced some powerful converts.

A few of these were members of the elite who had wealth and standing in society before the war. A friend and ally of Tourgée's, Thomas Settle, Jr., was a former slave owner who delivered perhaps the quintessential scalawag speech in Rockingham, North Carolina, in 1867. "Yankees and Yankee notions are just what we want in this country," Settle proclaimed. "There has been a general breaking up of the old ideas and we are now taking a new start in the world." Depicting the Reconstruction program as a great step forward in the progress of humanity, Settle urged his followers to emulate "Yankee" "intelligence," "energy," and "enterprise." Public education, he hoped—along with Tourgée—would instill Yankee work habits in the South, put an end to racial strife, and make useful citizens out of the former slaves:

> We must bury a thousand fathoms deep all those ideas and feelings that prompted those cruel laws against teaching these people and must quicken our diligence to see that the means of light and knowledge are placed within the reach of every one of them . . . we may hope that those who were a curse to the country as ignorant slaves, will prove a blessing as intelligent freemen.[64]

Though he conspicuously did not profess any confidence in the equality of the races, his willingness to support the Republican plan of equal education and equal opportunity indicates the real possibility of establishing an enduring biracial alliance.

Samuel F. Phillips was another of Tourgée's powerful white aristocratic allies. Considered by many to be the finest legal mind in the state, Phillips had graduated with highest honors from the University of North Carolina at the mere age of fourteen. He served on the North Carolina Court of Claims before the Civil War and, at the age of thirty-seven, became speaker of the State House in the reactionary moment of 1866. After Reconstruction drove him from politics in 1867, he ended up practicing law in Tourgée's courtroom from 1868 to 1870, during which time he became radicalized. To the horror of his prominent Conservative family, Phillips praised the 1868 State Constitution and returned to the State House as a Republican in 1871. In 1872, Ulysses S. Grant appointed him solicitor general, the nineteenth-century antecedent to attorney general, a position he would hold for thirteen years under four Republican presidential administrations.

Phillips's great admiration for Tourgée during these years probably did more than anything else to enhance his reputation as a judge among Conservatives, who still regarded the impressive Phillips with deep respect. His praise for Tourgée reached many ears, and he repeatedly spoke of him in high terms as "a man of extensive culture, of extraordinary intellectual gifts, a just and fearless judge, and a public-spirited citizen."[65] The profound impact Tourgée had on him on a personal level was made clear when Phillips wrote a heartfelt letter to the judge the day he closed his law practice in 1873. "Allow me to say now, Judge Tourgee, that as our relations as Judge and practicing lawyer are about to close," he told him, "I shall always retain . . . with me during my life a strong sense of the high ability with which you have administered your office in my sight and of the impartial and courageous manner in which you have administered the laws of North Carolina to all classes and colors." He went on to say that Tourgée had outclassed every judge he had practiced before, a list that included many venerated jurists in the state.[66] The respect was mutual. When a Supreme Court seat opened in 1878, Tourgée wrote a strong testimonial to President Hayes recommending Solicitor General Phillips for the spot, lauding him as a perfect choice to enhance sectional diversity and personally vouching for him as a man whom he "loves, admires, and respects."[67] The position went instead to another Southern Republican: John Marshall Harlan of Kentucky.

With such influential white converts as Settle and Phillips, the Conservatives had good reason to fear Republican electoral gains. While Radical ideology appealed to many, the revolutionary tones with which they pitched their message hardened the resistance of their opponents. In the political culture of Northern regions, such as the Western Reserve, it had been a mark of character to make a public stand on principle without regard to public disapprobation. Tourgée was determined, therefore, to be uncompromising, as he announced in the first issue of the *Union Register* in 1867, "The *Register* hopes never to be a 'mild' advocate of anything. We are aware that the advocacy of Union principles; or, if you prefer the word, radical principles, is anything but a popular movement in any part of the South." But he swore not to be dissuaded by opposition. Even more antagonistically, he declared that the mission of the *Register* would be to liberate the "poor, misguided and mismanaged South . . . from the slough of ignorance and prejudice."[68] To most Conservatives, this attitude was the very height of arrogance.

Tourgée's methods borrowed heavily from the confrontational style of abolitionists, and his political speeches were designed to have a shocking effect on his audiences. After one major speech in Greensboro before "the whole secesh [secessionist] *élite* of the country," for instance, Tourgée told a friend, with relish, of the "seething cauldrons of suppressed wrath" he detected in their faces as he pilloried the Conservative viewpoint for nearly two hours.[69] His audience likely reacted in the manner described in *A Fool's Errand* after the Fool's first public speech. As Tourgée described it, "the very audacity of [the Fool's] speech seemed to have taken away all power, if not inclination, to reply. Some of his audience regarded him with sullen, scowling amazement, and others just with dull wonder." Even those in sympathy with him stared blankly in "surprised silence," too awestruck to show any "manifestation of approval."[70]

Tourgée's blunt criticism provoked a variety of responses. A Conservative North Carolina lawyer later described the first time he heard Tourgée speak: "[He] let fly a speech at Andrew Johnson which, I reckon, made him the most hated man in all that community." However, the lawyer admitted, "while we listened in speechless disgust, I couldn't help admiring the persistence and pluck of the little devil."[71] Likewise, his ally Robert Dick reacted with horror after first hearing his neighbor speak in 1867, telling his Unionist compatriots, "Tourgee is either crazy or he is a bad man." Several years and political campaigns later, Dick had become used to Tourgée's style and he praised his oratory for its "originality of thought . . . forcible and brilliant style and delivery."[72] Tourgée enjoyed speaking extemporaneously and believed he was at his most effective when struck with sudden "flashes" of inspiration. In describing one effective speech to Emma, he explained his difficulty in remembering his exact phrasing by saying "like all good things I have ever said [it] was purely ex temporaneous . . . you know I never can recall those flashes." "Counted our best stump speaker" by fellow Republicans, he was kept in constant demand at political rallies despite — or perhaps because of — the sensation his speeches usually caused.[73]

Though few accounts remain of his political speeches, some of Tourgée's unrestrained responses to the personal abuses he received from the *Greensboro Patriot* suggest his tone. "Was it not a *mean, contemptible, sneaking lie* anyone but a hypocrite would be ashamed [of]?" he asked the *Patriot* in response to one of its more slanderous attacks, adding, "I do not envy the mental condition of the writer of that article. He is evidently a strange compound of malicious envy, insanity, and falsehood . . . whose prejudices are stronger than his regard for truth."[74] "You may talk of 'Southern pride' and 'Southern rights,' 'Southern principle' and 'Southern will,' " he taunted the *Patriot* editor in another instance, "but you will find that Human rights, eternal justice, and the will of the people will override all." Making an analogy to recent archaeological discoveries, he went on to predict that the overblown pride of the Southern planter would soon be reduced to a "microscopic particle" for geologists to study, and "the world will wonder [at the] fossils of slavery [and] the monsters of the 'ante-Reconstruction' period."[75]

Tourgée's bravado may have generated much excitement, but it did nothing to soften Conservative opposition. Though he made a show of shrugging off Conservative ridicule by dubbing his home "Carpet-Bag Lodge" and by announcing "I am not only a carpetbagger but I am proud of that fact," his attempts fell flat.[76] Once he even defended his conduct by declaring, "Jesus Christ himself was a carpetbagger." This last remark best encapsulated the conflict between Tourgée's views and that of his Conservative opponents. While he sincerely believed that he followed after Jesus in his unflinching devotion to spreading the gospel of human equality, the Conservatives could only perceive this statement as shocking. "Horrible Blasphemy!" declared one headline, following the remark.[77] After hearing Tourgée speak, one Conservative named David Schenck confided to his diary: "The white race will not suffer this outrage." The Radicals must be defeated, he vowed, even if by "assas[s]inations and secret means of revenge."[78] Schenck soon afterwards joined the Ku Klux Klan.

Radicalism clashed with the most fundamental beliefs of the Southern planter class, whose paternalist ideology was built upon the conviction that their black and white "inferiors" depended on their leadership for survival. Jonathan Worth, who served as head of the Conservative party from 1865 to 1868, may be taken as illustrative of North Carolinian conservatism. Fearing that blacks would "acquire bad habits if not governed" properly, this former slave owner complained, "with the Freedmen's Bureau here the necessary discipline cannot be used to bring them up so as to be useful men." Though he did not elaborate on what "necessary

discipline" entailed, Worth clearly believed that blacks could not be pro-
ductive laborers without the strong hand of an overseer. As he put it, "The
race never did work voluntarily and never will."[79] An experiment in "free
labor" in which the incentive to work efficiently was based, not on physical
coercion, but on the promise of upward social mobility—including the
goal of land ownership—was utterly anathema to him. Moreover, to
recognize either the right or the capability of their former slaves for
self-direction and individual autonomy was tantamount to an implicit
admission that the abolitionists had been correct in their critique of the
South's "peculiar institution." If Reconstruction succeeded, then all the
proslavery arguments would have been proved wrong. Southern honor
could never suffer such an admission, even implicitly.

To get rid of "the miserable set of jackasses, from Generals down to
Freedmen's Bureau men" was the only solution in Worth's estimation.[80]
With this goal in mind, North Carolina Conservatives took their cue from
other Southern states and countered the Radicals with intimidation, violence, and political assassination. At first, the conservative press charged
Tourgée and his followers with "mak[ing] war on capital" and promoting
agrarianism (i.e., land confiscation and redistribution). But when these
attempts to discredit the class aspects of the Republican program failed,
Conservatives quickly learned to focus their propaganda preponderantly
upon issues of race. The terrorist activities of the Ku Klux Klan were first
reported in North Carolina as the fall elections approached in 1868. Klan
members admitted that the politicization of poor whites into Republican
political clubs provided the impetus for the formation of their organization. Indeed, Klan activity in the state was strongest in those counties
where a biracial Republican alliance had been the most successful, while
it was minimal where the black population dominated the electorate.[81]

Conservatives spread rumors about the Loyal Leagues and other
Republican brotherhoods and accused them of plotting miscegenation,
rape, rebellion, and murder. One Klan member testified before Congress
that the KKK had been necessary because the "[R]epublican party had three
secret organizations in operation in the State . . . our friends thought it was
proper to organize a secret society for the purpose of counteracting that
influence." Another witness explained, "In 1868 the [R]epublican party was
gaining great numbers to its ranks through the instrumentality of the
Leagues, Red Strings, and Heroes of America. They had a newspaper at
Greensborough [sic] edited by one Tourgee [that was] devoted to the dis-
semination of these secret orders. A great many ignorant white men were
attracted to them." The phenomenon of "a great many ignorant white men"
joining these Republican political clubs struck fear into the planter class.[82]

Under the auspices of the Klan, the Conservatives would galvanize
their own cross-class alliance, one based explicitly on the brotherhood

of "whiteness." "WHITE MEN, ORGANIZE!" screamed Conservative editorials, "be true to your RACE[!]" "The GREAT and Paramount issue is: SHALL NEGROES or WHITE MEN RULE NORTH CAROLINA?" the *Raleigh Sentinel* claimed, exhorting its readers to keep "all other issues . . . secondary and subordinate."[83] Forging an *esprit d' corps* among whites—especially those who participated in the midnight raids and engaged in ritualized racial violence—while ostracizing those who tried to obstruct their movement, the Conservatives successfully fought back against the appeal of the Republican clubs.

Black communities were terrorized and blacks reported whippings, rape, murder, torture, and countless forms of humiliation inflicted by masked men in surprise attacks under the cover of darkness. Schoolhouses—the primary symbol of black advancement and Northern doctrines of racial equality—were inevitably attacked and burned down during Klan raids. Between the fall of 1869 and May of 1870, Tourgée counted "12 murders, 9 rapes, 11 arsons, 6 men castrated, and any number of houses broken open and men and women dragged from their beds and beaten or otherwise cruelly outraged," adding "barbarities that would disgrace our Indian enemies have characterized very many of these outrages."[84] In a remarkable psychological displacement of historical memory, the Republican leagues would be charged in the following decades by Southern apologists, such as Thomas Dixon, with having spread similar mayhem and committed acts including rape and murder. The very crimes committed by the Klan were, in retrospect, attributed to the leagues and these supposed "outrages" became the excuse for the Klan's extreme acts of "retaliation." Despite that later mythology, however, very few specific allegations were made against the leagues at the time, though many rumors circulated. Despite these rumors, according to the historian Otto Olsen, "*not one instance* of criminal activity by the Leagues was ever established in North Carolina."[85]

The seeds of later Reconstruction mythology were sown by the conservative press that printed wild rumors and blatant untruths. Tourgée was personally dogged at every turn by such conservative papers as the *Greensboro Patriot* and the *Raleigh Sentinel*, whose charges against him rapidly spread throughout the state. One of the most persistent charges, originally reported as hearsay in the *Greensboro Patriot*, was that Tourgée had spent four years in an Ohio penitentiary before escaping. Tourgée's initial sarcastic rejoinder to this wild rumor in, yet another, letter to the *Patriot* editor unfortunately refused to dignify it with a specific denial— inadvertently lending credence to the charge. Allusions to a shady or criminal past would be raised in conservative newspapers, speeches, and in unrecorded public gossip for more than a decade. "We were not aware he had ever publicly denied the allegation," one publication continued to insist many years later, despite his repeated denials and the detailed biographical profiles of him that had been published in Republican papers in the intervening years. It became almost a cliché among his opponents to allude to a shadowy past with such remarks as, "soon after the war he 'turned up' in Greensboro; from whence no one can say" and "the very name of the adventurer [is] evidently fictitious."[86] The ubiquity of these remarks indicate how insistently prototypical carpetbagger traits were applied to Radicals whether or not they had any basis in reality.

On the whole, Republicans did not have the resources to respond effectively to the demagogic charges of their opponents. Tourgée's own ventures into journalism simply failed to reach as wide a public as the established conservative press. Though he tried publishing an inexpensive weekly version of the *Register*, called the *Red String*, geared "for circulation among the poorer whites and blacks," he was unable to make the paper profitable.[87] Not only were much of his intended audience both impoverished and semiliterate, they were often prevented from getting copies of Republican papers due to Conservative obstructions, such as the systematic destruction of posted advertisements for the *Union Register*, which Tourgée believed was part of an organized campaign.[88]

When Tourgée traveled to Washington to solicit funding for his newspaper from the Republican Party leadership, he found a sympathetic ear in his former representative from the Western Reserve, Senator Ben Wade. Describing Tourgée's editorship as "thoroughly and persistently radical," Wade petitioned the Union Executive Committee on his behalf, explaining that "it is impossible [for Tourgée] to get advertising patronage as he is opposed in sentiment by nearly all the public business men."[89] But it was to no avail. In June 1867, the *Union Register* was discontinued after a mere six months, leaving the city of Greensboro once again without a Republican daily newspaper. With no reliable source of information, or even a counterpoint to the conservative press, Greensboro residents had to pick and choose what to believe from the abundant sources of rumor, gossip, and speculation.

Soon after abandoning his journalistic endeavors, Tourgée entered a new phase of his Reconstruction career when he arrived as a delegate to the State Constitutional Convention in January 1868. At twenty-nine years old, he would be the youngest man to participate in the historic gathering in Raleigh. By nearly all accounts, he made the greatest individual impact on its work. Moreover, Tourgée's contributions to the constitutional debates provide one of the fullest expressions of his political principles and the democratic philosophy underlying them. His participation in the Convention also brought attention to his considerable legal talent and launched his new career in the South as a jurist and reformer of the civil code. In this capacity, as we will see, he would achieve some of his most enduring legacies to the state.

5

The Unfinished Revolution

This plan would, no doubt, work a radical reorganization in
Southern institutions, habits and manners. It is intended to revolutionize their principles and feelings. This may startle feeble
minds and shake weak nerves. So do all great improvements in
the political and moral world. . . . Without this, this Government
can never be, as it never has been, a true republic.

—Thaddeus Stevens, September 6, 1865

As an interracial coalition of Republican delegates rewrote
the State Constitution at the 1868 Convention in Raleigh, Conservatives could do little but condemn the proceedings. Both in
the press and on the convention floor, they attacked the integrated body
of delegates and discoursed at length about the innate physiological
differences between blacks and whites. After suffering through one such
discourse by a Conservative delegate, Tourgée returned to his room and
composed a passionate refutation of racism. His chance to reply arrived
two days later, at the late evening session of the convention on Friday,
February 21. Holding the floor for over an hour, he delivered perhaps his
most salient speech yet on the subject of racial equality. Americans,
he told the convention, would no longer tolerate exclusions based on race
or color:

> "Man is man" is the keynote to our civilization . . . there is no color before
> the law[;] black and white are citizens alike of our glorious nationality,
> co-laborers in working out her destiny and heirs alike with the glories pur-
> chased with their mingled blood.[1]

The "mingled blood" symbolized the sacrifice of black and white Union
soldiers in the war that, in Tourgée's view, had fashioned an interracial
national identity.

A MAN KNOWS A MAN.
"Give me your hand, Comrade! We have each lost a Leg for the good cause; but, thank God, we never lost Heart."

Equal citizenship, in this illustration, is based on equal sacrifices on behalf of the nation. "A Man Knows a Man," from *Harper's Weekly*, April 22, 1865, p. 256. Courtesy of The Newberry Library, Chicago, IL.

Replete with themes that resonated in Radical Republican rhetoric across the country, his speech wove together several interdependent themes: an appeal to natural rights theory, to a Divine reckoning on the nation for the sins of slavery, and to the manliness of the black (and white) soldier. The principle that "man is man," whatever his skin color or social background, formed the core of his philosophical argument. Tourgée called this egalitarian creed America's "beacon light of promise and of joy, to the downtrodden peoples of the old world," and predicted that with its final realization in the Civil War "the historian will write [it] as the crowning glory of the nineteenth century."[2]

Closely wedded to this notion of equality was the belief that the attributes of manhood—including the capacity for self-sacrifice, self-denial, and duty to one's conscience—were the standard of good citizenship on which the success of democratic government depended. "The great idea of our American nationality and civilization is enthroned in that one word[,] the proudest of earthly names[,] *manhood*," he exclaimed.[3] In his estimation, and that of many Americans, soldiering was the most severe test of manhood. By exceeding expectations in their performance as soldiers, blacks had made an impressive claim to worthiness for full citizenship. Indeed, the campaign for black suffrage in the North would

A plea for the enfranchisement of African Americans, showing
a maimed Union soldier. "Franchise," from *Harper's Weekly*,
August 5, 1865. Courtesy of The Newberry Library, Chicago, IL.

be saturated with references to, and images of, the sacrifice of black
Union soldiers.[4]

Appealing to those skeptical of black equality, which included many
white Republicans, Tourgée sympathetically told the delegates: "I confess
it now with shame . . . I was one of those who were swayed and controlled
by that unmanly prejudice that has found such full expression on this
floor. . . . I too thought the negro a kin to the brute." But, he claimed, the
events of the Civil War had changed that and taught him that the Bible's
revelation that "of one blood are all nations of the earth" came with no
"proviso" for Africans.[5] To graphically illustrate this fact, he brought up
the ruthless slaughter of black soldiers at Fort Pillow, Tennessee, where
Confederate troops under General Nathan Bedford Forrest—who subsequently founded the Klu Klux Klan and who Tourgée described as "a fiend

who walks today unhung, and clamors for a white man's government"—
massacred a colored infantry "after a fair and honorable surrender."
Because the facts about this incident remained hotly disputed at the
time, Tourgée falsely claimed to have witnessed it firsthand. Asserting its
historical veracity, he solemnly vowed:

> If I ever forget that day and its lesson in noble manhood and ever fail to give
> my voice and strength for the equal, political, and civil rights to that race
> which gave one hundred and eighty thousand such heros [sic] in the darkest
> hour of the conflict to snatch the Banner of freedom from such foes, may
> God forget me and mine forever.[6]

Though Tourgée exaggerated the story of his own radical conversion for
rhetorical purposes, he accurately portrayed the importance of his war
experience in deepening his commitment to the cause of black freedom
and racial equality.[7] Indeed, if judged by his subsequent life, his vow to never
"forget" or "fail to give his voice" could not have been more genuine.

Furthermore, he assured the convention that racial restrictions on the
ballot that still existed in some Northern states were equally doomed.
Even in the North, he declared, "the cry [of prejudice] has lost its potency
[becoming] but the echo of a dead lie." Universal manhood suffrage "is a
dead issue, a settled question . . . it has been forever fixed and decided by
the colored man himself." Anticipating the Fifteenth Amendment, he
predicted that the egalitarian revolution against racial caste would soon
abolish the remnants of the old order. "No legal sophistry," he declared,
alluding to the Conservative speaker who had proceeded him, "no self
styled Science, no superficial lore, can stand before . . . the truth of
Almighty God written in the watch-fires of a hundred circling camps."[8]

Echoing the messianic spirit of military songs like "The Battle Hymn
of the Republic" that depicted the Union army as an avenging instrument
of God, wiping out the sins of slavery, Tourgée's speech was representative of radical thought at the height of its influence in Reconstruction. As
the abolitionists had, he merged Protestant religious values with American
democratic traditions. Having confessed his own complicity in antebellum
race prejudice, and thereby implicating the North along with the South
in past injustice, Tourgée suggested the need for a new start for both sections of the nation and a regeneration of American democracy—"a new
birth of freedom." Even more broadly, he connected the war's political
meaning to mainstream values of masculinity and meritocracy. Blacks were
not undeserving, passive recipients of the blessings of freedom and citizenship, he implied, but rather they had earned these rights by proving their
merit on the battlefield. This was a powerful combination of arguments
that proved valuable to the Radical cause outside the South at the time.

Within the South, the message received a less appreciative reception. In truth, very few white Republican delegates embraced the full racial integration of the state. If the Republican majority were to be lasting, however, it would be necessary for white Republicans to support fundamental political and economic rights for blacks, who were a critical element in their coalition. None recognized this more clearly than Tourgée. He seized the opportunity to push his Radical agenda, using the convention as a platform to preach the gospel of racial equality to this cross-section of the state Republicans. Adopting the mantle of a revolutionary, he sought to solidify black and white unity in a revolutionary class struggle against the old order that would sweep away the landed aristocracy and introduce color-blind citizenship and equal opportunity for all. The revolution that Tourgée sought ultimately fell short of his radical hopes, but it permanently changed the laws, institutions, and culture of North Carolina.

THE SPIRIT OF '68

The first Federal Reconstruction Act of 1867 had opened the way for revolutionary constitutional reforms. Having barred ex-Confederates from either electing representatives to the constitutional convention or voting on ratification of the Constitution, it excluded a large portion of Conservative leadership from participation. Eighty-nine percent of the convention's representatives were Republican, with eighteen carpetbaggers, fifteen African Americans, and seventy-four native whites.[9] Conservatives feared that this coalition was poised to rewrite the state constitution in such a manner as to upend state politics for the foreseeable future. Dubbed the "Gorilla Convention" in the Conservative press, the racial mix on the convention floor told Conservatives all they needed to know about the purposes of the delegates. While deeming the blacks "bestial," the papers regarded the whites as filled with a "demoniac hate to degrade us by asserting the Negro's right to social equality with our sisters, daughters, mothers and wives."[10]

Despite the apoplectic Conservative rhetoric, the convention would accomplish a democratic revolution that constitutionally transformed not just race relations, but class relations, and boosted individual rights for all citizens. Article I of the state constitution made clear the philosophy of this revolution. Opening with a "Declaration of Rights" of thirty-seven sections, the first section dedicated the state of North Carolina to the principles of the Declaration of Independence, with one notable addition. The section read: "We hold it to be self-evident that all men are created equal; that they are endowed by their Creator with certain inalienable rights; that among these are life, liberty, *the enjoyment of the fruits of their own labor,* and the pursuit of happiness."[11] Free labor, now added as a fourth inalienable right in Jefferson's democratic manifesto, would become the basis of the new economic order with all of the promise of upward mobility that the Northern free labor ideology implied.

Though his leadership was influential to the point that many would later refer to the gathering as the "Tourgee Convention," the convention majority still remained more moderate than Tourgée on the issue of racial equality.[12] Nevertheless, answering Tourgée's plea, the convention voted to adopt universal manhood suffrage, over the outcry in the Conservative press. But, the majority softened the blow to Conservatives by placing no suffrage restrictions on ex-Confederates, rejecting Tourgée's proposal to disqualify them as a necessary measure "to secure the rights of others."[13] While the convention eliminated black exclusion from the ballot box, jury service, courtroom testimony, marriage laws, the bar, and public schools, the prohibition against racial restrictions was not total. They were forced to compromise on interracial marriage and racially integrated schools.

Racial integration of public schools and miscegenation were inextricably linked, according to Southern ways of thinking. "Your children may be *forced* to go to school . . . with negroes," the *Wilmington Daily Journal* reported. "Your daughter, seventeen years old, may be compelled to recite with negro boys . . . they may make love to her, and call her pet names, and none can defend her."[14] In addition to their fear of adolescent sex play, Conservatives accused white schoolteachers of fostering "erroneous notions of social equality" and of "kissing and fondling" their black pupils.[15] Interracial affection—whether sexual or not—remained beyond all toleration, and Conservatives demonized any policy that they believed promoted miscegenation. The Conservative press effectively used extreme white phobia about racial mixing to their advantage. When the convention rejected a Conservative proposal declaring "all intermarriages between the Caucasian or white race, and the African or black race are forever prohibited," the press used their action as evidence that the convention intended to promote racial intermarriages.[16] Confronted with such explosive racial demagoguery, Republicans quickly became defensive.

Attempting to calm public fears, one Republican delegate urged his supporters not to "credit the misrepresentations" by the press and promised "there is no clause requiring whites & blacks to be enrolled in the same Militia Company, nor go to the same schools, nor to marry each other."[17] To offset Conservative propaganda, a black Republican delegate even proposed a resolution, subsequently passed, that "discountenanced" intermarriage and illegal intercourse between the races, and declared that "the interests and happiness of the two races would be best promoted by the establishment of separate schools." In fact, many blacks had no desire to force the issue of school integration.[18] In the end, the convention left it up to the legislature to decide these issues.

For his part, Tourgée was not content to acquiesce to school segregation without some constitutional provision to protect black schools from unequal conditions. Ironically, Tourgée proposed a "separate but equal" constitutional clause that read:

> That separate and distinct schools may be provided for any class of citizens in the State: *Provided*, That in all cases where distinct schools shall be established, there shall be as ample, sufficient and complete facilities afforded for the one class as for the other, and entirely adequate for all, and in all districts where schools are divided, the apportionment to each shall be equal.[19]

Unlike the later Jim Crow laws he would so adamantly oppose, Tourgée's clause was a compromise that sought to advance the principle of equality rather than that of separation. It did not *require* separate schools, but it did allow them to be segregated provided they were indeed qualitatively kept equal. This approach was shared by many black leaders, who understood that the choice was between allowing segregated schools or having no state-supported schools at all. Tourgée's clause might have guaranteed the best-case scenario for black education, but it was defeated.[20]

Despite the failure to prohibit segregation, the establishment of a state-supported public school system was a revolutionary achievement in itself. Section twenty-seven of the "Declaration of Rights" stated that "The people have a right to the privilege of education, and it is the duty of the State to guard and maintain that right."[21] For the first time, the state accepted in principle the responsibility for the education of all the children of North Carolina, black and white alike. "We propose to 'level upwards,'" the convention explained in a statement to the people of North Carolina, "to give every child, as far as the State can, an opportunity to develop to the fullest extent, all his intellectual gifts."[22] Education would be the cornerstone of a new state whose political structure would be based on the empowerment of the masses, black and white. Individual merit, not property ownership or family name, would be the basis of political and social power.

Tourgée's blueprint for a new state was taken more from Tocqueville than from Adam Smith. The lifeblood of democracy in the North, Tourgée believed, flowed upward from the local habits of self-rule. Tocqueville had attributed, in Tourgée's paraphrasing of him, "the superior intelligence and prosperity of the North" to its township system.

"That perfect crystallization of the primeval democratic idea," Tourgée wrote, the township system, was "the shield and nursery of individual freedom and action."[23] A vibrant local political culture was not only a necessary protection against the deprivation of rights from powerful forces at the state and national level, but also a kind of political school that nurtured grassroots political leaders. With its "open town meetings and untrammeled discussion of all matters, both great and small, affecting the interests of the municipality," ordinary citizens learned how to affect change and gained confidence in exercising "the higher duties and responsibilities of statesmanship."[24]

The Republicans, adopting Tourgée's proposal, divided counties into townships to be governed by popularly elected officials, school boards, and justices of the peace. Property qualifications for political office were abolished as well. This plan eliminated the powerful local magistrates, who had been appointed by the legislature and had dominated antebellum local politics. Tourgée also introduced and secured the popular election of superior court judges, previously another sinecure position from the antebellum era. While critics feared that the electorate would choose untrained men, Tourgée responded that party spoils and corruption were more likely to elevate unqualified men to the bench than the majority vote.[25]

In a similar vein, Tourgée proposed to modernize the antiquated legal system of the state by introducing code reforms modeled on those that had recently triumphed in New York and Ohio. A measure initiated by Tourgée alone, his proposal required a vast overhaul of legal procedures and civil codes.[26] The new codes would demystify the law for common folk and thereby make lawyers and judges more accountable to public scrutiny. Opposed by virtually all of the legal authorities present at the convention, Tourgée won passage of his measure by sheer force of argument. His evident expertise on this matter, representing "progressive" Northern views, prompted the convention to elect him to a three-year term as one of three code commissioners to help execute the massive project of re-codifying the state laws.[27]

On issues that touched on individual rights and humanitarian reform, Tourgée took a great interest. With Quaker support, Republicans successfully fought to abolish corporal punishment, including the stocks, whipping posts, and branding irons. Tourgée also spoke out against capital punishment—or "Judicial murder" as he termed it. Though privately chastised by some Quakers who, in his words, "cannot conceive that a soldier has any right to oppose Capital punishment," Tourgée saw no contradiction in his position.[28] He argued that the purpose of the penal system should be to reform rather than punish criminals—an idea derived from his perfectionist view of human beings as capable of moral improvement. No doubt he also agreed with other delegates who linked the death penalty to racial injustice by pointing out that capital punishment was disproportionately served in cases involving blacks. Ultimately, the convention substantially reduced the number of crimes that could be punished with death, were the legislature inclined to enact capital crime laws. Though it did not abolish the death penalty, the constitution did include Tourgée's clause that the "object of punishment" in the penal system was "not only to satisfy justice but also to reform the offender."[29] Later, this clause would assist Tourgée in his persistent efforts to reform the state prison system by creating more humane buildings.[30]

Finally, on economic matters, Tourgée consistently sought to protect the interests of the disadvantaged against those of the landed gentry. He argued strongly for the incorporation of a "Homestead Clause" that protected debtors from having their land seized by creditors and legitimated squatters' claims to empty land settled upon in years previous to the war. He rationalized this measure by arguing that the "right of eminent domain may be used in giving a homestead" as an extension of the state's right to combat poverty and provide "support of its needy citizens." This issue was of more benefit to poor whites than blacks, who held relatively few homesteads in 1868. The Homestead Clause was adopted by the convention, though later partially nullified by the U.S. Supreme Court, which declared its retroactive clause for squatters unconstitutional nine years later.[31]

Providing financial aid to railroads was also a popular issue among native white Republicans, but Tourgée showed little interest in it. Anticipating that support to railroads would result in higher taxes upon the landless, he stood virtually alone against bailing out railroad companies. Because supporting the railroads also meant honoring government bonds left over from the Confederacy, Tourgée considered it virtually treason to pay Confederate debts, insisting that the debts had expired with the Confederacy itself. But some of his Republican colleagues had taken over these debts from ex-Confederates with the hope their speculation would pay off when the new governments assumed the debt. While he was outvoted 56 to 15 on this issue, his stance indicates an unwillingness to promote economic development at the expense of fairness or the welfare of the underprivileged.[32] Though he recognized the importance of railroads for economic development, democratic revolution took priority over aid to financial and industrial special interests.

When the drafting of the constitution was finally complete, the document bore the marks of Tourgée's influence in nearly every article. One clause that particularly echoed his views was the section on religious liberty, which went beyond the First Amendment of the U.S. Constitution by declaring the freedom of conscience to be "a natural and unalienable right." It further elaborated that *"no human authority should, in any case whatever, control or interfere with the rights of conscience."*[33] While certainly representing the views of the Quaker community too, this clause nicely captured the deep respect for individual conscience that characterized Tourgée's democratic creed. Merging the power of the state with the ascendancy of the individual, the absolute protection of the rights of conscience promised to inscribe his radical individualism into the constitution.

The ratification of the North Carolina State Constitution in late April 1868, overcoming an intense campaign by Conservatives against it, must have felt like a personal victory for Tourgée. One disappointment, however, was that his party failed to nominate him as a candidate for United States Congress. During the convention, Tourgée campaigned behind the scenes for the congressional nomination, but instead Republican Party leaders nominated him to run for superior court justice. In part, this was a testament to the legal mastery he had demonstrated during the convention, and perhaps to his devotion to fairness and impartiality without regard to the political considerations, a predilection he flaunted in his unconventional and often nonpartisan proposals. While strict adherence to principle might serve well on the bench, Republican Party leadership considered Tourgée too unpredictable and independent-minded to be trusted in Congress. Tourgée had repeatedly bucked the Republican leadership during the convention—and worse still, he sometimes defeated them. He made a habit of arguing with friend and foe alike on the convention floor. At one point, he so infuriated the convention president by refusing to take his seat that he was placed temporarily under arrest, prompting the other delegates to rally behind him and demand his immediate release as "unlawfully arrested."[34] It was plain to see that he was almost constitutionally incapable of playing the "good soldier," as would be expected of a first-term congressman, and falling into line on command, which had been a problem for him even when an actual soldier. This temperament probably cost him advancement to the national level of the Republican Party.

But the choice of Tourgée as superior court justice would turn out to be an excellent one. Elected for a six-year term in the spring of 1868, he would excel in a position that would prove well-suited for his talents and temperament. Also, it provided a secure source of badly needed income for a much longer term than a two-year congressional seat. For the Republican Party's purposes, he would stand his ground against the Ku Klux Klan at the point of their attack, where their challenge most needed to be met. In far-off Washington, Tourgée might have proved less valuable to the cause of Reconstruction than he turned out to be as an eyewitness and an obstinate force of change within the state. When other Radicals were swept from power in 1870–1871, he would be left holding his ground and keeping the ideals of Reconstruction alive.

BEHIND THE CARPETBAG

By 1868 Tourgée had been so demonized in the press that he appears to have been regarded by some with genuine fear. "Considered by all good people to be a veritable monster," one description painted him as a story-book villain come-to-life:

> This Tourgée is the meanest looking man it has ever been our misfortune to meet. The Pirate; the cutthroat; the despicable, mean, cowardly, crawling, sneaking villain have been portrayed by nature, with a master hand, in every lineament of his countenance. The mark of infamy is stamped indelibly on his brow. . . .[35]

"Possessing a glass eye," another account remarked, "but with the other doing the observation of the eyes of twenty average men," his visage was unnerving to all who met him.[36] Children were purportedly afraid to look directly at him. So recalled one Greensboro resident of his childhood, "Judge Tourgee, we [children] looked upon him as some sort of pirate, mysterious and blackened by a thousand crimes, and we glanced at him covertly when he happened around."[37] Images of Tourgée from this period show him with a thick, jet-black beard and a perpetually scowling expression, looking almost as if he wished to reinforce his fearsome reputation.

If he relished his menacing and mysterious public persona, which his opponents took as confirmation of villainy, it may be because it served as a kind of deterrent. In one instance, a plot to assassinate him in his court-room went awry when Tourgée stared down the potential assassin and caused the man to lose his nerve. Two separate Ku Klux Klan plots against his life were abandoned, according to later testimony, by concerns that doing so may risk retaliation by a large force of armed men that Tourgée controlled and that it would require "300 men" to successfully kill him.[38] Indeed, Tourgée was believed to have organized an armed band of followers who lay in wait at his home, or at those of his allies, for expected Klan raids.[39] Such a villain as had been conjured in the public imagination surely could not be easily defeated.

Resolutely indifferent to the gawking of strangers, Tourgée sometimes found them amusing, privately joking to Emma when he traveled on his

Tourgée scowling in a photograph with his fellow Civil Code
Commissioners, William Rodman and Victor C. Barringer, 1868.
Courtesy of the Chautauqua County Historical Society, Westfield, NY.

judicial circuit that his courtroom was packed with those who came just
for "a chance to see if I have not really got hoofs and a forked tail."[40]
Braving public contempt for the sake of principle had been the highest
measure of moral rectitude in Tourgée's Western Reserve. The slanders
of the opposition, from this point of view, were a test of the Tourgées'
character and moral worth. But try as they might, Tourgée and his family
could not escape the psychological toll that came from being the subject
of such intense public disdain and frequent death threats.

Emma and her family lived a circumscribed existence, not venturing
to socialize beyond the familiar circle of Tourgée's political allies,
schoolteachers and missionaries, and other visitors from the North. The
hostility of local whites was so great that, by one report, "when
Mrs. Tourgee went along the street of Greensboro, the women of that
town made a wide circuit around her and gathered back their clothes as if
they were afraid of touching her."[41] Fear of attack or assassination was also
a constant source of great anxiety in their household. The Tourgées later
repeatedly told of how Emma's hair turned white overnight when the
Klan made a midnight visit to their house. Though details of this incident
are sketchy, the fullest account came in a newspaper article from 1880. "It

was during the Ku-Klux excitement of 1867, in North Carolina, that the Judge's house . . . was surrounded by a force of twenty to thirty midnight marauders," the article claimed. "The bravery and good fortune of the Judge saved his own life and those of his family, but the white hair of his faithful consort bears evidence of the anguish of that dreadful night."[42] An image of Emma from circa 1875 does not show evidence of a drastic change in the color of her hair, however, which suggests the possibility that Emma's complete graying of a few years later may have served for her, like Albion's blind eye, as a physical symbol of deeper, psychological scars that she carried from that time.

Emma rarely accompanied Albion to the obligatory social galas — probably for fear of unpleasant treatment by the wives of the elite — or on his journeys across the state on political and judicial business. He made a wide network of friends and acquaintances, including a few genuine friendships with members of the aristocracy, such as Thomas Settle and Samuel F. Phillips, who had converted to radicalism. But, he never gained social acceptance in their world. The refined culture of Southern elites confounded him and stirred up deep-rooted insecurities about his own unpolished upbringing. "These parties — dinnings and tea-ings — are dreadful ogres to me," he confided to Emma, "You cannot imagine, I fear, how terrible they are to me. I do not know of *anything* so fearful. All of my self-consciousness comes to the surface then and I cannot even breathe without fear of a *faux-pas*."[43] Completely out of his element, his performance at such gatherings probably did little to improve his public image. It was not that he lacked social charm — friends described him as "affable and entertaining," even "hilarious" in private company — but he made no effort to conform to the conventions of an elite culture that he instinctively disdained.[44] As the years passed, their exclusion from polite society grew more complete, as Tourgée warned an arriving Northern visitor in 1870, "We don't grow popular in the social acceptance of the town a bit, but rather the reverse."[45]

Not the least unpopular aspect of the Tourgées' conduct was their close association with African Americans and uneducated whites. The principle that "man is man" meant that no walls of exclusion should be maintained or respected, and the Tourgées tried to live this creed. They lived in an integrated neighborhood, with their property bordered on two sides by African American families.[46] Besides teaching at "colored" schools, the Tourgées frequented interracial political meetings, belonged to interracial fraternal societies, occasionally attended religious services in black churches, held dinners at their home for black guests, and even became the legal guardian of a black child who had been born in slavery. This unapologetic association with their supposed "inferiors" provided for endless speculation by whites, and for an educated white man to visit black neighborhoods for political meetings after dark was virtually unprecedented. "Very dark stories were whispered of his doings out in far-off Warnersville, the negro settlement out by the Methodist graveyard," reminisced a Greensboro resident. "He held meetings out there that we were almost prepared to say were a species of voodooism."[47]

His color-blind creed was class-blind as well. Tourgée was particularly ostracized, in fact, for his close association with John Walter Stephens, an uneducated native white Republican. Dubbed "Chicken" Stephens in the Conservative press due to an allegation that he once killed his neighbor's chickens, Stephens had committed the dual social breach of being poor *and* openly associating with blacks in both political and fraternal societies.[48] Stephens, despite his lack of formal education, became a justice of the peace after Tourgée personally tutored him in the law and administered his bar exam. Both were excluded from the genteel fraternization of the North Carolina State Bar Association. "Judge Tourgee had offended the lawyers, because he boarded with Stephens," one insider explained of the association's social snubbing of the judge, continuing,

> They considered it beneath the dignity of so high an official to make his home with a man so low in the social scale . . . they insisted that they would have treated [Tourgée] with respect, if not with cordiality, had he not shown these degraded tastes. . . . They believed that their only associates, on terms of equality, should be of their own order.[49]

Considering themselves "an educated aristocracy," the members of the bar believed that it was their duty "to inspire the plain people with the profoundest respect for their superiors," which Tourgée had undermined by treating "illiterate" and "unpolished" masses as equals.[50] Thus, it was virtually impossible for the Tourgées to find welcome among the "better sort" of North Carolinians who excluded him on principle of his conduct. "Judge Tourgee," the conservative historian J.G. de Roulhac Hamilton summed up in 1914, "although an able man and one who in time became an exceedingly strong judge, was throughout his public career in North Carolina, entirely shameless and without any sense of propriety."[51]

Tourgée's brazen flouting of Southern mores reached new heights in 1869 when he legally adopted a thirteen-year-old girl, Adaline Patillo, who was a former slave. Adaline, who usually went by "Addie" or "Ada," was the illegitimate child of a white man; she was light-skinned enough to pass for white and desperately impoverished.[52] It is not known how she first became introduced to Tourgée, but she lived in the neighboring county of Caswell and had connections to his friend Stephens. Soon after she was adopted, evidence shows that Adaline's mother, Louisa Patillo, and her younger sister, three-year-old Mary, moved into the Tourgées' home also.[53] It is clear that Tourgée considered Adaline intellectually gifted, and sympathized with her "unfortunate" financial circumstances. His interest in adopting her appears to be linked to his desire to send her to a boarding school where she could receive a superior education. In order to accomplish this, perhaps, he felt it proper to become her legal guardian.

At the time of Adaline's adoption, the Tourgées were childless. They had lost one child in 1867, who either died in its infancy or had been stillborn, and they were trying to conceive another when Albion hatched his plan to adopt Addie.[54] Albion would later tell Adaline that he regarded her as though she were his own daughter, and to some degree his interest in her may have stemmed from a desire to fill the void of their loss. Indeed, both Tourgées treated Adaline as a daughter, offering her all of the opportunities for intellectual and career advancement that they would later give to their own daughter, Aimée. Born eighteen months after Adaline's adoption in 1870, Aimée (nicknamed "Lodie") received artistic training in Europe as a teenager and then enjoyed a career as an artist and a writer before her untimely death in 1909. It appears the Tourgées held similar aspirations for Adaline. They sent her to the Hampton Institute in Virginia in 1871, where she became a classmate of Booker T. Washington.[55]

When Conservatives learned of Adaline's adoption, they were, predictably, horrified. On April 20, 1869, the Conservative *Raleigh Sentinel* seized the opportunity to imply that Tourgée's motives were something other than paternal: "This is generous of the Judge—very generous! Is Tourgee a married man?"[56] The public snickering was enough to sour Emma on the adoption plan, who voiced her misgivings to Albion soon after the embarrassing notice in the press appeared. But Albion—again, predictably—dug in his heels and prevailed upon Emma: "I know the course I have marked out—in the main—is for Ada's benefit, and *is right*—Your somewhat romantic supposition of the possibilities for a time somewhat discouraged me, but further reflection has entirely convinced me that, for the present at least, I must continue my guardianship of Ada." If anything, the public gossip hardened Tourgée's determination to take Adaline under his wing. He characteristically dismissed the town gossip, informing Emma, "I shall not ask my neighbors to define my duty for me, nor to dictate my course. If they don't like it, they may e'en let it alone."[57]

The few of Adaline's letters that survive overflow with affection and an unaffected intimacy with the Tourgées that belie any claim of illicit motives or improper conduct by Albion, and her correspondence also suggests that Emma quickly overcame her misgivings. From her boarding school, Adaline wrote effusive letters, telling the Tourgées in detail of her daily activities and thoughts. "Because I feel near to you & Mrs. T. I want you to know all I do," she explained in a letter to Albion. Of Emma and the infant Aimée, she wrote:

> I wish I could see my Darling little Lodie & take her in my arms this dreamy day and sing her off to sleep give a good kiss to her for me. I wish I was near so I would help Mrs. T. . . . Oh! she has been like a dear mother to me. I shall never forget her as long as I am in existence. I always remember her in my prayers.[58]

Adaline would make good on this promise to always remember. "Mary and I often talk of you," a thirty-seven-year-old Adaline, now married with children of her own, wrote to Emma in 1893:

> Many and many are the times I thank you & the Judge for my training and for my disposition. I am so thankful to have been placed under the care of one with so sweet a disposition as yourself. I try to be just like you . . . I well remember too, when the Judge used to read the bible & have prayers. I try to do that.

She also remarked about how she often walked by their old home in Greensboro just to see "the house where I have spent so many happy innocent hours."[59]

Although their relationship with Adaline occurred mostly outside the view of their white Southern neighbors, the Tourgées made at least one attempt to gain a measure of public acceptance for it. A neighbor recalled to the *Greensboro Record* decades later: "Tourgee adopted two negro girls," referring to Adaline and Mary—though Tourgée did not actually adopt Mary—and "on one occasion he brought them to the Baptist church with him, taking a seat near the front." The perturbed congregation quickly raised a committee to address this violation of the segregated church seating arrangement. Accosting Tourgée after the service, the committee informed him that "hereafter if he attended church he must not seat the girls with the white people." Unwilling to comply with this demand, the Tourgées never returned to the church.[60]

That they would be so bold as to directly challenge segregated seating in a Southern church is surprising, even for the Tourgées. Though the *Record* article did not mention Emma, she was surely present when this incident occurred and the attempt to bring the girls to church may have been her idea. Emma strongly wished to join a church. Not inclined to convert to Quakerism—where they certainly would have been welcomed —or to join the African American churches—whose energetic style was too alien for them—the Tourgées never found a home at either the Baptist and Methodist parishes that Emma preferred. Their daughter Aimée would not be baptized until after they left the South. Their unlikely attempt to bring Adaline and Mary to the Baptist services is indicative of Emma's determination on this issue.[61]

Though Albion managed to endure the social ostracism of his neighbors, even using it to fuel his revolutionary fire, Emma could not sustain her enthusiasm for Reconstruction under the harsh personal conditions. Her life in the South was generally unhappy, and her attempts to construct a viable family life never worked out to her satisfaction. She began to experience a change of heart about their work in the South, it seems, when during her first pregnancy, as she recalled, she was left in "a little log cabin, cold[,] hungry and alone" for several months before losing her baby in 1867. Albion's later recollections confirmed that "starvation" was threatening at that time, until his election to the constitutional convention, which came with a per diem salary, saved them.[62] Memories of this

Emma and Aimée "Lodie" Tourgée, ca. 1875. Courtesy of the Chautauqua County Historical Society, Westfield, NY.

terrible period haunted Emma, and her surviving letters afterward were markedly devoid of the encouragement for Albion's work that they had evinced when they first arrived. Emma, in fact, began to wish for a return to the North.

Just after the birth of Aimée in late 1870, Emma abruptly fled with her newborn to her sister's Angie's home in Erie. This was the first sign that their relationship had begun to split under the severe strain of social ostracism and constant state of danger. "I will go to Erie, to the West, anywhere, anywhere for your sake . . . as gaily and happily as I first came to your arms," Albion tried to reassure a frazzled Emma after her sudden departure, adding "Please do not ever intimate again that I desire your death."[63] Instead of leaving the South, he managed to coax Emma back to North Carolina a few months later. But tensions persisted. "I am so glad you are feeling good natured toward each other for it is so much for the best," Adaline remarked to Emma and Albion in an 1875 letter, attesting to their continued troubles.[64] Yet, Albion could not fail to recognize Emma's underlying unhappiness. "Your face has gathered a fixed patient look as if you were all the time carrying some burden," he told her. "Now and then you brighten up into my old Emma but it seems as if it were less and less often."[65] After periodic threats to leave, Emma finally had enough of her life as a social outcast and she returned to Erie without Albion in 1878, never to return again to North Carolina.

Among the several reasons for her final departure from the South were conflicts that stemmed from her desire to be part of a church. "By all means, join the church, and have Lodie baptized too," Tourgée conceded to Emma, soon after her return to Erie. "I have grieved a thousand times over what has been in regard to that. I do not know why, but it seems to have produced an isolation[,] almost an estrangement between us. I have always felt as if you half hated me, ever since." Ever since *what?* Tourgée did not say. Some incident—perhaps the one with Adaline and Mary— had prompted Albion to boycott the local churches, over Emma's objection. Hinting at an apology for having prevented Emma from joining a church without him, Tourgée concluded, "I . . . have always looked forward to our having a church relationship together but ought not to have made that a hindrance in your way. I do not suppose there is any reasonable prospect of my ever having any church connection again."[66] Their rejection from the local religious community had driven, or deepened, a wedge into their relationship. While Albion reacted by bitterly washing his hands of the local churches, Emma could not give up what had been so integral to her life before coming to North Carolina.

Emma's quitting of the South, however, did not indicate a weakening of her commitment to racial equality. In another letter to Albion sent soon after her arrival in Erie, Emma reported with apparent approval that eight-year-old Aimée had flouted Northern racial prejudice by befriending a "colored girl" at her school. "Lodie's sitting with a colored girl!" Albion exclaimed. "I am surprised at her doing so. I have been afraid she was getting demoralized on that head." It seems Emma and Aimée intended to carry on their crusade against racism in the North. Oddly, Albion advised Emma not to let Aimée do so. Predicting that she will be "laughed at," Albion suggested "a carpet-bagger's daughter had better not sit with a colored girl unless she is thicker-skinned than Lodie. I am afraid it would be a mistake to let her do so."[67] This surprising comment must be considered in light of the strained personal context. Written to an estranged spouse who had just given up on their crusade in the South, to which Albion remained committed, his comment might have been meant as an indirect criticism of Emma. If Aimée, like her mother, did not have the fortitude to sustain such a difficult undertaking, he may have intended to imply, then she perhaps should not begin what she would not be able to finish. Or alternatively, and less harshly, perhaps Albion simply did not wish his daughter to experience all of the pain and exasperation that her parents had suffered as a result of trying to revolutionize race relations.

The burden of living as social outcasts—following the dictates of their own consciences, associating with poor whites and blacks, and enduring the threats and abuse that followed from it—took its toll on the Tourgées. The psychological and personal consequences of carpetbagging should not be forgotten in the historical understanding of the downfall of Reconstruction. As effective as violence and intimidation by the Klan was, the social exclusion and smear campaigns of Conservatives could be just as successful in driving off or silencing their opponents. The harder one pushed for social change in the South—and few pushed harder than Tourgée—the harder the Conservative South pushed back. It took an unusual personality, as well as an extraordinary commitment to the project of Reconstruction, to maintain hope for change and stick around as long as Tourgée did.

"UPLIFTING" THE BLACK SOUTH

Though truly egalitarian in his social relations, Tourgée nevertheless considered himself the agent of a higher civilization that would "uplift the South." This implied a sense of superiority over his neophyte Southern brethren, both black and white. The ideology of uplift was especially important to his relationship with Southern blacks, as it challenged the racist orthodoxy of the planter class that blacks were fitted only for slavery and also presumed blacks would embrace its goals. But how did blacks react to this crusade to "uplift" them to Northern standards of civilization? To better grasp Tourgée's role in Reconstruction, it is important to examine his relationship with Southern blacks more closely in the light of his notions of moral progress.

Invited to address an assembly of freedpeople on Emancipation Day, 1870, Tourgée took as his theme "The Slave's Wages." Attempting to place slavery into an historical perspective, he described it as an "apprenticeship . . . under a hard master" that was not an unmixed evil. "What did two and a half centuries do for the slave?" he asked rhetorically. It had rescued them from savagery, he answered: "Year by year [the slave] rose above his brutish origin. Skill came to his hand and life to his brain." Slavery was, in fact, part of a divine plan. In a statement that virtually overlooked white responsibility for slavery, he declared that through their abduction from Africa, "God had brought them within the scope of Christian teaching and religious light" and "opened to the slave not only the pathway of civilization but the gate of Heaven." Salvation was theirs and despite the harsh, unrequited toil, "the weak, groveling, incompetent savage, was nursed and molded by Slavery into the strong, active, enduring efficient laborer. . . . Mighty steps! Glorious results!"[68] These were the wages paid to the slave.

For Tourgée to express such views is surprising, especially considering their close association with the racist arguments of slaveholders themselves. Tourgée, however, marshaled his arguments in an attempt to compliment the former slaves for the terrific "progress" they had achieved. He asked the audience to compare themselves with the first generation of African slaves brought to American soil. "The distance between them and the freedmen seems enormous," he said:

> The original slaves represented simple barbarism—whether higher or lower than some other tribes and races is a matter of little importance. It was [in] all its essential features barbarism—of thought, of life, of religion, mental and moral darkness and degradation.[69]

While this was mostly a simple reiteration of colonialist ideology, he believed nevertheless that all "tribes and races" were capable of progressing from barbarism to civilization, and his comparison was meant to prove that much progress had occurred already for the African race. In fact, he continued on to say, "the freedman of 1865 was as well prepared . . . to provide for his own sustenance as the average American citizen, much better, in this point of view, than the average white man of the South."[70] Tourgée's seeming total disregard for the value of African culture and traditions was harsh, but not unlike his view of Southern aristocratic culture, which he deemed, similarly, a barbarous obstacle to be overcome. He acknowledged too that his points were the same "arguments by which Slavery sought to defend itself," but he begged his audience not to confuse his message with those of proslavery writers who painted a purely benevolent picture of the institution. Tourgée stressed the crimes and inhumanity of the system, recalling slaves' accounts of "whipping and torture, of murder and crime and cruelty of every form and character."[71] Nevertheless, his advice was not to dwell on those horrors but only the good that came of slavery—bitterness would be of no use to the future.

One reason for Tourgée's emphasis on the "benefits" of slavery was his fear that resentment for the injustices of slavery had begun to impede black progress. It was common, he said, among the freedmen to feel that "the past is his debtor" and to expect that the account would be settled with some kind of economic reparations in the near future. "This view is eminently hurtful to the Freeman as tending to make him less regardful of his present opportunity and less and less inclined to rely upon himself for the amelioration of the future," he warned. "[I]t nourishes a sense of injustice and ingratitude which is quite inconsistent with the cheerful recognition of their true status, and the performance of the duties of citizenship in an unprejudiced and impartial spirit." Rejecting the idea of reparations as impossible—"it never could be paid if it were actually his due"—and dismissing the desire for them as itself debasing, Tourgée urged his audience to consider the debt of slavery already paid. It would be better for blacks to treat whites, including former slaveholders, as equal citizens—in an "unprejudiced and impartial spirit"—rather than as cheats and unrepentant adversaries.

There is no direct evidence of the freedpeople's response to Tourgée's speech, but the Conservative papers praised his "impressive talk" and reported that his "excellent advice . . . [was] spoken of highly by everyone."[72] It is telling that Conservatives approved of his comments. There were points that Conservatives might have quibbled with, but on the whole, the message was one on which white Radicals and Conservatives could find common ground: blacks needed white instruction to become "civilized," and they were best served by not seeking redress for the injustices of the past but rather by being grateful for the opportunities of the present. In consecrating American customs and denigrating African ones, the ideology of "civilization" was fundamentally hierarchical and paternalistic, requiring some degree of white tutelage over blacks. Yet, the similarities of Tourgée's "civilizationism" to traditional planter paternalism could easily be overstated.[73]

While Tourgée understood his actions within the larger project of a civilizing mission, his profound individualism tempered the most intolerant and oppressive aspects of this ideology. His respect for individual worth, basic human empathy, and his own distrust of institutionalized authority, differed considerably from the paternalistic temper that discountenanced the autonomy of others.[74] Though he could be condescending in tone—to whites as well as blacks—he rarely strayed from the overriding goal to prepare the freedpeople for economic success and equal participation in the democratic polity. Whereas conservative planters sought to perpetuate black economic dependence and subordination, Tourgée sought to end it. Indeed, almost without exception, black leaders of nineteenth-century America embraced the ideology of uplift just as Tourgée did, except that their emphasis on the goal of black autonomy and self-direction was even more pronounced.[75]

Tourgée's relationship with Southern blacks and his various attempts to empower them, suggest both the possibilities, and limits, within the civilizing mission. For instance, Tourgée's concern for economic advancement and his support for black land ownership was evident from his arrival. He understood that political equality and education would be an empty achievement without the opportunity for economic advancement that would truly liberate freedpeople from the control of white landowners. "The highest good of the Freedmen and of the country demands that as soon as practicable the great majority of them should become owners of the soil they now till," he wrote to a Freedmen's Bureau agent in 1867. "[I]t is as nearly self-evident as any social, moral or political problem can be . . . it *must of necessity* come either by *excessive taxation* or *confiscation*."[76]

Yet Tourgée never publicly came out in favor of governmental confiscation. Indeed, his Emancipation Day comments suggested that he did not approve of the government issuing land compensation to former slaves. Rather than excite backlash among white landowners and others who denied the government's right to directly redistribute property, he favored limited government action, including a progressive tax on land in addition to the homestead policy that he wrote into the 1868 constitution. These policies ensured squatter's rights and encouraged planters to sell off their uncultivated land, forcing it onto the market, and thereby indirectly achieving land redistribution. Unlike confiscation, these policies enjoyed widespread support among North Carolina Republicans.[77]

After deciding that land must be redistributed primarily as a result of market operations, he became involved in several private ventures designed to sell land to freedpeople. Like many other Southern cities after the war, in 1865 Greensboro experienced a large influx of black refugees who crowded on empty or abandoned lands on the edge of the city. Tourgée took a special interest in helping these refugees secure land and better housing, and he assisted Yardley Warner, a Quaker missionary, in establishing a housing development on the southern edge of Tourgée's Greensboro property (later to be named Warnersville after Yardley Warner). It appears that Tourgée brokered land transfers and may have sold some of his own land to Warner and his missionaries.[78]

Following Warner's lead, Tourgée proposed to Freedmen's Bureau Commissioner General Oliver O. Howard in 1867 that "a Freedmen Land Agency be established in each state" that would facilitate the purchase of land by Northern capitalists who might then resell it to freedpeople on good terms, with minimal down payment. "I have no fear whatever of the profit of the thing if [done well]," he promised. "There are hundreds of estimable freedmen who are anxious to buy land on such terms, all about me." He vouched for the freedmen as "reliable purchasers of real estate," arguing that they had already shown their ability "to pay for small lots and horses which they purchased at extravagant rates" from local whites. The difficulty was to circumvent the distrust between planters and freedpeople. He explained the dilemma to the Freedmen's Bureau agent: "the land owners have little if any confidence in the negro as a buyer and almost universally refuse to sell to him on time or at a reasonable price. The negroes as a rule have a strong reciprocal feeling in regard to the land owners, and much dislike to purchase of them."[79] Thus, the agency would serve as a broker and mortgage lender.

When the Freedmen's Bureau failed to act on Tourgée's proposal, he attempted to establish a Land Agency on his own. "I wish you would send me a plot of the plantations you wish to sell at once, with full descriptions of the same," he asked his friend Quaker Nathan Hill in July 1867. "[I]t is my impression that I can sell them off at once." He explained his plan: "I am ready to convince people here that it is policy to sell, and people North that it is policy to buy." With Emma working "as treasurer and accountant for which she is fitted," he promised to handle all the advertising and promotion if Hill would contribute the one hundred dollars in capital that was needed to get things started.[80] But Hill, unconvinced, did not back the venture, so the scheme never materialized.

Though he hoped his entrepreneurial ventures would benefit the freedpeople, Tourgée also intended to make a profit. His vision of capitalism presumed that labor and capital would prosper together as the market economy expanded. His confidence in this theory was confirmed in 1870 when, as a judge, Judge Tourgée was called in to "settle some complications . . . among the partners" of a small wood handle business, the Snow Turning Company. He discovered a thriving factory that employed a largely black labor force on good terms. "I was perfectly *thunderstruck* at the profits," Tourgée told a friend. "It had been going on within sight of my house for nearly two years and I had not dreamed that the capital invested was paying more than an ordinary profit. . . . It has been kept *very* quiet."[81] Perhaps because Southern whites did not approve of blacks and whites working side-by-side, especially in a factory setting, the owners, including another carpetbagger, William H. Snow, had kept a low profile. Its potential was so great that Tourgée convinced them to expand under his guidance. Soon, they found a new market for their wood handles and spokes in the North, and their enterprise was transformed into the North Carolina Handle Company.[82]

Elected president of the company, Tourgée assiduously courted Northern investors, found Northern distributors for its wood handles, and even tinkered with the invention of a more efficient wood-cutting machine. When he failed to attain backing by the Freedmen's Bank, a quasi-governmental institution created to assist blacks, he borrowed twenty-four hundred dollars to invest in the business. At its height, the company employed as many as seventy-four workers and became one of the largest handle-producers in the country. The owners reportedly organized interracial baseball games among its employees, in which the thirty-five-year-old Tourgée may have taken part, if the health of his back allowed. Unfortunately, as was often the case with his business ventures, prosperity was short-lived. The company was overextended, "with liabilities amounting to $30,000," when a financial panic that hit Wall Street in 1873 caught its investors off guard and led to the bankruptcy of the company. Though he was able to convert the company's debts "into mortgages upon real estate," Tourgée was crushed by the loss of a business that had not only brought handsome profits for himself but had been such a boon to the black community of Warnersville where many of its workers lived.[83]

Tourgée's confidence in free-market capitalism was not broken by the 1873 crash or the subsequent six-year-long depression. Though he was ruined financially, he consoled himself that he had brought much-needed capital into the state and provided good wages for those who needed it most. "I have the consolation too of knowing that I did not hold money and let it rust . . . but so used it that others received good from it," he wrote to Martin B. Anderson, a friend who he knew would appreciate his capitalist efforts. Looking out upon the neighborhood of Warnersville, he boasted to Anderson, "I can sit by my window and see scores of snug homes that would never have been built but for the steady work and good wages which their owners derived from my enterprise."[84] By 1879 the wood handle company had returned to prosperity under new ownership and still employed an interracial labor force. The *Greensboro North State* ranked the establishment of the Handle Works as one of Tourgée's main achievements while a resident of Greensboro. "The 'North Carolina Handle Works,' which owes its origin to Judge Tourgee, is now the property of other parties—purchased after the panic of 1873—doing a prosperous business, and giving employment to many of our people," the paper observed in 1879.[85]

Despite his efforts to make market capitalism work to the benefit of the freedpeople, the staunch opposition of Southern landowners and creditors ensured that little economic advancement would come to blacks without strong government action. Distrust between blacks and whites pervaded economic relations, and Tourgée was not exempt from this tension. Indeed, though he preached and practiced the gospel of racial equality, Tourgée stood to benefit economically and politically from African Americans that worked and voted for him. The Conservative press was quick to point this out. Attempting to turn blacks against him, the *Greensboro Patriot* once quoted a freedman who claimed, "when Tourgée wanted to be Judge he ate with me, mashed my potatoes and poured gravy over them and, now, he won't even speak to me on business." While Republicans dismissed this man's story as fabricated, the *Patriot* more seriously asked Tourgée, "Are you and your party the real friends of the colored people? If so, did you ever nominate one for any office that had any pay attached to it?"[86] This was indeed a very delicate subject, as blacks found it suspicious when Republicans passed over black candidates for nomination too regularly.

One incident in 1876 dramatically illustrates Tourgée's inability to overcome this racial distrust. When James E. O'Hara, an African American candidate for presidential elector, won the Republican Party nomination, Tourgée feared that his presence on the party ticket would have adverse consequences for the other Republican candidates. Choosing his words carefully, he composed an unsolicited letter of advice to O'Hara, whom he had known as a colleague at the 1875 constitutional convention. "You may perhaps be surprised at the tenor of this letter from me, since you are well aware how little I am accustomed to heed the clamor of our weak-kneed Republicans upon the question of color," he began, and proceeded to plead with O'Hara to step down for the good of the party on account of his race. Professing to "despise the prejudice as much as you can," he nevertheless insisted that the only way to overcome it was to put Republicans into office, which O'Hara's candidacy would not help to do.

Tourgée, who was not a candidate and had no evident ulterior motive, concluded: "I hope you will not consider me impertinent and I am sure you will not attribute to me any motive other than the one I avow."[87] But this hope was misplaced.

James O'Hara wrote a furious response that Tourgée described as a "torrent of angry abuse." Though O'Hara's letter has not survived, Tourgée's two responses have. Positively fuming, his first one accused O'Hara of exhibiting "the worst kind of race prejudice" that sought to "wreck revenge" even on those whites who were not responsible for black ills. He bitterly claimed that vengeful black men like O'Hara had ruined Reconstruction in Louisiana, Mississippi, and South Carolina and would put back the cause of black freedom "two or three hundred years." But after this imprudent outburst, Tourgée prudently put aside this letter, and wrote a second, less accusatory one. "I have no desire to see you forced off the ticket or 'driven' or 'dictated to' in the least," he more coolly explained:

> I am at a loss to understand however, how a colored man will claim any especial credit for his conduct should it result in the defeat of his party, the [annulment] of the Constitutional amendments, and the general prejudice of his race. It is all very fine to complain of unfair treatment, "masters" and "servants" and etc. but it is the result which tests ideas. When the colored man was made a citizen he was not made angelic (as your letter proves) nor was he exempted from any of the ills of humanity. . . . It makes no difference how black or white you may be you cannot subvert realities . . . this is not a question of what *ought* to be but of what *is*—as you will find out before the campaign is over.[88]

Tourgée presumably sent the second letter. O'Hara did subsequently withdraw from the ticket, though surely not due to Tourgée's urging alone. The 1876 election results were a disaster for the Republicans nonetheless, with widespread reports of fraud and ballot box stuffing by Democrats resulting in a landslide that mocked Tourgée's strategic tinkering with O'Hara's nomination.[89]

Tourgée's conflict with O'Hara demonstrates how fragile interracial relationships could be. Though he may have believed that he could step outside his identity as a white man to offer an objective analysis to O'Hara, his advice was still that of a white man pressuring a black man to take a subordinate position on account of his race. Moreover, his accusation that the conduct of black men had undermined Reconstruction elsewhere shows how susceptible even he could be to racial thinking— though his more considered second thoughts appeared to revoke this train of thought. Finally, it is revealing that O'Hara accused Tourgée of acting as a master toward a slave. Above all, emancipation meant for blacks the promise of autonomy from white control. White dominance, even in the Republican Party, continued to grate as a vestige of slavery.

Despite his role as "uplifter" of the black South, Tourgée's ultimate goal was to see blacks achieve individual autonomy. But what was required before this autonomy could be achieved? Certainly in the arena of politics, he felt that blacks would be dependent on the Republican Party until the time when both parties accepted them as political equals. But, what of cultural Reconstruction? At what point would blacks no longer need the tutelage of Northern whites? In this regard, it is instructive to examine Tourgée's relationship with Adaline Patillo in more depth and his deeper reflections upon cultural reconstruction in his fiction.

Recognizing her as a gifted individual, Tourgée urged Adaline to strive for self-improvement and upward mobility into the middle class. This did not come easily and it required strict discipline and self-control. In one letter, Adaline suggested that she had been reprimanded at school for misunderstanding the nature of freedom: "I regret so much that I have the wrong idea of independence for I think it can make a ___ of any one so quick. I hope as I grow older I shall get rid of them." What exactly she got wrong was not clear, but the remedy she adopted was to rededicate herself to middle-class respectability: "I don't know, of showing my independence in but one way and that is in living as a lady," the eighteen-year-old wrote, adding appreciatively, "there are few of my position that are ladies."[90] She even imagined herself assimilating into the Northern middle class. When the Tourgées sent her to visit Ohio, she exclaimed upon arrival: "Can't I stay [?] I *want to be* a northerner."[91] No doubt the Tourgées approved of these sentiments.

While it is possible that Tourgée imagined Adaline becoming a future leader of her race, in the mold of a female writer, such as Francis Ellen Watkins Harper, another intriguing possibility is that he hoped Adaline would choose to pass for white. In fact, Adaline had passed on occasion. In 1875 Adaline wrote to the Tourgées that she and her companion were mistaken for being white by her Ohio hosts, who had been expecting "colored girls." Even after she revealed her racial identity, she reported, the Northern man insisted on calling her white, meaning that he regarded her as a member of his race because of her complexion.[92] Considering Tourgée's fascination with people of indeterminate race in his fiction and in the law, one wonders whether he might have encouraged Adaline to move to the North after finishing her education, and pass for white.

Adaline and Mary Patillo, ca. 1873, shown here as the picture of
middle-class respectability, reflecting their own aspirations for
upward mobility and middle-class assimilation. Courtesy of the
Chautauqua County Historical Society, Westfield, NY.

One bit of hearsay evidence suggests this was indeed Tourgée's
ambition for her. When the Conservative press first learned of Adaline's
adoption, the *Raleigh Sentinel* reported the following regarding
Tourgée's motives:

We understand that the Judge formed such a partiality for a "yaller girl" in Yanceyville that he prevailed on her mother to let him take her home with him and "educate" her. He said if she remained at home the probability was she would marry a negro, whereas he would take her and, educating her, "marry her off to the best advantage."[93]

Considering the Conservative source, which goes on to imply that Tourgée had a sexual interest in the girl — her age, thirteen, is not mentioned — this statement must be taken cautiously. It is certainly possible that he *did* make the statement about Adaline marrying "a negro," but that the newspaper took his comment out of context — it was not unusual for the Conservative press in North Carolina to distort the facts in this manner. It seems unlikely, however, that Tourgée's main purpose in educating Adaline was to improve her marital chances, even though he may have speculated in conversation about the possibility of her moving North and marrying a white man. This would be in keeping with his belief that one should not be marked for life into any caste because of their birth. In fact, her success in assimilating into white Northern society, after being born a slave and a "colored" girl, would be proof of the foolishness of caste. Since Albion left behind no recorded firsthand comment about Adaline's complexion or about her passing, this is merely an extrapolation based on scanty evidence.

Adaline's letters indicate that she was conflicted about fulfilling the role that Tourgée had marked out for her. She wrote to Albion in 1875: "It always makes me feel *so sad when you* say you feel towards me as a daughter for I cant see how you can feel towards such a girl *as I am* as a daughter. I often think to myself can it be true." Reminded of her own humble beginnings as a slave and her illegitimacy, she remarked: "I never have yet had a Father but what I was ashamed to own."[94] Not quite willing to accept the role of daughter, she also never quite accepted Tourgée's aspirations for her to join the cultural elite. In the end, she discovered that her own priorities outweighed either becoming a Northerner or aspiring to middle-class achievement. Without finishing her studies or receiving her degree, Adaline chose to give up school and return to Greensboro, where she would remain for most of her life.

Although her reasons for doing so are obscure, Adaline had a change of heart in her fourth year of study. She mentioned "feeling uneasy . . . every day" about the failing health of her mother who was "lame & nearly worn all out." Desiring to return home, Adaline hinted that she was ready to give up school, remarking about her mother, "if [her] life lasts, in the future [I will] try to do something towards supporting her if I *never* graduate." Anticipating Tourgée's words of discouragement, she justified her decision,

"I may have to labor hard . . . [but] she has labored hard for me when I could not for myself." Since her mother, Louisa, was living with the Tourgées, her health may have been only a pretext for her decision. Imagining a life surrounded by her friends and family, she wrote, "I do want a home of our own & I will not feel content until I get one." She did not reject the idea of higher education as an advantageous route for a young woman, but she made up her mind that time had come to give up school and to work for a living. In her speculations about the future, she declared that, "If in time I shall marry a man[,] I shall take [her sister] Mary and try to educate *her.*"[95]

After teaching for two years, Adaline married Leroy William Woods in Greensboro in 1878, perhaps reuniting with her mother and sister under their own roof at last. The couple eventually would have seven children: their sixth, born in 1894, was named Albion Tourgee Woods. Owning two barber shops in which Adaline would assist her husband, the Woods family lived in relative prosperity for Greensboro's black community. There, Adaline spent the rest of her life trying "to do some Christian work among my people and help them in every way I could," as she reported to Hampton Institute in 1920.[96] She also kept up with what Evelyn Brooks Higginbotham has called the "politics of respectability," a strategy by which black women "boldly asserted the will and agency to define themselves outside the parameter of prevailing racist discourses" by adopting middle-class "manners and morals."[97] Evidence suggests that Adaline never regretted her decision to return to Greensboro despite its limited upward mobility for blacks, but her frequent visits to the Tourgée's old home and her wistful recollections of being raised by "the Judge" also suggest that she never forgot her ambitions of that earlier time. The last Adaline's voice is heard from in the documentary record, she was still talking of those old times. In 1925, a white patron of her husband's barber shop reported to the *Greensboro Record*, "Addie Woods, the colored girl whom Judge Tourgee adopted in Greensboro and educated in the North, told me the other day, while washing my hair, that he and his family lay awake many a long night dreading a visit from the Ku Klux."[98]

Her life was probably not the one Tourgée imagined for her. One can only speculate how Tourgée viewed Adaline's decision to choose the life of limited advancement for blacks in Greensboro over the intellectual achievement and middle-class status she might have achieved elsewhere. It seems he respected her choice and may have even come to sympathize with it, as there is no evidence that he begrudged her decision and he continued to be a source of financial and moral support for Adaline and her family well into the 1890s.[99] Turning to Tourgée's fictional representations of Reconstruction, it is clear that he came to possess a keen awareness of black ambivalence about white middle-class culture. In fact, one of the most compelling explorations of the relationship between a white teacher and black pupil in all of nineteenth-century fiction can be found in Tourgée's 1880 novel *Bricks Without Straw.*

A sequel of sorts to *A Fool's Errand, Bricks Without Straw* attempts to tell the story of Reconstruction from the vantage point of the freedpeople. In the novel, Eliab Hill, a black preacher and community leader, is chosen by white missionaries to become a schoolteacher. As a slave he was unable to work in the fields because of an illness that left him crippled, but Eliab took advantage of his misfortune to learn, somewhat imperfectly, to read, and he acquired vocational skills as a shoemaker. His mental training and keen powers of observation attracted the notice of the Northern teachers at Red Wing who desired, in Tourgée words, "to accustom the colored people to see those of their own race trusted and advanced."[100]

Under the tutelage of a New England "schoolmarm" named Mollie Ainslie, Eliab undertakes to complete his education and become a competent teacher. But the relationship between Mollie and Eliab turns out to be a somewhat vexed one. The main Northern character in the novel, Mollie is a flawed heroine whose racial egalitarianism is less of the heart than of the head. Tourgée describes her as experiencing a "terrible isolation" in the black community of Red Wing where she is afflicted by "a hungry yearning for friendly white faces." Despite an unvanquished "zeal for the unfortunate race she had striven to uplift," Mollie remains aloof from her students and never feels "any inclination to that friendly intimacy which would have been sure to arise if her pupils had been of the same race as herself."[101] Her lack of warmth, Tourgée implies, was not an unusual disposition of the New England schoolmarms toward Southern blacks. Historian Robert C. Harris is probably correct in observing: "Mollie Ainslie is a complex individual. Too complex, in fact, to have been a totally fictional creation."[102] Most of Tourgée's characters were based on real-life individuals, including Eliab Hill, who bore a resemblance to a crippled South Carolina preacher named Elias Hill. The conflict between Molly and Eliab might even be viewed as a summation of Tourgée's own experience and observations as an educator during Reconstruction.

Eliab spends hours after class in tutorials with Mollie in which she grows increasingly frustrated with his progress. "She had heard him pour forth torrents of eloquence on the Sabbath, and felt the force of a nature exceptionally rich and strong in its conceptions of religious truths and human needs," the narrator explains, "only to find him on the morrow floundering hopelessly in the mire of rudimentary science, or getting . . .

an imperfect idea of some author's words, which it seemed to her he ought to have grasped at a glance." Her inability to fully sympathize with him and his difficulties comes to a head when Eliab, overcome with his own frustrations, finally tries to explain them to her. Pointing out to her the vast cultural gap between his background and the knowledge she takes for granted, he explains:

> There are thoughts and bearing that I can never gather from books alone. They come to you, Miss Ainslie, and to those like you, from those who were before you in the world, and from things about you. It is the part of knowledge that can't be put into books. Now I have none of that. My people cannot give it to me.[103]

Picking out a passage from one of his books as an example, Eliab says of the author: "If I knew all about his life and ways, and the like, I could tell pretty fully his meaning." But he cannot because, as Eliab tells Mollie, "his thoughts are *your* thoughts and his life has been *your* life. You belong to the same race and class. I am cut off from this, and can only stumble slowly along the path of knowledge."[104] Despite Eliab's stunningly clear explanation of the obstacles that he is struggling against, Mollie is unable to see things from his viewpoint.

Overcome with despair and agitated by Mollie's coldness, Eliab impulsively chooses to discontinue his studies with her. "Education is something more than I thought—something so large and difficult that one of my age, raised as I have been, can only get a taste of it at the best," he concludes. Slipping back into the dialect, with which he spoke at the outset of his studies, he insists that Mollie spend the hour formerly reserved for him training the most promising younger students: "The time is precious— precious, and must not be wasted. You can't afford to spend so much of it on me! The Lord can't afford ter hev ye, Miss Mollie! I must step aside, an' I'se gwine ter do it now." Utterly taken aback by this outburst, Mollie reluctantly agrees to do as he wishes. Tourgée ends this dramatic confrontation with an ironic commentary on Mollie's inability to empathize with the cultural chasm that torments Eliab:

> "I declare, Lucy," said Mollie Ainslie that evening, to her co-worker, over their cosy tea, "I don't believe I shall ever get to understand these people. There is that Eliab Hill, who was getting along so nicely, has concluded to give up his studies. I believe he is half crazy anyhow. He raved about it, and glared at me so that I was half frightened out of my wits. I wonder why it is that cripples are always so queer, anyhow?"

Making sure that the irony of this dialogue does not elude the reader, Tourgée's narrator concludes:

She would have been still more amazed if she had known that from that day Eliab Hill devoted himself to his studies with a redoubled energy, which more than made up for the loss of his teacher's aid. Had she herself had been less a child she would have seen that he whom she had treated as such was, in truth, a man of rare strength.[105]

Her failure to properly comprehend the needs of "these people," he implies, had made her tutelage more of an obstacle than an asset to Eliab's education.

After an attempt on his life by the Ku Klux Klan forces Eliab to leave Red Wing, he travels North where he completes his education, immersed in that middle-class culture that he believed was such a necessary component of it. After receiving a college degree in the North, Eliab demonstrates the depth of his loyalty to Red Wing by turning down an opportunity to teach at "a colored school in one of the Northern states" and—like Adaline—returns home. A firm believer in the benefits of education, Tourgée concludes his novel with Eliab assuming the role of schoolmaster at Red Wing. Eliab does not have to fear violence anymore, but he finds that Mollie and the other teachers have gone with the collapse of the Reconstruction government and the people have returned to "the dull, plodding hopelessness of the old slave time."[106]

As he settles down to work toward the advancement of his people, Eliab achieves a final reconciliation with Mollie. He is glad when he learns that Mollie has continued her work of educating African Americans as a missionary in Kansas. Assuming that she probably regretted having "ever been a teacher in a colored school," he writes to thank her for her efforts at Red Wing and to explain himself.[107] He sums up his intellectual journey since discovering the path to black self-reliance:

> I now see, more clearly than ever before, that we must not only make *ourselves* free, but must overcome all that prejudice which slavery created against our race in the hearts of the white people. It is a long way to look ahead, and I don't wonder that so many despair of its ever being accomplished. I know it can only be done through the attainment of knowledge and the power which that gives. . . . I think that the Lord has dealt with me as he has in order that I might be willing to stay here and help them, and share with them the blessed knowledge which kind friends have given to me.[108]

Tourgée's denouement implies that the future of cultural uplift for Southern blacks rests with educated blacks like Eliab rather than white missionaries like Mollie.

Bricks Without Straw may encapsulate the personal conclusions Tourgée drew from his experience as a participant in cultural Reconstruction. Anticipating Du Bois's strategy of the "talented tenth," or the National

Association of Colored Women's slogan "Lifting As We Climb," Tourgée looked to the educated African American elite as the best agents of cultural uplift. In this, he recognized the inherent racial tension within the white "civilizing" mission and the preference of blacks for ownership of their own education. Perhaps he even endorsed the desire of black leaders to forge their own definition and standards of civilization that were not restricted to Euro-American tradition. The exercise of individual autonomy by the fictional Eliab Hill and the real Adaline Patillo, which did not fully conform to the expectations of their white tutors, was evidence of that desire. Each broke free of white control and exercised their own self-determination by focusing on improving the lives of their own family and community. *Bricks Without Straw* suggests that Tourgée recognized this and approved.

THE COLLAPSE

The Republican ascendancy in North Carolina was remarkably short-lived. In the fall elections of 1870, the Conservatives regained majority control of the State Assembly largely because of the intimidation of Republican voters who stayed away from the polls in districts where Klan activity had been high. Then, in 1871, W.W. Holden became the first governor in American history to be successfully impeached. All of Holden's "crimes" were derived from his vigorous prosecution of the Klan; in particular, his suspension of habeas corpus in Alamance and Caswell counties that had overstepped his expressed constitutional powers. Though Holden's successor, another moderate Republican, would hold onto the executive office until 1876, the progress of Reconstruction in the state ground to a screeching halt.[109]

The events that led to Holden's downfall began with the murders of two of Tourgée's close associates. On February 26, 1870, a gang of Ku Klux Klansmen seized Wyatt Outlaw, a black leader, and lynched him from a tree that stood just outside the Alamance County Courthouse, where Tourgée held court. A Union veteran and the president of the Union League of Alamance, Outlaw had been one of the most respected black Republican leaders, and his murder shocked his community.[110] Then, in what would be remembered by some as "one of the most atrocious political murders on record," John Walter Stephens, now a state senator, was assassinated in the basement of his own courthouse in neighboring Caswell County on May 21.[111] The effort by law enforcement to bring the killers of both men to justice led to an escalating cycle of intimidation and retaliatory murders against witnesses by Klan members. In response, Holden suspended the writ of habeas corpus in Alamance and Caswell and send a militia force of three hundred men under the command of Colonel George W. Kirk to round up suspects.

Before Kirk's forces could arrive, Tourgée was due to hold his circuit court in Alamance in June 1870. "You should not hold the Court at Alamance," Governor Holden advised him, admonishing, "You would be in personal danger to do so." Some of Holden's advisers, however, suggested that it would be admitting defeat if he did not go, and one remarked to Tourgée that he knew his personal safety would not be a concern for him, "though it would be with any other."[112] This remark was perfectly calculated. Briefly torn by indecision, Tourgée decided to hold court, reasoning that not to do so would undermine the legitimacy of the law.

Fearing his own death, he wrote several letters to friends and politicians explaining the situation. He reported to Martin B. Anderson that the Klan had sentenced him to death, and informed him with "notices of the time appointed, a coffin placed at my door, a paper pinned to the gate with a knife stating that I had been doomed . . . and etc. etc. I still live but really do consider the tenure very precarious."[113] To U.S. Senator Joseph C. Abbott he made a poignant and well-reasoned appeal for federal action against the Klan. "Our friend John W. Stephens, State Senator from Caswell, is dead," Tourgée informed him. Calling Stephens a "brave" and "honest" Republican, he wrote:

> Warned of danger, and fully cognizant of the terrible risk which surrounded him, he still manfully refused to quit the field . . . he was accustomed to say that 3,000 poor, ignorant, colored Republican voters in that county had stood by him and elected him, at the risk of persecution and starvation, and that he had no idea of abandoning them to the Ku-Klux.[114]

After describing in great detail the criminal activities of the Klan in the region, Tourgée intimated that he was prepared to follow his friend's example. "My steps have been dogged for months," he wrote:

> I have little doubt that I shall be one of its next victims . . . and with this conviction I say to you plainly that any member of Congress who, especially if from the South, does not support, advocate, and urge immediate, active, and thorough measures to put an end to these outrages . . . deserves to be damned.[115]

Deeply affected by Tourgée's letter, Abbott showed it to many colleagues on Capitol Hill, where it may have had some influence.[116] In it, Tourgée

also made a forceful case that the Fourteenth Amendment had unquestioningly empowered the federal government to intervene in state affairs
in order to protect citizen's rights, and he proposed several measures
to counter the Klan, one of which would ordain that "going armed and
masked or disguised in the night time, an act of insurrection or sedi-
tion."[117] The first Federal Enforcement Act, or anti-KKK Act, already
under debate, would be passed shortly afterward enacting just such a law.
The following year, Tourgée would be called to Washington to consult
with the congressional investigators into the "Klan conspiracy." Though
he did not officially testify before the Joint Congressional Committee,
he advised them on their investigative strategy and on June 13, 1871, was
given a private audience at the White House with President Grant, who
almost certainly had been shown Tourgée's letter the previous year. No
account of their conversation survives, but Tourgée was so impressed by
Grant that he became utterly convinced of his intention to support equal
rights in the South—a faith that would remain unshaken even through
Grant's wavering second term in office.[118]

But, all of this would come months later. The immediate impact of his
letter to Abbott was not quite so triumphant. Somehow Tourgée managed
to survive his court session in Alamance without incident, but he faced
new trouble when his letter to Abbott made its way into the hands of the
New York Tribune's editors. Its publication on August 3, 1870, in the
nation's most widely read newspaper sparked a furor across the state
reminiscent of the fallout from his speech at the 1866 Philadelphia convention. Conservatives charged him with having exaggerated the facts,
and their editorial outcries unleashed a new torrent of threats, both overt
and covert, with demands for retraction from all directions.[119] Tourgée
stood by what he had written, although, according to him, the *Tribune*
had enhanced a few statistics cited in his letter: four arsons had become
fourteen, and 400 to 500 break-ins had become 4,000 to 5,000. Tourgée
suspected his letter had been doctored before it had been passed to
the *Tribune*.[120] Once again, the controversy over the precise accuracy
of his statements obscured the fact that the break-ins, whippings, arsons,
castrations, rapes, and murders he described were perpetrated at an
alarming rate by masked gangs who continued to evade capture and
prosecution.

In response to the publication of his letter, the *Greensboro Patriot*
sneered: "Judge Tourgee resides with his family in this city, and if there
has ever been an attempt on his life, or even a *threat*, we have yet to hear
it."[121] Though it stopped short of providing directions to his house, the
Patriot's rebuff sounded more like a challenge to the still-rampaging Klan
than a denial of their activities. Friends and family were now begging

Albion to quit the South. "What in thunder [is] the use of staying there any longer?" wrote Joe Warner from Ohio, exasperated with Tourgée for having gone to Alamance against his advice:

> Let business go to the d-d, or someone may send you there. Just you pack your duds[,] take Emma on your arm and make a straight "shirt tail" for the North . . . we are all very anxious to hear from you. I couldn't sleep the night I got your letter . . . how I wished I had hold of your collar. I would have jerked you out of that infernal hole quicker'n lightning could scorch feathers.[122]

A friend from Erie also insisted, "do not fail to come stay with us and let some of the natives fight the KK's for a while."[123] Uncharacteristically, even Albion began to consider beating a strategic retreat.

For her part, an expecting Emma desperately wished to return to Erie, at least until the danger passed. "If I don't go my wife will die of hysteria at my first prolonged absence from home," Albion told a friend, "and I would not have her suffer as she does now."[124] Torn between his compulsion to stand "manfully" against the Klan as Stephens had done, and his duty to his pregnant wife and family (and perhaps, his desire to live), Tourgée hatched a brilliant compromise. He would quietly attain a diplomatic appointment that would take him out of the country for a while. In this way, he would not be entirely abandoning his allies or acting cowardly. He told Senator Abbott that a foreign appointment might allow him "to get away from KKK cords and daggers for a year or two. I am not giving up my grip but just let go to get a new hold."[125] When he learned that a position as minister to Peru was available, he lobbied for it aggressively. Courting the support of Thomas Settle, he wrote, "I would rather go to South America than elsewhere, as I am proficient in Spanish and could make out better there."[126] But he chose the wrong man to lobby for him. Soon afterward, Settle himself was offered the Peru ministry, and he accepted it.[127]

As with other crises that had come in North Carolina, Tourgée outlasted this one. The Klan began to dissipate as many of its members were arrested or held without charges, while, at the same time, a sweeping electoral victory by the Democrats in August lessened the perceived need for further terrorism. As public attention turned toward the movement to impeach Governor Holden in the fall of 1870, the threats receded. This did not prevent Emma, however, from escaping with her newborn child to Erie in December of that year, as previously discussed.

Though he conveniently forgot having done so, Tourgée once had encouraged Holden to take whatever measures necessary to save the Republic from "defeat, ruin and disgrace," even at the risk of his own impeachment, urging him that bold action would make Holden a hero to his party.[128] Now even Tourgée turned against Holden. Feeling that Holden, whom he long distrusted, had botched the prosecution of the Klan by holding them in military rather than civil courts, Tourgée joined in the abuse heaped upon his former ally. He even accused Holden of having doctored his letter to Abbott and giving it to the *Tribune*. "We have had enough of Holden," a Republican confrere agreed with Tourgée, "if we ever expect to regain the State we must drop him."[129] The Republican coalition was crumbling.

After Holden's ousting from office, North Carolina Republicans began six years of conciliatory policies in an effort to temper the forces of reaction. Though Conservatives were anxious to roll back the revolution, their ability to do so was limited by a significant Republican minority and the popularity of most of the Republican constitutional reforms. In 1875, for instance, when Conservatives succeeded in calling a new convention to amend the 1868 constitution, they managed to elect only a threadbare majority of delegates. Again Tourgée was an outspoken participant, but this time he assumed a defensive posture in leading the Republican attempt to block any revision of their 1868 work. Despite much drama and fanfare, the convention adjourned, having done little more than to inscribe into the Constitution the already existing legislation that enforced school segregation and banned interracial marriage, as well as to modify the township system to reduce local political control. Otherwise, the 1868 civil, judicial, educational, penal, and suffrage reforms were fundamentally preserved.[130]

In 1874, Tourgée passed up an opportunity to sell off his assets, and leave the state when his six-year judicial term had expired. Instead, he persisted for almost a year in searching for a local position until he finally attained appointment by President Grant himself to become federal pension officer in Raleigh. Despite the drastic lowering of his status, he accepted the position, explaining to a Northern correspondent, "I *like* living here." Having worked so hard to reform the state, he found it now impossible to sever his connection to it. "I have strung so many sweet hopes and bright dreams here that I seem almost to have knit my heart into the land," he later told Emma.[131]

When Tourgée packed up his Greensboro home to move to Raleigh, quite a few residents of the town were not sad to see him go. One of them, a fourteen-year-old named William Sydney Porter (later to become a famous author under the pseudonym "O. Henry"), published a sardonic sketch of the judge. Depicting Tourgée as a bird of prey taking leave with nothing but the carpetbag he brought with him, and a handkerchief to catch the tears falling from his one good eye, Porter cast Tourgée as a pathetic and defeated figure. But if Porter's ridicule was meant to suggest total victory over "carpetbagger rule," he underestimated the impact of the Reconstruction years. The seeds of equal citizenship had been planted, and whatever the future of race relations in North Carolina, there would be no returning to the world of 1865.

O. Henry's sketch of Tourgée, ca. 1875. Courtesy of The Greensboro Public Library.

PART III

The Counterrevolution

6

The Politics of Remembering Reconstruction

The Southerner will regularly bring forward the horrors of the
Reconstruction governments and "black domination." These
memories are in a sense to be cherished. They serve as a vital
defensive function to the white South . . . [that] needs to
believe that when the Negro voted, life was unbearable.
The myth of the horrors of Reconstruction . . . are, in our
terminology, false beliefs with a purpose.

—Gunnar Myrdal, *An American Dilemma*, 1944

So the South cursed "carpetbaggers," because they were of
the North; and the North cursed them because the South set
the example . . . not knowing whom it denounced, and not
pausing to inquire whether they were worthy of stripes or not.

—Albion W. Tourgée, *A Fool's Errand*, 1879

PUBLISHED IN 1879, *A Fool's Errand* was one of the first shots fired in
a struggle over the historical meaning of Reconstruction and the
political lessons to be drawn from it. Had he not written *A Fool's
Errand*, Albion Tourgée would likely have disappeared into history like
most other Republicans who survived a career on the front lines of
Reconstruction. The unexpected success of this book, however, catapulted
him to national fame and launched a second career for Tourgée as a
political writer who was determined to keep the fires of Radical
Republicanism alive. What is most surprising about Tourgée's success
with *A Fool's Errand* was that its argument ran counter to the Conservative mythology of Reconstruction that had gained credence in the
Northern press in the mid 1870s. Tourgée's analysis of Reconstruction
became the subject of widespread discussion; it even influenced the 1880
Republican presidential platform. The reception of *A Fool's Errand*

indicates that, in spite of the government's withdrawal from Reconstruction, the public meaning given to its history was far from settled. Radicalism may have waned after the ratification of the Fifteenth Amendment, but the public sentiment that had supported Radicalism had not necessarily repudiated its work. Not yet.

The 1880s were a transitional decade in which the opportunity still existed for the federal government to promote black interests in the South by protecting the ballot box and allowing for modest progress in property ownership, education, and professional advancement. Race relations in the South remained somewhat in flux, if not to the degree C. Vann Woodward once postulated. It remained to be seen whether or not conditions would regress under long-term Democratic rule.[1] Often overlooked was the real possibility of a renewed intervention on behalf of black civil rights by the federal government, especially with regard to aid to public schools in the South. How Reconstruction was remembered would play a vital role in determining all future policies toward the South, and Tourgée's was a powerful voice of vindication for the Radical approach.

THE END OF THE DREAM

While assassination and intimidation did their work well, the Conservative propaganda machine probably inflicted the most long-lasting damage on the Republican Party in the South. As Reconstruction unraveled, Northerners had to choose whether the cause of social turmoil in the South was primarily the result of black "misrule," as Southerners claimed, or white racism, as Southern Republicans insisted. But, exaggerated stories of "carpetbagger-scalawag-negro" misrule were accepted by many Northern editors and politicians virtually without question by the mid 1870s. Horace Greeley, the once-Radical editor of the *New York Tribune*, had been among the first Northerners to uncritically accept the Conservative viewpoint. After touring the South in 1871 and meeting almost exclusively with white planters, Greeley returned deeply influenced by their viewpoint. Greeley issued the single most influential Northern indictment of carpetbaggers, proclaiming:

> The thieving carpet-baggers are a mournful fact; they do exist there, and I have seen them. They are fellows who crawled down South in the track of our armies . . . [who] at once ingratiated themselves with the blacks, simple, credulous, ignorant men, very glad to welcome and to follow any whites who professed to be champions of their rights.[2]

Voted into office by blacks, Greeley claimed, the carpetbaggers immediately began "disgracing" the Republican Party by "stealing and plundering" the riches of the Southern states by excessive taxation. Amazingly, he attributed the rise of the Ku Klux Klan and everything else that had plagued the South under Reconstruction to the malevolent influence of Northern carpetbaggers, concluding: *"They are the greatest obstacle to the triumph and permanent ascendancy of Republican principles at the South, and as such I denounce them."*[3]

Using "corruption" as an opening to attack Ulysses S. Grant's Reconstruction policies, a group of Republicans revolted from the party in 1872 and launched a presidential campaign under the banner of "Liberal Republicanism," choosing Horace Greeley as their candidate. Greeley's 1872 campaign, which focused particularly on opposing the policies of Reconstruction, exposed a rift within the Republican Party over the limits of federal power that would eventually paralyze Reconstruction efforts. His campaign witnessed a revival of states-rights constitutionalism in the North, and rehearsed laissez-faire arguments increasingly heard among powerful Northern intellectuals that couched themselves in the Darwinian rhetoric of "survival of the fittest." Greeley himself notoriously declared during the campaign that the time had come for freedmen to "Root, Hog or Die" without assistance from the national government. Though his campaign was an embarrassing failure, it presaged the shape of things to come in Northern thinking about Reconstruction. After weathering the Liberal Republican challenge, Grant was noticeably more cautious about his support for Reconstruction during his second term.[4]

Following a disappointing four years under Grant, the elections of 1877—marked by a tidal wave of fraud and disputed returns in three Southern states that were unresolved for months—brought Tourgée to new depths of despair and disillusionment. When the dust cleared, his friend Thomas Settle, back from Peru, was defeated in the epic North Carolina gubernatorial race of 1876, ending the nine-year Republican hold on the executive branch in the state.[5] Former Confederate Governor Zebulon B. Vance took office in the spring of 1877 as newly elected President Rutherford B. Hayes simultaneously announced his "let alone" policy toward the South. Patronage for Southern Republicans seemed unlikely as Hayes declared the beginning of a new era and promised to reach out to Southern Democrats. Tourgée personally lost his position as pension agent, his main source of dependable income since 1874. Following Hayes's inaugural address, Radical die-hard Wendell Phillips exclaimed in disgust, "Half of what Grant gained for us at Appomattox, Hayes surrendered in Washington on the 5th of March." "No, the epoch has not ended," he predicted, "the battle is only adjourned."[6]

One month after Hayes's inauguration, the disputed governorship of South Carolina was awarded by default to ex-Confederate general Wade Hampton. President Hayes's refusal to take sides in the electoral dispute or protect the Republican incumbent, Daniel Chamberlain, with federal troops allowed Hampton to take the governor's mansion by force. His victory represented the triumph of naked violence and fraud over "black Republican" rule, as Hampton's Red Shirts had suppressed enough votes from the state's numerical black majority to assure his victory. Echoing Wendell Phillips, Tourgée rued the bitter irony of what he considered a betrayal of the Union cause in the Civil War. "On the 9th of April 1865 Lee surrendered to the army of the United States, because the people of the United States were determined that a lawful majority should rule," he wrote to Martin B. Anderson. "On the 9th of April 1877, Chamberlain surrender[ed] to Hampton because it was unlawful to use the army of the United States to hold in check or put down a lawless minority!"[7] But Phillips's and Tourgée's dissent from Hayes's "let alone" policy was drowned in the chorus of approval from the Democratic and moderate Republican press.

Reports of the return to peace and tranquility in the South began flowing out of the Conservative press. Later that same April, an old friend wrote to Tourgée from Brooklyn, New York, conveying his belief that the "times are getting better there" and "prospects are brightening" in the South thanks to President Hayes's new policy. Tourgée angrily replied: "[Don't be] such a fool as to believe that everything [is] all lovely and serene at the south mere[ly] because somebody chattered about a new policy . . . [in] all of that time I have lived here yet I have never seen an hour when political bitterness has been so intense and hostility to Northern men so fierce as it is today."[8] Interestingly, Tourgée regarded President Hayes as a true "lover of liberty" and "a fair exponent of the mind and heart of the North," who had been tragically misled by the Conservative misinformation campaign. Had he understood the true conditions of the South, he believed, Hayes would never have followed such a terrible path. "It is not a matter of *policies* . . . it is a question of *facts*," he lamented, "The same old clan who *lied* for *two* generations about slavery—systematically, deliberately, and continuously—are [now] the only ones who can be believed."[9]

After a sleepless night two months later, Tourgée rose one Sunday morning with a sudden clarity about the situation. Waking Emma, he informed her: "I am going to write a book and call it 'A Fool's Errand.'"[10] Drawing from his own experiences, he would vindicate Southern Republicans and open the eyes of Northerners to the true circumstances regarding the overthrow of Reconstruction. In a burst of inspiration, he wrote the first four chapters that Sunday, only to put aside the project. Perhaps a gnawing feeling of the futility of the effort overtook him. It would be eighteen months before he returned to it.[11]

In the meantime, Tourgée busied himself with other writing projects, including a series of controversial political letters published under the initial C that excoriated North Carolina's Democratic leaders. The "C" letters were hailed as "masterful," and their author praised for his "genius," "learning," and "remarkable intellectual resources."[12] Tourgée was not yet ready to let go of North Carolina politics. Protected by his anonymity, he enjoyed in helping to undermine an old nemesis, David Schenck, in his bid for a Supreme Court nomination and in watching other Democratic leaders squirm under his withering commentaries. Buoyed by the unexpected success of this venture in attack journalism, he answered the Republican Party's call for a congressional candidate in 1878. It turned out to be his final stand against counter-revolution in North Carolina.[13]

The campaign of 1878 was a disaster for him both personally and politically. Realizing that he was no more than a sacrificial lamb, Emma refused to support his congressional run, to Albion's great dismay. His nomination prompted her final return to Erie in August 1878, taking Aimée with her.[14] That Emma's absence kept Albion disturbed and distracted is documented by the steady stream of letters he wrote to her complaining that her departure was hampering his ability to conduct the campaign and might cost him the election. His letters oscillated wildly between unrealistic hopes of victory and morbid self-pity. One stated: "Oh, my Darling, why did I ever bring you here to experience sorrow. How happy we should have been if we had remained in Erie. I do think it was the greatest mistake of my mistaken life." Predicting his own assassination, he concluded, "I do not think I shall live long."[15] Though he wisely moderated his rhetoric during the campaign, sticking largely to a defense of "hard" currency and avoiding racial issues, his efforts were futile. With his crushing defeat in November, failing to win even a single district, he spiraled further into a depression. "Why did I not die in the campaign? Why did I not die years ago?" he moaned.[16]

The novel that would bring Tourgée his greatest fame and success was written at perhaps his lowest point in a life full of extreme highs and lows. Secluding himself in his Greensboro home and working eighteen-hour days, he chained himself to the task of completing three unfinished books, including *A Fool's Errand*. His letters to Emma were infrequent during this intense period of seclusion, and he described being driven to the verge of "insanity" and struggling with his "old depression." But the act of writing *A Fool's Errand* had a therapeutic effect. Emerging from his study in January 1879, Albion triumphantly announced to Emma, "I have got over the shock of the past and am as full of determination as ever. I knew that if I did not tie myself down to this work I should die—give up and die of the shocks of disappointment. I am over it now."[17]

Having finished his books, Tourgée negotiated a reconciliation with Emma, reaching a protracted compromise about their future. Unable to endure the "humiliation" of returning to Erie, he told Emma, "I hate Erie about as much as you do N.C." and proposed instead that they follow Greeley's old advice to "go West."[18] Emma agreed to relocate to Denver, where an opportunity for Albion to become a partner at a law firm had materialized. "I have won back my wife, never to lose her heart or confidence again, for one moment, with God's help," he confirmed, and announced to Emma, "hereafter *we two* must be of *one mind*, thoroughly and positively."[19] Only forty-one years old, Tourgée left North Carolina at last and expected, by all indications, that the dramatic years of Reconstruction would be thereafter a closed chapter in his life.

THE POLITICS OF *A FOOL'S ERRAND*

Published anonymously as *A Fool's Errand By One of the Fools*, his novel appeared in print in November 1879 with no fanfare and little expectation of success. Tourgée seemed more hopeful about another recently finished novel, *Figs and Thistles: A Romance of the Western Reserve*, that had preceded *A Fool's Errand* into print in October. He deemed *Figs and Thistles*, the story of a young man's rise from humble origins during the Civil War, worthy of being shopped to the more prestigious publishing houses, including Harper & Brothers. But when he returned to his old publishers, Fords, Howard & Hulbert, with the rejected manuscript, he simply offered *A Fool's Errand* with it. Within six weeks of its publication *A Fool's Errand* had sold 5,281 copies; by June it was a runaway best-seller with 43,653 copies sold. "No book on the shop counter sells better and the fame of it has been carried on the wings of newspapers into every state if not county in the land," the *New York Tribune* declared.[20] Speculation over its authorship fueled public interest in the volume, with Tourgée's name mentioned along with better known carpetbagger politicians like Daniel Chamberlain and Adelbert Ames. Some even believed it the handiwork of that most successful of political novelists, Harriet Beecher Stowe.[21]

With glowing reviews that declared the unknown author "the long-looked-for native American novelist who is to rival Dickens, and equal Thackeray" and "the Victor Hugo of America," it was evident that another world was opening itself to him.[22] The Tourgées were hardly settled into their new home in Denver when Edward Ford, of Fords, Howard & Hulbert, arrived at the Tourgées' door to discuss contracting Albion to publish more volumes for his firm. Ford convinced him to return to New York to prepare a second edition of *A Fool's Errand*, in which he would reveal his identity and supply an appendix of evidentiary support to vouch for the novel's historical accuracy. As word of his authorship spread, Tourgée ensconced himself as a celebrity among New York City's leading Republicans and mixed with the cultural elite. He especially frequented the Union League Club, which would hold a dinner in his honor in 1881.[23] Within a year, the Tourgées sold their property in Denver and took an apartment near Union Square in New York City, where, at the urging of his publishers, he began work on a second book that addressed the same theme.[24]

Anointed the successor to Stowe, he soon became acquainted with the great political writer herself and was invited to Stowe's annual birthday celebration, where he mingled with a distinguished list of attendees that included Fredrick Douglass, Oliver Wendell Holmes, John Whittier, William Dean Howells, and Henry Ward Beecher.[25] Judging from its reviews, *A Fool's Errand* had tapped into a growing discontent with Hayes's Southern policy—which had been proven a disaster by 1879—and uncovered a lingering sympathy for the original goals of Reconstruction. Nearly all of its commentators remarked upon the novel's political message, and several believed it possessed the potential to revive Northern intervention in the South. "If every representative and senator in Congress were given the book," one New York reviewer remarked, "we should be nearer a solution of the problem of reconstruction."[26] *The Nation*, normally at slumber on Southern issues, proclaimed of its message, "this Macbeth doth murder sleep!"[27]

Southern Republicans, buoyed by its vindication of their part in Reconstruction, wrote to the publishers offering to peddle it to their colleagues in the South, where most bookstores refused to carry it. "I think [it] will do our Southern Cause much good," Northern missionary John Emery Bryant wrote to his wife. "Judge Tourgee is a very able man . . . the book will do great good because it will turn the Northern mind to the subject, and will, I think help to arrest the attention of the Northern people."[28] Many Southern editors fearfully agreed. The *Raleigh Observer*, for instance, called it "a powerfully written work . . . destined, we fear, to do as much harm in the world as 'Uncle Tom's Cabin,' to which it is, indeed, a companion piece."[29]

Unlike Harriet Beecher Stowe, Tourgée wrote from direct personal experience. "The one merit which the story claims," he announced in the preface, "is that of honest, uncompromising, truthfulness of portraiture.

Its pictures are from life."[30] His careful adherence to the historical record is demonstrated by the well-documented evidence of Tourgée's own experience. The most significant incidents of the book are taken from actual events. The lynching of the character Jerry Hunt matches that of Wyatt Outlaw in exact detail, and John Walter Stephens is memorialized in the life and death of the character John Walters. The many letters and newspaper accounts included in the novel are based on those in Tourgée's own letter book and scrapbooks.[31]

The emotional power and pathos of the story are derived from the reader's sympathy with the Fool's righteous cause, and the terrible sense of injustice the reader experiences by the manner of its downfall. The protagonist of the novel, Comfort Servosse, is made into a "fool," not because his beliefs are foolish, but because the Republican leaders in Washington abandon him and his Southern Republican compatriots to the wolves when faced with determined opposition. Servosse is no Radical. Tourgée fashioned his character to appeal to the widest possible Northern audience. A "broken down" Union veteran, he relocates to North Carolina for health reasons and naively believes—in accord with the advice of his esteemed mentor, Dr. Enos Martin—that the South would be rapidly transformed by the introduction of free labor. From the moment of his arrival in the South, he is impressed by the loyalty of poor white Unionists who bravely resisted the Confederacy during the war, and he is amazed by the rapid acquisition of property and education by the freedpeople. Reluctant at first to support universal black suffrage, Servosse converts to Radical measures only as he comes to appreciate the depth of planter opposition to the modest and peaceful advancement of the freedpeople and poor whites.[32]

Though most of the novel's scenes are adapted directly from events in Tourgée's life, A Fool's Errand cannot properly be called a fictionalized autobiography. Servosse sometimes speaks Tourgée's views, but he is not Tourgée. Rather the omniscient narrator of the story, who maintains a broader perspective on events than Servosse, consistently offers Tourgée's own commentary on events freely using the advantage of hindsight. The narrator describes the architects of Reconstruction with scathing sarcasm as the "Wise Men" and depicts their plan as a cynical mixture of "party necessity and political insincerity." According to his view, the Wise Men should have listened to tough-minded leaders like Thaddeus Stevens, who—along with Tourgée's protagonist, Servosse—concluded that "the North is simply a conqueror [and] she must rule as a conqueror."[33] Like many modern historians, Tourgée believed that Republicans in Congress ultimately bowed too much to the voices of caution and conservatism for fear of alienating their moderate constituents.

The primary flaw of Congressional Reconstruction, as represented in *A Fool's Errand*, is that it turned over the administration of Reconstruction to the state governments too quickly, not realizing that the white South would oppose a government based on a black electorate with a ferocity matching that of Lee's Army. Congress secured equal rights in law, but it failed to provide any means to ensure that these rights would be respected once their possessors tried to exercise them. It had falsely assumed that the ballot box alone would automatically protect black interests by forcing Southern whites to court black electoral support. Tourgée presents the Radical plan as one that "neither shirked nor temporized" but rather struck at the root of the evils. The plan would have abolished the former Confederate States altogether, allowing them to "molder in the grave of rebellion—the bed they had themselves prepared."[34] In their place, he suggests:

> [The South] should be divided up into Territories without regard to their former statal [*sic*] lines, and so remain for a score of years under national control, but without power to mold or fashion the national legislation—until time should naturally and thoroughly have healed the breaches of the past, till commerce had become re-established, and the crude ideas of the present had been clarified by the light of experience.[35]

This radical reorganization of the South, it should be noted, is offered as an alternative to building Reconstruction on the foundation of universal black manhood suffrage. By making the South truly "prostrate" before the federal government (as opposed to a perceived black majority), this plan would have brought about gradual change and allowed the use of whatever force was necessary to achieve the assimilation of former slaves into the body politic.

One of the themes of *A Fool's Errand* was that the North and the South had been "two divergent civilizations." Failure to appreciate the cultural chasm between Northern and Southern political cultures, especially, had doomed Reconstruction to failure. As Tourgée explained to one admirer, "I am glad that you so fully appreciate the lesson of 'A Fool's Errand.' I think the struggle which it feebly shadows forth, between two conflicting civilizations[,] is the great question of the near future. If the work shall awaken the country to this fact the author will feel well repaid for whatever it may have cost him."[36] At the heart of this conflict are two irreconcilable attitudes regarding the relationship between race and democratic citizeship.

In one of the most important passages in *A Fool's Errand*, Tourgée illuminates the Northern viewpoint on race:

> The South was right in believing that the North cared little or nothing for the negro *as a man* but wrong in the idea that the theory of political

equality or manhood suffrage were invented or imposed from any thought
of malice, revenge, or envy toward the South . . . the idea that "of one blood
are all of the nations of the earth," and that "race, color, or previous condition of servitude" can not be allowed to effect the legal or political rights
of any *was* a living principle in the Northern mind, as little capable of
suppression as the sentiment of race-antagonism by which it was met.[37]

Here Tourgée explains the coexistence of racism and egalitarianism in
Protestant, middle-class Northern thought. Though misleadingly he uses
the word *Northern* when he refers only to the middle-class, Protestant element of it, his insight is nevertheless persuasive. The antislavery culture
of Tourgée's youth espoused the moral principle that every individual
should have the opportunity for self-improvement and advancement,
regardless of gender, color, or creed. To deny this to any class would be
a sin. But "equality of opportunity" was also no guarantee of success.
Whatever middle-class Northerners believed about the inherent capac-
ities of black people, Tourgée insisted, few would deny their *right* to all
of the benefits of citizenship. This was an important concession, even if
many Northerners suspected that—all things being equal—blacks were
destined to fail on their own merits anyway. Indeed, many were quick to
conclude afterward that blacks had been given an opportunity during
Reconstruction and proven themselves incapable as citizens.

A *Fool's Errand* showed that blacks had been given no such opportunity. The racial ideology of the South would not tolerate equal rights for
blacks in theory or in fact. Servosse composes a letter to "one of the wisest
of the Wise Men" in the U.S. Senate (perhaps Ben Wade or Charles
Sumner), in which he explains that Congress had vastly underestimated
the depths of planter race-prejudice. "You say that the *interest* of the
Southern leading classes will compel them to accept and carry out in
good faith your reconstructionary [*sic*] plan," but Servosse warns him that
no amount of reason or self-interest can overcome Southern hostility
to black advancement. "This utter and thorough disgust and scorn for the
race—except in what they consider its proper place—[is] a feeling more
fatal to any thing like democratic recognition of their rights as citizens
than the most undying hate could be," he explains. Northerners could
hardly fathom this feeling: "Hate is a sentiment mild and trivial compared
with it."[38]

A *Fool's Errand* depicted the cultural conflict between North and
South as a struggle between individualism and free speech on one side
and political censorship and oligarchy on the other. The appeal of the
Klan was merely symptomatic, in his view, of the continuing hegemony
of landowning families over poor whites—whose support had been
necessary to sustain slavery. Political power in the South, he lamented,

rested upon "the influence of family position, social rank, or political prominence" whereas in the North it resulted from the quality of one's ideas and the force of one's arguments. "Leadership," he observed, "in the sense of a blind, unquestioning following of a man, without his being the peculiar exponent of an idea, is a thing almost unknown in the North: at the South it is a power."[39]

Servosse discovers that public discussion among blacks and poor whites were confined to secret political meetings held in "that refuge of free thought at the South, the woods."[40] When the carpetbagger Servosse tries to bring this political discussion into the public sphere, his life is immediately endangered. "The Southern man is by habit and training intolerant," Tourgée explained in a *New York Tribune* interview. "Evidence of good will, sympathy, identity of interest are all disregarded as soon as the outsider expresses a difference of opinion."[41] The South simply lacked the fundamental building blocks of democratic culture. Near the end of the novel, he observes, "the men who engaged in . . . these acts [Ku Klux Klan violence] were simply no better and no worse than their surroundings and training made them."[42] Northern-style democracy could not take root until the proper soil was prepared.

Education, Tourgée believed, would not only provide upward social mobility, it would eventually ameliorate class and racial friction through cultural assimilation. He insists that the entire nation, not only the South, protected and fostered slavery and thus should bear the moral responsibility to make amends. "Make the spelling-book the scepter of national power," Servosse suggests to his mentor Dr. Martin:

> Let the Nation educate the colored man and the poor-white man *because* the Nation held them in bondage, and is responsible for their education; educate the voter *because* the Nation can not afford that he should be ignorant. . . . Let it educate those whom it made ignorant, and protect those whom it made weak."[43]

Significantly, he includes both poor whites and blacks as victims of slavery. Tourgée realized that the culture of slavery had created a ruling class that excluded poor whites, as well as blacks, from the means to power and demanded political servility from both.

The public school could be a culturally nationalizing force—teaching Southerners democratic values and the virtues of a capitalist, free labor system. Cognizant that public education presents a challenge to their hegemony, Servosse warns that the planters are adamantly opposed to it: "the South—that *pseudo* South which has the power—does not wish this thing to be done to her people and will oppose it with might and main." It "must be an act of [National] sovereignty, an exercise of power."

Servosse concludes, "whether the State-Rights Moloch stand in the way, or not."[44] Just as it once served to prevent federal interference with slavery, Tourgée argued, the "States-Rights Moloch" now was employed simply to prevent federal interference with racial oppression. "This demon required a million lives before he would permit slavery to be abolished," Servosse observes, pondering how "many more would induce him to let the fettered souls [of the freedpeople] be unbound and made free."[45]

A Fool's Errand directly challenged the efforts of the Liberal Republicans to make scapegoats of Southern Republicans by putting the blame for Reconstruction's shortcomings at the feet of Northern Republicans. "We Republicans of the South will go down with the reconstruction movement," Servosse tells one of the Wise Men, but he says they will not accept the responsibility: "That will rest now and for all time with the Republican party of the North—a party the most cowardly, vacillating, and inconsistent . . . that has ever been known in any government."[46] Tourgée reserves special contempt for Liberal Republicans, such as Greeley, who uncritically accepted the Conservative propaganda about carpetbaggers. He mused:

> Perhaps there is no other instance in history in which the conquering power has discredited its own agents, denounced those of its own blood and faith, espoused the prejudices of its conquered foes, and poured the vials of wrath and contempt upon the only class in the conquered territory who defended its acts, supported its policy, promoted its aim, or desired its preservation and continuance.[47]

The calculated lies of Southern planters were a natural and unavoidable tactic, but the acceptance of their viewpoints by Northern Republicans was incomprehensible.

In some of its most bitter passages, *A Fool's Errand* accuses Republicans of the North, among other things, of lacking manhood. "I begin to seriously fear that the North lacks virility," Servosse fumes. Returning to the appeals to masculinity that once rallied men like himself to enlist in the war in the first place, Tourgée implies that the "manhood" of Union veterans was once again being challenged by their old Confederate foes. The North has shown "sheer weakness" in its "cowardly shirking of responsibility" and its "sniffling whine about peace and conciliation," while the South has stolen back the fruits of their victory by showing manly determination and daring in pursuit of their aims.[48] The Ku Klux Klan was entirely a political organization, not an outlet for mere sadism or vengeance: "It was not the individual negro, scalawag or carpetbagger, against whom the blow was directed, but the power—the Government—the idea which they represented."[49] Instead of acting boldly in defense of their agents, the government adopted the weak social Darwinian rationale suggested by Greeley. Tourgée wrote, "[They] abandoned these parties like cocks in a pit, to fight out the question of predominance without the possibility of national interference. They said to the colored man, in the language of one of the pseudo-philosophers of that day, 'Root, hog, or die!' "[50] It was a disgraceful shirking of duty and responsibility.

Thus, *A Fool's Errand* encompassed an interpretation of history, a critique of policy, a challenge to Northern Republicans, and a specific proposal to renew Southern reform through nationalized education. The public response was illuminating.

THE PUBLIC RESPONSE

It is hazardous to generalize too much about the public reaction to *A Fool's Errand.* The book offered a perspective on the history of Reconstruction that seemed to take its readers by surprise: *powerful* is the most ubiquitous word its reviewers used to describe the effect, neither an endorsement nor a rejection, of its arguments. Though *Harper's Magazine* found it "one sided, but intensely earnest," other reviewers praised the book's "freedom from political rancor" and "spirit of fairness," and admired its "intensely realistic view of social life in the South."[51] "His trenchant sword cuts both ways," the *Erie Dispatch* wrote of the unknown author: "He does not spare the follies of his friends, nor fail to respect the honest prejudices of his foes."[52] The *Atlantic Monthly* reviewer wrote: "It is rare to find an author with wrongs before him like those which are portrayed in *A Fool's Errand,* who has the courage and the conscience to turn, so clearly as he does, the best side of the wrong-doer before one." Indeed many readers were drawn to Tourgée's portrait of Southern conservatives as products of a culture that trained them to be superior, proud, and defiant. The *Atlantic Monthly* concluded, "It is because this best side [of the Southerner] is in part the explanation of the wrong that the historical honesty of the book is forced upon the reader."[53]

Despite its defense of Radicalism, and that dozens of notices compared the book to *Uncle Tom's Cabin,* many Southerners commented favorably on the novel. One former Klan member suggested that much could be learned from *A Fool's Errand's* discussion of the Klan. "You would hardly expect a man thus detested and scorned by a people to be able to appreciate any of their good qualities," he added, with evident pride in Tourgée's depiction of the Klan. "But he does and this proves that he was himself far superior to ordinary carpetbaggers."[54] Cornelia Phillips

Spencer—a Conservative who once orchestrated Tourgée's removal from the University of North Carolina Board of Trustees—admitted in a private letter to her brother Charles: "I have just read Tourgee's 'A Fool's Errand.' It is very smart, & the only book on South and North that presents a true picture. He has done it very well & tells the truth as nearly as a C-bagger & a Tourgee could possibly be expected to do."[55]

While it unequivocally defended the cause of reform in the South, *A Fool's Errand* also gave a forceful expression to the feeling of disillusionment over the failure of Reconstruction. Some readers responded more favorably to its bitter sarcasm than its call for a renewed commitment to the "Northernizing" of the South. Starting with the title, irony was Tourgée's predominant narrative device. "The title of the book is a stroke of genius," the *Atlantic Monthly* remarked, "and throughout the book the irony of the name Fool is skillfully used." Tourgée played upon the fact that Reconstruction had been widely repudiated as "a fool's errand" for reasons other than those to which he ascribes in the novel. Embracing this phrase, he deliberately twists and defies his readers' expectations. Some, without having read it, jumped to their own conclusion about its political message, like one Northern schoolteacher in Virginia who wrote home: "Have you read Tourgee's *A Fool's Errand*? I think from all I hear of the book, it must be my own story of my life here in Virginia. How hopeless it seems ever to educate the Southerner up to Northern civilization!"[56]

As Tourgée's authorship became known, some Northern papers sent correspondents to Greensboro, where most residents confirmed that "the book did not exaggerate the facts at all."[57] Greensboro Conservatives, in fact, were reported to have taken great pride in Tourgée's description of their ferocious opposition to his political beliefs. "The feeling against the judge was quite as strong as had been represented," one reporter stated, but he was told nevertheless that "as a man and a judge Tourgee was and is still liked and respected by the intelligent class of people of this neighborhood."[58] One reporter who went to Greensboro hoping to discredit Tourgée came up rather empty, discovering only that Tourgée had sometimes missed his mortgage payments and revealing that he once cheated a "poor negro man" of his life savings, though no names or specifics are given. Asserting that the man had "died of a broken heart" after Tourgée failed to repay a loan that "represented the savings of a lifetime," the reporter used this story to make the point that "the poor negro has had to suffer . . . more from his professed friends than from his enemies."[59] The threadbare quality of this story merely underscores the inability of detractors to dig up damaging tales in North Carolina.

Other Southerners recognized the great ideological stakes involved in letting Tourgée's historical interpretation go unchallenged. The

Louisville Evening Post and News was among the first to register a dissent and proffer the outlines of a Conservative counterinterpretation. In order to boost its Southern sales, Fords, Howard & Hulbert confidently sent copies of *A Fool's Errand* to Southern editors, with a letter that quoted from newspaper reviews attesting to its impartiality. After pursuing the volume, however, the *Evening Post and News* editor responded that "an examination shows all such claims to be unfounded. It is eminently unfair, unjust, and untruthful; it perverts facts; it misrepresents sentiments; and it makes statements impossible for the author to substantiate." This editor went on to enumerate the omissions that skew Tourgée's historical portrait. "In this story we are not told that field hands were placed in the Legislature," he complained, nor did Tourgée mention that "men who could neither read nor write were elected Sheriffs and Constables." Finally, "there is no hint in these pages of the fact that a servile race just released from bondage, clothed with almost unlimited power, was guilty of any crime or disorder." Implicitly calling on Southerners to respond to its "distortions" of history, the article warned its readers: "'A Fool's Errand' is having a very wide sale in the North, and its misrepresentations are received as gospel truths by those who know nothing of the South."[60] This editor astutely perceived the necessity of reaching the Northern reading public to challenge any attempt to establish a dominant historical memory of Reconstruction that ran counter to the Conservative one.

Within five years, several books would be published responding directly to *A Fool's Errand* and challenging its overarching historical interpretation. Former editor of the *Virginia Commonwealth*, William L. Royall, offered the most comprehensive non-fictional response to it in his ninety-five-page *A Reply to 'A Fool's Errand, by One of the Fools'* (1880). Royall's attack dealt mostly in generalities that followed in the vein of the *Louisville Evening Post and News* except that it dredged up an old accusation that Tourgée had accepted a bribe from a notoriously corrupt railroad speculator in 1869. Tourgée explained this loan easily enough in a letter to the *New York Tribune* which, in turn, dismissed Royall's rants as having no substance except to declare *A Fool's Errand* "'false as hell'— a mode of reasoning which can hardly be called conclusive."[61] *A Fool's Errand* spawned responses from writers of fiction as well: a reissue of J. H. Ingraham's 1860 novel about a Northern abolitionist who is "converted" to proslavery views under a new title, *Not "A Fool's Errand": Life and Experience of a Northern Governess in the Sunny South* (1880); North Carolinian William Simpson Pearson's *Monon Ou; or, Well-nigh reconstructed, A political novel* (1882) included a parody of Tourgée himself as the scheming Judge Gaurdees; and finally, Virginian and ex-Confederate officer N.J. Floyd's sprawling six-hundred-page novel *Thorns in the Flesh: A Voice of Vindication from the South in Answer to "A Fool's Errand" and Other Slanders* (1884), which was touted in Southern papers as "a romance of closer adherence to reality and yet of greater and more thrilling power than 'Uncle Tom's Cabin' or 'A Fool's Errand.' "[62] Although none of these books received much notice, each of them rehearsed arguments that would become central to the reconciliation mythology concerning slavery, the Civil War, and Reconstruction.[63]

Of these books, Floyd's *Thorns in the Flesh* is the most significant because of its pioneering attempt to turn Tourgée's arguments back on themselves in literary form. A broad fictional portrait from a Conservative viewpoint, the novel contrasted markedly with the later portraits of novelists Thomas Nelson Page and Thomas Dixon. Agreeing with Tourgée that the North and South had been distinct civilizations, Floyd reversed the presumption behind Northern attempts to "uplift" the South by declaring of the Virginia planter class, "We possess a higher civilization—North as well as South—than was ever known to any people who engaged in civil strife on a large scale."[64] Though he decried slavery as a "necessary evil," Floyd spends the greater portion of his novel rehashing the old proslavery arguments that celebrated the attainments of Southern gentlemen over their coarse and rapacious Northern brethren.

For the most part, his glowing portrait of an unoffending—but much offended—Virginia gentry skips over the messy details of Reconstruction. In fact, the Ku Klux Klan make only a belated and somewhat apologetic appearance in the final pages of the novel. "Acts of violence that were not fully justified by the crimes committed, were perpetuated here and there, by mobs of persons styled 'Ku-Klux Klans,' acting under sudden impulses of outraged feelings," Floyd conceded, "as all Fools who did errands have testified and can testify."[65] Because he hailed from Virginia, where blacks never attained much political power and where the Klan had been nonexistent, perhaps, Floyd has relatively little to say about the heroism of the Klan or the supposed horrors of "black misrule" but much to say about the nobility of the Confederate "Lost Cause."[66] Blaming the North for all of the evils of the Civil War and its aftermath, he chose to focus his critique of Northern civilization on an interesting target. At the root of the sectional conflict, he argues, was that most uncharitable and overbearing moralizing that he defined as *Puritanism*.

According to *Thorns in the Flesh*, a fanatical "Puritan religionism" that had been "substituted for Christianity" in the North was responsible for "the different qualities of the two civilizations" between North and South. Puritans are shown by Floyd to be the true "negro-haters" whose slave ships brought blacks to America in the first place and who would now rather see the freedmen starve than be cared for by their paternalistic former masters. In a strangely apt blending of stereotypes, he defines the carpetbagger as "the Wandering Jew turned Puritan," come to exploit the devastated South. Tourgée himself is denounced in the preface as a "radical Puritan notoriety-seeker" who profits by abusing the South with his "clever witticisms or stinging sarcasms upon our humanity, Christianity, civilization, and social characteristics."[67] Because the concept of Puritanism is never specifically defined in the novel, except as a rough synonym for "hypocrisy," Floyd's historical analysis fails to achieve any real explanatory power. Unable to comprehend the Northern mindset except as motivated by a mysteriously malicious fanaticism, his counter-punch to *A Fool's Errand* ultimately falls flat. In many ways *Thorns in the Flesh* even confirms Tourgée's portrait of the planter class. Floyd's attacks on capitalism and his strident defense of class rule and white supremacy reveals him as thoroughly bound up in an aristocratic worldview.

There were abundant ideological materials for fashioning a more extreme Conservative response to *A Fool's Errand*, yet for over a decade no Southern author was willing to attempt anything like Thomas Dixon's toxic Reconstruction novels. Interestingly, James. S. Pike, a Northern Liberal Republican, wrote the most direct precursor to Dixon's novels when he penned the extremely negrophobic chronicle of Reconstruction in South Carolina, *The Prostrate State: South Carolina Under Negro Government*, in 1873. A journalist who had once been Horace Greeley's associate editor at the *Tribune*, Pike was dismayed by the failure of the Liberal Republican movement in 1872 and soon thereafter visited South Carolina to see the results of Reconstruction for himself. His influential indictment, punctuated with bestial descriptions of blacks—though the Dixonesque "black rapist" does not appear—and impassioned assertions of their utter racial inferiority, was a controversial sensation in the North. But, no Southerner who had actually experienced Reconstruction followed Pike's lead in the realm of popular fiction.[68] Whether or not a receptive public existed in the North for the more extreme white supremacist interpretation of two decades later, no Southerner with eyewitness credentials to match Tourgée's stepped forward to offer them.

In 1882, a writer for the University of North Carolina monthly magazine predicted with shrewd accuracy that Tourgée's success with *A Fool's Errand* and its sequel, *Bricks Without Straw*, would prove to be transient and that a more pro-Southern interpretation would take hold in the near future. "His writings form a mirror in which Northern prejudice may see its distorted face, hence their present popularity. So soon as this Northern prejudice vanishes, as vanish it will, then will Tourgee's writings sink into merited oblivion," assured this anonymous columnist. Though he admitted that an unbiased view of Tourgée's works could recognize "the beauty and force of style exhibited in these writings in spite of the unpalatable ideas they contain," they had no place in the future.[69] He looked forward to an era of reconciliation in which all perpetrators of sectional animosity must and will be forgotten.

THE POLITICAL IMPACT

In the years following *A Fool's Errand*, Tourgée committed an enormous amount of energy to advancing the cause of nationalizing public education, convinced that his success was a sign of widespread public approval for this idea. He drew attention to this proposed remedy again in the documentary appendix he prepared for the second edition of *A Fool's Errand*, titled *Part II. The Invisible Empire*. With 130 pages of evidence drawn from public records to authenticate his depiction of Reconstruction, this addendum also reiterated his thesis that the culture of slavery must be truly eradicated before the "Southern problem" could be solved. Introducing his evidence, he asserted: "The opinion has been ventured in 'Fool's Errand' that only GENERAL EDUCATION—*universal enlightenment of whites and blacks alike*—can be relied upon to change the spirit which moved these horrors, and that it is the first great duty of the Nation to provide for such enlightenment." Suggesting that it should be a bipartisan issue, he insisted that nothing "can make the South an honored and equal partner of the North, except such an *education of the masses* as shall make that beautiful portion of our land genuinely 'democratic' and truly 'republican.'" "Ask any reader to consider the pages that follow," he challenged, "and then deny that doctrine if he can—if he dare."[70]

Tourgée's insistence that a final resolution to the problems of the South could be achieved through education had a multivocal appeal. Even those who blamed the turmoil of Reconstruction on black misrule could have agreed that a more literate and informed citizenry would produce better results. When Tourgée first advanced these arguments in a series of newspaper articles in the 1870s, North Carolina Conservatives were quick to conclude that he no longer supported the Fifteenth Amendment and regretted the enfranchisement of an uneducated majority. But Tourgée denied this conclusion, replying: "It has been stated, that I thought the negroes should have been educated before they were allowed to vote. In one sense this is true and in another false. I think an ignorant man has the same *right* to self-government as a wise one. . . . At the same time, I think that the government *owed* both education and training in the duties of civil life, to the slave" as well as to "illiterate whites whom slavery had kept from knowledge." He regarded education, not as a prerequisite, but as a supplement to the Fifteenth Amendment. It was both "an act of justice" and a wise policy.[71] Nevertheless, this distinction was not always made clear in Tourgée's crusade for public education and perhaps intentionally so. While radicals could embrace education as a means for black social advancement, moderates could support it as an antidote to the failures of Reconstruction.

The idea of a national public education system was a decade old by the time *A Fool's Errand* was published in 1879. Though generally neglected by historians of Reconstruction, it was in many ways the uncompleted capstone to the Radical program. After the ratification of the Fifteenth Amendment, such Radical Republicans as Henry Wilson and George Hoar looked to the establishment of a national educational system as an important supplement to it and, in historian Ward McAfee's words, a means of "pushing Reconstruction to the next level of intensity."[72] Tourgée could truthfully claim to have been among its original proponents. As early as 1869 he campaigned for improved public education in North Carolina and advised President Grant that "the only remedy" for the "ignorance and consequent weakness" of Southern Republicans "is general education." Concerned more with long-term effects than a quick fix, Tourgée wrote candidly to Grant: "It will act slowly but surely. It is no magic . . . but [it] is the only remedy that will cure the disease, and the general government is the only power that can apply it."[73] Within six months of this letter, Tourgée and other North Carolina Republicans were campaigning on the educational issue all over the state. In June 1870 Tourgée's Greensboro neighbor William Scott informed the "colored men" of Salem, "[The Republican Party] will not rest until a grand elementary system of public education is established all over our American Union for the education of every child," but most especially for their own "moral and intellectual advancement." "Work, work, work day and night in your town and all through your country," Scott advised, "every other interest . . . should be subordinated to this."[74]

On a national level, Massachusetts senator Henry Wilson—soon to become Grant's vice-president for his second term—announced nationalized education as a "New Departure" in the Republican Party agenda in a prominent article in the *Atlantic Monthly* in 1871.[75] Following soon after this announcement, a bill "To Establish a National System of Education" was introduced in Congress by Massachusetts representative George F. Hoar. A coalition of Democrats and Liberal Republicans opposed the bill as both a potential attack on parochial schools and an unnecessary centralization of power into federal hands. More explosively, the bill was accused of being a back-door measure to pave the way for racially integrated schools. The Education Bill was purposefully conflated with Massachusetts senator Charles Sumner's controversial Civil Rights Bill that was proposed to ban segregation in total, including public schools. That the most outspoken proponents of these measures, Hoar, Wilson, and Sumner, were all from Massachusetts only seemed to confirm that these were two sides of the same Radical coin.

The issue of integrating public schools had been moot virtually everywhere in the South since 1869. Tourgée had long since resigned himself to the impracticality of the measure. The survival of "colored" schools was precarious enough as it was, as they were understaffed and still subject to midnight torching by unreconstructed whites. Most were desperately short of books and completely lacked desks, blackboards, and even floors. These schools hung on through a combination of black contributions, state funds, and Northern white philanthropy. Tourgée understood the great improvements that could come from federal funds, and he abhorred Charles Sumner's obsession with a Civil Rights Bill that insisted on school integration. Privately he excoriated Sumner as one of the self-congratulatory "Wise Men" of the party whose short-sighted and impractical polices had condemned Reconstruction to fail.[76]

When the Senate finally passed Sumner's Civil Rights Bill in the spring of 1874, with the school provision intact, Tourgée was livid. He wrote to Martin B. Anderson: "I have no use for those who prescribe for disease without knowing [its] nature. Sumner knew no more of the actual condition of the colored man here than he realized his condition on the Gold Coast. The bill with all respect to its author, is just like a blister plaster put on a dozing man." Despite the fact that it embodied "good doctrine" and "fine theory" in Tourgée's view, the bill was "pure folly" when applied to the actual circumstances blacks faced in the South. Tourgée predicted:

> If it becomes law, it will constantly be avoided. No man can frame a statute which some other cannot avoid. For all its beneficent purposes it will be a dead letter. For its evil influences it will be vivid and active. . . . It will utterly destroy the bulk of our common schools in the South. . . . It simply delays—puts back—the thorough and complete rehabilitation of the South ten or twenty years.[77]

This caustic assessment, as it turned out, was prescient. The public school provision would eventually be stricken from the Civil Rights Bill by the lame-duck Republican Congress in the spring of 1875, but too late. Before the final bill was amended, the Republican party suffered one of the most devastating defeats of any party in American history in the congressional elections of 1874, losing their former control of both houses by wide margins. The cry of "racial amalgamation" echoed throughout the Democratic campaign from beginning to end—a potent cry in both the urban North and the South—fueled by Sumner's Bill. Though historians often attribute the 1874 reversal of the Republicans' fortune to the onset of economic depression, Tourgée was convinced that Sumner's Bill had handed the Democrats the election. In the South, especially, racial issues far outweighed economic ones in campaign rhetoric.[78]

Tourgée recognized that the gains blacks had made were not yet secure, and he was fearful of a backlash that might undo all of the work of the 1860s. Unlike the 1890s when he would take bold action to stave off the tide of reaction, he counseled caution in the mid 1870s. Aiding the cause of education generally, he believed, would promote black interests far better than pressing for fuller racial integration at that moment. He concluded:

> The most important thing in the world is to let the South forget the negro for a bit: let him acquire property, stability, and self-respect; let as many as possible be educated; in short let the race itself get used to freedom self-dependence and proper self-assertion; and then let his [Sumner's] bill come little by little.[79]

This strategy might have been the wiser one, but Sumner had refused to listen to it. His Radical colleagues, including such black leaders as Senator Hiram Revels, had urged him to back down on the school integration issue but to no avail.[80] Ironically, Tourgée's decision twenty years later to challenge segregation in the *Plessy* case could be subject to the same charge of imprudence that he leveled at Sumner. Both visionaries had to make difficult strategic choices, but in each of these cases the backlash that resulted was devastating to their cause.

The public discussion of massive federal aid to schools throughout 1870–1873 ended abruptly with the panic of 1873. Sumner's Civil Rights Bill took over the Radical agenda in the mid 1870s instead. But, federal aid to schools had not been entirely forgotten. As another presidential election approached in 1880, the "Southern problem" returned to center stage. The mass migration of blacks to Kansas in early 1879 captured national attention and called attention to the worsening conditions of Southern blacks since the "compromise" of 1877.[81] Even President Hayes virtually admitted the failure of his "let alone" policy and began to call for a new enforcement measure for ballot-box protection in the South. Before stepping down, Hayes set the tone for the 1880 campaign by suggesting that no Republican candidate should "be sustained unless [he pledges] . . . to carry out in good faith" the federal protection of "the rights of colored citizens." He declared, "to establish now the states rights doctrine of the supremacy of the states, and *an oligarchy of race,* is deliberately to throw away an essential part of the Union victory . . . equal rights and the supremacy of the laws of the nation are just and wise, and necessary. Let them not be surrendered."[82] With President Hayes appealing to the Radical meaning of the Civil War, and *A Fool's Errand* a national best-seller, Tourgée approached the upcoming election with renewed faith in his party.

Tourgée attended the 1880 Republican National Convention in Chicago and enjoyed the attention of fellow delegates who had recently learned his identity as author of *A Fool's Errand* in the second edition, which had just been published. To his delight, the Republican platform for the first time officially included a plank that endorsed aid to public education as a "duty of the National government." He strongly supported a third-term nomination for Ulysses S. Grant, with whom he had personal access and, he believed, some influence. (Grant's praise for *A Fool's Errand* on the campaign trail later that summer suggested some basis for this belief).[83] When Grant failed to receive an unprecedented third-term nomination, Tourgée was consoled by the convention's compromise nominee, James Abram Garfield. An acquaintance from childhood, Garfield was another man with whom Tourgée had a personal connection—they had been inseparable companions the summer that ten-year-old Albion visited his cousins in Chester, Ohio. When Garfield personally asked him to campaign on his behalf, Tourgée agreed to do so but insisted on first finishing his new Reconstruction novel, *Bricks Without Straw.* Convinced that it would be influential in the campaign, he completed the book in time for it to appear in print in September. Like *A Fool's Errand,* the novel concluded with another passionate call for national aid to education.[84]

Once finished, Tourgée joined the campaign and stumped for Garfield energetically and effectively in twelve states. After receiving word from an aide that "[Tourgee] is a good 'popular talker' and make no mistake," Garfield ordered his staff to "get Mr. Tourgee for as many appointments as possible" and pay all of his expenses. Tourgée later reported that he gave "his almost undivided attention to that single provision" of aid to public education and he "found it everywhere received with approval."[85] Relying on his knowledge of Southern conditions, he told his audiences what he had witnessed of the freedpeople's zeal for education: "the colored man or woman who does not honestly desire that their children shall be taught all that [they] possibly can acquire is so rare that he may almost be said to be yet undiscovered." But this admirable enthusiasm for education, he explained, was met by intransigent opposition from the planter class, who sought to block their advancement, and from "perhaps a majority" of poor whites, who "care nothing about education for themselves or anybody else." Also, criticizing missionaries who aspired to be above politics and content with private efforts, Tourgée strongly argued that federal supervision alone could ensure that black education would be protected and nourished.[86]

If the campaign's official songbook is any indication, the Republican effort reverberated with odes to the Radical interpretation of the war. Dozens of Union Army favorites were adapted to the campaign themes. A rendition of "John Brown's Body" declared that "What was won upon the battle-field we will not now let go/ . . . the principles for which they bled forever shall abide/ We'll pay the debt Rebellion made, we'll guard our public schools/ . . . The men who saved the nation still shall make its laws and rules." And to the tune of "When Johnny Comes Marching Home," Republican crowds chanted: "We must have equal rights for all, Hurrah! Hurrah!/ By this we either stand or fall, Hurrah! Hurrah!/ Free schools, free speech, free thought, free press/ We will have these and nothing less/ With Garfield leading, We are marching on."[87] Tourgée was apparently so enthused by this atmosphere that he turned down a personal request to meet with Garfield so that he could stay with the campaign, suggesting that the candidate might perhaps have more important things to do than to "spend [his] time *visiting.*"[88]

Garfield carried the election by a slim margin of less than one-half of one percent of the popular vote. Elated, Tourgée took it upon himself to make certain that Garfield did not abandon the South. "You cannot be a mere cipher like your predecessor. You cannot adopt a negation and call it a policy," he boldly admonished the president-elect. "I sincerely hope that your life and fame have not reached their climax in the fact of your election."[89] In a detailed fifteen-page letter, he urged Garfield to reward Southern Republicans with patronage, especially blacks whose "miraculous faithfulness and unquenchable" loyalty had "carried the party through these four years." Most importantly, he reminded Garfield that "the educational plank in the Republican platform is the master-key of the situation" that could become the "glory" of his term in office. It was "a great thought—a grand idea [that] awaits its true development and con-secration at your hands," and in addition, it would "strike at the roots of the 'exodus' by enabling the laborer to guard himself from fraud by the terms of his contract."[90]

In the *North American Review*, Tourgée's views on the subject were published as "Aaron's Rod in Politics," which expanded on his recom-mendations to Garfield for an influential national audience. The article provided a detailed plan that emphasized the importance of raising a national fund to be distributed directly to "the officers or teachers of schools in towns or districts, according to the number of illiterates therein" and to be overseen by "a thorough system of inspection and supervision of the schools . . . [with] full and accurate reports of all matters necessary to direct future legislation on the subject." The purpose of the fund was to wipe out illiteracy—not to bolster the education of those already privileged. Therefore it was essential to Tourgée that distribution of the fund bypass state government machinery. Otherwise, "such a fund is liable to be diverted from its legitimate purpose for the benefit of a class or a sect," instead of "curing the illiteracy of all classes and both races." He elided constitutional arguments against federal intervention in states' actions since the issue was a matter of national self-preservation. "It is not the Constitution but the law of national existence that flows from the Constitution that gives us this right," he wrote.[91]

Garfield was clearly sympathetic to Tourgée's ideas, though it is doubtful that he would have endorsed the degree of federal supervision Tourgée required. Education was attractive to Garfield as a new approach to the "Southern problem." Public education had been the source of Garfield's own rise from poverty in the rural Western Reserve. Having excelled at his studies at an Ohio academy, Garfield was able to attend Williams College in Massachusetts and returned to become a professor and then president of the Western Reserve Eclectic Institute (later renamed Hiram College). The Civil War brought him further success, as he rapidly rose through the ranks to brigadier general and then got elected to Congress in 1863 as successor to Joshua Giddings. A devoted supporter of Thaddeus Stevens, Garfield was a staunch Radical Republican in the 1860s and an early advocate of black suffrage. In the early 1870s, he voted in favor of Hoar's National Educational Bill.[92]

By the time of his nomination in 1880, Garfield had shifted away from Radicalism toward safer ground. He even participated in the 1877 Wormley Hotel talks, in which the bargain was struck to withdraw federal troops from Louisiana and South Carolina—though it must be said that the Republicans at the talks did extract promises from Southern Democrats to continue state support for black education. Initially, he supported Hayes's "let alone" policy and conspicuously denounced the exploitation of "sectional issues" in the political campaigns of 1878. But, he now regretted this approach. Deploring Hayes's Southern policy as a "dreary failure" that had "turned out to be a give away from the start," Garfield repeatedly promised to protect black rights and support education during the 1880 campaign.[93]

Yet, Garfield dropped hints that he entertained the same misgivings that had haunted Hayes: the limits of constitutional power. In an 1880 campaign speech to a black audience, Garfield ominously promised them "an equal chance and nothing more," which he explained as a "fair

A political cartoon of James Garfield from the last days before
the election. The caption read "FRIEND OF THE FREEDMEN:
'Now that we have made them free, we will stand by these black
allies! We will stand by them until the sun of liberty shall shine
with equal ray upon every man, black or white, throughout the
Union!' — General Garfield August 6, 1880." *Harper's Weekly*,
October 23, 1880, p. 685. Courtesy of The Newberry Library,
Chicago, IL.

chance, within the limits of the Constitution, and by the exercise of its
proper powers."[94] Did an "equal chance" include federal funding to
schools, or did that overstep the limits of constitutional power? Did "nothing more" mean that federal power would not be used to protect their
voting rights? Garfield's position remained unclear.

In the weeks leading up to the inaugural, Garfield, Tourgée, and
Burke A. Hinsdale — Garfield's closest friend and most trusted adviser —
carried on a serious correspondence about the education issue. Hinsdale,

Garfield's successor as the president of Hiram College, was a natural advocate of universal education, but he counseled Garfield to proceed with caution lest he antagonize the states-rights crew. Although he believed *A Fool's Errand* was "a book of great power," Hinsdale doubted whether Tourgée's prescription of more federal intervention would have "averted the last twelve years." He also perceived "great difficulties" in the particular scheme of federal supervision over school funding proposed in "Aaron's Rod in Politics," telling Garfield: "A good deal of discussion must precede doing anything on an extensive scale." But he added, "I hope you will say enough in your Inaugural to precipitate debate all over the country." For his part, Garfield appeared to embrace Tourgée's "two civilizations" thesis wholesale and he agreed that "modernization" of the South was the only remedy. "I have no doubt that the final cure for the 'Solid South' will be found in the education of its youth, and in the development of its business interest," he acknowledged, but cautioned "both of these require time."[95]

On March 4, 1881, Garfield delivered a surprising Inaugural Address that seemed to demonstrate the influence of Tourgée on his thinking. Over one-third of his address was devoted to issues of black civil rights and national support for public education. Garfield called "the elevation of the negro race from slavery to the full rights of citizenship" the most significant "political change we have known since the adoption of the Constitution of 1787." Emphatically, he declared that there could be "no middle ground between slavery and equal citizenship. There can be no permanently disfranchised peasantry in the United States." With this principle in mind, he noted that the national government remained "under special obligation to aid in removing the illiteracy which it has added to our voting population." But Garfield also equivocated on this latter point by calling on "all of the constitutional power of the nation *and* of the states *and* all of the volunteer forces of the people" to eradicate illiteracy. The goal of universal education affected all Americans and required universal cooperation. He concluded by appealing for color-blind, non-sectional bipartisanship: "in this beneficent work sections and races should be forgotten and partisanship should be unknown."[96]

Although unable to attend the Inaugural Ball, Tourgée was "heartily pleased" when he read of Garfield's address and immediately wrote to congratulate his friend in the White House. "That document presages the dawn of a new and brighter era," he predicted.[97] Within weeks, Washington newspapers were commenting on Tourgée's ubiquitous presence at the White House and mentioning his name among those likely to receive positions from the new administration.[98] Breaking an earlier promise to Garfield that he would not ask for an appointed office,

Tourgée now lobbied for a position on the United States Court of Claims. "I prefer a judicial appointment," he told Garfield, frankly admitting, "I shall then have such leisure as will permit me to continue my literary studies and labors."[99] But before he received an appointment, it seems their relationship became strained, a development that perhaps began with Tourgée's aggressive lobbying on behalf of his old North Carolina allies, particularly African American ones, which drew fire from Southern critics in political gossip columns and may have irritated Garfield.[100] Much later, Tourgée told the inside story of this conflict, and the embarrassing moment when he realized Garfield's limits on the principle of racial equality.

Having been invited to the White House "for the purpose of 'talking over' the question of an appointment to the Court of Claims, which had been more than half promised me and which I greatly desired," Tourgée explained, "it chanced that a colored man was also an applicant for the place—for which he was fairly competent." Upon learning this from Garfield, Tourgée offered to withdraw his candidacy on the understanding that the "colored man" had a more important claim to party favor: "There was an impressive silence. Then the President said, 'Do you think I would appoint a *negro* to the bench?'" When Tourgée indicated that he had indeed thought so, Garfield told him that he would not because he himself could never practice law in court before a black judge, "no more than I would invite him to my table." It was a terribly disillusioning moment for Tourgée, who found it incredible that Garfield—"a Republican, a patriot and [a man who] stood very near the head of a great Christian sect"—could entertain such blind prejudice. Soon afterward he learned: "the colored man was not appointed nor I either—probably because of my folly in broaching the subject."[101]

Whether Tourgée would have continued to have influence in the Garfield administration after this incident, or attain a satisfactory appointment for himself, will never be known. He continued to visit the White House and lobby for patronage for his Southern allies, but without much success. Then, merely four months into his presidency, Garfield was assassinated by Charles Guiteau—who was, coincidentally, a disgruntled supporter who had been passed over for federal patronage. Shot on July 2, Garfield lingered until September 19, when his death officially passed the presidential torch to Chester A. Arthur.

President Arthur had demonstrated little in the way of interest for civil rights during his career as Customs House collector for the port of New York; in fact, his presence on the ticket had been a concession to the Conservative wing of the party. Arthur's indifference to both the South and to the educational issue was evident in his initial message to

Congress, which was the first presidential message to Congress that did not mention Southern issues since the Civil War. Privately considering federal aid to education unconstitutional, he turned the initiative over to Congress, declaring that only Congress could decide the "momentous" question of aiding public education.[102] Hinsdale and Tourgée were devastated, convinced that public education would have been Garfield's top priority. Just after his death, Hinsdale told a reporter, "his heart was fixed upon this as a prominent feature of his administration—national aid to public, and especially to Southern, education."[103] What Tourgée had called a "new dawn" turned out to be a sunset.

7

Radical Individualism in the Gilded Age

The most tremendous forces have moved with unprecedented energy toward the subjection of the individual . . . the segregation of capital in a few hands has been equaled only by the restriction of opportunity. A few already control one-half the valuation of the country . . . fewer still control the opportunities for labor. . . . Organization has practically eradicated the individual.

—Albion Tourgée, *Murvale Eastman: Christian Socialist,* 1890

The law of the survival of the fittest was not made by man and cannot be abrogated by man. We can only, by interfering with it, produce the survival of the unfittest . . . the sentimentalists have been preaching for a century notions of rights and equality, of the dignity, wisdom, and power of the proletariat, which have filled the minds of ignorant men with impossible dreams.

—Professor William Graham Sumner, *Sociology,* 1881

THE 1880S WERE CHALLENGING TIMES FOR TOURGÉE. A profound intellectual transformation was taking place in the North, and he began to fear that Americans were losing faith in the very egalitarian premise of democratic government. Beginning with the assassination of Garfield, personal and political setbacks ended his brief period of insider influence in national politics after the success of *A Fool's Errand.* That euphoric experience was soon replaced by a growing feeling of disconnection to his times. This feeling was captured perfectly in Tourgée's collection of satiric essays, *A Veteran and His Pipe,* published in the mid-1880s. A wide-ranging rumination on the meaning of the Civil War, filled with cutting sarcasm, these essays extolled the higher ideals of Civil

War veterans such as Tourgée that, in his view, had been forgotten by so many beneficiaries of their sacrifice.

Written in the first person, Tourgée assumed the identity of a disgruntled, one-armed veteran who feels scorned by the society that begrudges him even the modest pension that he needs to survive. A memorable alter ego, the veteran prefers to spend his days alone, soliloquizing to his lit pipe about the decay of the nation's morals since the end of the war. "We are told the day of sentiment has passed, and the era of practicality has begun," he tells his pipe. "Devotion to the rights of man is an innocent weakness, gain the one thing needful. The capitalist's margins are more important to the nation than justice to the oppressed. This is the wisdom of today." Affectionately nicknamed "Blower," the pipe he holds, and to which his discourses are addressed, was pressed into his hands at Chickamauga by a comrade whose last words were "Tell them I died for freedom—and the right."[1] A symbol of peace, the pipe represents the victory so dearly won in the war, now tossed aside by those who were willing to exchange the hard-fought victory for sectional "reconciliation" based on states rights, limited government, and white supremacy.

Much more than emancipation for the enslaved, the Union victory had meant the triumph of "free labor" principles that rejected all forms of individual economic and political subjection. "'Freedom and the right,'" the veteran explains, meant "the right of every man to equal power and privilege with other men! . . . A right to liberty and life, to free access to that golden gate of opportunity!"[2] But, in the North, the very idea of equal opportunity was being undercut by men whose economic theories disdained even a soldier's pension as a dangerous precedent of government assistance.[3] Leading the opposition to soldiers' pensions in the North were members of the Northern intellectual elite whose aristocratic pretensions the veteran regarded with disdain. "To smoke a pipe and believe in human right as a practical, tangible thing—a sentiment that ought to outrank and overpower all other political ideals," he fumed, "is in the highest degree absurd to one who sucks rice-paper cigarettes, glorifies the Anglican ideal, and studies political philosophy in the sweet seclusion of his club."[4] Somehow the ideology of the Southern master class, including its sense of racial superiority, now began to thrive among the apologists for capitalism who exploited their laborers in the North with equal abandon.

The overriding theme of these essays was that the radical meaning of the Civil War had to be preserved against the claim that emancipation had never been more than an unintended consequence of the war. Putting the war into a larger historical context, the veteran asserts, "one side represented the rights of man, the other the rights of the master. The one meant equal rights for all; the other special privileges for a class. It was only one phase of the mighty conflict which is as old as man—the rights of the many against the encroachments of the few." Yet, the claim that the Union's purpose only had been to preserve the nation had become a popular rationale to disavow federal efforts to protect equal citizenship. "There are some who teach to-day, and many who believe that the cause for which so many died was of a narrower scope, and its upholders animated my meaner motives," he concedes while still insisting, "We better know the story of that day, Blower, but we are getting old, and our ideas growing sadly old-fashioned, too."[5]

A tone of resignation and regret permeates *A Veteran and His Pipe*. Indeed, Tourgée may have been ready to concede defeat in 1885 in the midst of a difficult period of cultural adjustment and professional rejection during which he penned these essays. Yet, after intense soul-searching and philosophical introspection, Tourgée would return reinvigorated in his preferred role as idealistic reformer and public agitator. His radical understanding of the Civil War would expand accordingly to meet the new justifications of political and economic values proffered in the Gilded Age.

RISE OF THE MUGWUMPS

After the death of Garfield, formidable obstacles stood in the way of new efforts to advance the cause of equal citizenship in the South. One of these was the rise of a powerful faction of reformers, known in the colorful political language of the time as the mugwumps. Originally a derogatory term, the word *mugwump* referred to the unapologetic elitism of these reformers and has been said to be a mock-Indian term for "Big Chief."[6] A small but influential group of disaffected Republicans, the mugwumps were a second coming of the Liberal Republican movement of 1871–72, driven by similar purposes and led by many of the same prominent figures. Deeply disillusioned by the corruption of the two-party system, and by the failings of popular democracy generally, mugwumps shaped a powerful critique of the egalitarian excesses of the Reconstruction era. In terms of policy, they advocated limited government and civil service reform—believing that the professionalization of government would eliminate the rampant cronyism and corruption the worst examples of which they cited as both the Northern urban political machines and Southern Reconstruction governments. Their condemnation of Republican carpetbagger governments proved an extremely useful rhetorical tool, despite the ending of Reconstruction, because it enhanced their claim to nonpartisanship and helped to court Southern Democratic support. Yet,

the gusto with which they assailed those Republicans who wished to protect black civil rights suggested profound philosophical differences at the
root of their criticism.[7]

The mugwump arguments for limited government can be viewed as a
direct refutation of the Radical Republicanism of the 1860s. Their political critiques had a pronounced deterministic and secular flavor and a
strong hint of social Darwinism.[8] To cleanse government of corruption,
some mugwumps even began to press for the elimination of the "ignorant
vote" from the electorate altogether, through such devices as literacy tests
or poll taxes, and regarded the primary flaw of democratic government
to be the empowerment of the "unfit." Tourgée was particularly horrified by this anti-democratic trend in their thinking, which he assailed in
a series of 1885 articles in the *Chicago Inter Ocean*, entitled "Letters to
a Mugwump." In his view, it was the obligation of the educated to

This Thomas Nast cartoon, captioned "The Ignorant Vote—Honors
Are Easy," captured a growing sentiment among Northern
intellectuals that would become associated with the mugwumps.
The "ignorant voters," drawn here as racially inferior brutes, one
black, one Irish, are blamed as the source of political corruption for
both parties. *Harper's Weekly*, December 9, 1876, cover page.
Courtesy of The Newberry Library, Chicago, IL.

eliminate ignorance in the electorate by education, not exclusion. "Even if this bugbear of 'the ignorant and vicious masses' were a veritable fact," he fumed, "their exclusion from the rights of the citizen would be an act of such gross injustice as to be unfit for consideration as a remedy."[9]

Like the Radical Republicans of twenty years before, mugwumps had an influence far greater than the number of their professed followers. They enjoyed a wide hearing because they represented Northern intellectuals and held, as one historian put it, "a virtual monopoly on the periodicals read by the refined Northern middle classes."[10] Tourgée recognized their growing influence as well. Not only did the leading periodicals propagate their elitist views, college professors were training the next generation of intellectuals to adopt them. That "the educated man, so called, is by that very fact entitled to leadership," Tourgée lamented in 1887, had become the maxim of the "political thought which has recently characterized the college life and general culture of the East."[11]

The mugwump influence in politics reached its height in the years after the assassination of Garfield. Chester A. Arthur's unexpected devotion to civil service reform and his disdain for sectional issues may have been just the formula to encourage its growth. One sign of the times came in 1882 when *Harper's Weekly* editor George William Curtis experienced a "permanent change in [his] thinking" that caused him to pronounce the "race issue" dead and devote his editorials henceforward to "nonsectional" issues, though it had been leaning away from such issues for years.[12] Curtis joined other mugwump editors, such as E.L. Godkin of *The Nation*, in leveling savage criticism at Republicans who "waved the bloody shirt," accusing them of cynical opportunism and intellectual bankruptcy. In 1884, the mugwumps showed their electoral power when their temporary revolt from the Republican Party—precipitated in part by presidential candidate James G. Blaine's inclusion of race and sectional issues in his campaign—helped throw the election to the Democrat Grover Cleveland.[13]

The charge of "waving the bloody shirt" summed up the mugwump opposition to the federal intervention in the South. This phrase at the time referred not to the bloodshed of the war, but to the public sentiment in support of Reconstruction. Although its use became common only after 1874, the phrase may have referred originally to a congressional speech by Radical Republican Ben Butler in 1868, who made an emotional appeal for a stronger Southern policy while reportedly displaying the bloodied nightshirt of a Mississippi carpetbagger who had been assaulted by the Ku Klux Klan.[14] The charge of "bloody-shirt" politics sometime thereafter came to refer to politicians who, like Butler, supposedly exploited Northern moral outrage to serve party purposes. By 1875, the *Boston Globe* defined a "bloody-shirt waver" as "a man to whom a horrible outrage in the South is a political boon, and garments rolled in the blood of a negro like the banner of Constantine."[15] A term of ridicule, like the counter-term *mugwump*, it served quite effectively to tarnish the motives of those who called for governmental protection of black rights— or even sought to discuss the race problem at all. As Tourgée put it, "To consider the causes of revolution and counter-revolution, to trace the course of prejudice and caste, to tell the tale of violence is to be 'a stirrer up of strife,' a 'waver of the bloody shirt,' a 'ranter on dead issues,' a party insubordinate, and a pestiferous political nuisance."[16]

The plan for federal aid to education was a special target for mugwump attacks. For another decade after Garfield's death, the issue survived in Congress, kept alive by such determined supporters as Senators Hoar from Massachusetts and Henry W. Blair from New Hampshire. By 1884, a greatly watered-down compromise measure known as the Blair Bill seemed the last best hope for federal aid to schools but still faced determined mugwump opposition. "My mugwump friends," Senator Hoar explained in 1885 regarding the Blair Bill, "[accuse us] of waving the bloody shirt. They tell us that, if we will hold our tongues about these things, they will come back to us perhaps, and give us a majority." Hoar called on his fellow Republicans in the Senate not to capitulate to this electoral blackmail. "For one, it is not with me a question of majority or minority. It is a question of God's truth," he intoned, "the Republicans of Massachusetts will serve this standard [the bloody shirt] and will keep it flying. This is a contest between good and evil."[17] Reconstructing the South, and promoting equal rights, still elicited the language of the higher law, as Hoar's references to "God's truth" and "good and evil" evinced. For some, equal citizenship continued to be a matter of conscience.

From a mugwump perspective, Tourgée was the archetypical bloody-shirt waver. His public comments about the South often unwittingly reinforced the perception of him as mired in the anti-Southern animosity of the war generation. Though he had begun to moderate his rhetoric in some of his more carefully worded essays and books, he continued to lash out with bursts of pugnacious language in speeches and newspaper articles, just as he had during his North Carolina days. On one occasion, for instance, he complained to the editor of the *New York Sun*:

> I am surprised to see you refer to my works as full of "resentment" toward "the South." I am sure I do not feel any. I believe most thoroughly in the South—no not the gnarled, cramped and dwarfed product of a bastard civilization which now arrogantly styles itself "the South," but the free, tolerant, prosperous, intelligent South which shall arise . . . when free speech and free labor shall abide there in peace and honor.[18]

Lost in Tourgée's denunciation of the planters as representing a "bastard civilization" is an important point in that the South should not be thought of strictly in terms of the interests of the white, planter class. But, his most even-handed writings found it difficult to get a fair hearing.

The reception of Tourgée's *An Appeal to Caesar* (1884), one of his most tempered works, highlighted his philosophical differences with the mugwumps. This book was written at the suggestion of Garfield, who, shortly before he died, proposed to Tourgée that he expand the arguments of his *North American Review* article into a full-length study with more evidentiary support. Overcoming the discouragement that he felt after Garfield's assassination, Tourgée belatedly fulfilled his obligation to complete the task. Although the book begins with a melodramatic description of his final meeting with President Garfield, Tourgée rightly concedes that the book does not represent Garfield's position on aid to education, which had yet to be formulated. The "Caesar" of the book's title, he explained, referred not to his attempt to convert Garfield to his views, but rather his appeal to "that other and greater Caesar whom none so devoutly revered—the AMERICAN PEOPLE."[19] Bordering on a sociological study, and making extensive use of census data, *An Appeal to Caesar* is full of compelling insights and observations on race and sectional relations; the book has been called by historian George Fredrickson "the most profound discussion of the American racial situation to appear in the 1880s."[20]

Casting its arguments as broadly and dispassionately as possible, *An Appeal to Caesar* offered both an analysis and a dire warning about Southern race relations. First, it directly challenged white supremacist claims that blacks would not be able to compete with white labor in a free labor economy. Despite widespread predictions that they would die out as a race without the institution of slavery, Tourgée showed that blacks not only continued to thrive twenty years after emancipation, but their population had increased at a much faster rate than whites in the decade 1870–1880.[21] Their progress toward the acquisition of property and education since the war, he claimed, had far outstripped the poor white class of the South. In fact, this rapid material advancement, rather than indolence or criminality, had been the reason for white violence against blacks during Reconstruction. "It is an inflexible rule of development that the inferior class when free has always an upward tendency and inclination to rise and become, sooner or later, the dominant power," he hypothesized. "The white race can never prove or maintain its superiority simply by excluding the negro from all opportunity for growth and development."[22] Rather, whites were better off to accept this advancement at its steady pace, or else they risked a violent revolution and full-fledged racial war.[23]

Reaching out to his opponents, Tourgée took especial pains to respond to their anticipated objections. Of the long-standing arguments that insisted upon the racial inferiority of blacks, he reasoned, "We do not know whether this belief is well founded or not. We have no special knowledge of the divine purposes in establishing distinctions of race, nor do we believe that any other human being has." Yet, he suggested, "the events of the past quarter of a century would seem to be sufficient to convince any one of the possibility of a mistake in regard to such a theory."[24] Citing the military record of blacks during the Civil War, the rapid proliferation of churches and schools in their communities since emancipation, their vigorous population growth, their surprising gains in material progress despite "the most adverse circumstances," the racist arguments of the past appeared questionable indeed. By deliberately excluding blacks from opportunity, white supremacists contradicted their own professed theory of innate black inferiority—for if blacks were truly inferior there would be nothing to fear from their competition. What whites truly feared, he implied, was the testing of their racist theories. "Whether the colored man is the equal, the inferior, or the superior of the white race in knowledge, capacity, or the power of self direction has not been specifically revealed," he insisted, and truth can only be discovered if all are given an equal chance: "if he is not capable of competing with the white race after enjoying such [a fair and equal] opportunity, certainly no harm will have resulted from allowing him to approach as nearly to that level as he is capable of attaining."[25]

Because he understood the race problem to be a problem of white racism at its roots, Tourgée offered that education is the only possible panacea. From Washington's farewell address to Garfield's inaugural, the enlightenment of the masses had been a cherished goal of national leaders that was still unheeded by a national enactment. The benefits of supporting public schools with national aid, therefore, would have positive effects far beyond the realm of racial or sectional harmony. Even so, he was not optimistic about the time frame for Southerners to overcome racial strife given the deep mistrust between the races at the present time. "We speak of the past as dead," he wrote. "Fortunately or unfortunately, as the case may be, it cannot die. . . . To-day is as Yesterday made it, and To-morrow will be shaped by To-day."[26] Without expectation of a quick fix therefore, Americans needed to proceed with determined support for peaceful progress and upward mobility for both black and white as their last, best hope. The oppressive conditions that might spark revolution would be removed, as the pathway to advancement opened for all. Blacks would finally prove the truth or falseness of racial theories, as they either failed or succeeded on their own merits.

Though otherwise widely and favorably reviewed, criticism of *An Appeal to Caesar* came especially from those expressing distinctively mugwump views.[27] For instance, a critic for the *Saturday Review* remarked upon "the contrast which the reality of his pictures presents to the unreality and even absurdity of his proposed remedy." Betraying his predilection for the "hard facts" of social science, the writer commended the sociological descriptions in the first half of the book, but expressed sincere disappointment in the specific proposals offered in the second half: "Judge Tourgee, shrewd, keen, and profound in noting political tendencies and national character, has a pupil-teacher's reliance on the infallible virtues of elementary education, an American child's implicit confidence in the self-evident truth of democratic principles." While not elaborating on his dim view of the benefits of education, or the self-evident falsity of democratic principles, the long review concludes with a a favorite phrase of unreconstructed Southerners: " 'This is a white man's country.' "[28] By putting this phrase in quotation marks, the reviewer refused to own it but submitted to its dictation nonetheless. If white supremacy was inevitable and irresistible, Tourgée's proposal became an "absurdity."

In a review that exceeded seven columns of its paper, the *New York Commercial Advertiser* took Tourgée to task with an explicit Darwinian rationale that dismissed the whole idea of a race problem as a figment of his imagination. Regarding Tourgée as a bitter pessimist, the *Advertiser* suggested that he had failed to understand the nature of black people. If the black population has increased faster than whites, the reviewer theorized, it meant only that "[the 'Negro'] alone of what Darwin calls the inferior races, has shown his capacity to survive the process of civilization by contact with a more civilized race. He has abundantly proved his fitness for life and will live."[29] Because this has occurred "by force of natural law," the country can rest assured that "it will not bring danger to our institutions or harm of any kind to the country in our judgment."[30] Tourgée's dire prediction of an impending racial war in the South was ridiculous. The black population's increase, the writer conjectured, reflected their sustenance and their contentedness as field laborers in the Cotton Kingdom. "So far from being a burden, the multitudinous children of the negro laborer are a source of positive profit to him" because they allowed "men whose wants so simple as those of the negroes' to work less, and yet still make a comfortable living by increased number of cotton-picking 'hands' per family."[31] In other words, the population statistics demonstrated that the race problem was solving itself and that blacks were settling into their natural station in society.

Interestingly, the *Advertiser*'s reviewer regarded his own attitude toward blacks as far more charitable and optimistic than Tourgée's. "Mr. Tourgee seems to think that the negroes are a race of wholly uneducated barbarians" who stood ready to "set the law at defiance" if their rights are not respected.[32] The reviewer replied, on the contrary, that Southern blacks were a peaceful people, thoroughly "under the influence of the moral law," who posed "no danger to the community."[33] As if describing the folk wisdom of Joel Chandler Harris's "Uncle Remus," the writer remarked, "However ignorant some of their preachers are of bookish theology, they are stern moralists and *no mean* teachers of practical ethics."[34] In his view, therefore, blacks seemed to have little need for book learning: "They know nothing of the spelling book, it is true, but it is a very shallow conception of education which regards the spelling book as a specific for ignorance or a panacea for moral and social ills."[35] Having adopted a comfortable social Darwinian view of the matter, the reviewer was convinced that natural laws would resolve all problems without human interference and that the "lower" races, if they survived natural selection at all, would remain subordinate to the "more civilized" ones.

Both of these reviews rejected Tourgée's premise that education could place blacks on an equal footing with whites by implying that racial inequality was biological and unchangeable. Interestingly, the country's leading mugwump journal, *The Nation*, did not express this view—at least explicitly. *The Nation* gave the book a grudgingly positive review, though not without confessing the source of some of its political biases against Tourgée. "We wish to do a piece of justice, and frankly confess that we had a strong prejudice against Judge Tourgée as an embittered sufferer from dispelled illusions," *The Nation's* critic admitted. "This prejudice was not lessened . . . by the opening sentimental account of an interview with President Garfield" nor by "the foreshadowed proposal of national interference in State affairs." Disliking political appeals to sentiment, and the expansion of federal power, this reviewer also went on to express contempt for those "bloody-shirt Republicans" who made the most out of every new Southern atrocity. Stories of atrocities "have been manipulated for the sole purpose of keeping the men who call themselves the leaders of the Republican party . . . in power," he insisted. "Government information is . . . perfectly worthless" with regard to the conditions of the South. The writer thus welcomed an independent source, stating that "trustworthy private information as to the conditions of the South is of great importance."[36] But did this reviewer trust the facts about the South as reported by a first-hand source such as Tourgée?

While it is not clear whether *The Nation* found Tourgée's description of Southern conditions credible, its reviewer put aside his predilections against Tourgée when he considered the specifics of his plan. "When we came to his plan of national education, we would not deny its reasonable

and statesmanlike character," he wrote approvingly. "[T]here is no question of handing over sums of money to the jobbery of State officials, nor
again of the Federal administration of school affairs in the States." Having
avoided the pitfalls of aiding machine politics or extending the federal
bureaucracy into constitutionally questionable areas, the reviewer could
find no other reason to object to his plan. "We say to him, Brother, be of
good cheer," the review concludes. "The seed that thou sowest, it shall
yet bear grain."[37] Despite this surprising endorsement, there is no statement in the review that takes the position that racial equality would be
advanced, or blacks achieve upward mobility, if federal aid to education
was enacted. Rather the writer seemed willing to concede his support to
a moderate plan that might satisfy bloody-shirt wavers but posed little
danger to the status quo in the immediate future—or in the long term, if
one subscribed to scientific theories of black inferiority.

Despite the modest support for Tourgée's plan by *The Nation*, the
political will in Congress to overcome mugwump opposition and unite
the old Republican Party alliance behind some moderate legislation, as
we shall see, would never materialize. Though their Darwin-influenced
racial determinism often remained just below the surface, the mugwump
lack of enthusiasm for the educational solution betrayed their deep
skepticism about the principle of human equality on which democratic
government was based. Perhaps determinism becomes especially attractive in post-revolutionary times, when expectations for great social reforms
have been disappointed. Even Tourgée would struggle to keep his revolutionary fire burning in the mid-1880s.

FORTUNE AND MISFORTUNE

The success of *A Fool's Errand* and *Bricks Without Straw* brought Tourgée
substantial fame and fortune. But while his fame would last throughout
his life, his fortune would be short-lived. According to Emma, the
Tourgées had "made $11,000 in the first 60 days of sale on 'Bricks Without
Straw'" and "$24,000 in the first 6 months on 'A Fool's Errand'," which
would equal roughly $5 million in 2004 dollars.[38] Anticipating a lifetime
of royalties from these works, Albion began planning for a comfortable
career as a man of letters. In the spring of 1881, he purchased for ten
thousand dollars a country estate of fifty acres, with an impressive twenty-
three-room gabled home that overlooked Lake Chautauqua in western
New York, not far from his and Emma's childhood home on the Western
Reserve. Fancifully christening his new estate "Thorheim," or "Fool's
Home," he imagined it would be used primarily as a summer retreat.[39]

Never inclined to limit himself to only one profession, Tourgée hoped to pursue literature while simultaneously attaining another position of political or social influence. Soon after Garfield's assassination, an opportunity arose that promised to fulfill his grand ambitions. Robert S. Davis, a wealthy Philadelphia businessman, recruited Tourgée to be the editor-in-chief for a new weekly literary magazine to be called *Our Continent*.[40] If successful, Tourgée, as the editor of an important national magazine, would enjoy prestige and intellectual influence far beyond that of any likely political or judicial appointment he might have attained from Garfield. And *Our Continent* could serve to keep radical principles alive in the intellectual culture of the North. It was exactly what he wanted, and he threw himself into the work with characteristic abandon without any apparent concern for the high rate of failure of such ventures.

Sadly, *Our Continent* did not live up to expectations. More than merely another disappointment, it turned into a professional and financial disaster as great as any Tourgée had experienced. Staking his entire life savings on the success of the magazine, he lost an estimated $150,000 in personal fortune and incurred debts in excess of $70,000 that left him embroiled in lawsuits and battling creditors for twelve years after the magazine's collapse. In one moment of desperation, he even mortgaged the future sales of his books to his creditors. The failure left him emotionally demoralized and financially devastated. Emma regarded *Our Continent* as Albion's greatest setback, lamenting to a family friend, a month after his death in 1905, "How his life was embittered, ruined, by his trying to do what he had no capacity to do. His mind was too large to take in business details, and without that ability no one can succeed in such ventures as the *Continent*, which took all his fortune, his ambition, his hopes— everything but his wife!"[41]

Called a "brilliant and ambitious attempt" by the distinguished historian of journalism Frank Luther Mott, *Our Continent* was probably too ambitious for its own good.[42] It promised to revolutionize the periodical scene by offering the quality of a literary monthly on a weekly basis. Davis and Tourgée chose to publish the magazine out of Philadelphia, which itself seemed almost a defiant act against the magazine-publishing establishment that was almost exclusively based in New York. Employing a team of accomplished illustrators and columnists, *Our Continent* was an expensive enterprise, paying high prices to attract the best contributors— including $1,000 to Oscar Wilde for an original poem to launch its first issue—yet charging only ten cents per issue for sixteen quarto-size pages. In response to advice that he commission more work from cheaper and less esoteric writers, Tourgée indignantly declared that he would "stubbornly adhere" to his motto "the best is none too good for 'the masses' of

American readers."[43] Although the first issue impressively sold over 58,000 copies, Mr. Davis sold his share of *Our Continent* a few months afterward, apparently alarmed at Tourgée's propensity for extravagance and his high-minded inattention to the bottom line. Indeed, it was only after anticipated yearly subscriptions did not materialize in significant enough numbers that Tourgée bowed, after six issues, to the necessity of including advertisements in the magazine.[44]

By the time he awoke to the deteriorating finances of the magazine, the end was near and his ill-advised attempts to, in Tourgée's words, "resuscitate the corpse" by taking out personal loans and selling overvalued stock to investors only compounded the disaster that followed. "Had I been brave enough to cut expenses down to bed-rock, I should have succeeded," he insisted, "but I was not."[45] In 1883, he attempted to save the magazine by publishing it monthly, renaming it *The Continent*, and moving its headquarters to New York City, where he hoped to benefit from closer association to financers and other major publishers. This move nearly worked, but it came too late. The following year Tourgée attracted the interest of Mrs. Frank Leslie, wife of the great magazine mogul, who considered buying out the magazine and retaining Tourgée as editor. Before the deal could be completed, Mr. Leslie squashed it for fear of becoming embroiled in *The Continent*'s impending lawsuits. Thus, publication of *The Continent* ceased on August 13, 1884, with its final circulation having dropped below 4,000.[46]

After the magazine's demise, the Tourgées gave up their New York apartment and withdrew to Thorheim, where they would spend the majority of the next thirteen years. The property was protected from Albion's creditors because it had been given to Emma as a gift and owned solely in her name—a happenstance that led to a practice of putting all of their property, including the copyright to each new book Albion wrote, in either Emma's or Aimée's name. From the seclusion of Thorheim, Albion took a hard view of his predicament and the demeaning measures he was forced to adopt to forestall his creditors. "I feel humiliated, and it would be hard indeed to expect a friend to overlook what I am so clearly conscious of," he explained to a former *Continent* colleague. His deeply-lying Puritanical belief in the justice of a "free labor" system made him regard his business failure as an adverse judgment upon his own character. In his mind, he bore a stigma "as one who has failed to accomplish his undertakings" that bespoke of some terrible inadequacy, a serious moral or intellectual lacking that made him almost undeserving of his famous name. "Before I have any right to ask others to put me on the level I occupied before," he declared, "I have to work my way back to self-esteem by self-achievement and retrieve this failure."[47]

This burden wore heavily on him as the years passed. "For two years after my disaster I fought and hoped," he would admit a few years later. "Since that time, I have not hoped . . . I never expect again to see my family have more than daily food and decent clothes."[48] Tourgée would write book after book, trying to replicate the success of his two Reconstruction novels, but each new book seemed to bring diminishing returns. Earning a small income through lecture tours, from newspaper and magazine publications, and occasionally from book advances, Albion refused to succumb to the need to return to a regular profession—such as teaching or practicing law—and instead waited for a financial miracle that never arrived. Seemingly intent on recouping his entire lost fortune in one heroic act of individual achievement, he even turned to the quixotic dream of patenting a new invention. A steel harness, a shock-absorbing wheel, an improved propeller, and other similar projects were patented, whose conception and design occupied many precious hours, but none of which caught on with manufacturers.[49]

Emma's remark that the *Continent* disaster had taken everything "except his wife" expressed her own sense of martyrdom but also a con-firmation of her self-conscious decision to remain and support Albion. Although their relationship was often strained by their crushing debts, both Albion and Emma were determined to put the storminess of the 1870s behind them and remain together. Unlike in North Carolina, at Thorheim Emma was able to create the kind of family life she had imagined, with regular church attendance, her family members nearby, and indulgent neighbors proud of their famous local author. Emma's beloved older sister Angie continued to teach at the Erie Academy but spent nearly every vacation with the Tourgées. Excepting her distress over their financial straits and her periodic frustration at Albion's inability to break them, Emma experienced a large measure of contentment at Thorheim.[50]

After the *Continent*'s collapse, Albion came to depend upon Emma's emotional, intellectual, and managerial support more than ever before. Though he had often taken her for granted previously, he had fallen almost completely to pieces emotionally when Emma left him in the 1870s. Now, he could not take yet another desertion from the one person who had always been there to nourish his self-esteem with her boundless faith in his talent and intellect, if not always in his judgment. Aided by her editorial skills and her whip-cracking encouragement, he produced a remarkable quantity of writing from Thorheim, and he later gave her credit for his productivity, speaking of her as a "sweet co-laborer" and "tireless collaborator" in his literary work. "It is hardly too much to say, that for her clarifying touch, little had ever come off the work-bench on which so much had been heaped," Albion affirmed. "[M]any an uncompromising sketch has grown under her prudent nursing, to a lusty volume."[51] For example, immediately upon their arrival at Thorheim after *The Continent* folded in the summer of 1884, Emma would not allow him to wallow in self-pity and insisted that he finish his long-planned *An Appeal to Caesar*. At her insistence, he dictated the book to her from a sickbed, where he lay depressed and immobilized by a severe recurrence of his back trouble.

Emma kept a diary that covered most of the years from 1881 to 1898, chronicling her efforts to motivate Albion and keep them afloat financially. She spent endless hours criticizing, proofreading, copying, and re-copying his work, often staying up late into the night to prepare manuscripts for morning deadlines. "Looked over what Albion had written," she exhaustedly recorded in one diary entry, "find many alterations necessary which it pains me to call to his attention but it must be done."[52] With his mind "too large" for business details, Emma managed their finances, as she had done throughout their marriage, while at the same time keeping Albion's schedule, supervising the help, being a mother to Aimée, and caring for her often-ailing younger sister, Millie, and her aging mother, Mary. Though they might have sold some of their property and possessions to reduce their debts, Emma and Albion opted to live beyond their limited means. This sometimes involved the humiliation of buying groceries on credit, explaining missed mortgage payments to the bank, and selling fruit from their orchard for extra cash—tasks that inevitably fell to Emma to perform.[53]

Even more significant than her moral and managerial support, Emma encouraged Albion's adherence to the moral values of their youth. They had shared the same radical individualist outlook since antebellum times and now they reinforced each other's views. Having spent a decade and a half away from the North, they found the North to which they had returned differed greatly from the one they left in 1865. Each rejected the secularization of political and social thought and remained intellectually anchored to the world of the 1850s. It was surely no accident that they chose to live in western New York—in a town, Mayville, that closely resembled the texture of life as they had known it before the war on the Western Reserve. They seemed to deliberately isolate themselves from the drastic economic and social changes that they encountered while living in New York and Philadelphia from 1880 to 1884, during which time they escaped to Thorheim as often as possible. Though deeply cognizant of these changes, and alarmed by them, they preferred to avoid them in their daily experiences and thus chose a community well removed from the buzz of urban life.

At Thorheim, August 18, 1887. Front row, from left: Aimée (Lodie) Tourgée, age 16; Sarah Emillia (Millie) Kilbourne, age 40; Mary Kilbourne, age 79; Angie Kilbourne, age 49; Emma K. Tourgée, age 46. Woman standing at back and woman with hands on Emma's shoulders have not been identified. Courtesy of the Chautauqua County Historical Society, Westfield, NY.

The environmental surroundings at Thorheim encouraged Albion's sense of individual separateness and moral self-determination. Typically, he spent half-days working feverishly in his office only to rush off to his fishing boat to spend the remainder of the day in tranquil peace on Lake Chautauqua. These trips seemed to have less to do with a love of fishing than for the meditative isolation they offered—as attested by the fact that he rarely brought home any fish. He also took extended hunting trips at least once a year, often without companions. Reflecting upon his lifelong penchant to retreat alone into nature, he explained, "I love to be alone—to feel that I am alone . . . I like to bathe in solitude as in a sea, and know that I am king of a realm no other lives to dispute with me." Though he regarded excessive isolation from one's fellows to be morally unhealthy, Albion cherished these little retreats as a chance to banish "life's burdens . . . until the weariness has passed away" and he was prepared to "go forth into the battle of life again."[54] The frequency with which he took these rejuvenations suggests how heavily he felt those burdens.

As he wrestled with the demons of failure in the 1880s, Tourgée began to look upon his daughter Aimée as his greatest hope for redemption. Encouraging Aimée's interest in art and literature, the Tourgées enrolled her in the Philadelphia School of Design for Women in 1890 despite the extra financial burden, and later they sent her to study art in Europe and Canada. Though she preferred art, Albion sought to "coax and tease" Aimée into a literary career. Since she was very young, he had involved her in his imaginative process by inventing stories for her amusement. The novel *Button's Inn*, for instance, began as a yarn he spun for Aimée about the abandoned inn they passed on their daily drive to and from her academy. Aimée must have contributed to his stories or created some of her own, because by the time she was a teenager Albion had become convinced that she had inherited his literary gifts. He imagined that one day this child prodigy would surpass his own literary success.[55]

Never did Albion or Emma discuss Aimée's future in terms of marriage or motherhood; rather, they concentrated exclusively on her career. As with Tabitha Holton and Adaline Patillo, Albion often showed a keen interest in women's professional advancement. Whether his aspirations for her were a manifestation of an emerging feminism or a displacement of his own disappointed dreams is a matter of pure speculation. For her part, Aimée was an award-winning student, but she seemed hesitant about living up to her parent's expectations. As an artist, she published many sketches and illustrations but never seems to have attempted anything too ambitious. As a writer, she eventually would publish a few travel pieces and short stories. Among the family papers is a lengthy manuscript she wrote about an Irish family in a New York tenement district. Entitled *The Culwin Luck Stone*, the book is unfinished, and it is not clear whether she abandoned it or died before completing it. In her Last Will and Testament, written a few days before she died of heart disease at the early age of 38, Aimée identified her profession as "spinster."[56]

Though she adored and admired her father, Aimée sometimes chafed under the pressure of Albion's overbearing "encouragement" and his impatience for her to achieve great things. One exchange between Albion and twenty-year-old Aimée indicated the effect on her of his unrelenting spur. Writing to Aimée at her art school, Albion mentioned his disappointment at her reluctance to illustrate one of his forthcoming works and chided her for timidity. Threatening to "go insane or something" at his implication that she had been too timid to accept the task, she answered "the harder I work the less approval I get, it seems. . . . I don't seem able to satisfy you anyway for which I am very sorry."[57] Albion replied reassuringly, "Your papa loves you. . . . [you are] doing well . . . and developing splendidly." Nevertheless, he entreated, "Do not get worried, if I did advise you to begin *to do* . . . I have thought that you are like myself too much inclined to cumbersome exhaustiveness of preparation." Urging her toward greater self-confidence, he offered the lessons of his own life in an interesting manner:

> I have trembled with dread at every step in my life. I was afraid of my class-mates in college—half jealous of them. I have lived—to find out when it was too late to be of value—that only one of them was anything like my intellectual peer . . . If I had thought myself fit to command a company at the outset, I should have been a Maj. General before the war was closed. I did not, so I served under men who were my inferiors everyway except that they believed in themselves. The fear of starvation and shame led me to fight for a place as a member of the Constitutional Convention of 1868. I found myself the strongest man in it. I suffered almost mortal agony over the task of undertaking the duties of the Judgeship in 1868. It was easy to me and I am known in it . . . never mind it, now . . . it [self-confidence] may not come to you until you are forty as it did to your father. It may not come until you are sixty.

Each of these events was meant to demonstrate how bold and daring action had been rewarded with success while a lack of confidence had served only to prevent him from achieving much more. This statement, with its mixture of egotism and self-reproach, excessive pride in accomplishment and talent, and excessive self-blame at failure and weakness, makes it easy to comprehend why Aimée feared that she would never satisfy him. He would never be satisfied with himself. He concluded by telling her, "If you learn nothing from my failures I might almost as well not have lived."[58]

Despite the tension in their family relationships, the Tourgées were exceptionally close and life at Thorheim certainly had its share of happiness. But these years witness the solidification of Albion's self-image as a heroic failure: increasingly, he identified with the "Fool," that semi-fictional character he had created—a romantic hero who had been unjustly defeated, whose ambitions and ideals were set too high to be realized in his lifetime. Public acceptance and acclaim were somehow incompatible with this self-image, and coping with the failure of *Our Continent* enhanced his sense of alienation and sharpened his social criticism.

LITERARY POLITICS

Tourgée's literary output in the 1880s was prodigious: In that single decade he published nine novels and three novellas, one collection of short stories, and four books of essays or social criticism.[59] Add to this, dozens of newspaper, magazine, and journal articles, and the volume of writing he produced during these years is almost staggering. Not surprisingly, the quality of his work was uneven.

As a writer of fiction, Tourgée employed his craft largely to serve political causes, and he saw little use in fiction "without a purpose." Therefore, he rarely wrote anything that did not either attempt to mobilize his readers to action or deepen their understanding of a political or historical issue. His novels often had imaginative premises and invariably contained eloquent political discourses, insightful social commentary, and grippingly realistic scenes. Yet, even the best books suffered from an intrusive didacticism and repetitiveness that might have been less detrimental had he taken editorial advice from anyone other than Emma, who reinforced his predilection. At one point, publisher John R. Howard, knowing her influence, asked Emma to do something about Albion's reluctance to "spare anything he has written"; he jokingly added that if Albion could obtain his own parish where he could "preach twice Sundays & once Wednesday night," perhaps it would "relieve his internal moral commotion; then he could write *stories* without *sermons*."[60] But the stories meant little to Tourgée without the sermons.

Emma and Albion firmly believed that fictional writing should maintain an uplifting moral purpose. They also shared an aesthetic preference for the conventions of mid-Victorian literature that included intricate plotlines and fantastic deus ex machine solutions—among his favorites were the unmasking of disguised identities, miraculous coincidences, and mysterious genealogies that lead to unforeseen inheritances. Albion's favorite novelists were James Fenimore Cooper, Victor Hugo, and Sir Walter Scott.[61] At the same time, Tourgée had an exceptional talent for realistic description, and he often incorporated actual events—that he had experienced or had intimate knowledge of—into his novels in passages that rivaled those of the leading realists of the day. Since his time, there have been a few champions among literary critics who classify him as a realist; Eric Sunquist, for example, judged that "if realism is measured by the fusion of historical materials and imaginative action, Tourgée . . . has few peers."[62] Nevertheless, Tourgée explicitly rejected the aesthetic of literary realism.

In Tourgée's view, the philosophy of realism undercut the moral purpose of fiction by belittling human attempts to shape events. He began his assault on realism from his weekly editorial column in *Our Continent*, in which he attacked William Dean Howells and Henry James as "novelists of first-rate abilities with second rate purposes." He criticized them not so much for their techniques as for their subject matter that reflected a "belief that life has nothing good or noble . . . worth the novelist's while to seek out and portray." Regarding them as "over refined dilettanti" whose interest was limited to the psychological lives of the rich, he scoffed at their "eternal analysis of the most trivial and insignificant motives" that "may be very real life," but it was "the life of a vacuum." In a memorable comment that underscored his perception of their elitist, class-bound perspective, Tourgée remarked: "Mr. James has looked at us [humanity] through the large end of his opera glass, till convinced we are small enough for the microscopical examination he has inaugurated." "Whatever his art may represent," he concluded of James, "it has no fellowship with the noblest and deepest facts of life."[63]

Though he conflated the philosophy of Naturalism—which is explicitly deterministic—with realism more generally and described James's fiction better than Howells's, Tourgée was correct in his assertion that realist writers, as a rule, debunked individual heroism and often depicted efforts to achieve good in the world as hardly less than futile. The most prestigious literary critic of his time, Howells had lavishly praised the literary Naturalism of Europeans Emile Zola and Leo Tolstoy, who portrayed humanity's subjection to forces beyond its control, and he beseeched American authors to follow their example of banishing moral didacticism from fiction.[64] Thus Tourgée felt he was defending the idea of "the novel with a purpose" against the glorification of novels that ended in moral ambiguity and political confusion. Within a decade, this criticism would have less validity as many realist writers, including Howells, tackled larger social and political issues and began to adopt their own mode of "social protest." Edith Wharton, a realist in the Jamesian mold, would later remark, "[No] novel worth anything can be anything but a 'novel with a purpose,' & if anyone who cared for the moral issue did not see in my work that I care for it, I should have no one to blame but myself."[65] While we do not know how Tourgée would have responded to Wharton's *The House of Mirth* (1905), he could find no moral purpose in the early novels of James and Howells.

What is most interesting about Tourgée's attack on realism is that he seems to have regarded its philosophy as a rejection not merely of his literature but of his life. "A novel without a purpose," he observed, "is the counterpart of a man without an object."[66] Guided by the belief that individual action could achieve great results, he had self-consciously tried to live a hero's life: "It is an infamous theory," he fumed in reference to Tolstoy, "this notion that . . . heroism and love and the impulse to do good to others, are mere figments of a vain and deluded fancy." Without these ideals, he felt, the motivation to act on behalf of something greater than oneself would be lost. Perhaps thinking of his own life, he wrote: "If he had only learned the philosophy of 'realism' before he plumed his wings for flight, there would have been no bitter Icarean plunge! True enough; but he would never have been so near the sun, either." "Love may be a myth," he admitted, and "few—possibly . . . none—[are] fortunate enough to realize all their dreams, to attain all their ideals. But how much sweeter the world is for their having believed in them! How many *more* have struggled towards them, and how much *higher* have they climbed than if they had set out with the thought that all of these things are vain." Few would ever "strive for an ideal [they] may never reach," he concluded, had they imagined beforehand that their success was impossible. Arguing for the utility of belief systems as the foundation for human action, Tourgée anticipated the philosophy of William James.[67]

Tourgée's brazen challenge to the literary establishment, so characteristic of his personality, probably did little to enhance his own reputation with his contemporaries. He probably would have done better to articulate the philosophy behind his own aesthetic. For, despite his affinity with romantic novelists, his literary style incorporated a great deal of what later critics have come to classify as realism. He had no objection to realism insofar as it was a technique that evoked the textures and sounds of lived experience, and he prided himself in particular on his use of dialect, as he told an editor at *McClure's* in 1894: "You know I am a realist, in a much broader sense than those who claim the name, and my realism compels me to represent men as talking as I find that they really do."[68] Attempting to record life as he encountered it, Tourgée's fictional portrayals, especially of black culture in the South, have become some of the most important historical documents of the Reconstruction Era. Two scenes from his successful Reconstruction novels illustrate his realist method and his choice of subject matter.

In *A Fool's Errand*, Tourgée describes an African American church service the Servosses attended at the invitation of their radical ally "Uncle Jerry." The scene is told from the perspective of Emma's fictional counterpart, Metta, who describes their experience in a letter to her sister. As they enter the church, a hymn is being sung with the chorus, "Free! free! free, my Lord, free! An' we walks the hebben-ly way!" which Metta is shocked to learn had been a favorite during slavery times—"How the chorus came to be endured in those days I cannot imagine," she remarks. Metta's reaction to what she calls the "strangely weird" religious practices of the freedpeople is a mixture of fascination and fear. She reports:

> One man began weaving back and forth on his knees, and shouted, in a voice which might have been heard a mile, for fifteen or twenty minutes only one sentence—"Gather 'em in! O Lor', gather 'em in! Gather 'em in! O Lor', gather 'em in!"—in a strange, singing tone, the effect of which on the nerves was something terrible. Men shouted, women screamed. Some

sprang from their knees and danced, shouting, and tossing their arms about in an unconscious manner, reminding me of what I had read of the dancing dervishes of the Orient.

Metta describes herself as "clinging to Comfort's arm in almost hysterical fright" at the intensity of the ceremony. "I begged [Comfort] to take me away," she confessed, "but I am glad now that he did not." After a while, many of the dancers collapsed to the ground from exhaustion until "finally the see-sawing shouter himself fell over . . . in five minutes the assemblage was as quiet as any country prayer meeting in Michigan." The emotional outburst of the shouting and dancing is followed then by a mystical sermon preached by Uncle Jerry that concludes with a prophetic vision that Jerry delivers in a trancelike state—"he 'talked with God,' oh how simply and directly!" Metta exclaims in appreciation.[69] Tourgée's fascination with black spiritualism is evident here, and his description of this cultural encounter of white radicals and freedpeople should be of interest to any student of black-white relations during Reconstruction.

Tourgée's fullest attempt to portray black Southerners realistically in fiction can be found in *Bricks Without Straw*, however. In his representation of the diverse characters in the black community of Red Wing, he self-consciously set out to correct the "burnt cork minstrels and the exaggerations of caricaturists . . . [that] have come to represent the negro to the unfamiliar mind."[70] One character may be considered representative of Tourgée's method. Berry Lawson, the banjo-strumming entertainer of Red Wing who at first seems to resemble the stereotypical plantation minstrel, provides an alternate perspective in the community, one that is skeptical of the work of "cultural" Reconstruction. "A consummate mimic," Tourgée writes of Berry, "his fellows never tired either of his drolleries or his songs. Few escaped his mimicry, and nothing was too sacred for his wit." Berry gently ridicules and challenges the community leaders, Eliab Hill and Nimbus Ware, who strive to advance the community both economically and intellectually, and he provides an interesting critical foil to their project of uplift. At one point, Berry is singing to a crowd when Nimbus happens by and, seeing Nimbus, Berry begins an ironic song about the planters' ability to undermine every attempt of the "black man" to succeed economically:

> De brack man's gittin' awful rich
> The people seem to fear
> Alt'ough he 'pears to git in debt
>   A little ebbery year.
> Ob co'se he gits de biggest kind
>   Ob wages ebbery day,

> But when he comes to settle up
>   Dey dwindles all away
>
> Den jes fork up de little tax
>   Dat's laid upon the poll.
> It's jes de tax de state exac's
>   Fer habben of a soul!

While Berry's song is a protest against the poll tax, it is also a challenge to Nimbus, who has worked tirelessly toward establishing a profitable tobacco plantation at Red Wing and attempted to compete with the planters as an economic equal. However hard Nimbus works, the planters have the power to keep him in his place. Four stanzas long, the song concludes: "When cullud men was slaves, yer know / T'was drefful hard to tax 'em; / But jes de minnit dat dey's free, God save us! how dey wax 'em!"[71]

While some of the lyrics were likely altered by Tourgée, he borrowed the tune from a political song that was popular with the black community during 1865–67. Originally publishing it anonymously as the "Poll Tax Song" in the *Anti-Slavery Standard* in 1867, Tourgée interestingly did not claim any credit for its lyrics.[72] As it was typical for him to incorporate contemporary material nearly verbatim into his fiction, both the song and the character Berry Lawson were undoubtedly from real life. In any case, they shed important historical light on the political culture of the black community during Reconstruction and offer a glimpse of the wry humor characteristic of African American folktales and secular songs of the nineteenth century.[73]

As editor-in-chief of *Our Continent*, Tourgée showed a distinct preference for stories, poems, and essays that addressed issues related to African Americans and the Civil War.[74] In addition to his own fiction, he published works by such authors as Harriet Beecher Stowe, J. T. Trowbridge, Rebecca Harding Davis, Constance Fenimore Woolson, Edward Everett Hale, and Joel Chandler Harris, whose quaint dialect stories did not yet carry the neo-Confederate bent of his later Reconstruction novels. But, the writer whose work Tourgée most wished to see in the pages of *Our Continent* was George Washington Cable. A white Southerner, Cable had deeply impressed Tourgée with the "beautiful spirit of justice and charity towards the [Negro] race" exhibited in his 1880 novel *The Grandissimes*. Tourgée read *The Grandissimes* aloud to his family and subsequently made Cable an impressive offer of $7,500 to serialize his forthcoming Civil War novel in his magazine. According to Cable's biographer, his new novel, *Dr. Sevier*, was "still a long way from the type-setters" when the offer was made and Cable had little choice but to decline. Tourgée nevertheless took it personally, complaining to Cable,

"I have the misfortune to be one of your pet aversions."[75] Evidence suggests that Cable indeed may have been wary of the ex-carpetbagger with his reputed anti-Southern, "bloody-shirt waving" proclivities. Despite their similar literary interests, the two men would never establish a strong alliance. Even without Cable's contribution, however, the magazine had no trouble maintaining a radical agenda.

It is difficult to determine whether its political tone or literary quality was to blame for *Our Continent's* failure to capture a regular national readership. The publication of Tourgée's own serialized novel *Hot Plowshares* that ran from July 1882 until May 1883 corresponded with the magazine's precipitous drop in circulation. Dealing with the causes of the Civil War, focusing especially on the impact of the Fugitive Slave Law and the radicalization of the North in the 1850s, Tourgée called his novel "a history, wrought out with infinite pains, of the thought of a great section of the American people . . . true in every detail."[76] An ambitious idea, the book was not able to successfully combine its fictional plot with digressions into historical analysis. The most dramatic moment in the novel comes when the characters are temporarily led to believe that the heroine—a transplanted Southern belle named Hilda Hargrove—is the daughter of a nearly-white slave woman, a fact that readers had been led to suspect all along. The revelation of her "negro blood" exposes the depth of racism among her Northern classmates at a New England boarding school and puts Hilda in the position of being a fugitive slave pursued by her rightful owners. The plot twist briefly energizes the novel and raises interesting dramatic possibilities, the most powerful of which is when Hilda stares frantically into the mirror, looking madly at her skin, her eyes, and her hair for evidence of "the one drop of darker, baser blood," and is unable to answer with certainty the question "was it possible?"[77] Before Hilda and her Northern beau are forced to emotionally accept her new racial identity, however, they are rescued from the predicament by the unlikely arrival of absolute proof of her pure white ancestry. Thus, Tourgée dulled the critical edge of his story and undercut its radicalism by pulling back from an exploration of racial prejudice that might have truly discomfited his readers.

The shortcomings of *Hot Plowshares* were partly the result of Tourgée's inexperience with writing in a serial format and the fact that he had written it under difficult conditions. As he later explained, "it had just been commenced when it became necessary for the writer to assume the entire control and management of the *Continent*, both editorially and as a publisher."[78] Attempting to be both an editor and main contributor was, no doubt, ill-advised. Reviews were not enthusiastic. Complaining of incidents that strained the reader's credulity, *The Nation* noted: "the author

. . . has gathered much geographical and historical detail, but that makes brilliant essay writing, not the picture of life." "If the book were more important," the reviewer continued, "the fairness of some of the statements about even Northern affairs would doubtless be impugned." By restricting his commentary to the book's artistic weaknesses, the reviewer avoided engagement with the historical argument it advanced.[79]

At times criticism of Tourgée's aesthetics seemed a mask for hostility toward his politics. A private letter from Richard Watson Gilder, the editor of *Century Magazine*, to George Washington Cable in 1890 hinted as much. Having once been among Cable's most avid supporters, Gilder became impatient with Cable's repeated use of fiction to protest issues of racial injustice. Like other mugwump editors, Gilder had been increasingly disenchanted with sectionalism and began to self-consciously promote sectional reconciliation in the mid-1880s.[80] By 1890, Cable's politics had became unbearable to Gilder. Rejecting his Reconstruction novel *John March, Southerner*, Gilder effectively ended his literary relationship with Cable by telling him: "I could weep for disappointment. Instead of a return to literature, an attempt to fetch everything into literature save & except literature itself . . . Shades of Tourgee!"[81] Just what Cable had "fetched" into literature that made Gilder think of Tourgée was not simply a penchant for didacticism—common among contributors to *Century*— but more likely a particular concern for racial injustice in the South. Not coincidently, both Cable and Tourgée experienced declining sales in the 1880s, and neither would enjoy another popular success after 1890. Literary realism and mugwump politics had combined with a growing culture of North-South reconciliation to marginalize their novels as much for their politics as for their style.

Tellingly, the most critically acclaimed Civil War novel of the nineteenth century exemplified the kind of evisceration of politics from the memory of the Civil War that Northern editors so favored. Stephen Crane's *The Red Badge of Courage* (1895), regarded as a masterpiece of realism, used the war as a vehicle to study the pathos of humanity's struggle to survive in an amoral universe—a Darwinian theme if ever there was one. Crane depicted the soldiers as completely indifferent to slavery and the political issues of the war—topics never even mentioned in the book—and concerned primarily with the desire for prove their manliness and valor. The war appears in the book as virtually meaningless and without purpose, while the soldiers' effort to do their duty in the face of its horrors is both pathetic and yet ultimately honorable.[82] This was a far cry from the radical meaning of the Civil War that Tourgée propagated.

Critical reception of *The Red Badge of Courage* praised its psychological and descriptive realism at the expense of previous novelists of the Civil

War. Novelist Harold Frederic, reviewing it for the *New York Times*, applauded the novel's "effect of a photographic revelation" and compared Crane favorably to Civil War "writers of the elder generation . . . [like] Judge Tourgee." Although Crane had not personally fought in the Civil War, he noted, other writers who "saw tremendous struggles on the battlefield" firsthand nevertheless had failed to convey their experiences convincingly—"to put the reality into type baffles them." Frederic commented in particular on Tourgée's lack of subjective insight into the soldier's experience: "At best, he gives us a conventional account of what happened; but on analysis you find that this is not what he really saw, but what all his reading has taught him that he must have seen."[83] For Tourgée, however, fiction's similitude to lived experience was far less important than its political purpose. "Literalness is by no means synonymous with truth," Tourgée wrote in 1894, as if anticipating Frederic's criticism, "its [realism's] reality is that of half-truth which is the worst of all lies, because the most difficult to detect."[84] Truth, for him, was something different than what it felt like to be there.

Despite the prestige of realism in the highest literary circles, sentimental and romantic fiction remained the dominant style of the day, and a deluge of popular fiction offered yet another challenge to the radical memory of the Civil War. The late 1880s and 1890s witnessed the rise of popular novels and stage shows that celebrated the Old South as a pastoral Eden, with harmoniously hierarchical race relations, and mourned the lost Confederate cause as the last gasp of honor and chivalry in America. These themes appealed to those in the rapidly modernizing North who longed for simpler times.[85] Southern writers especially dominated this literature of the lost cause, a well-worn genre by the time it reached its apex with Margaret Mitchell's *Gone with the Wind* in 1936.

Tourgée addressed this trend in a notable 1888 article in *The Forum* entitled, "The South as a Field for Fiction." "Not only is the epoch of the war the favorite field of American Fiction today. But the Confederate soldier is the popular hero," he observed. "Our literature has become not only Southern in type, but distinctly Confederate in sympathy."[86] Tourgée was alarmed that Southern writers had claimed literary authority over the South yet left out much of the historical truth about the Civil War and Reconstruction. "About the Negro as a man, with hopes, fears, and aspirations like other men," he observed, "our literature is very nearly silent."[87] Likewise, "poor-whites," if mentioned at all, existed only as a foil to the Confederate officer. "So far as our fiction is concerned," he quipped, "there does not appear to have been any Confederate infantry." Tourgée appealed to aspiring writers, specifically "the children of soldiers and slaves," to correct these flaws and "advance American literature to the very front rank" of literary history. "The Negro race in America may itself become a power in literature," he predicted.[88]

African American writers and critics, indeed, would become the greatest caretakers of the radical memory of the war and the force in American literature he foresaw. Kept alive by such enthusiasts as Anna Julia Cooper, Charles Chesnutt, and Sterling Brown, Tourgée's own works would enjoy a critical standing and influence among African Americans long after his works fell out of the mainstream cannon. In 1892, Anna Julia Cooper wrote glowingly about Tourgée's novels in her pioneering book *A Voice from the South.* Ranking him first among the "champions of the black man's cause through the medium of fiction" with novels read by "five to ten millions," she judged, "in presenting truth from the colored American's standpoint Mr. Tourgee excels, we think, in fervency and frequency of utterance any living writer, white or colored." Comparing his treatment of racial issues favorably to those of George Washington Cable, she observed that while Cable never forgets that "he is a white man," Tourgée "speaks with all the eloquence and passion of the aggrieved party himself." Although Cooper tempered her praise with an honest assessment of his shortcomings, deeming him more of a "preacher" than a novelist, and predicting that it was "mainly as a contribution to polemic literature that most of Tourgee's works will be judged," her book began a tradition of including Tourgée in African American literary tradition that would be continued by early twentieth-century critics Sterling Brown and Hugh Gloster.[89]

Tourgée's call for challengers to the white domination of Southern literature was best answered in his lifetime by Charles W. Chesnutt, regarded by many critics as the first great African American novelist. Born in 1858, Chesnutt was raised in Tourgée's North Carolina, where he was educated during Reconstruction in a freedmen's school founded by the American Missionary Association in Fayetteville. As he often liked to recall, Chesnutt's attempt at a literary career was directly inspired by Tourgée's *A Fool's Errand* and *Bricks Without Straw.* An entry in Chesnutt's private journal in 1880, in fact, documents his initial reaction to these novels. "If Judge Tourgée, with his necessarily limited intercourse with colored people, and his limited stay in the South, can write such interesting descriptions, such vivid pictures of southern life and character as to make himself rich and famous," the twenty-two-year-old wrote, "why could not a colored man, who has lived among colored people all his life . . . write as good a book[?]"[90] A few weeks afterward, Chesnutt confided to his diary, "I think I must write a book . . . it has been my cherished dream, and I feel an influence that I cannot resist calling me to the task." Moreover, he declared emphatically, "If I do write, I shall write for a purpose, a high, holy purpose, and this will inspire me to greater effort."[91]

When Chesnutt began to publish his first short stories in the mid-1880s, he wrote to Tourgée for encouragement and editorial advice. Tourgée proved a responsive mentor, taking an active interest in Chesnutt's career and mentioning him as a promising author in his *Forum* article. In private letters, he urged Chesnutt forward, elaborating on his own views of African Americans' potential in the field of literature. In one such contemplation, he prophesized:

> I incline to think that the climacteric of American literature will be negroloid in character. I do not mean in form—the dialect is a mere fleeting incident,—but in style of thought, intensity of color, fervency of passion and grandeur of aspiration. Literature rather than politics, science or government is the branch in which the American Negro—not the African for there is really but little of the African left—will win his earliest, perhaps his brightest laurels. . . . Power will not flow to their hands for many generations, but art and literature will be the field of their achievements and triumphs.[92]

In this brief passage, Tourgée not only anticipated the artistic bent of the "New Negro" movement of the early twentieth century, but he foresaw the central place that African American culture would eventually occupy in American culture. One wonders if Tourgée would have defined his own literature as "negroloid in character." He never elaborated on these views, but at the very least, this passage indicates that he perceived within African American culture distinctive renderings of the human condition that were of great value, destined to be of great influence, and worthy of imitation. Whether, or how, those elements might have influenced his own fiction, he left for the literary historians to discover.

Despite Tourgée's encouragement, Chesnutt proceeded cautiously. He considered his own "dialect stories" of minor importance and informed Tourgée in 1893 that he was still "biding his time" in preparation of fulfilling his dream of writing a novel.[93] Eventually, Chesnutt would publish three novels, all of which paralleled Tourgée's in their style and subject matter, most especially *The Marrow of Tradition* (1901), a political novel that directly protested Southern racism and segregation. When delivering the manuscript to his publisher, Chesnutt remarked that he hoped that the novel might "become lodged in the popular mind as the legitimate successor of 'Uncle Tom's Cabin' and 'A Fool's Errand' as depicting an epoch in our national history."[94] Yet, Chesnutt had waited too long to write his radical novel. *The Marrow of Tradition* would not duplicate the popular success of *A Fool's Errand*, and its financial failure would hasten Chesnutt's retirement from fiction in 1905. Ironically, another novel modeled after *A Fool's Errand* and inspired by *Uncle Tom's*

Cabin achieved phenomenal success in 1902. That book was Thomas Dixon's *The Leopard's Spots.*

TOWARD CHRISTIAN SOCIALISM

As he grappled with the cultural transition that seemed to be leaving the antislavery ideals of the Civil War era behind, Tourgée fell back upon bedrock principles. The elitist skepticism about democracy he perceived all around him led him toward deeper philosophical introspections of his own political principles. In a series of books published in the late 1880s, the religious basis of his radicalism came to the forefront as he searched for a solid foundation on which to base his beliefs. The result was Tourgée's own version of the Social Gospel in which he merged the ethical teachings of Christianity with his unwavering commitment to democratic government.

His first philosophical exploration, a collection of essays entitled *Letters to a King*, specifically addressed the generation that had grown up since the Civil War. Formulated as a series of letters written to the (probably fictional) son of a fallen comrade, the book catechized on the duties of citizenship and the "ethical principles of our government" and afforded him the opportunity to venture into political philosophy in the guise of juvenal advice literature. The survival of democracy, the book argued, depended upon one's obligation to act ethically towards fellow citizens. Democracy, he pointed out, was optimistic of human nature; it assumed that "a majority of the citizenship will always be wise enough . . . honest and patriotic enough to demand what is for the general good." For citizens to practice this kind of virtue, they must respect the rights of others as they would their own. "He [the citizen] is responsible not only for his own action, but for his fellow's opportunity," he asserted. "He must not only stubbornly assert and maintain his *own* privilege, he must see to it that neither fraud, violence, bribery, terror, nor any other malign influence, shall be allowed to neutralize the conviction, bias the judgment or thwart the will of his fellows."[95] In other words, Tourgée rejected the view of a democratic citizenship based only on negative liberty—that is, freedom from encroachment on privately enjoyed rights—and moved toward one based on positive liberty, which demands that citizens actively pursue the common good.

Throughout *Letters to a King*, Tourgée reiterated that a democratic system was designed to protect the lower classes from domination by the powerful and educated. It was to the poor, the weak, and undereducated who otherwise lack the means to protect their interests, he wrote, "to such the ballot is at once a sword and a shield. . . . It is their only hope.

Unfortunately, intelligence does not always imply righteousness or justice; and even against the best, the lowest and the meanest of every land need always to stand on their guard."[96] Citing Lincoln as an example, he pointed out that the "natural" leaders of a republic did not come from privilege but rather sprang from the ranks of those who best understood the sufferings of the common people. "It is not the rich, the wise, the refined and cultured elements of the world's life who have pushed forward the cause of humanity and right," he observed, "the man who feels the popular want, understands the demands of the popular heart . . . becomes the political leader in a republic."[97]

While Tourgée did not systematically explore the ethical code of democratic citizenship in *Letters to a King*, his subsequent essays on the theme developed the argument that he had first put forth in his ca. 1876 lecture "the Ben Adhemite Era": the Golden Rule was an absolute moral standard for democratic conduct. As he had written in a newspaper column in 1889, " 'Whatsoever ye would that others should do unto you, do ye even so to them' is the only divine measure of Christian conduct. It is the universal standard of just relations between man and man in private and public capacity, and without exception as to race or color."[98] This principle, he argued, had given rise to the antislavery movement and it was at the heart of democracy as a political system. "As ethical systems, Christianity and democracy have the same purpose," he concluded, "neither can fully secure the results it professes without the cooperation of the other. . . . Christianity and good citizenship are identical."[99] This was the language of the higher law, as it had been employed in the Western Reserve of Tourgée's youth. The Golden Rule's instruction to treat others as you would yourself contained within an implicit message of the oneness of humanity and the entitlement of all to fair treatment and equal justice. By making this doctrine an explicit element of democratic ethics, Tourgée imagined that social turmoil could be alleviated.

In the 1880s, a host of Protestant ministers and religious thinkers were reaching similar conclusions. They refuted the popular notion that individuals were motivated solely by economic self-interest—a notion supposedly confirmed in the law of "survival of the fittest"—and they advocated a radical application of Christian ethics. In 1886 Washington Gladden's *Applied Christianity* denied that the "maxims of Smith and Ricardo" were true regarding the economic imperative to pursue self-interest, and they proposed instead that the rule of conscience and the Golden Rule would achieve better results in both prosperity and social harmony. Richard T. Ely, a leading economist who once contributed an essay to *Our Continent*, declared in his book *The Labor Movement in America* (1886) that the Christian doctrine of universal brotherhood should be the rallying cry and the animating principle of the labor movement. Like Tourgée, these thinkers were suspicious of governmental intervention into the economy, but they unhesitatingly supported the interest of laborers and called on capitalists to reform their own business practices. "The first duty of man in trade, as in other departments of human employment," Ely suggested, "is to follow the Golden Rule."[100]

Influenced by this thinking on economic injustice, Tourgée was particularly energized by the success of Edward Bellamy's utopian novel, *Looking Backward* (1888), which was a didactic expression of the author's Christian social ethics. As a reform novel, this book surpassed *A Fool's Errand* in the political excitement it ignited that also drew comparisons to *Uncle Tom's Cabin*. The receptive response to its devastating moral critique of corporate capitalism inspired Tourgée with the hope: "The spirit is gaining force with amazing rapidity in our land that the welfare of the many is immensely more important than the engorgement of the few."[101] While he agreed with Bellamy's diagnosis that rampant selfishness and greed by corporations were at the root of working-class poverty and social unrest, Bellamy's remedy of a nationalized economy managed by an informed elite disappointed him. Not only did it seem impractical, it called for a degree of government intervention into "all the environments of life" that he found dangerous to individual liberty. Though he supported government control over some elements of the economy—telegraphs and public utilities, for instance—he could not imagine a complete rejection of free enterprise. Yet, he began to imagine the possibility of a moral awakening on economic injustice akin to the one that swept over the North in the 1850s in opposition to the extension of slavery—an awakening that embraced Bellamy's principles if not his specific plan.

Emboldened by Bellamy's success, Tourgée infused his next three novels with his concerns about the labor problem, democratic ethics, and of course, the race problem, each book honing its message more effectively than the last. The first and most experimental of these, *Eighty-Nine; or the Grand Master's Secret* (1888), creatively critiqued corporate capitalism by drawing a comparison between the anti-democratic views of Northern corporate leaders with that of the Southern planter aristocracy. Borrowing a plot device from *Looking Backward*, *Eighty-Nine* purports to be a personal account of future events recorded by an eyewitness—though it is indicative of Tourgée's sense of urgency that his setting is not the distant future of 2000 but the very near future of 1889. In that year, a neo-Confederate secret political order, "the Order of the Southern Cross," and the corrupt Rock Oil Trust conspire to orchestrate a stalemated presidential election in 1888—reminiscent of the election of 1876—which results in the permanent suspension of the Constitution and divides the country into two separate nations: a Northern one dominated by Rock Oil's political and economic monopoly and a Southern one dominated by the neo-Confederate planter class. In this shady cross-sectional conspiracy, the Northern industrialists and Southern agriculturalists crush their "labor problems" by reconfiguring their political power to secure absolute control over their laborers and dissolving democratic government.[102] While Tourgée did not integrate the elements of this outlandish tale very coherently, he did manage to draw unsettling comparisons between the oppression of Southern black laborers and the Northern industrial working class. The misfired experiment of *Eighty-Nine* was soon improved upon by two novels that would more effectively promote his new interests.

Pactolus Prime; or the White Christ (1890) began as a short Christmas story published in the *Chicago Advance*, a weekly religious periodical, and grew into a full-fledged serialized novel as readers demanded to know more about the mysterious character from which the book takes its title. One of the most unusual African American figures in all of nineteenth-century American literature, Pactolus Prime is both a vehement black separatist and a self-hating internalizer of white racism. Striking in appearance with his completely bald head and deep blue-black complexion, Pactolus wears dark glasses at all times and works as a boot black in an upscale Washington, D.C., hotel. There, he spends his days debating issues related to the race question with senators, ministers, Supreme Court justices, and other powerful men who, while sitting in his chair for a shoeshine, humor him in conversation. Having mastered the intricacies of legislation and law at some point in his mysterious past, he is an intellectual match for anyone who sits in his chair—and he holds back nothing in his unsparing denunciation of the hypocrisy of both Christianity and American democracy.

All of the action of the novel takes place on Christmas day, providing the theme for the novel and allowing Pactolus—and Tourgée—to take white Americans to task for their unchristian treatment of blacks. Utterly contemptuous of Christianity, Pactolus is asked at one point whether he at least believes in Santa Claus. "I've heard that Santa Claus was really some sort of heathen god just made over to suit later notions," he replies. "He might not be troubled at my complexion—might be color-blind, you know; but the Christ, Mr. Ca'son, your white Christ don't ever make such mistakes."[103] Preferring the "heathen gods" to the Christian ones, Pactolus makes repeated references to Christ's "whiteness" and the inapplicability of Christian teachings across the color-line. Probably to shock his readers, Tourgée allows Pactolus to be killed tragically in an accident without ever recanting his blasphemous talk or being reconciled to Christianity.

Tourgée undoubtedly meant Pactolus Prime to be a tragic figure—the editor's preface calls him the "Oedipus of American literature"—and his fate a dire lesson about the perverse consequences of racism on American ideals. The mystery of Pactolus's life is revealed when an autobiographical manuscript is found among his papers that recounts a fantastic tale of racial passing, miscegenation, love, betrayal, and remarkable accomplishment. As it turns out, Pactolus had been a light-skinned slave, the son of his master, who escaped and passed for white until his skin was turned blue-black as the unfortunate side-effect of a medical treatment. Thwarted in his desire to escape his racial identity, he is forced to live out his life suffering the full prejudice against his race, despite having attained a university education and secretly amassed a fortune through real estate speculation accomplished with the aid of a white lawyer who conducts the transactions in his name. Working as a humble bootblack, he is embittered toward, and defiant of, white society. His greatest desire is to bequeath his secret fortune to his light-skinned daughter, Eva, who has been kept ignorant of the identity of her father and unknowingly passes as an orphaned Southern belle in Washington high society, enjoying the privileges of being wealthy and white in America. Pactolus's elaborate will is foiled by Eva's own investigation, which uncovers the truth. In the end, Eva joins a convent, adopts the name Sister Pactola, and devotes the entire fortune and the rest of her life to the uplifting of her race.

Because Tourgée imbues Pactolus with many of his own political views, along with his acerbic profanities, the reader is led to identify with him and cannot fully condemn him for his shocking "blasphemies." Undeniably for the reader, the talented Pactolus has been deprived of deserved career advancement and prevented from enjoying his self-earned wealth on account of the unchristian prejudice against his race. Moreover, Tourgée effectively uses the character's strangely chameleonic and conflicted racial identity to suggest both the instability of racial classifications and the perverse psychological consequences of racism on those stigmatized by those classifications. On this last point, Charles Chesnutt reacted strongly against *Pactolus Prime*'s denouement because he felt that Tourgée had punished Eva as if she were a fallen woman by sending her into a convent when her only sin was the "taint"—in Chestnutt's words—of black ancestry.[104] But Tourgée probably intended Eva's devotional turn as a means of redemption for her father's unredeemed soul, not to suggest impurity for having mixed ancestry. His ending was in keeping with the tragedy he intended the story to be and consistent with the values of the presumed Christian readership of the *Advance* whom he expected to scandalize with the story. Tourgée believed the book, even with its watered-down conclusion, to be so blasphemous that he later conjectured, " 'Pactolus Prime' if it gets into a household is usually stowed away where the children will not get a hold of it."[105]

While he addressed the theme of racial injustice and Christian ethics in *Pactolus Prime*, Tourgée simultaneously had begun work on a major novel that would apply his interest in Christian social ethics to the labor problem. Consumed with the desire to match Bellamy's political impact on this issue, he spent nearly a year meditating upon the plot before he began. Emma described his seriousness of purpose in her diary: "the agony—I can use no other word—of decision was intense. He wishes to do so well—to put forcibly the truths which have weighed on him so long."[106] The story succeeded *Pactolus Prime* in the *Advance* from October 1889 to July 1890 under the title "Naziremea or the Church of the Golden Lillies" and was subsequently published in book form as *Murvale Eastman: Christian Socialist* (1890). The novel sold better than most of Tourgée's recent books, although it did not approach the great breakthrough he aspired to achieve. Only a few years later, the most wildly successful of all social gospel novels, *In His Steps* by Rev. Charles Monroe Sheldon, which boiled Christian social ethics down to the immortal question "What Would Jesus Do?" was serialized in the *Advance* in 1896.

Most reviewers praised *Murvale Eastman*, and it attracted enough attention in England, where Christian socialism originated, that a conference of ministers held a discussion of the book in 1893. Ex-President Rutherford B. Hayes recorded his approval of *Murvale Eastman* in his private journal, declaring "It is his best book; puts the question of our time admirably. He has hit the nail on the head. More that is good and less that hurts than in any book I have seen on the question."[107] Even Southern reviewers applauded Tourgée this time, and the *Atlanta Constitution* was particularly glad he had taken on Northern issues, remarking that at last "his nose is pointed in the right direction."[108] *Murvale Eastman* has been viewed favorably too by the few twentieth-century critics who have written about it, even deemed by one to be "among the best of the works of the last two decades of the century on the economic and social problems of an expanding capitalism."[109] The book at least belongs on any short list of important works in the social gospel tradition.

Murvale Eastman tells the story of the moral awakening of the affluent minister of one of the richest Episcopal parishes in an East Coast city (likely New York City). Described as a "skilled sportsman and a yachtsman of renown," Murvale Eastman had "sprung from a family both old and rich" and he enjoys a comfortable, aristocratic lifestyle. Revered and flattered by his admiring congregation, Eastman is unbothered by the social turmoil of industrialization and seems an unlikely candidate to become an agitator for the labor movement. But he is transformed when he witnesses the near-killing of a "scab" streetcar driver, whose car is over-turned by rioting strikers during a tumultuous streetcar strike. "It aint any more'n I deserve," the old driver tells Eastman as he lays near death on the sidewalk, "to keep myself from starvation I helped the company keep up its slaves' hours and starvation wages for others. And this is what I've got for it!"[110] Even more, the old driver turns out to be a Civil War veteran who has been unjustly deprived of his pension though he con-tinues to suffer from his war injuries. Horrified, Eastman impulsively decides to hold down the man's job until the driver is well enough to resume the position.

Because the company maintains a dehumanizing policy of refusing to know its drivers' names and referring to them only by their license numbers—as if they were "jailbirds," one character says—Eastman is able to take over the identity of "number forty-six" and brave the danger of cov-ering the man's route while he recuperates. As such, Eastman experi-ences the brutalizing conditions of the job and comes to sympathize with the strikers' demands for higher wages and a ten-hour day. Eventually, he negotiates a settlement with the company on behalf of the laborers, winning all their demands as well as an annual profit-sharing bonus. Using his charisma and moral reasoning, Eastman thus prevents violence between the strikers and management and persuades the board of direc-tors to treat their workers at least as well as their prized horses (ironically one of the board members is a zealous leader of the American Society for the Prevention of Cruelty to Animals and scrupulously keeps the com-pany's horses pampered, well fed and not overworked).

Tourgée's descriptions of the strikers and the conditions at the streetcar company are effective, but the main conflict of the novel takes place at the Church of the Golden Lilies where Eastman attempts to translate his experience into a new religious doctrine for his congregation. Led by the quiet opposition of its "chief factotum," Wilton Kishu, the rich congre-gation revolts against the minister—at first—when he begins to preach a code of conduct that he calls "Christian socialism." "The fundamental idea of the Founder of Christianity . . . [is that] it is the duty of the strong to assist the weak—*not* to devour them," he chides his congregation, "the *social* function of Christianity is not merely to relieve want or exercise 'charity' but to *incline the hearts of men in their individual, corporate, and political relations to refrain from doing evil* . . . [and to] make the welfare of their fellows the first and highest object in life."[111] Though it embarras-ses his congregation, Eastman's pronouncement captures the attention of the press, which descends on the Church of the Golden Lilies and prevents the powerful Wilton Kishu from summarily dismissing Eastman from his post. Foiled, the scheming Kishu nevertheless covertly undertakes to destroy Eastman by character assassination, employing a private investigator who dredges up a convincing accusation that Eastman fathered a child out of wedlock. Using his control over the press, Kishu reveals his pastor to be a hypocrite and forces him to resign in disgrace.

Perhaps the most interesting character in the novel, Kishu voices the corporate perspective and represents the prototypical Captain of Industry. Perhaps modeled on J.P. Morgan—who acted in a similar role at St. George's Episcopal Church in New York—Kishu exercised a dictatorship over the Church of the Golden Lilies, where he "managed the finances; engineered the Sabbath-school; looked after the Mission" and contributed generously to its coffers.[112] Like all men of his class, he instinctively opposed anything that challenged his power and he ferociously protected his interests against all "socialistic" schemes of the labor movement. Because it was the rich man who "builds the churches [and] endows the schools," Kishu assumed, Tourgée tells us, that he should be "allowed to plunder at will, in order that he may disburse at his own good pleasure."[113] A self-made man, he cannot sympathize with those who did not succeed as well as himself. Kishu possessed, "the universal American contempt for the man who does not achieve, do something for himself. It is the inheritance of our distinct individuality. With all of his snobbery, this was at the bottom of Wilton Kishu's character."[114] But in the end, Kishu is miraculously converted to Christian Socialism when he comes to admit that his own success had been purchased only through ruthlessness and the unchristian treatment of his fellows (in particular one dark instance of cheating his fellow man which put him on the road to success). The novel concludes optimistically with Eastman exonerated from all moral suspicion and Kishu launching the Society of Christian Socialism to promote the ethical precepts of the Golden Rule and human brotherhood. The society declares itself to be open to atheists and nonbelievers, although Tourgée makes little effort to make the society seem welcoming to non-Protestants.

Murvale Eastman is Tourgée's most extended application of his egalitarian principles toward a critique of corporate capitalism. But his analysis does not fail to address, and assimilate, his views on racial injustice. In the didactic conclusion of the novel, one of the characters explains to Wilton Kishu that the callous disregard for human life in the process of European colonization and imperialism around the globe has come home to roost in the attitude of men like himself toward their own laborers. Interjecting Tourgée's own views in an extended indictment of white supremacy, the character observes:

"We said to the Indian, the Negro, the Sandwich Islander, to the weaker, dusky peoples of all the lands we coveted: 'Give us what we desire; become civilized; accept our forms of life and government; give up what you prize—or we will kill you. If you accept our terms, you must furnish a market for our rum and opium and submit to our lust and rapacity. If you cannot stand before our civilization under these conditions, you must accept it as the will of God that you should disappear from the face of the Earth."

"I suppose that is so, Mr. Underwood [Mr. Kishu responds] but what has that got do to with the plans you spoke of? There aren't any heathen about here."

"True enough; but the philosophy which has justified, defended, exalted Anglo-Saxon civilization, in spite of its terrible record of slaughter and destruction of the weak, has now turned itself upon our own life, don't you see?"

"I—I don't believe I do—exactly—"

"What we call 'the law of civilization' has been that we had the right to seize the lands, destroy the government and social system of any weaker people and require them to adopt ours—and if they grow restive or resisted, kill them. This was on the theory that an uncivilized people have no rights a civilized people are bound to respect, or in other words that strong peoples have a right not only to control weaker ones, but to prescribe what is best for them and under what conditions they may be permitted to live. This we call 'the immutable law of progress' .... This idea—that the strong have, somehow, a right to control the weak—used to be a question of race, nationality, or class, but now it is a question of individuals . . . the big fish are constantly swallowing the little ones, and are themselves growing greater and fewer. All forms of business are going into the control of fewer and fewer men."[115]

In the final analysis, Tourgée implies, this monumental injustice can be reduced to a question of individual morality and lack of ethical conduct. The justification of the strong to dominate the weak will lead to greater and greater social injustices—first between races, then between nations, and finally between individuals. The end result is the exultation of the few. Humanitarianism toward all, on the contrary, will lead toward greater social justice and the exultation of the many.

Despite its subtitle, *Murvale Eastman* does not support socialism in the sense of introducing greater government control over the economy. Tourgée's preface to the book made clear that the author "has not sought to indicate specific methods of amendment" but only the "moral tendency from which amendment must arise."[116] Indeed Eastman repeatedly warns against "the overthrow of all existing systems" and emphasizes the need for a gradual, moral transformation rather than a sudden, convulsive revolution. He pragmatically suggests, at one point, that the commandment to "bear ye one another's burdens" might be carried out "sometimes through governmental action, sometimes through voluntary associations."[117] *Murvale Eastman* concludes with the founding of a society to propagate this social ethic and the conversion of a powerful capitalist, but unlike Bellamy's novel, it does not provide a specific blueprint toward the full realization of these ideals.

Nevertheless, some of Tourgée's readers accused him of promoting socialism—an anathema for many who equated it with anarchism or atheism. He exasperatedly replied to one university professor that "Murvale Eastman is not concerned with the means or method . . . but only asks the question 'how may . . . the Golden rule be applied?"[118] In an exchange with Bishop John H. Vincent, the Methodist founder of the Chautauqua Institute, Tourgée rebuked Vincent for his narrow view of Christian doctrine. "The Church is not entirely in accord with the prevailing impulse for human betterment . . . because it clings to the theory of the supernatural nature of Christ," Tourgée insisted. "This is not only illogical but absurd . . . there must be a common ground for Christian social-political activity in which the question of faith should not arise."[119] Disappointed that his secularized gospel should "seem so strange and sometimes incomprehensible" to religious leaders whom he expected to welcome it, he nevertheless had reason to feel that his message had struck a chord in some influential circles and that at last his voice was joined with others in an attempt to rally the social conscience against economic injustice.

Although the social gospel movement presented a sharp indictment of laissez-faire capitalism, Tourgée himself never abandoned the meritocratic economic model. He remained wary of the labor movement, especially when the rhetoric of its spokesmen appeared to reject capitalism for such extreme alternatives as anarchism or communism. For Tourgée, the promise of a meritocracy in which talent and hard work would be rewarded with success had to remain the underlying principle of the economic system. This accorded with his notion of justice. But considering his own financial circumstances, it was not difficult for him to believe that something had gone terribly wrong with American capitalism, as is illustrated by Kishu's ethically warped doctrine of success. "The 'wealth of nations' has proved a delusion," he wrote in the book's preface regarding the postulation that market forces could alone administer economic justice; "wage earning is not slavery, but when it becomes a fixed condition it is one of sheer dependence."[120] As it was for the race issue, individual autonomy and self-direction was his measure of liberty and justice. And rather than place his faith in deterministic laws of supply and demand or of inevitable class struggle, he as always looked to individuals, guided by conscience, to attain this standard of justice through their own ability to act in ethical and humane ways.

8

Beginning the Civil Rights Movement

The most popular white man in the country today with Afro-Americans is that staunch friend of the race, Judge Albion W. Tourgée.

> —Harry C. Smith, *Cleveland Gazette*, November 21, 1891

I know I voice the sentiments of thousands of my race [in wishing] that the Bystander may live long to speak with clarion voice against wrong and injustice.

> —Ida B. Wells to Tourgée, February 22, 1893

You are fighting a great battle, Judge. You are, if not the only one, the foremost militant apostle of liberty in the whole land. You are doing an immense good to the blacks of the South . . . instilling in them a spirit of resistance. You are rendering a great service to the whites of the North by opening their eyes to dangerous and criminal conditions in the South.

> —Louis A. Martinet to Tourgée, May 30, 1893

NOT LONG AFTER HE PUBLISHED *AN APPEAL TO CAESAR*, Tourgée mused, "[I have probably] done my last work and written my last word" on the subject of race.[1] Having made his case for national education repeatedly and at length, he imagined little else he could do to advance the cause of racial equality. He hoped that steady economic and educational progress, aided by the federal government, would enhance African Americans' ability to exercise their hard-won civil and political rights. Yet, he failed to anticipate just how far back the counterrevolution against Reconstruction was about to swing. A rash of lynchings and white mob violence against blacks that started in the South and spread rapidly into the Midwest in the late 1880s heralded a frightening new reassertion of white supremacy. State-mandated racial segregation and the wholesale disenfranchisement of Southern blacks were soon to follow in the 1890s.

These developments drew Tourgée inexorably back into the national dialogue about race. With a renewed sense of urgency, and discarding moderation, he returned as a firebrand of racial equality, regarded by many as the second coming of William Lloyd Garrison.

THE BYSTANDER

Tourgée's newfound stature was achieved through a weekly newspaper column in the *Daily Inter Ocean,* Chicago's leading Republican newspaper. Having contributed several well-received special series to the paper in the 1880s,[2] its editors hoped that Tourgée's brand of fearless social commentary, and his famous name, would bring the kind of attention that Henry Demarest Lloyd had brought to its Democratic rival, the *Chicago Tribune.* Tourgée made the most of this opportunity. Outspoken and controversial, he attained hero status among black readers for his unrelenting assault on white racism, and as a leading editorial voice in the nation's second largest city, he was beginning to be taken quite seriously by politicians. Though the title of his column, "A Bystander's Notes," implied that Tourgée had intended to remain critically detached and outside the political fray, the success and popularity of the column quickly drew him off the sidelines back into the fight.

The *Inter Ocean's* chief editor, William Penn Nixon, was an ex-abolitionist of part Indian ancestry who greatly admired Tourgée both for his novels and for his lifetime of commitment to Radical Republicanism. Tourgée had a warm but often conflicted relationship with Nixon and the paper. Its editorial staff took pride in their "advanced position" on race and called their paper "primarily and always a radical republican newspaper" that maintained "a reputation for extreme friendliness toward the colored race."[3] But, the *Inter Ocean's* radicalism had limits. Its motto— "Republican in everything, independent in nothing"—was taken seriously. Nixon often found himself in the uncomfortable position of warning Tourgée not to level too harsh criticism at Republicans. His editors too would spend a great deal of time pleading with him to " 'turn his guns' on the right party."[4]

Within weeks of its inaugural column, in fact, "The Bystander" blasphemed by conceding that the Democrats held a "worthy position" on the tariff and by referring to the "monopolists" who controlled the tariff as "cannibals."[5] To distance themselves from irregular positions like these, the paper, to Tourgée's annoyance, prefaced his columns with such statements as: "Whether politicians agree with him or not, whether he strikes at them or with them, they always find in what he writes something worth reading and thinking about."[6] His ten-year relationship with the *Inter Ocean* as "The Bystander" would be turbulent, with editors at times censoring portions of the column, at times refusing to run columns they found thoroughly objectionable, and twice dropping the column altogether only to bring it back after patching up relations with Tourgée.

The early days of "A Bystander's Notes" were consumed with the approaching 1888 presidential election and Tourgée's political commentary instantly entangled him in a personal feud with the Republican Party leadership. Fearing that the Republican Party, still reeling from the mugwump defection of 1884, would abandon "sectional issues" in the campaign, "The Bystander" called for Republicans to stand loyally by their Southern supporters by initiating a bold campaign in the South. To crack the "Solid South," he called upon the Republican National Committee (RNC) to "put its orators on the stump and its organizers in the field" in Southern states, arguing that "the stranger can do at the South what is utterly impossible for the resident of that section to accomplish" when it came to speaking freely about their Democratic opponents. Though he predicted that some blood would be shed, he estimated one hundred speakers in regions where blacks dominated the electorate would produce a large Republican return to Congress and perhaps secure crucial electoral votes for Republican candidate Benjamin Harrison.[7]

When the RNC calculated that it could win the election without wasting its resources in the South, Tourgée was appalled. His anger was compounded by the RNC's decision not to employ Tourgée as a stump speaker, which contradicted an earlier promise. Their turnabout came only after Tourgée had refused to agree to deliver a single, prefabricated speech that had been supplied for him. "I couldn't wear a gag. If I had tried my work would have been of no value," he later told Ben Harrison. "I was excluded from the list of campaign speakers . . . from a deliberate, set purpose to exclude me from the campaign. . . . I know very well the purpose was to keep my mouth shut."[8] Tourgée described himself as shocked and "humiliated" to find his work unappreciated by the party for which he had actively campaigned since 1860.

He did not take his exclusion passively. Arranging his own speaking engagements, Tourgée independently campaigned for Harrison and used "A Bystander's Notes" to publicize his irregular party views. Privately, he began a correspondence with Harrison that presumptuously advised him on strategy, urging him directly to undertake his proposed "Southern Raid." Declaring himself one who was not "willing to kiss a presidential candidate's backside for the sake of hanging upon his coattails," he proceeded to frankly criticize Harrison's conservative campaign in a half-dozen letters, remarking at one point, "I would go forty miles barefoot to have you do something—well, a little *startling*."[9] Harrison, anything but startling as a politician, campaigned for a higher tariff to the near exclusion of other issues, but defeated Cleveland in an election in which a remarkable two-thirds of Southern votes were cast for the Democrat, causing Harrison to lose the national popular vote. Their worst showing in the South since Reconstruction, the Republicans suspected widespread ballot box fraud and intimidation of black voters.

Soon after Harrison's election, "The Bystander" turned his attention to the condition of African Americans in the South. An account in the black press caught his attention that made reference to the suppression of a "Negro insurrection" in Kemper County, Mississippi. Tourgée expressed amazement at the lack of details forthcoming from the local authorities, as well as the inattention of the mainstream Northern press to the story. According to his informants, the so-called Negro rebels were a quiet farming community of law-abiding citizens who were raided by whites after a minor act of "impudence" on a street corner. Tourgée imagined the scene: "We have again the old, old story of the mustering of armed men from half a state to put down the revolt of a half-dozen negroes at some country cross-roads!" He lamented "the same sickening tale of murder of those who dared resist unlawful violence; the same hunting of the refugees in the swamps and hills as if they were wild beasts [and] the same care to prevent a true version of the facts from reaching the northern press." To emphasize the true motivation behind this raid, he reported in boldface type: "**ALL THE NEGROES KILLED OWNED LITTLE FARMS.**" This was nothing less than "a ruthless war on the unoffending Negroes of Mississippi, the driving out of prosperous colored men and seizing their possession."[10] This fate, he believed, would befall other Southern blacks who attempted to improve their economic standing if they were to be abandoned by the Republican Party.

Within weeks, another episode of white supremacist violence caught Tourgée's attention. This time occurring in the North, a shadowy group of vigilantes calling themselves the White Caps had lynched and threatened dozens of blacks in a rash of incidents in Indiana and Ohio that were designed to drive off black residents. Calling them "nothing more or less than Northern Ku Klux," Tourgée warned his Northern readers that "an organized body of lynchers is the most dangerous development that can occur in a self-governing community." It was a sign of the nation's faltering commitment to democracy and the rule of law. What most offended Tourgée was the tolerance of the White Caps by such public officials as Republican Governor Joseph B. Foraker of Ohio, who had had practically excused White Cap lynchings by citing the "inefficiency and delay of the courts" as the cause of their actions—a statement which presumed the guilt of the gang's victims. The previous year, Foraker had rejoiced at the repeal of the last Ohio "Black Law," yet he seemed unfazed by this white mob violence. "To all intents and purposes," Tourgée coolly asserted, "the Governor of Ohio might just as well be a member of the gang himself. He has hopelessly embarrassed the administration of justice in the state."[11]

Without the protection of civil authorities, Tourgee advised blacks to meet "White Cap" violence with their own violence. "If every one who receives a [White Cap] warning would straightaway arm himself and fill his assailants so full of buckshot that they would forget to go away, it would put an end to this evil very quickly," he shockingly proposed. Every man had the legal right to self-defense, he reasoned, and perhaps "a few respectable funerals" might chasten the perpetrators of these crimes. "The Bystander has always advised the killing of Ku-klux," he recalled, reminding his readers that many Northerners had advised the same when the disguised assailants were white Southerners.[12] But Tourgée was not simply defending the right to self-defense, he called for active violent resistance:

> Every colored man who kills a lyncher ought to have his name inscribed very high up among the race's heroes and benefactors. Such a man does more to secure the rights of his people than a whole generation of "eloquent leaders." If the Bystander were a colored man, he would keep the names of such as a saints' roll, giving every one his day until the whole year should be a calendar of brave deeds.[13]

Responses to "A Bystander's Notes" came from all over the country averaging about fifty letters a week.[14] The column was frequently reprinted in the black press in such leading papers as the *Cleveland Gazette*, the *Indianapolis World*, the *New Orleans Crusader*, the *Detroit Plaindealer*, the *Richmond Planet*, the *Chicago Conservator*, the *Washington Bee*, and the *New York Age* as well as in a great many small town papers throughout the South and West. So far-reaching was its readership that one journalist referred to "A Bystander's Notes" as "a source of strength and encouragement" to "multitudes" of rural black Mississippians who subscribed to the *Weekly Inter Ocean*. Indeed, Southern blacks wrote hundreds of letters to Tourgée, many of them detailing incidents of oppression and expressing their hope for deliverance from white allies in the North. Reading these letters left him with no illusions about what impoverished Southern blacks, with no voice in Northern newspapers, were facing.[15]

These letters were sometimes barely intelligible because of the sender's poor writing skills. "Please excuse bad Penmanship," asked one writer, "the whip was my pen before the war." A letter from "the women of

"The Bystander" at his office at Thorheim, ca. 1890. Courtesy
of The Huntington Library, San Marino, CA.

Wayne County Miss" reported: "We cannot live here much longer . . .
the white people of this county . . . beat a young man nearly to death this
week . . . the men have to pay too dollor Poll Tax and them that cannot
write cannot vote." Some were written in a state of immediate danger and
some asked for assistance. One stated: "I hav ben in Prison ever since 21 of
June for represntin your work . . . the Dimocrat beat me and curs you and
I want you to get me out of this fix." Another group, seeing no alternative
but to shoot their way out of the South, asked for assistance of a more dangerous kind: "Wee the friends of liberty have concluded to [inform] you
of the fact that wee are needing ass. aid such as sending us arms . . . wee
are amongst our enemies the only way for us to protect our leaving is for
you to send us arms." Confident that Tourgée, the champion of armed
resistance, would deliver, the author added the postscript: "Dont certify
what is in the box Just say hard ware."[16]

    Most letters echoed the sentiments of a self-identified "negro minister"
who assured him that blacks will "tell your name to our children as do we
those of the immortal Lincoln, Sumner, Garrison and others," and another

who stated, "as a race we owe more to Albion W. Tourgée than to any man living."[17] One man wrote, "I take that paper just to get your weekly letters. They are all the light I have . . . I go to see my wife every Friday or two & take my Inter Ocean with me and we go off to some secluded spot and I read aloud to her . . . at times you plead our cause so eloquently [that] we find ourselves in each other's arms weeping."[18] Such letters kept Tourgée acutely aware of the continued racial crisis in the South and the desperate state of those who continued to fight for equality. Often making reference to them in his column, he personally responded to most of these letters, which affected him as profoundly as any public response he had received in his career.[19]

Tourgée's prestige among black radicals soared over the next several years as he continued to bring attention to lynchings and pressured Republicans to act in "A Bystander's Notes." His various calls for anti-lynching legislation were answered in 1894 by Harry C. Smith, editor of the *Cleveland Gazette*, who had been elected to the Ohio State House of Representatives. Smith turned to Tourgée for advice in framing an anti-lynching bill, and he responded by proposing a comprehensive law in an open letter to Ohio governor William McKinley (Foraker's successor), published in Smith's *Gazette*. Arguing that lynchings "*never occur* except in a community whose citizens favor and approve such outrage[s]," Tourgée proposed a law that would, in addition to regular criminal proceedings against participants in lynch mobs, penalize the counties in which lynchings occurred by entitling the victim, or the victim's heirs, or the state itself, to sue for up to $10,000 if the victim is killed, and up to $5,000 if the victim is seriously injured. By levying a "penalty tax" on the entire county, he argued that the "pocket-nerve" of the county would motivate residents to discourage mob actions and encourage respect for the rule of law.[20] Capitalizing on his national prominence, Congressman Smith introduced the bill as the work of Tourgée—who later testified in Columbus on its behalf—and he worked tirelessly for two years to secure its passage. During that time, two more brutal lynchings took place and Governor McKinley finally lent his support to the Anti-Lynching Bill in 1896. That year the bill passed, though the maximum penalty had been reduced to $5,000 from Tourgée's original plan.[21]

Though some critics doubted its constitutionality, upon passage the Ohio Anti-Lynching Law was widely praised and quickly became the model for legislation passed in nine other states.[22] In 1912 the NAACP would launch an anti-lynching campaign using the Ohio law as its model. There is some evidence to suggest that the law's effectiveness in reducing the crime of lynching was considerable. In 1897, when a white mob in Urbana, Ohio, took a young black man who pled guilty to a rape charge from police custody and brutally tortured and lynched him, it prompted the first lawsuit filed under the new law by the relatives of the victim, asking for maximum damages. Predicting that the law would never be enforced, the *Washington Post* scoffed that "no power . . . could force Champaign County [OH] to pay $5,000 to the heirs of the wretch that was killed at Urbana last Friday."[23] Indeed, the County Court ruled the Anti-Lynching Law was unconstitutional and dismissed the case, but their ruling was subsequently overturned first by the Circuit Court in 1898 and then by the State Supreme Court that confirmed its constitutionality in 1900. Over the next decade, only two incidents of lynching took place in Ohio, a drastic reduction from the previous decade. The perception, at least, that lynching had been curbed by legislative action was widely held. When Tourgée's law survived another judicial review in 1908, an elated Harry Smith felt moved to write to the widow Emma Tourgée: "Ohio's mob violence or anti-lynch-murder law passed in 1896 has been adjudged constitutional by the State Supreme Court and has been a success *a grand* success, thanks to *Judge Albion W. Tourgée*, our *grand friend* for so very many years."[24]

Though Tourgée's importance as an early agitator against lynching has been virtually ignored by historians, his contemporaries, such as Ida B. Wells and Catherine Impey, recognized him as the trailblazer for their own anti-lynching crusades. "A Bystander's Notes" preceded Wells by three years in its national campaign against lynching, and Tourgée's analysis of the phenomenon presaged her main contention that white violence came out of fear of black upward mobility rather than the protection of white womanhood. Wells surpassed him, however, when she confronted in a much more direct manner than he had the "old thread bare lie," as she termed it, that most black victims of lynching had been accused of raping white women.[25]

When Wells published the sensational series of articles in T. Thomas Fortune's *New York Age* that made her national reputation in 1892, Tourgée sent her a letter of congratulations and encouragement that she gladly acknowledged by paying tribute to him as the leading voice of radicalism on the subject. "I feel more reassured," she responded, "when I can have the approbation of one who has done so much for the race; one whom, more than all others is the credit due for awakening the sluggish consciences of the M.E. Church and the party of great moral ideas." But she also told him that her greatest wish was to vindicate "the Negro race . . . of the foul charge" of rape, and she challenged, "will the Inter Ocean or any other white man's journal do that much?"[26] Henceforth, Tourgée seemed to do everything in his power to promote Wells and her views.

As Carolyn Karcher has recently argued, Tourgée and Wells were kindred spirits who both chose to be outsiders by refusing to conform to either the gender or race expectations of their own social groups. They forged an unlikely, mutually admiring friendship and became each for the other a fierce and reliable ally. In 1893, when Wells appealed to Tourgée for legal assistance in her potential libel suit against a pair of black Memphis lawyers, she expressed confidence that only he could provide "a clear, impartial opinion" about the wisdom of her undertaking the suit and told him that she regarded him as her most trustworthy white "friend." While he did not take on her case himself—apologizing that he "could not afford to do more gratuitous work," but even so, not wishing to be "a very bad friend," he arranged for a colleague, Ferdinand L. Barnett, a lawyer and general editor of the *Chicago Conservator*, to assist Wells at no fee. Wells had a special reason to thank Tourgée for this connection, for two years later she married Barnett.[27] On another occasion, Tourgée publicly defended Wells against Francis Willard, the white woman president of the interracial Women's Christian Temperance Union (WCTU), who accused Wells of misrepresenting the WCTU's position on lynching and of defaming the virtue of white women in America. While black leaders Frederick Douglass and Bishop Henry McNeal Turner publicly defended Willard against Wells, Tourgée unequivocally sided with Wells. In an installment of "A Bystander's Notes" that declared her remarks to have been "literally true," he took Willard—who he considered a dear friend also—to task for her organization's capitulation to the rationale for lynching. A dismayed Willard wrote to Tourgée in protest, while Wells thanked him profusely for the "opportune" words and "expressions in behalf of justice that [Tourgée] alone seemed moved to make."[28]

In another instance, when Wells sought his support in her boycott of the World's Columbia Exposition in 1893, Tourgée made the ingenious suggestion that "the colored people put out a strong, brief, compact yet comprehensive pamphlet in two or three languages and circulate it freely at the Fair" in order to "give a realistic representation of a Southern Lynching" as well as other issues. Wells enlisted Frederick Douglass's support behind this idea, which resulted in the powerful pamphlet *Why the Colored American Is Not in the World's Columbian Exposition*. Tourgée declined to contribute to the pamphlet because he planned to participate in the World's Fair. He assisted in the preparation of the pamphlet nonetheless, and when Wells sent him the final product she remarked, "I understand that you did not wish to appear in this matter is why no reference has been made to you . . . I wish to . . . beg your pardon for the unintentional appropriation of your language in the closing paragraph." She inscribed a copy of the pamphlet to him: "To Judge

A.W. Tourgee whose suggestion it was that originated the preparation of this volume, 2000 of which were distributed at the World's Fair."[29]

British Quaker Catherine Impey, who founded the anti-imperialist journal *Anti-Caste* in 1888, sought out both Tourgée and Wells when she visited the United States in 1892 to research the phenomenon of lynching. Impey headed an organization that stood squarely for racial equality, working actively, in her words, "to promote brotherly fellowship and sympathy between white and dark races everywhere, throughout their social, civil, and religious life; believing that only by such untrammeled intermingling in the common affairs of life can the fires of prejudice be extinguished."[30] Impey wished to bring the facts about lynching before the British people and tried to arrange for both anti-lynching crusaders to lecture on the subject in Great Britain. Wells agreed, but Tourgée did not, citing too many

This page and opposite: Front and back of a photograph of a lynching near Clanton, Alabama, that took place on August 21, 1891, with children posing triumphantly afterward with the corpse. Sent to Tourgée by a member of the lynch mob. Courtesy of The Chicago Historical Society.

commitments at home. Undoubtedly, it was the lack of funds that prevented him from joining Wells, who, herself, was paid barely enough to cover her travel costs.[31] When Impey personally visited Tourgée at Thorheim, however, he lent her a chilling photograph that had been sent to "The Bystander" by the perpetrators of a lynching. It showed a black corpse hanging from a noose, in front of which white children cheerfully posed for the camera. On the back of it, the lynchers had boasted: "This S.O.B. was hung at Clayton, Ala. Friday, Aug. 21 '91 for murdering a little [white] boy in cold blood . . . He is a good specimen of your 'Black Christians—hung by White Heathens.'" Impey published an artist's rendering of the photo on the front page of *Anti-Caste*, and promptly passed the picture to Wells, who used it to great effect on her speaking tour of England. The photograph provided stunning visual evidence for the skeptical audiences that Wells encountered on her first British lecture tour.[32]

FAC-SIMILE OF BACK OF PHOTOGRAPH.

Wells's first tour of Britain attracted enough attention that the *Inter Ocean* hired her to publish dispatches for her second British tour in a special column entitled "Ida B. Wells Abroad." This was the first time a white mainstream paper had hired a black woman journalist as a regular, paid correspondent, and it is likely that Tourgée played a key role in this groundbreaking move.[33] Whether or not he directly suggested it to chief editor Nixon, Tourgée clearly felt vindicated by Wells's overwhelming success in her second tour of Britain. During one of his disagreements with Nixon, Tourgée boasted: "On the 'Race Question' it would no doubt, have ruined the Inter Ocean if it had taken the Bystander's position at the outset," but because of his work, the *Inter Ocean* had "crystalized sentiment" against lynching overseas and earned an international reputation for doing so. Significantly, Wells gave sole credit to Tourgée for radicalizing the *Inter Ocean* when she told a Manchester audience of the lack of outcry in the American press: "I can point to nothing which has been done on this score, save the voice of the Bystander, which has been heard so long through the columns of the *Inter Ocean*. He *only* has insisted on justice full and free to every American citizen."[34]

Like Wells, Catherine Impey continued to recognize Tourgée as the leading white radical against lynching and continued in her efforts to bring him to Britain. After Wells returned from her second tour, Impey came to him with a new proposal:

> What if you and Mr. [George Washington] Cable should come both of you and together? His name is much more *generally* known here than your own—because his novels have been circulated so wide in our best literary circles . . . but he could not talk as *you* could talk. It is you above all others that I want to have speak just now. Couldn't you manage a just a month or so, if no more?[35]

But Tourgée would never go to Britain. His activities during 1893 and 1894, as we will see, would keep him more than occupied at home.

While Tourgée discovered new allies and enjoyed new influence through his column, he also earned the intense vilification of opponents both in the North and the South. Angry letters to the Bystander reasserted white supremacy and freely proposed "disenfranchisement," "deportation," and even "extermination" as solutions to the race problem, exemplified by one Southerner who replied to Tourgée's warnings of a black uprising that "if they ever dare attempt to burn us out . . . we will exterminate the whole race—men, women, and children."[36] Northerners expressed similar views. One Michigan reader proclaimed "the noble Aryan race" that had proven its superiority through "ages of natural selection" had been chosen to rule the country "according to the immutable laws of nature." He favored "compulsory deportation" of blacks as the "only hope" for maintaining the purity of the white race.[37] Racist, and even threatening, responses were not surprising. More ominous were the many sympathetic voices that expressed simple fatigue on the race issue. "The American people have tired of color politics and race legislation," one reader complained. "I can see no good accomplished by keeping up a fight . . . for negro rights. I think this fight has come near breaking the back of the Republican Party, and has done the negro no good."[38]

Unswayed by such obstacles, Tourgée continued to believe that the old, antislavery conscience of the North could be mobilized into action if only the facts were put before the American public. For a brief period, this strategy appeared promising. In 1890, the moment appeared ripe for federal action. The race issue returned to the center stage of national politics, and a political showdown took place that would have long-term consequences for the cause of racial equality.

THE TIPPING POINT

For the first time since their disastrous defeat back in 1875, the Republicans won a majority—albeit a narrow one—in both houses in the fall congressional elections of 1889. With a Republican in the White House, and in control of both houses, the path suddenly cleared for Republicans to implement their long-deferred plans for a more effective "Southern policy." In the Senate, Henry Blair reintroduced his Education Bill, while in the House, Henry Cabot Lodge introduced a Federal Elections Bill that promised to protect black voting rights against the kind of extralegal fraud and intimidation that presumably kept Southern blacks from the ballot box in 1888. The Blair Bill and the Lodge Bill (dubbed the "Force Bill" by opponents) became the centerpiece of an intense yearlong public debate, both inside and outside the halls of Congress, that touched upon the history of Reconstruction, scientific knowledge about race, and the constitutional scope of federal power. With well-known views on each of these subjects, Tourgée found himself in constant demand.

In early 1890, Tourgée traveled to Washington to testify before congressional committees on the Blair and Lodge bills. Before he did so, he met privately with President Harrison and House Speaker Thomas B. Reed and told them that both bills lacked adequate protection against state governments.[39] He instead offered his own measures that would both aid public schools directly, and hold national elections separately from state elections under more thorough federal control. Some were enthusiastic about his measures, including Harrison Kelley from Kansas, who introduced both of them on the House floor, and Speaker Reed, who for several weeks preferred Tourgée's election bill to Lodge's. "He is leading the leaders," Harrison Kelley wrote to Emma in admiration.[40] But, in the end, the compromise measures suggested by Blair and Lodge had a much better chance of success and ultimately received the endorsement of Republican leadership. While he reluctantly supported the Lodge Elections Bill, Tourgée could not bear to see the federal aid for schools given over to Southern states for disbursement. Perhaps unwisely, he took a bitter stand against the Blair Bill.

Although he had been one of the most outspoken advocates for National Aid to Education, he now personally lobbied congressmen to oppose perhaps the last opportunity to aid education in the South. Of the Blair Bill, he said "I do not like this bill . . . I think it would be better a thousand fold to give nothing in aid of National education than to throw millions unconditioned and unlimited into the treasuries of the southern states."[41] Previously, the Blair Bill had passed the Republican-controlled Senate three times, in 1884, 1886, and 1888, only to fail in the Democratic House. In his view, the efforts to reach out to Democrats over the years had watered-down the bill to the extent that Southern state governments could easily deprive "colored" schools of their fair share of the fund. Even in the very best scenario, he felt, "the *colored* schools of the South would receive one-third and *white* schools two-thirds of the fund, though the colored schools represent *two-thirds* of the illiteracy."[42]

By contrast, his own measure proposed that the federal funds would be used only to pay teacher's salaries directly, thus bypassing state bureaucracies, and the amount would be earmarked according to racial illiteracy rates. Tourgée's bill stated that, "in case the State within which any district is located prescribes separate schools for white and colored pupils," then the fund must be apportioned to each race according to their illiteracy rates, and "neither of these sums shall, under any circumstances, be used to aid a school for the benefit of the other race."[43] Just as he had in 1868, Tourgée explicitly accepted the racial segregation of schools in his "race conscious" legislation in order to assure the equity of resources. Most black leaders were willing to accept separate schools; Senators Blair and Hoar opposed any appearance of sanctioning segregation. "Separate schools are not a positive *wrong*," Tourgée reasoned to an unknown colleague about his willingness to accept school segregation, "a colored man is not *wronged* or hurt if on one corner is a white school and on the other a colored one. The wrong is when there is none."[44] Thus, his willingness to compromise on segregated education, as opposed to all other public forms of segregation, came out of a pragmatic awareness that white Southerners would accept no public education at all—for black or white—before they accepted integrated education.

While Tourgée was undoubtedly correct that black schools would not see anything like an equal share of the fund, blacks themselves still overwhelmingly supported the Blair Bill. While noting its inadequacies, the newly formed Afro-American League, representing a broad national coalition of black leaders, favored the bill mostly out of their keen awareness of "the absence of anything tangible to take its place."[45] If nothing else, the bill would have lent symbolic federal support to black education. But Tourgée could not stand to see the proposed $77 million squandered with so little protection against fraud, and he could never quite accept that his widely praised counter measure had been rejected. Moreover, he was certain that a majority of Northern whites would turn against future measures for black education by pointing to their support of the Blair Bill and saying, "We gave you what you wanted and now you are whining about it."[46]

When the Blair Bill fell six votes short of passing in the Senate, where it had previously passed, political observers were shocked. A few of the Republican Senators who joined the Democratic opposition cited Tourgée as a factor in their decision, and at least one scholar has attributed his influence to be decisive in turning seven votes (though the evidence is inconclusive). Watching the vote from the Senate gallery, Tourgée exalted when the Bill failed and told the press, "it was a lucky thing for the colored people of the South that the Blair bill did not pass."[47] After ten years of political debate and legislative maneuvering, the struggle to provide federal aid to education was dead. With it went Tourgée's last effort to employ moderate and conciliatory measures.

After the Blair Bill failed, a ten-month struggle ensued to enact the Lodge Federal Elections Bill. While Congress debated, Tourgée published a flurry of articles on race and citizenship rights in prominent Northern journals and newspapers.[48] Attracting the most attention was Tourgée's debate in *The Forum* with Alabama senator John Tyler Morgan. Leader of the opposition to the Lodge Bill, Morgan made an unapologetic case for the disenfranchisement of blacks in his article "Shall Negro Majorities Rule?" basing his case on the "horrors of enforced Negro rule" during Reconstruction and the ineradicable inferiority of blacks.[49] Tourgée's rejoinder, "Shall White Minorities Rule?" reasserted that "the rule of the majority is the fundamental principle of our government," and without a constitutional amendment the attempt "to restore the term 'white' as an essential qualification for citizenship" violated the Constitution. That Senator Morgan ignored this basic fact was unsettling. Blacks only voted as a block because they were treated as a class apart, Tourgée argued, if all citizens rights were respected alike, majorities would be neither black nor white. He also argued that, once conferred, the franchise became a right not a privilege. To disenfranchise, whether legally or extra-legally, would be a catastrophic attempt to reverse the march of progress that would likely ignite a race war. "It should not be forgotten that there are 50,000 [blacks] still living who wore the federal blue and fought for the freedom of their race," he warned, and any attempt to oppress such men "through the instrumentality of the shot-gun, the cow-hide, the falsified return, or perjured election officials" would never succeed for long.[50]

In response to Morgan's racial theories, Tourgée also indulged in his own observations regarding bloodlines. Mimicking Morgan's propensity to discuss ancestry in terms of blood "drops," he wrote, "It may be doubted whether taken drop for drop there is not nearly pretty much as much white as colored blood in the veins of those ranked as Negroes in this country." Morgan had portrayed a vast gulf between the white ruling class, with its great statesmen and timeless intellectual achievements, and the barbarous African race who created nothing in their history in Africa or America. While calling attention to the extensive history of sexual transgressions of the color line in the South, Tourgée also questioned the very notion of a separate white heritage when he pointed out, "this white infusion represents the very best stocks of the South. Hardly a noted family can be named that is not as fully represented on the colored side as on the white."[51] He thought it strange that Morgan and other racial philosophers believed that their invincibly superior white blood was so easily defeated in its greatness by a few drops intermixture from a so-called weaker breed.

In June of 1890, Tourgée participated in another national debate when he attended a major conference on the "Negro Question" held at Lake Mohonk in upstate New York. Evolving out of previous conferences on the "Indian question," the gathering brought together Northerners and Southerners, ex-abolitionists and slaveholders, and included such distinguished individuals as former President Rutherford B. Hayes, Hampton Institute founder General Samuel C. Armstrong, former head of the Freedmen's Bureau, General O.O. Howard, and Plymouth Church Pastor Lyman Abbott. Stirring controversy even before the conference began was the organizers' decision to extend invitations only to whites on the theory that the discussion may not otherwise be entirely candid and uninhibited. George Washington Cable boycotted as a result, and Tourgée privately compared the approach of the meeting to the Colonization Society's white supremacist approach to ending slavery. Most of the participants came to promote the separatist, self-help rhetoric increasingly heard from black leaders, especially in the wake of the Blair Bill's defeat.[52] Discussion topics included vocational training, moral improvement, and strengthening the black family. At one point, Abbott went so far as to proclaim that there was no "race problem" anymore.[53]

Tourgée put in a masterful performance in his effort to disrupt the complacent consensus of the meeting. Since blacks were unable to speak for themselves, he protested their exclusion by entitling his main lecture "The Negro's View of the Race Problem" and used it to shame the organizers for excluding blacks by reminding them, "the man who wears the shoe knows better than anybody else where it pinches." After listening to the previous speakers, including Abbott, he sarcastically told the distinguished gathering: "I am inclined to think that the only education required is that of the *white* race." Their knowledge of the negro, he told them, was based on a mixture of misinformation and false suppositions, most egregiously that black poverty resulted from "racial qualities, and not fortuitous, resulting conditions." The "race problem" could not be alleviated through charity, as so many of them supposed. "We congratulate ourselves on what we have contributed to his mental and religious development," he told philanthropists, "but forget that for every dollar we have given . . . he had before given a thousand to our enrichment [under slavery]." Invoking his own authority as one who spent fourteen years in North Carolina and employed hundreds of blacks himself, he insisted:

> [After] constant study of their conditions since emancipation, I do not hesitate to say that the colored people of the South have accomplished more in twenty-five years, from an industrial point of view, than any people on the face of the earth ever before achieved under anything like such unfavorable conditions.

He concluded that blacks were not especially in need of philanthropy from whites, but only pure and simple justice. President Hayes recorded the tremendous impact of his speech in his personal journal, noting that Tourgée was "an orator—pungent, dramatic, original, and daring."[54] A newspaper account echoed Hayes calling Tourgée's "magnetic oration . . . the most striking, exciting and intellectually interesting feature of the conference."[55] Disappointed by the attitude at the Mohonk conference, Tourgée afterward resolved not to attend racially exclusive meetings in the future and he subsequently refused an invitation to the second annual conference in 1891 (still exclusively white).[56]

Although most Northerners at Mohonk probably supported the Lodge Bill, the conservative tenor of their conference that lauded private rather than public action, did little to apply pressure to Congress as it weighed a major new intervention in the South. The Lodge Bill would have empowered federal supervisors to control and count ballots in federal elections, wherever the electorate petitioned Congress to do so. Thanks to the aggressive leadership of House Speaker Reed, the bill passed the lower chamber in June. But opponents, such as Senator Morgan, intensified their rhetorical campaign against it, effectively raising the specter of a vast federal bureaucracy controlling and sustaining a black Republican electorate in the South, and playing blatantly on race-hatred with more allusions to the horrors of "Negro domination." British critic James Bryce, in the *North American Review*, joined in the Southern chorus and dismissed the Lodge Bill as "an attempt to overcome nature by law," attributing Southern opposition to mere "self-preservation" in the face of a threatened return of that "dismal period" of Reconstruction.[57] Indeed, the Lodge Bill stalled in the Senate as Democrats resorted to desperate parliamentary tactics, including a lengthy filibuster. In exchange for Southern support of the Sherman Silver Purchase Act, Republican Senators cut their losses and finally abandoned the Lodge Bill in January of 1891. What had appeared to be widespread sympathy for the Democratic opposition in the press, cast a pall over any further talk of federal intervention in the South.[58]

The defeats of 1890 and 1891 marked a watershed in the history of black civil rights. They began a new era of race-relations, which Howard University historian Rayford Logan memorably described as the "nadir" of the African American experience. The inability of the Republican Party to pass either of its "Southern" measures despite its majority control over both houses of Congress had far-reaching consequences. In August of 1890, even as the Lodge Bill was argued before the Senate, Mississippi Democrats called a constitutional convention for the expressed purpose of eliminating blacks from the electorate. The new state constitution they produced pioneered the legal disenfranchisement of African American voters by employing the use of literacy tests and poll taxes, supplemented by a so-called understanding clause—clearly designed for uneducated whites—that allowed illiterates who could demonstrate a "reasonable interpretation" of a passage from the State Constitution that would be read to them would be exempted from the voting restrictions. The defeat of the Lodge Bill encouraged the rapid proliferation of similar measures throughout the Southern states over the next decade. Furthermore, between 1887 and 1892 nine Southern states passed laws, each increasingly bold in character, that required racial segregation on railway transportation. The debates of 1890 had helped to reenergize the politics of reaction in the South. Ironically, as Rayford Logan observed, "the nadir was reached . . . not because of lack of attention [to the condition of Southern blacks]. On the contrary, the plight of the Negro worsened because of the efforts made to improve it."[59]

With reasonable hope for federal action all but dashed, African American politicians were thrown into political confusion in the 1890s. The setback hastened the rise of a philosophy of accommodation among a growing number of black leaders, to be made famous by Booker T. Washington, who regarded political agitation as futile and who preached that blacks should not look for others to do what they needed to do for themselves. Others, such as A.M.E. Bishop Henry McNeal Turner, turned to the dream of voluntary emigration to Africa as the ultimate deliverance for black Americans. Still others, though disillusioned, remained committed to the strategy of pressing for full civil and political rights by exerting pressure on the Republican Party as a loyal constituency. Finally, some considered third party alternatives, with many black sharecroppers joining farmer's alliances and forging a real possibility of an interracial alliance of farm laborers in the People's Party. In this political morass, Tourgée pressed forward with his agitation in "A Bystander's Notes" and soon became involved in a final crusade to stem the tide of reaction.

THE MOVEMENT FOR COLOR-BLIND JUSTICE

In July 1890, the Louisiana Legislature passed Act 111, which purported "to promote the comfort of passengers on railway trains." This law, quickly dubbed the "Separate Car Act," required that all state railway companies provide "equal but separate accommodations for the white and colored races" in the form of "separate coaches or compartments" for each. Companies who failed to provide racially segregated cars were subject to a fine from $100 to $500, while conductors who failed to enforce the proper assignment of passengers were liable for either a stiff $25 to $50 fine or twenty days imprisonment. The innovative formulation of "equal but separate"—or "separate but equal," as it would be remembered—presented a rationale for racial segregation to meet the conditions of the "equal protection" clause of the Fourteenth Amendment.

Tourgée immediately denounced the act in "A Bystander's Notes," as it seemed to him the most blatant violation yet of the Fourteenth Amendment's imperative that "no state may pass any law" infringing upon the "equal protection of the laws" of its citizens. Though appalled at the brazenness of the Louisiana legislature, he was heartened by a protest against the law filed by several New Orleans black leaders under the auspices of the American Citizens Equal Rights Association of Louisiana (ACERA). Two longtime political activists and self-proclaimed Radical Republicans, Dr. Louis A. Martinet and Rodolphe Desdunes, led ACERA's resistance to the Separate Car Act. Members of the light-skinned Creole population of New Orleans, these men represented the professional middle class of the city, who had achieved a greater degree of integration into the public sphere than any other nonwhite group in the South. The rise of *de jure* segregation in New Orleans was therefore particularly galling to them. One of ACERA's younger members contacted Tourgée in August

1890 seeking advice on how "to test its constitutionality in the Federal Courts" and thanking him "on behalf of the 7,999,999 of my race whose interest and whose rights you have ever championed." Tourgée's response was so encouraging its recipients had it published.[60] But more than a year would pass before he heard anything more of the protest in Louisiana.[61]

A physician, lawyer, and editor of the *New Orleans Crusader*, Martinet was an avid reader of "A Bystander's Notes" and an admirer of Tourgée. Martinet was the author of ACERA's official protest to the legislature, which was reprinted and circulated broadly afterward. In it, he foreshadowed several lines of argument that Tourgée would later develop in the *Plessy* case. The Fourteenth Amendment, Martinet explained, had established the principle that "citizenship is national and has no color," and its purpose had been written to reaffirm the national commitment to the proposition that "all men are created equal." The Separate Car Bill proposed a caste system that would "insult, humiliate, and otherwise maltreat inoffensive persons, and especially women and children who should happen to have a dark skin." Finally, he hinted that racial classifications themselves were unscientific and arbitrary distinctions: "Will it seriously be contended that such a problematical proposition as the ethnical origins of color is a sufficient cause for a deliberate interference with settled rights?" he asked.[62] New Orleans Creoles like Martinet, who could often pass for white, were in a better position to appreciate the "problematical proposition" of the "origins of color" than most nineteenth-century Americans.

In Martinet, Tourgée discovered an ideological soul mate whose fiery editorials and uncompromising political style matched his own. Described by Desdunes as "courageous," "conscientious, energetic, and talented," Martinet ambitiously hoped to spark a statewide boycott of segregated railroad cars through his editorials in the *Crusader*.[63] He soon grew frustrated by the lack of support in the black community, which he partly attributed to the widespread belief that earlier Supreme Court decisions had already upheld state-mandated segregation. "It has been said," Martinet observed, alluding to the Court's striking down of Sumner's 1875 Civil Rights Act, "that the Supreme Court of the United States has already passed upon the rights of States to enact such unjust laws." He vehemently denied this and attributed the spread of this belief to Conservative propaganda. He urged his readers, "[do] not be discouraged by such reports; they have been invented and put in circulation by the enemy to stop the wheels of progress."[64] Indeed, even while striking down Sumner's legislation, the Court had explicitly reaffirmed the Fourteenth Amendment's prohibition on state-imposed violations on civil rights as opposed to actions perpetuated by "private" individuals.[65]

By August 1891, Martinet's boycott was abandoned and the ACERA itself had dissolved due to conflicts over its failed strategy. Suddenly, a new organization appeared. On September 5, 1891, Martinet, Desdunes, and eighteen other prominent black leaders of the city formed a new organization called the "Citizens' Committee to Test the Constitutionality of the Separate Car Law." Having decided that "defeat is more honorable than flight or surrender," they determined to go forward with a test case no matter what the consequences. Desdunes declared in an editorial in the *Crusader*: "We are American citizens and it is our duty to defend our constitutional rights against the encroachments and attacks of prejudice. The courts are open for that purpose and it is our fault if we do not seek the redress that they alone can afford."[66]

Tourgée clearly had a hand in the resurrection of the movement. Martinet wrote to Tourgée on October 5, 1891, offering him the committee's entire fund of $1,412.70 to serve as "lead counsel in the case from beginning to end" with full "power to choose associates." Martinet also remarked in this letter, "the revival of interest in the Jim Crow car matter is owing to you more than to anyone else."[67] It is likely that Martinet had received a second letter from Tourgée urging them to pursue the constitutional challenge. But whatever immediately prompted Martinet's offer, Tourgée readily accepted the position but refused remuneration despite his continuing financial woes. The committee's fund instead was used to hire a local Republican lawyer, James C. Walker, a white man who normally practiced criminal law. Over the next two years, Tourgée oversaw the case from Thorheim, and he developed every detail of strategy and argument through a long-distance correspondence with Martinet and Walker. In this correspondence, the two New Orleanians occupied a decidedly advisory role, responding to Tourgée's inquiries about state laws and local customs and offering their input on his proposed lines of argument.[68]

From the outset, Tourgée and Martinet were determined not to restrict their activities to the courtroom. As veteran editorialists, they naturally hoped to mobilize public opinion by publicizing their activities as widely as possible. A national civil rights organization would serve their purpose. The ACERA had failed, Martinet lamented, because "the proper men were not at the head." The Afro-American League, founded in 1887 by T. Thomas Fortune, by its very moniker was perceived as an organization for blacks only—it had no white members. Martinet had criticized its racial exclusivity in the *Crusader*, ridiculing its innovative phrase *Afro-American*, whose hyphen, he said, "keeps the 'Afro' always just so far away from the 'American.' "[69] He would later tell Tourgée that the league would "not take with the best of our people here" in New Orleans, because it reinforced "the color line."[70] So he was pleased when Tourgée proposed an interracial organization. Martinet wrote, "I heartily approve your suggestion for a national organization without the color or race line, to speak for the oppressed & defend their rights . . . we want no distinct association [for blacks] & no distinct appellation, except when necessary for descriptive purposes."[71] Thus, their organization would embody the principle that citizenship was both national and color-blind.

Armed with the New Orleans Citizen Committee's approval, Tourgée announced his challenge to the Louisiana Separate Car Act and on October 17, 1891, called for the founding of a national civil rights organization in "A Bystander's Notes." Addressing himself directly to his white readership, he placed the onus of launching the movement on the readers themselves. Asking for "positive evidence" that "any considerable portion of the American people . . . still believe in equality of civil right," Tourgée provided a small printed form at the bottom of his column that he asked readers to cut out and mail to the *Inter Ocean* if they "approve the object of forming a 'Citizens' Equal Right Association.'" He asked, "Will the people of the North stand by the colored citizen in his appeal to the law?" Moreover, he challenged his readers to demonstrate a civic responsibility comparable to that of the black citizens of New Orleans. "It is a wonderful thing," he observed, that "by dimes and half-dimes, an oppressed and an impoverished race who are asserted to be incapable of self-government or co-operation are raising a fund to bring before the courts of the land the question of their rights as citizens." Whites who had no reason to fear retribution had remained shamefully silent over the Separate Car Act, he chastised, while Southern blacks risked everything to protect the legal integrity of national citizenship. "Thanks to the civic instinct of an 'inferior' race," he concluded, "we shall see whether justice is still color-blind or National citizenship worth a rag for the defense of right."[72]

The response to Tourgée's call was overwhelming. Letters of support, along with enrollment forms, poured in, numbering some twenty thousand by the end of 1891. On November 16, he received a letter from "the colored citizens of New Orleans" bearing several hundred signatures.[73] But, Tourgée was more taken by surprise by the extent and fervor of the responses by his white readership. Many referenced the meaning of the Civil War, such as one who recalled that Abraham Lincoln had accomplished his "great and good work" by always keeping "the principles of the Declaration of Independence . . . uppermost in his mind."[74] The National Headquarters of the Ladies of the Grand Army of the Republic echoed these sentiments by calling on its members to join the association, and the students of Oberlin College pledged to recruit five hundred new

NCRA members.[75] These letters gave Tourgée new hope for optimism. He told a friend, "I had long given up hope of visible results in my day but kept on week after week striking a blow which, however feeble, fell always in the same place." All at once, it appeared his weekly laments had not fallen on deaf ears: "The progress of the last year is altogether amazing. The white people of the North are rapidly coming to a clearer comprehension of the situation."[76]

In keeping with the agreement to avoid "the color or race line," Tourgée christened the new organization the National Citizens Rights Association (NCRA). Its stated purpose was to "collect and publicize" violations of civil rights of all citizens, black or white, and to use the courts to strike down oppressive laws like the Louisiana Separate Car Act. Tourgée proclaimed that his goal was to enlist one million members (membership was free) and to use the organization to pressure legislatures and political parties. "Today the voice of public opinion is more potent in shaping the action of peoples and nations than ever before. A million names on our roll will command the attention of every phase of the world's thought," he announced to prospective members. Evidence of strong support, he believed, would sustain the fading hopes of Southern blacks. "Show the colored citizen that he is not to be abandoned," he implored, "that the sentiment of liberty, justice and equality of opportunity is not a mere evanescent whim on the part of the northern people."[77]

The NCRA's principles and objectives were outlined in a thirty-two-page pamphlet entitled *Is Liberty Worth Preserving?* The *Inter Ocean* agreed to print 25,000 copies of this pamphlet in 1892, although it did so on the understanding that Tourgée would cease to use "A Bystander's Notes" to promote the NCRA and circulate its subscription forms. Having "eroded the good nature" of Nixon on the subject, Tourgée agreed to find another platform for his organization.[78] In the end, *Is Liberty Worth Preserving?* would be the only significant publication under the auspices of the NCRA.

In the pamphlet, Tourgée stated that the NCRA would combat "the suppression of free speech" in the South and the rise of "class legislation," such as the Separate Car Act and the amended Mississippi Constitution. He also stated unequivocally that race-prejudice—not racial inferiority— was the true cause of persistent black poverty and illiteracy throughout the nation. He declared, "The ignorance and poverty of the colored race are neither the result of ethnic qualities nor of individual inclination on their part but are the ineradicable evidence of the reckless greed, injustice, and neglect of the duty of the white race." Just as Lincoln had imagined the Civil War to be a divine reckoning for the national toleration of slavery, he described "race war" of "inconceivable horror" that would be visited as a divine judgment on the nation if it did not act. The bloodbath, Tourgée imagined, "may spring from resentfulness at the 'Jim Crow Car'; it may result from lynching a man who defends his wife's honor . . . cities may be burned, railroads destroyed, and civilization in all its forms be forced to do penance for injustice and oppression."[79]

By the summer of 1892, the NCRA had considerable momentum behind it, claiming over 100,000 members and described by Tourgée as "very strong in Illinois, Michigan, Wisconsin, Kansas, Nebraska, and . . . rapidly growing in Indiana, Ohio and other states."[80] At the Republican National Convention, the NCRA received acknowledgement from several party leaders whose show of respect indicated that the Republican Party took it seriously. Privately, however, Tourgée feared that the Republicans may "come out a 'White Man's Party'" at the convention. Even congressional radicals, he lamented, preached caution lest they provoke "the cry of 'Bloody-shirt' which would scare about 1/3 of the Republicans into fits."[81] Attempting to rally the confidence of his congressional sympathizers, he told anyone who would listen that "a very large minority at least" of Northerners still "believe in justice and equal rights without regard to race or color." The NCRA distributed circulars supporting House Speaker Reed for president, who privately assured Tourgée that he would not let the "Southern question" slip from his party's platform if he were to be nominated.[82] Harrison narrowly won renomination, to Tourgée's great disappointment, but the 1892 platform did include a staunch declaration against "Southern outrages" and a reaffirmation of the Lodge Bill's principles—concessions that probably had less to do with the NCRA than with fear of losing the black vote to the newly established People's Party.

Tourgée left the convention discouraged about the direction of his party. "The Republican party have accepted the idea that greed is the strongest motive that can be appealed to," he grieved. "They no longer say 'this is the party of liberty and justice;' but, 'this is the party of self and profit.'"[83] Yet he refused to break with Republicans and even used the NCRA to campaign for Harrison. One follower of the maverick People's, or Populist, Party wrote to him asking, "I know you are too staunch a Republican to change your political views. But on the face of the platform what do you think of the people's party?" Tourgée replied: "I am perfectly willing the People's party should agitate any of the questions they propose in their platform. In several of them I quite agree, but I have no hope of any good from them since I know its Southern members to be the worst enemies labor ever had." In short, he had no interest in joining a party dominated by disaffected Southern democrats. Moreover, he viewed all third parties as ineffectual, except to lobby the establish parties to adopt their viewpoints, as the NCRA was trying to do. "I do not expect any good from the Alliance or third Party except incidentally," he explained. "It may do two things: 1. It may encourage free-speech and independence of thought among the southern whites. I think it is doing this. . . . 2. It may serve to spur the Republican party up to its [destiny]."[84]

In spite of its growing following, Tourgée was unsure of how to best realize the NCRA's potential as a weapon of political influence. NCRA letterhead and circulars listed the names of its Executive Council, which included Ida B. Wells, Charles W. Chesnutt, George Washington Cable, and Florence A. Lewis; but he promised them that they would not be burdened with any actual responsibilities, particularly Cable, who had only reluctantly joined.[85] In fact, the organization was run entirely out of Thorheim, with Emma and Aimée keeping the records of membership and answering much of the correspondence. Inquiries about holding a national convention, or establishing local chapters, were put off with evasive responses. He confessed to one confidante of his hesitancy for fear of taking a wrong step: "I may almost be said to be superstitious in regard to the NCRA. It began so strangely and has kept on growing so steadily that I am very loath to interfere with the method which has yielded such results." Rationalizing that he was protecting its grassroots origins, he added: "Besides that, I am always doubtful about building from the top down. Thus far this is purely a people's movement. There has been no particle of personal or partisan influence."[86] He hoped "to give everyone an opportunity to work according to his own inclination and capacity and in his own way" without centralized control. Avoiding a national conference would also prevent "bickerings, jealousy, distrust, and excess of machinery" that undermined recent attempts to create a national organization "among the colored people."[87]

But beneath these explanations, another fundamental dilemma lurked. An interracial organization required interracial meetings. After his recent experience at Mohonk, and after a lifetime of tripping over the color line, Tourgée feared that this issue alone could destroy the movement. He explained to one white member of the NCRA: "Thousands who say they are willing the colored citizen should have equal rights would abandon all idea of it if they had to attend a public meeting . . . this is very foolish and wrong but true. Even our Mohonk people dare not ask a Negro to consult with them. How shall this be avoided?" His answer was to avoid public meetings altogether. There will be "no conventions, no delegates, no speeches, no parades, no eloquence," Tourgée insisted. "I see no use of these instrumentalities now but their employment would kill our work." To any whites who needed reassurance, Tourgée would insist that the NCRA "is not a colored movement." It was a movement for *citizen's* rights: "They are oppressed because they are colored. But that is not the reason they are entitled to protection, justice, and equal opportunity. That is because they are human beings, citizens of the United States, and people whom we have wronged until our sin has ripened into curses."[88]

Tourgée may well have asked himself whether his "color-blind" organization had capitulated too much to the realities of the color line in order to build up its white membership. By accepting the common distinction between "social equality" and "civic equality," he rationalized that the NCRA need not insist upon the intermingling of whites and blacks. For his own part, he explained, "I don't care anything about the prejudice. I treat a colored man as a gentleman, if he is one and esteem a colored woman a lady, if she is one." But this was his personal choice. "Others must do as they choose, also. I do not think I have any right to endanger good results by trying to compel compliance with my notions," he decided.[89] Since the time of the abolitionists, the charge of promoting "social equality" had frightened off whites who otherwise supported the notion of formal equality before the law. The phrase "social equality" reverberated with implications of "miscegenation," of blacks marrying whites, forcing themselves into white homes and parlors, joining elite social clubs and other privileged spaces. His strategic evasion of this issue was understandable, yet it greatly restricted the NCRA's field of endeavor.

An international scandal involving Catherine Impey in 1893 merely confirmed the danger of inviting charges of "miscegenation." Impey, who had openly advocated for the "untrammeled intermingling" of the races, fell in love with a black dentist, Dr. George Ferdinands, a man who was treated almost like a son by Impey's wealthy Scottish benefactor Isabelle F. Mayo. When Impey confessed her "affections" to Ferdinands, encouraging him not to withhold a marriage proposal because of the color bar between them, he showed the letter to Mrs. Mayo who promptly became uncontrollably enraged. Denouncing Impey as a "nymphomaniac" and threatening to publish her letter, Mayo withdrew her funding of Ida B. Wells's lecture tour and wrote letters to civil rights leaders on both sides of the Atlantic imploring them to shun Impey and calling her dangerously unstable.[90] Wells, who witnessed Mayo's confrontation with Impey, called it "the most painful scene in which I ever took part." When Wells stood by her friend Impey, Mrs. Mayo "cast her into outer darkness with Impey," thus also severing her relationship with Wells.[91]

Tourgée was flabbergasted when he received Mayo's condemnatory letter. While others who received it, like Frederick Douglass and T. Thomas Fortune, waffled in their response, Tourgée wrote back defending Impey in the strongest terms possible:

I cannot imagine anything more infamously brutal and heartless . . . [than] to make her the subject of two continents prurient suspicion by writing letters of this sort . . . Catherine Impey fought a battle, which though slight and indeterminate, was a poem of truth in an age of greed . . . Impey has wrought for justice, liberty and equality for all with a singleness of purpose and a faith under all discouragement which few can pretend to rival and none in our time can claim to exceed. So I will continue to give my loving respect to the poor woman whose fervid aspiration it was a gratification to know and my profound contempt to the male or female jackals who would magnify themselves by blackening her good name.[92]

While it is unclear what motivated Mayo's extreme response—whether it was Impey's attempted initiation of an interracial romance, or Mayo's own complicated feelings for Ferdinands—the revelation of a white female civil rights leader throwing herself at a black man and being spurned had potentially devastating consequences for their cause. The widely known scandal was kept out of the press, but Impey resigned from her civil rights organization before long.[93]

Despite his reluctance to challenge the NCRA's white membership on the question of "social equality," Tourgée remained committed to integration as a long-term goal. To this end, he seemed less reluctant to encourage his black followers to test the boundaries of the color line. Citing a controversy in Brooklyn over a "wealthy and refined colored man" who moved into a white neighborhood, he called upon blacks "who have bank accounts" to integrate "fashionable neighborhoods" in spite of white protest they might incur. In addition, he proposed that every black Christian should attend a white church once a month across the North. Although few Christian churches actually barred blacks from attending, the customary segregation of churches by race, North and South, reflected the vast social and cultural divide that continued between blacks and whites. He proposed that blacks should present themselves "humbly, persistently . . . as a witness of that Christ spirit of which he is an equal heir" and to remind whites of the Biblical doctrine that "God made 'of one blood all the nations of the earth.'" One wonders whether Northern whites would have reacted as Southerners did when Tourgée brought Adaline and Mary Patillo to church with him in the 1870s. Other than letters of protest that accused Tourgée of "inciting colored people to go where they are not wanted," there is no evidence that anyone acted on his proposal.[94]

Tourgée's most promising strategy for the NCRA was to establish a major journal, to be called *The National Citizen*. Just as Du Bois's *The Crisis* would do for the NAACP years later, Tourgée imagined that *The National Citizen* would be able to provide focus, a consistent public voice, and tangible recognition for the NCRA. Tourgée described his proposed journal as a twelve- to twenty-page weekly of literary and political character. Its features would include "a monthly Lesson Leaf on the duties of the citizen, and a monthly record of outrages upon the citizen," and most importantly, " 'A Bystander's Notes' will appear only in its columns."[95] But the failure of *The Continent* probably made investors and publishers wary of supporting a journal under Tourgée's editorial control. Emma, fearful at the prospect of another *The Continent* disaster, was utterly unenthusiastic. On the other hand, Ida B. Wells strongly endorsed the idea and aggressively pursued investors on Tourgée's behalf.[96]

Most encouraging among Tourgée's preparations for *The National Citizen* was his successful pursuit of Charles Chesnutt for associate editor. Chesnutt was at first skeptical: "I recognize the need for such a journal," he told Tourgée, but "were it not for the large roll of the Citizen's Rights Association, I would doubt the existence of such a demand, so far as the white people are concerned." Though not convinced the journal could succeed, he was willing to put forth the effort as long as Tourgée would employ him as a true colleague and not as a racial token: "I do not suppose that you want an associate editor merely for ornament," he wrote to Tourgée. "I certainly would not care to be a mere figurehead in such an enterprise."[97] After he traveled to Mayville to discuss the position with Tourgée in person, Chesnutt was assured that, unlike his position on the NCRA Executive Council, this would entail real responsibility and be a truly collaborative enterprise. Both Chesnutt and Tourgée agreed, however, that they would *not* make a go of it "without ample capital," and Chesnutt himself pledged a few hundred dollars.[98]

While the long-term future of NCRA rested upon finding backing for *The National Citizen*, Tourgée gave the organization shape in the short term by lecturing on its behalf and writing strategic letters on the NCRA letterhead. In one instance, an African American NCRA member, Mrs. H. Davis of Omaha, requested that Tourgée correct the grammar of her personal appeal to President Harrison to prevent lynching and forward her letter to him. Through the moving words of a humble citizen who placed personal responsibility for tolerating lynching at the president's feet, Tourgée sent the letter under the auspices of the NCRA and seized the opportunity to publicize it in "A Bystander's Notes." The letter, which detailed the atrocities against blacks, entreated Harrison, "I call on you, Mr. President in God's name to help us. It lays in the hands of this government to protect all citizens. . . . Will you help my people?"[99] With little choice but to respond, Harrison's feeble reply was that, despite his deepest sympathy, "as President, the Constitution and the laws limit my powers and, in such cases as those to which you refer, these powers do not extend."[100] Having forced Harrison to address the issue, Tourgée now excoriated the president both publicly and privately for missing the opportunity to speak out strongly against the hundreds of racial lynchings and murders that had occurred during his administration. It was not a matter of constitutional power, he lectured Harrison, but rather the moral force of a "resolute and earnest" message from the president. He wrote in exasperation, "If you had but 'protested' officially what I do not doubt you felt personally, your words would have moved not only the heart of the nation but of the world."[101] As always, Harrison's leadership had failed.

In another instance, Tourgée used the NCRA to chastise Cornell University professor Jeremiah W. Jenks for a public lecture in which he cited the history of Reconstruction as evidence of black racial inferiority. Accusing Jencks of making the "superficial study of unrelated phenomena" the basis of purportedly "scientific conclusions," he demolished both his logic and evidence. "I do not believe it is scientifically decided that the Negro is inferior to the white man because I know of no scientific formula by which superiority and inferiority may be determined [in relation to] intellectual quality," Tourgée rebuked him. Whereas Jenks had cited the financial mismanagement of "Negro" governments during Reconstruction as evidence of their inferiority, Tourgée retorted, "Is this a racial quality? How many of the States had 'Negro' governments? What constitutes a 'Negro' government? Does financial mismanagement of public affairs imply racial inferiority?" Pointing out that more white politicians than black had been guilty of financial mismanagement in American history, Tourgée went on to pour contempt on the intellectually bankrupt claims of pseudo science and on Jenks in particular for having lent not only his name, but also the "repute of a great university and, to a certain extent, the much abused name of science" to logically absurd statements. Jenks, he wrote, taught that the "law of life, of civilization, is merely that which rules the destiny of the brute—'the survival of the fittest,'" yet he did not consider the evidence that environment, not biology, played a greater role in the determination of "intelligence and power." After a spirited defense of nurture over nature, Tourgée ended by appealing to Christian values as a counter to Jenks's biological determinism:

> When the American people read the words of a "Professor" upon any subject they naturally expect the highest degree of accuracy in connection therewith . . . God grant that they who teach our young men may learn that there is a truth more beautiful than that which governs the brute's existence and that two elements of it are justice, equal right and equal opportunity for all of the children of our common father—not to be measured by race or color.[102]

Whether or not his scolding successfully cautioned Jenks from making future public statements on race and Reconstruction, the weight of a letter from a national organization at least let him know that his views were not uncontested.

As Tourgée developed his arguments in the *Plessy* case, he became increasingly outspoken against the claims of science regarding race. His most thorough reflection upon this topic came when he delivered a paper, "The Negro in the United States," at the African branch of the Ethnological Congress at the World's Columbian Exposition in Chicago in 1893. Celebrating five hundred years of "progress" since Columbus, the 1893 World's Fair indulged in a great deal of theorizing about, and hierarchical classification of, human "races," "civilizations," and "types." Once again disturbing a smug consensus, Tourgée injected a voice of profound doubt regarding the validity of the new social scientific theories. Though he complimented "the marvelous experimentation and profound subtlety of Darwin," he insisted that the theory of evolution did little to solve the fundamental question of human origin or provide much certainty regarding the rate or capacity for "progress" or "advancement" in human beings and their civilizations. Historically speaking, great civilizations appeared relatively suddenly, created by peoples that had appeared to remain static for eons previously. Once awakened, progress occurred astonishingly quickly. How could the theory of evolution predict when or which peoples possessed the potential for awakening to progress? Moreover, Tourgée registered his unequivocal "protest against the terminology which still afflicts the supreme science of human existence" in regard to racial categories. The "physical differences of what are termed 'races of men' are so great and attach with such uniformity to specific groups, that they could not fail to attract attention" from scientists, he admitted, yet none could even define *race* with any accuracy, much less formulate a coherent theory of racial superiority or inferiority that resolved the conflicting evidence:

> Anthropology—including ethnology and ethnography which have no substantial differences of signification—very naturally accepted these long-established classifications by race and tried most faithfully to fit the Noahian myth [of Ham's sons] to the facts of human existence, but facts are not only stubborn things—they are also multitudinous.[103]

The point of Tourgée's lecture was that, despite all of its hubristic claims of certainty, science had solved nothing regarding the significance of race. Indeed much of its work had been a simple endeavor to justify age-old prejudices.

Tourgée's activities through the NCRA and "A Bystander's Notes" attracted a great deal of attention and admiration. The summer of 1893 probably marked the height of the NCRA's prestige and Tourgée's personal influence. Susan B. Anthony was suitably impressed to invite Tourgée back to the World's Fair to speak on "Citizenship and Suffrage" on a distinguished panel with Elizabeth Cady Stanton as part of a week-long conference on suffrage in August 1893, sponsored by the National American Woman's Suffrage Association, of which Anthony was president. When extending the invitation, Anthony told him, "I do not know of a single person—man or woman—who feels the need of every citizen's being a voter as you do—unless it is my friend Mrs. Stanton."[104] Other speakers at the conference included Frederick Douglass, Lucy Stone, Francis E.W. Harper, ex-Senator Blanche K. Bruce, Julia Ward Howe, and Clarence Darrow—an impressive group of radicals to be sure. Tourgée was also honored to receive the hospitality of the newly established Tourgée Club on Dearborn Street on his return to Chicago. Named in tribute to him by Ferdinand Barnett and other black leaders of the city, this gentleman's club entertained distinguished "race visitors" to the World's Fair. One day of each week the club was reserved for "ladies day," hosted by Ida B. Wells, which laid the groundwork for the first black woman's club in Chicago.[105]

Overall, Tourgée had made an impressive start with the NCRA, although its future remained precarious. The greatest challenge ahead remained managing a successful constitutional challenge to racial segregation by presenting a convincing case to the United State Supreme Court. Just getting their case to the court would be difficult. A series of ill-timed personal events would make it even harder.

9

The Rejection of Color-Blind Citizenship: *Plessy v. Ferguson*

The object of the [Fourteenth] Amendment was undoubtedly to enforce the absolute equality of the two races before the law, but in the nature of things it could not have been intended to abolish distinctions based upon color, or to enforce social, as distinguished from political equality, or a commingling of the two races upon terms unsatisfactory to either.

—Justice Henry Billings Brown, *Plessy v. Ferguson*, 1896

The colored man and those white men who believe in liberty and justice—who do not think Christ's teachings a sham—must join hands and hearts . . . without both united, there is no hope of success.

—Tourgée to Louis A. Martinet, October 31, 1893

HE ASKS NOTHING AS A NEGRO," Tourgée appealed on behalf of blacks in 1890. "It is as a citizen merely that we are called on to consider what rights and privileges he is entitled to exercise."[1] The "color-blind" argument, however, became increasingly difficult to maintain as the legal evisceration of the Reconstruction Amendments proceeded into the 1890s. In fact, the language of color-blind "equal citizenship" had been used by Justice Joseph Bradley in his Supreme Court majority opinion in the *Civil Rights Cases* (1883). Bradley wrote, "There must be some stage in the progress of [the "Negro's"] elevation when he takes the rank of mere citizen, and ceases to be the special favorite of the laws, and when his rights as a citizen are protected in the ordinary modes by which other men's rights are protected."[2] Although crudely misrepresenting the purpose of the Civil Rights Act of 1875 as turning blacks into the special favorites of the laws, Bradley's logic foreshadowed the appropriation and transformation of the principle of equality before the law to forestall government action on behalf of racial justice. The growing myth that Reconstruction itself had been an attempt to elevate black over white fed into the Conservative perception that civil rights agitators simply called for more special protections for the rights of black citizens, who were too weak to protect their own rights as white citizens did.

This phenomenon presented a formidable ideological obstacle to Tourgée's case against segregation as well as to his attempts to mobilize an interracial, color-blind citizens' rights organization. Constitutional precedents weighed heavily against a direct argument for color-blind equality, as the Supreme Court had marshaled their constitutional interpretations of the Reconstruction Amendments to limit the power of the federal government to protect its citizens from racial discrimination. Meanwhile, Tourgée firmly believed that an organization devoted to the rights of all citizens, regardless of color, was the most effective method of mobilizing the public against Jim Crow laws, but other civil rights leaders had different ideas. Some black leaders responded to the congressional failures of 1890, and the Conservative co-option of color-blindness, by turning to self-help strategies and political organizing separate from whites. Related to this, a strategy of accommodation to Jim Crow became increasingly popular among black leaders who regarded political agitation as futile and who sought a gradualist strategy as a way to calm antiblack violence and lessen white obstruction of their economic advancement.[3] In this context, Tourgée would struggle mightily to keep the radical version of color-blind citizenship alive, even as he developed groundbreaking legal arguments that moved beyond this principle and struck against segregation in new ways.

BUILDING THE CASE

Historians have sometimes questioned Homer Plessy's lawyers for their decision to not challenge the material "inequality of accommodations" on the Louisiana railroad cars. This criticism badly misunderstands their constitutional predicament. By providing that the separate coaches for white and black passengers must be made substantially "equal," the Louisiana State Legislature's "equal but separate" formulation paid lip service to the requirements of the Fourteenth Amendment.[4] To insist that the railroads fully comply with the law was not to challenge the constitutionality of it. Tourgée made note in his brief to the court that in fact the law's requirement of "substantial equality of accommodation" had *not* been enforced on the railroad cars, but he acknowledged that this was not an issue in their challenge. "The gist of our case," he insisted, "is the unconstitutionality of the assortment: *not* the question of equal accommodation . . . the State has no right to compel us to ride in a car 'set apart' for a particular race whether it is as good as another or not."[5]

The wording of the Louisiana Separate Car Act made it an elusive target for abstract arguments about equal protection of the laws. What made categorization by race inherently unconstitutional? That the social stigma of race was perpetuated when states required the separation of races by law was not likely to be considered by the Court. Inclined toward legal formalism, the Supreme Court justices were not disposed to look beyond the internal logic of the law to the larger social context. The law itself pretended that no such stigma existed, as Tourgée would tell the Supreme Court:

> The Statute itself is a skillful attempt to confuse and conceal its real purpose. It assumes impartiality. It fulminates apparently against white and black alike. Its real object is to keep negroes out of one car for the gratification of whites—not to keep whites out of another car for the comfort and satisfaction of the colored passenger.[6]

Yet to prove injurious discrimination within the confines of accepted constitutional law would be challenging. To broaden their attack on the law, Tourgée and his colleagues chose to introduce other elements into the case to raise as many thorny legal complications as possible. Their most important strategy in this respect involved picking a plaintiff who himself defied easy racial classification.

In spring 1892 Tourgée instructed his local counsel to choose a plaintiff who had "not more than one-eighth colored blood" and would be able to pass as "white." Originally he had suggested to Martinet that a "nearly white" woman would make a good choice as a plaintiff, but he was advised that in New Orleans no such lady would be refused admission to the railroad car.[7] Martinet informed him: "people of tolerably fair complexion, even if unmistakenly [*sic*] colored, enjoy here a large degree of immunity from the accursed prejudice" that afflicted the darker-skinned blacks. Martinet himself rode in whatever car he wished and never feared exclusion from any segregated public accommodations. But Tourgée's purpose was strategic: he intended to exploit the Louisiana legislature's failure to define race and to introduce the inconclusiveness of scientific evidence on racial categories and definitions into evidence. "That race is a scientific and legal question of great difficulty," he pointed out to his co-counsel, "is a question [the Court] may as well take up, if for nothing else, to let the court sharpen its wits on."[8] Moreover, Tourgée preferred a female plaintiff because it would underscore the uncivilized and unchivalrous act of forcible expulsion from a segregated car that would not be highlighted by a male plaintiff.

In order to make Tourgée's suggestion work, the Citizens' Committee arranged in advance with the railroads to have their light-skinned plaintiff expelled from the white car. The railroad companies, as it turned out, were overwhelmingly opposed to the Separate Car Act because of its extra cost and inconvenience. For unstated reasons, the committee rejected the idea of a female plaintiff and instead enlisted Professor Daniel Desdunes, the twenty-one-year-old son of committee leader Rodolphe, who fit Tourgée's description of not being discernibly "colored." The choice of a male plaintiff probably came from the committee's desire to project an image of "manly resistance" to the public—as well as its recognition that the plaintiff would be hauled off to jail and put in a position of vulnerability while in police hands. After Desdunes was arrested for boarding a white-only car, Martinet praised him in the *Crusader* as a American patriot, proclaiming, "The young Professor Desdunes is to be congratulated on his manly assertion of his right, and his refusal to ride in the Jim Crow coach. The people should cherish the performance of such patriotic acts and honor the patriots."[9] A heroic American patriot fit much better with the Citizens' Committee's vision of their movement than a female in distress.

The Daniel Desdunes case ended when the state dropped its prosecution in May 1892—a consequence of the Louisiana Supreme Court's having struck down the Separate Car Act's application to interstate travel. Tourgée and Martinet had Desdunes board an interstate train at co-counsel Waker's suggestion that they invoke federal supremacy over the states in the regulation of interstate commerce. At first, they received this development as a great victory, but they soon realized that it would have little effect on the majority of railroad cars within the state and amounted to little more than a loss of money and time. Thus, the case began again on June 7, 1892, with a new plaintiff, Homer Adolphe Plessy—a thirty-year-old friend of Rodolphe Desdunes and another man who was also to all appearances white. When he purchased a ticket on an East Louisiana railroad heading to an intrastate destination, Plessy did not identify himself as "colored," but he did so to the conductor after the train had left the station. Arrested for refusing to leave the first-class car, he submitted to police quietly without any commotion or disturbance of the peace, following the committee's instructions. Plessy put down a $500 bail bond at the police station, which was paid for by the committee, and returned home to await his arraignment.[10]

One myth about the *Plessy* case, repeated by even top scholarly authorities, is that the light skin color of Homer Plessy sparked controversy within the black community of New Orleans. An influential 1993 *Harvard Law Review* article has even claimed that Tourgée's request for "a fair-skinned plaintiff" was carried out "over vigorous opposition from organized Black leadership," who "objected that such a strategy, even if successful, would mitigate conditions only for those blacks who appeared to be white."[11] This statement is utterly without foundation. No evidence has ever been offered, nor can be found, to support the claim that anyone, much less "organized Black leadership," objected to Tourgée's arguments or his suggestion for a light-skinned plaintiff. Yet, the implication that Plessy's lawyers were somehow more concerned about the rights of the light-skinned Creole community rather than that of African Americans has persisted in historical and legal literature. This unfortunate misinformation is derived from a second-hand report of comments made by *one* local black preacher coupled with persistent confusion over the intent behind some of Tourgée's arguments. The history of tension between the light-skinned and dark-skinned communities of New Orleans, moreover, has also served to make this urban myth seem plausible.[12]

The "trouble" was reported from Martinet to Tourgée in a letter of December 7, 1891. Martinet remarked that Reverend Alexander S. Jackson of New Orleans had charged the Citizens' Committee with representing only the interests of those who "were nearly white, or wanted to pass for white." This report came before the Desdunes case had even begun and before Tourgée made his suggestion of a light-skinned plaintiff. Martinet adamantly dismissed Jackson's accusations as "absurd and malicious" and "a lot of nonsense."[13] Indeed, the Citizens' Committee, which included fully dark-skinned members, such as its Vice-President C.C. Antoine, had stood unequivocally for the rights of all blacks—or as one member had put it "the 7,999,999 *of my race*."[14] As it turned out, Reverend Jackson was no enemy of their cause. He had joined Tourgée's NCRA upon its inception a few weeks earlier in October, and he had written Tourgée a personal letter expressing great admiration for him, praising his novels and comparing him to William Lloyd Garrison. Perhaps Jackson's desire to establish a local NCRA chapter with himself at the head fueled his oppositional comments against the Citizens' Committee. After writing to both men, Tourgée was able to smooth out the conflict between his two allies. He even hinted that Martinet may have been misinformed about Jackson's comments. "I am glad that Reverend Jackson has been misrepresented," Martinet somewhat grudgingly replied a few weeks later. Still regretting that Jackson had "talked so much and tried so hard to obstruct our movement," he nevertheless assured Tourgée, "You need have no fear; what you call my combativeness will not interfere with the NCRA or with the progress of any good cause."[15] It is not clear whether Jackson and the Citizens' Committee collaborated afterwards, but Jackson's public criticism ended. It was a relatively small bump on the road for the test case that had nothing to do with Desdunes, Plessy, or Tourgée's later arguments to the court.

As Tourgée researched his arguments in the case, he found few precedents to support his position that the Constitution barred racial segregation—and many against it. The precedent that spoke most directly to the issue was *Roberts v. The City of Boston* (1850), discussed in chapter one, in which Charles Sumner argued directly for color-blind citizenship, insisting that citizens were guaranteed equality before the law "without distinction of color." Sumner's argument failed to persuade the Supreme Judicial Court of Massachusetts, whose chief justice, Lemuel Shaw, ruled that classification and segregation by race was a "reasonable" and non-invidious policy, akin to segregation by gender or age. The *Roberts* precedent would be cited by Tourgée's opposing counsel in the *Plessy* case, and the failure of Sumner's arguments served as a warning to Plessy's lawyers about basing their entire argument on Sumner's color-blind logic.[16] Although Tourgée would insist that the Reconstruction Amendments had mooted the *Roberts* decision, which the Supreme Court need not have followed anyway, *Roberts* nevertheless provided a tempting rationale to uphold segregation—from the State of Massachusetts, no less—that he needed to dissuade the court from adopting.

Whether one believed the *Roberts* decision had been rendered moot by the Fourteenth Amendment depended upon whether or not one believed that racial segregation had been prohibited by the amendment's strictures. Neither the wording of the Fourteenth Amendment nor the congressional debates over its adoption resolved this question. Some congressmen argued for a clause that would have struck at segregation by prohibiting states from making "any distinction in civil rights" based on "race, color, or descent." But this language was rejected in favor of a more ambiguous phrase guaranteeing the "equal protection of the laws," which lent itself to greater interpretation and avoided any clear resolution of the segregation issue.[17] Adding to the perception that the amendment did not prohibit segregation, many Republicans, including Tourgée himself, had been willing to accept the existence of segregated schools. Yet, at a time when a state-supported public school system itself was an innovation—as yet far from established as a permanent fixture of public life, especially in the South—there were distinctions to be made. Tourgée, for instance, never supported the state-mandated *de jure* segregation of schools. Where local communities had formed racially exclusive schools of their own accord that reflected the all-black or all-white geographic communities in which they were formed, it was tolerable to him and preferable to no schools. But such exceptions to the rule fed into the widely held perception that the amendments had not prohibited segregation.

Further weakening the case against segregation, a string of Supreme Court decisions in the 1870s and 1880s greatly curtailed the scope of the Thirteenth and Fourteenth Amendments. In the *Slaughter-House Cases* (1873), the Court ruled in a narrow five to four decision that the Fourteenth Amendment had not been designed to fundamentally alter the balance between state and national citizenship that existed in judicial interpretations prior to its adoption. Adhering to a theory of "dual citizenship," the majority insisted that the Fourteenth Amendment could be applied only to state infringements on the "privileges and immunities" of *United States* citizenship as distinct from *state* citizenship. Its equally narrow interpretation of the intention of the Thirteenth Amendment in *Slaughter-House* seemed to render that amendment impotent in its application to any circumstance other than Southern slavery as it had existed before Emancipation.[18]

In addition, *U.S. v. Cruikshank* (1876) ruled that politically motivated mob actions against blacks in Colfax, Louisiana, did not violate a citizen's rights within the purview of the Fourteenth Amendment because it applied only to *state* action, not to the actions of individuals. The effect of this ruling was to relegate most civil rights cases to state courts rather than to federal courts, leaving blacks at the mercy of state judges and juries. Finally, in its most widely noted decision, the *Civil Rights Cases* (1883), the Supreme Court struck down Charles Sumner's 1875 Civil Rights Act that, among other things, prohibited segregation in most public and quasi-public services. Its rationale, resting upon *Cruikshank*, argued that voluntary segregation by restaurants, hotels, and other privately owned businesses were individual acts of discrimination that did not fall within the scope of state action.[19]

Despite this bleak record, there were many ambiguities and close decisions in these cases that Tourgée hoped to exploit. The controversial *Slaughter-House* ruling had been publicly denounced by several framers of the Fourteenth Amendment, and four justices vigorously dissented from its majority opinion. Justice Stephen J. Field, who wrote the most influential dissent in the case, had become a venerable force in the intervening years, and he was the last holdover from *Slaughter-House* court at the hearing of *Plessy*. A ruling in *Plessy* that revisited the scope of national citizenship as defined by the Fourteenth Amendment might enable Field to use his influence to reverse the close *Slaughter-House* decision. In addition, the public outcry against the *Civil Rights Cases* gave Tourgée some hope that *Plessy* might be used to restore some of its lost credibility on citizens' rights. Justice John Marshall Harlan's widely celebrated dissent in the *Civil Rights Cases* asserted unequivocally that both the Thirteenth and Fourteenth Amendment contained affirmative rights that gave broad power to the federal government in the protection of citizens' rights. Tourgée believed that some of the other justices who heard the case had come to regret the decision.[20]

The lead attorney for the plaintiffs in the *Civil Rights Cases* had been none other than Tourgée's good friend, Samuel F. Phillips, the U.S. solicitor general. Tourgée kept up a warm correspondence with Phillips over the years and even dedicated an 1888 collection of short stories to him, effusively praising his "faith in divine justice" and his "sympathy for humanity."[21] Phillips's brief in the *Civil Rights Cases* provided some of the material for Justice Harlan's dissent and may have inspired Tourgée's heartfelt tribute. Phillips and Harlan, as fellow Southern Republicans appointed during Reconstruction, socialized together in Washington and shared a similar worldview. Having dinner one night in 1878, they discussed Tourgée, and Phillips wrote afterward to tell him, "Justice Harlan . . . spoke in high terms of your brief in the homestead case"—the case had arisen out of North Carolina and had been recently reviewed by Harlan on the Supreme Court.[22] Phillips's thirteen-year tenure as solicitor general ended in 1885, but he continued to live in Washington and practice law. With his long experience practicing before the Supreme Court and his personal influence on Harlan, Phillips gave Tourgée reason for optimism when he agreed to join the *Plessy* legal team in early 1893. Once the case was successfully appealed to the Supreme Court, Phillips would contribute a brief of his own and he would guide the case through the final procedures of its appeal.

While Tourgée studied the arguments of Sumner in *Roberts* and Phillips in the *Civil Rights Cases* closely, another brilliant legal brief against racial segregation surely captured his attention, one that was never submitted to a court of law. Robert Green Ingersoll, in the aftermath of the Court's adverse decision in the *Civil Rights Cases*, joined Frederick Douglass and others at a mass protest in Washington, D.C., on October 22, 1883. Several speakers made impassioned speeches denouncing the decision, but Ingersoll, a talented lawyer and renowned orator, delivered a point-by-point rebuttal to the Court's majority opinion that amounted to one of the most cogent statements of Radical Republican constitutionalism. Ingersoll employed the metaphor of color-blindness in his description of the impact of the constitutional amendments on American citizenship. In reference to the Thirteenth Amendment, in particular, he said, it had "abolished not only slavery, but every 'badge and brand and stain and mark of slavery.' It abolished forever all distinctions on account of race or color. . . . From the moment of the adoption of the 13th Amendment the law became color blind."[23] In addition, Ingersoll asserted that the Thirteenth and Fourteenth Amendments carried with them "affirmative rights" that vastly expanded the scope of national citizenship. The Court's restricted interpretation of the Reconstruction Amendments, he said, had "undervalued the accomplishments of the [Civil] war" by failing to recognize that the old distinction between state and federal citizenship, which gave primacy to the former, had been eradicated. He proclaimed:

> In construing the Thirteenth, Fourteenth and Fifteenth Amendments the courts need not go back to decisions rendered in the days of slavery—in the days when narrow and constrained construction was the rule, in favor of State sovereignty and the rights of the master. These amendments utterly obliterated all such decisions. The Supreme Court should begin with the Amendments. It need not look behind them. . . . They laid a new foundation for a new nation.[24]

Tourgée's arguments in *Plessy* would echo Ingersoll both in his appeal to civic color-blindness and in his interpretation of national citizenship. But he was planning an attack on racial segregation unlike any that had ever come before.[25]

Moving beyond the color-blind argument, Tourgée was planning to question the very categories of race, to probe the social power of whiteness, and to turn conservative arguments on behalf of property, marriage, and family against the Separate Car Act. Unlike Ingersoll—and Justice Harlan for that matter—Tourgée would not argue that the Reconstruction Amendments, either as a whole or the Thirteenth in particular, had specifically inscribed a rule of color-blindness into the Constitution. Instead, he would suggested as a higher principle of jurisprudence that "the law ought at least to be color-blind" in its treatment of individual citizens. This was more in keeping with his previous uses of the term, going back to 1870, and it emphasized the flexibility of the means toward this end. His pragmatism, in the end, is what would make Tourgée's *Plessy* brief extraordinary and distinguish it from all preceding ones.

In October 1892, Homer A. Plessy's challenge to the constitutionality of the Separate Car Act was heard by Judge John Howard Ferguson, a carpetbagger from Massachusetts who served in the criminal district court for Orleans Parish. Judge Ferguson, referred to as "our friend" by James Walker, upheld Plessy's conviction and affirmed the constitutionality of the Separate Car Act. Plessy's appeal of Ferguson's ruling was quickly upheld by the Louisiana Supreme Court in December which added little to Ferguson's reasoning. Thus, in January 1893, the case of *Plessy v. Ferguson* appeared on the United States Supreme Court docket.[26] When the October term of the Supreme Court arrived in 1893, the Citizens' Committee awaited word upon whether the Court would take up the case. Although their challenge had been executed impeccably thus far,

Tourgée suddenly urged a change of course. "I have been having some very serious thoughts in regard to Plessy's Case of late, as my preparation for the hearing has extended," Tourgée ominously began a letter to Martinet on October 31, 1893. He asked Martinet to gather the entire Citizens' Committee together and lay his letter before them.

After assessing the legal and political inclinations of the Court, Tourgée concluded that their chances of winning at the present time were slim. He observed that the makeup of the court and the political context had changed since they first began the case in 1890. "It is of the utmost consequence that we should not have a decision *against us*," Tourgée warned. "It is a matter of boast with the court that it has *never reversed* itself on a *constitutional question*." All three of the new appointments made by Benjamin Harrison had disappointed Tourgée, especially his lame-duck appointment of Tennessee Democrat Howell E. Jackson in January 1893, which prompted his outraged article entitled "Ben Harrison a Traitor Too!" Thus, in fall 1893, Tourgée counted only one justice, Harlan, known to be favorably disposed to their case, while four justices were known to be unfavorably disposed and "will probably stay where they are until Gabriel blows his horn." Of the remaining votes, he believed one inclined toward them "legally" but not "politically" and two others "may be brought over by the argument."[27] Thus, the best they could muster was four votes out of the eight sitting justices. A ninth seat on the court remained unfilled at the time of Tourgée's letter, but it would soon be filled by Edward Douglass White, a Louisiana Democrat and former Confederate soldier with a rumored Ku Klux Klan past.[28]

The implication of Tourgée's assessment was clear: they should either delay or drop the case. For the present, his advice was to delay. "Leave the case to come up when it will and [let us] not attempt to advance it," he proposed. In the absence of pressure from the plaintiffs, it might be a few years before *Plessy v. Ferguson* was heard, buried in the Supreme Court's large backlog of cases. "We have nothing to hope for in any change that may be made in the court," he admitted, "but if we can get the ear of the Country, and argue the matter fully before the people first, we may incline the wavering to fall on our side when the matter comes up."[29] What was required now was a major new effort to reach the public. He believed, "[I]f we can wipe out the indifference of the white people of the North upon this subject, there is a chance that the Supreme Court . . . when moved by the awakened and potent conscience of the people, may grant its edict against caste."[30] In his view, they would have the means to do it, if his plans for the *National Citizen* came to fruition. Reluctantly, the Citizens' Committee agreed. The case would be put off while Tourgée attempted to rouse the public's indignation against segregation.

THE FRACTURED CRUSADE

On September 6, 1890, a small newspaper article from Buffalo announced "Mrs. Tourgée Goes to Prison." Emma must have been mortified, and not a little alarmed, to read of her own prison sentence in a story that was picked up by newspapers across the country, including the *New York Times.* The story explained that Judge Lewis of the New York Supreme Court had fined her thirty-five dollars and sentenced her to thirty-five days in jail for disobeying a court order and "failing to appear before a referee . . . to answer as to the financial relations existing between herself and her husband Albion W. Tourgée."[31] Earlier that year, Tourgée's creditors decided to press their claims on his income, attracted by his sudden return to national prominence, his well-known Bystander's column, and his newly awarded Civil War pension (which he began to receive earlier in 1890). Emma had continued to keep their property and bank accounts in her name, and through this financial legerdemain they had been able to evade their creditors. Now they came after her.

Both Albion and their family attorney urged Emma to testify, assuring her that she could refuse to answer any questions she wished. But she feared that in doing so she might be threatened with contempt charges; and if forced to respond, she would have to choose between lying under oath and risking perjury or disclosing the truth and facing financial ruin. In the end, Emma served no jail time. After their challenge to the court order failed, the Tourgées worked out a deal with their creditors and resumed modest payments. The charges were dropped, but the ordeal left Emma humiliated and shaken at having faced the prospect of imprisonment. Consequently, she began to withdraw her moral support from Tourgée's civil rights work, believing that his first priority should be to lift their debts.[32]

Within two weeks of the *New York Times* story, Emma executed her own plan of action that showed both her sense of desperation and her diminished faith in Albion's ability to keep them from utter ruin. Having heard about the recent philanthropic works of John D. Rockefeller, Emma took advantage of Albion's absence on a lecture circuit and traveled alone to Cleveland to appeal to the generosity of the world's first billionaire. Rockefeller's sister-in-law gently declined Emma's request for a personal interview and turned her away at the door. But she prevailed upon Emma to state her case in writing, and a few days later, she did so.[33]

"You doubtless know who my husband is," Emma wrote to Rockefeller on September 26, 1890. Excusing her imposition as an act of "a wife's devotion to her husband," she described Albion as an idealist who had "done some good to humanity in the past" and whom Rockefeller might enable "to do much more" in the future. After detailing their financial predicament, she told of Albion's tortured psyche as "a proud, sensitive man, battling with ill-health and ill-fortune," and frankly admitted that he was totally unable "to retrieve himself." "He is no business man," she explained, "and since his failure he has attempted nothing looking toward management of our affairs, leaving all such things to me." She asked for a no-interest loan of $25,000 to lift the crushing pressure of his debts so that he might be free to pursue his humanitarian work. Offering as collateral Albion's $30,000 life insurance policy, which she had kept up diligently over the years, Emma assured Rockefeller that she could pay him back in ten years or upon Albion's death, whichever came first. "Whether my plea is heard or not," she concluded, "I feel I have done no wrong, and what a true, loving woman will do for her husband—that is not wrong!"[34] Her long letter has survived in the Rockefeller family archives. If Rockefeller replied, which he likely did, his refusal, whether kind or unkind, was quietly destroyed by Emma, who never told Albion what she had done.

Conflict with Emma ate away at Albion's commitment to the NCRA as he tried to press forward with his civil rights crusade. On November 7, 1893, just one week after Albion's letter to Martinet advising delay in the *Plessy* case, Emma recorded her frustration in her diary: "Albion wrote again to Bishop Turner. I have no faith in what he is doing—merely wasting time which should be given to other work, whereby we could have something to live on. My heart is very heavy."[35] Emma did not suffer in silence. Albion's letter to Bishop Turner bears evidence that Emma's concerns were weighing upon his mind. Complaining to Turner that his work was not sufficiently supported by certain black leaders of influence, he warned: "I feel that the time has come for me to cease troubling myself about these things and give my attention more fully to the problem of 'ways and means' for my own little group of human wayfarers."[36] This empty threat, made at the exact moment he had pledged to redouble his efforts to reach the Northern public, illustrated the emotional toll Emma's opposition had on his morale.

Without the full support of Emma and his household, Tourgée's own enthusiasm for the NCRA began to waver. Making things worse was his growing awareness that Northern black leaders were not fully behind him, confirmed by reportage in various newspapers, even from the beginning of the case: The *Philadelphia Times* had gleefully reported opposition to the NCRA in 1892 with the blaring headline, "Won't Indorse [*sic*] Tourgee: Leading Colored Men Regard Him As An Alarmist." Two black leaders in Philadelphia were quoted at length belittling the NCRA's denunciation of lynching and dismissing Tourgée's predictions of an impending "race war." Robert Purvis, a wealthy ex-abolitionist, told the

Times, "Judge Tourgée does not voice the sense of the thinking colored people of the South . . . these lynchings that he refers to have been almost without exception visited upon colored men who have outraged white women." Accepting unquestioningly Southern justifications for lynching, Purvis remarked that he could almost fancy taking part in lynch mobs himself to protect female virtue: "Death, and death alone appears to be the one punishment that will discourage this crime," he was reported to have said.[37]

Even Frederick Douglass, in his final years, failed to publicly support either the NCRA or the Citizens' Committee. Douglass infuriated the Citizens' Committee by answering their appeal for his support with a chastising letter disapproving of their efforts. According to Martinet, Douglass presumed that they wanted a donation and he refused to give one declaring that he "saw no good in the undertaking." "Of course, we were not after his money," Martinet explained, "we wanted his endorsement and moral support rather."[38] In light of Douglass's vociferous denunciation of the *Civil Rights Cases* in 1883, his lack of support for the *Plessy* case is puzzling. Curiously, echoing Robert Purvis, he privately admitted in 1892 that he "had begun to believe it true" that black victims of lynching in the South were signs of "increased lasciviousness" toward white women. Douglass told Ida B. Wells that it was only after reading her series of articles in the *New York Age* that he realized the true injustice of the situation. Yet, he remained strangely reluctant to act publicly during the reactionary crises of the 1890s and often required a great deal of cajoling from Wells to support her or collaborate with her even after his favorable comments about her work.[39]

Why Douglass never joined the NCRA also remains a mystery. Although very few letters between them have survived, Douglass and Tourgée were well acquainted. They may have discussed the NCRA at the Republican National Convention in 1892: "I should have called to see you yesterday," read a note Tourgée passed to Douglass on NCRA letterhead at the convention, "I am especially working here in behalf of the rights of the citizens of the United States in the various states. It seems to us that the time is ripe to declare that a man who is not free everywhere is free nowhere. I enclose our [literature] and hope that I may see you before I leave."[40] Did they meet? Did Douglass explain why he had not publicly supported the NCRA's efforts? Douglass's response is unknown, and it may have been deliberately kept so by Tourgée. Without the support of black leaders of the most significant stature, the prospects of failure for the NCRA were high indeed.

Tourgée was frustrated and confused over the situation. Just a few days after his note to Douglass in June 1892, he implored a black confidante,

Florence A Lewis of Philadelphia, to explain the lack of response of Northern black leaders. "The white people of the North respond by thousands and scores of thousands. The colored people of the South send me their piteous tear-stained appeals for aid. The colored people of the North remain indifferent, unresponsive—doing nothing," he complained. "Candidly, madame, I am afraid the colored man of the North feels very little the wrongs of the colored people of the South and does not realize the importance of the subject to him and his people." He even detected a certain animosity among them: "Most of them seem to wonder at the intensity of my conviction and I'm not sure that many of them do not feel a mild contempt for me on account of it. . . . The NCRA has for its roll ten white names for every one colored. What does it mean?"[41] Lewis could offer little by way of explanation, suggesting only that Tourgée clarify his position to them and publicize his views as widely as possible to counteract misinformation.[42]

With each passing year, Tourgée became more convinced that certain Northern black men, whom he referred to discreetly only as "the leaders" —a group that may have included Douglass, Purvis, and even Thomas T. Fortune—secretly worked against the NCRA. An editor for the *Allegheny Republican*, Thomas W. Griffin, reported to Tourgée early in 1894 that, after consulting with "men of means and influence . . . among them editors of the race papers," he had found widespread complaints that they had not been "consulted or invited to cooperate" with him before the NCRA was launched.[43] Yet, Griffin, a Tourgée enthusiast, remained convinced that once *The National Citizen* was established all black leaders would rally behind it. Still believing that "the leaders" presented an obstacle to the NCRA, however, Tourgée came up with an inventive strategy for neutralizing them. "I shall take the colored *men* from the South and the colored *women* from the North and so checkmate the 'leaders,'" he confided to Martinet. "I am going slow but they have got to get out of the way without any fuss."[44] Many prominent black women, like Ida B. Wells and Florence Lewis, felt as marginalized in Northern civil rights circles as he did. Sex presented yet another fissure that seemed to prevent the coming together of black activists behind a single strategy or organization.[45]

In truth, Tourgée had not made much of an effort to reach out to Northern black leadership before he launched his movement. It would have been especially wise to do so with respect to the leaders of the Afro-American League, who very likely regarded the NCRA as a hostile competitor and successor to Martinet's ACERA. Tourgée's associates in New Orleans had formed ACERA as a color-blind alternative to the league, and Martinet had conspicuously criticized the league after they were reluctant to change the name of the organization at the 1890 meeting in

Chicago. Tourgée himself bore some resentment against some delegates at the Afro-American League 1890 meeting who, as a symbolic act of declaring their independence from white guidance, had wanted to refuse his letter of advice and support. Newly elected League President Joseph C. Price helped defeat this motion and Tourgée's letter was read at the convention, but newspapers reported on the controversy his letter precipitated. Afterward, Tourgée congratulated Price and reaffirmed his support of the league, while pointedly suggesting that he control the "pitiable fools" who offered him "the almost unprecedented insult" of suggesting the return of his letter. "It will not pay to kick a faithful champion because he is white," he complained, "such conduct won't hearten people up to advocate your rights."[46]

If organizational rivalry and bad feelings were at the root of the conflict, they remained mostly out of the public sight. T. Thomas Fortune, the league's founder and successor to Price as its president, kept up a friendly correspondence with Tourgée throughout this time. After Fortune declared the Afro-American League dead in August of 1893, he became especially interested in working with him. In November of 1893, he made Tourgée an extraordinary offer. He declared that he could guarantee five thousand dollars of stock if Tourgée agreed to have the proposed *National Citizen* absorb the *New York Age*, and employ Fortune as its managing editor. He had been thinking of launching a "high class monthly" for some time: "We can never reach the better class of whites through a race newspaper," he told Tourgée. "New York is naturally the publication field of the newspaper . . . [the *Age*] enjoys the confidence of the colored people and the respect of the leading editors of the country. We have 5,000 subscribers [and] the addition of your prestige and influence would undoubtedly double these figures within a reasonable time."[47] It was an impressive offer that promised to heal past conflicts, real or perceived. "I have become dissatisfied with race journalism," Fortune confessed. Apparently ready to support the interracial, color-blind strategy, he urged Tourgée to consider his proposal, persisting, "We are so fully agreed on so many points."[48]

Without hesitation, Tourgée rejected his offer, though he invited Fortune to come to Thorheim to "talk the matter over." Surprisingly, he defended the importance of "race journals" to Fortune and insisted that the *Age* and the *National Citizen* each would be more effective as allies working in conjunction. "*The Age* has its own field; and a most necessary one," Tourgée told him. "As long as the colored man is distinguished against in any way, he must keep up his distinctive sentiment, organization, speciality [*sic*] of interest in sheer self-defense." Moreover, he promised that the *National Citizen* would "make liberal and frequent excerpts from race journals . . . so [as to] bring them into notice by people who do not now, and would not otherwise see them." Group advocacy and self-assertion by blacks, in his view, should continue independent of the effort to reach a white audience. The *National Citizen* "could not combine with *The Age* without spoiling both," he insisted.[49]

Tourgée offered his rationale as strategic and pragmatic rather than a matter of principle or personal preference. White readers not already inclined to support black rights would stay away if the journal appeared to be an organ established solely for the advancement of blacks. The *National Citizen* "cannot accomplish results . . . by antagonizing those to whom it must appeal," he said, "however deplorable, [race prejudice] is still a fact and like all prejudice must be overcome by patience and example as much as by argument." With Charles Chesnutt already enlisted as associate editor, he told Fortune, they will have done enough to "make plain [our] disapproval of race distinctions and thus gradually accustom people to disregard such prejudice." Thus, somewhat paradoxically, Tourgée seemed to conclude that only with a white man as general editor could his publication truly be viewed as "a journal of citizenship without regard to color."[50] He was probably correct, although it might have been wiser to exchange his vague hope of capturing the moderate white audience for uniting Northern black leadership behind the NCRA. But Tourgée might have rejected the offer simply because he regarded Fortune, whom he had long distrusted in private as an unprincipled self-seeker, as the wrong man to become spokesman of their movement. One wonders whether he would have responded the same had the offer come from a more trusted ally like Chesnutt, Martinet, Ferdinand Barnett, or Ida B. Wells.[51]

In retrospect, Fortune's offer turned out to be the best opportunity for the *National Citizen*. Plans for the journal would unravel nine months later, when Aimée Tourgée became seriously ill in August of 1894. Continuously plagued by fits of pain from an undiagnosed ailment, her condition became severe and required treatment by a New York specialist. "I am greatly troubled," Albion wrote a friend, "Mrs. Tourgée and I leave tonight for New York and the daughter's treatment. . . . [I] trust that her beautiful life is not destined to be forever clouded with pain and her promising career cut short."[52] But the treatment did little to ease their concern. Soon afterwards, Tourgée wrote to McGerald & Sons Publishing Company to back out of their plans for the *National Citizen*, citing Aimée's ill-health and family priorities. His wife and daughter, he added, were also too fearful of the strain and the economic risk involved in the venture. "I do not wholly share their feeling," he admitted, but without their support he would be forced to withdraw from the project.[53]

A year after the Citizens' Committee's decision not to press the hearing of the *Plessy* case, Tourgée had experienced nothing but setbacks. Not only had plans been abandoned for the *National Citizen*, even "A Bystander's Notes" had been unceremoniously dropped from the pages of the *Inter Ocean*. His promotion of the NCRA had "eroded the good nature" of Mr. Nixon who, caving to its readers' demand, restored the column after a six-month suspension only when Tourgée agreed not to make further mention of the organization in his column. The NCRA, Tourgée lamented, was left "without any regular medium of expression" and "the cause of equal rights without any recognized exponent in American journalism."[54] Public opinion had not been favorably mobilized, rather just the opposite.

The year 1895 brought even worse developments. Booker T. Washington's famous "Atlanta Compromise" speech in September captured national headlines and ushered in what has been called—with exaggeration—the era of African American accommodation. What made the speech so remarkable to observers was that Washington had proposed that blacks accept segregation and disenfranchisement in exchange for economic and educational progress. Purposefully conflating agitation against segregation with support for social equality and "amalgamation," he declared, "the wisest among my race understand that agitation of questions of social equality is the extremist folly."[55] After the death of Frederick Douglass in February 1895, many whites embraced Washington as the leader of a new generation of blacks who accepted their place in the social order and who compared favorably to the radicals of the abolitionist generation. This came only six months before the *Plessy* case was finally heard and handed the court just the reverse of what Tourgée had envisioned: evidence of public acceptance, even from black leadership, of separate-but-equal segregation.

The Washington speech did not come from out of the blue. The mantra of black self-help had been gaining ground among black leaders for years and was part of the support for the Afro-American League's self-directed black organization, although the league certainly never disavowed civil rights agitation. "The Booker Washingtons, the [Joseph C.] Prices and others have their uses and are doing a useful work," Louis Martinet allowed as early as 1892 about these two great educators. Noting the similarity in their self-help ideology, he regretted that they did not teach their pupils "the spirit of true manhood of manly courage and resistance to oppression."[56] However frustrating and gratuitously ingratiating of white supremacy their message of quiet self-improvement could be, the accommodationists had a point. Even Martinet and Tourgée at times questioned the wisdom of agitation for equality. "Are we helping the race or advancing the cause of justice by the method we are pursing?" Martinet wondered during the summer of 1893. "I have grave doubts myself," he sadly concluded, "whenever the colored people show any spirit 'white supremacy' is sure to assert itself, rise up and crush it."[57] Likewise, Tourgée's suggestion that the case be put off implicitly agreed with Washington's analysis that there might be more to be lost than gained by a direct challenge to Jim Crow.

Publicly, Tourgée remained outspokenly critical of the accommodationist rationale. Before a black audience in Boston in April of 1894, he told of a letter he recently received from "a leading colored minister" which urged him not to agitate on issues of political equality. "What our people want," the man had written to Tourgée, "is not their rights but work." The audience burst out in cheers when he quipped in response, "That's just what slavery gave—lots of work and no rights at all. Slavery ought to have suited him!" Rather than follow the advice of accommodationists, Tourgée advised his audience to imitate those leaders who refused to capitulate to the Jim Crow exclusion:

> When T. Thomas Fortune sued a New York saloon-keeper for refusing him a glass of beer [in 1890], he did a service to his race that cannot be measured in money. When the colored citizens of Louisiana raised the money by dime subscriptions to test the validity of the Separate Car Law, by carrying the case of *Plessy vs. Ferguson* to the Supreme Court, they attested their right to the free exercise of the privileges of citizenship as few white men have ever done.[58]

Fortune, who had been one of the most militant voices in the Afro-American League, had recently won a substantial settlement from a white bar owner in New York. Mere months after Tourgée praised him as a model of agitation, however, Fortune republished Washington's "Atlanta Compromise" speech in the *Age* with glowing commentary that asked whether the "Negro Moses" had been found. By 1896, the *Age* was receiving financial support from Tuskegee and had become a mouthpiece for Washington.[59]

In December of 1895, Tourgée was given the perfect opportunity to respond to the "Atlanta Compromise" speech when asked to deliver the public eulogy for Frederick Douglass at Faneuil Hall. Indirectly he did so when he called upon the black members of his audience to continue Douglass's work of unrelenting agitation. "Let the life of Frederick Douglass be an example to those who must take up the conflict where he was obliged to lay it down," Tourgée suggested. Alluding obliquely to Douglass's curious absence from the civil rights movement of the 1890s, he said "[Douglass] relied on the provisions of the XIVth Amendment.

They seemed to him sufficient; but as they were bent and twisted, in the process of legal construction[,] he gave up that hope. . . . He recognized his inability to cope with the new problem." Perplexed by the legal negation of the Reconstruction Amendments, according to Tourgée, Douglass's final wish was that a new generation of black activists would carry forward his lifetime struggle for full political and civil equality to its final victory: "Other hands must forge new weapons. Other hearts must bear the burden. Other souls must endure the scath [sic] of impending conflict . . . one Douglass born out of slavery is the forerunner of many to be born out of the semi-freedom which is all that Caste permits his race [today]."[60] Thus, he seized a posthumous endorsement from Douglass for his strategy of direct action against oppression. Though his rallying cry was applauded in the black press, the tide was turning against the abolitionist tradition.

Tourgée's strategic delay in the *Plessy* case had backfired. But, he did not revisit the idea of dropping the case. Martinet's *Crusader* of February 1895 ran an editorial explaining that they had "urg[ed] their counsel" that "the Jim Crow case—the Plessy case—will be had at the present term of the United States Supreme Court."[61] But the spring term passed without *Plessy* being called, as did the fall term. By spring 1896, Tourgée and his colleagues—believing that the upcoming presidential election might aid their cause should a Republican win—were once again hoping for a delay. But then, the case was called at last. As oral arguments in *Plessy* were delivered before the Supreme Court in April of 1896, a new era in race-relations began to take root.

THE ARGUMENT

The U.S Supreme Court hearing of *Plessy v. Ferguson* did not begin auspiciously for the plaintiffs. On April 3, Tourgée, in Mayville, received a cable from Samuel F. Phillips inquiring about how to proceed in the case without him since it had been called on the Court's docket the previous day and Tourgée had not been present in the courtroom. The fault was evidently with Phillips, who should have known that the policy of the Court was to notify local counsel only, with the expectation that he would notify his co-counsel. Believing that the hearing of the case had begun, Tourgée wrote a furious letter to the Supreme Court Clerk hoping that somehow the case could be carried over until he arrived. "There is a . . . mistake somewhere," he fumed. "I have been ready for the hearing for three months, waiting every day to know when it would probably be reached but have never heard a word from you. . . . On account of the importance of the case—*involving the personal right of half the population of a state*—three other counsel desire also to take part in the argument and only waited to hear from me in regard to it." He continued on in disbelief:

> I represent an association of about 10,000 colored men of Louisiana who raised the money to prosecute . . . and now by some inscrutable mishap they are deprived of the service they had secured, and I am put in the attitude of neglecting a case over which I have exerted the most scrupulous care and to which I have given years of labor and study. . . . Just how you could do this without notifying me I do not quite understand.[62]

Fortunately his alarm was premature. The case had been called, along with several others, on April 2, but the hearing had not yet been held. When informed of this by the clerk a few days later, Tourgée boarded a train for Washington on April 10 and arrived in time to take part in oral arguments. Walker and Martinet were notified too late to appear.[63]

On Monday morning, April 13, arguments took place in the old Senate chamber of the United States capitol building where the Court had met since 1860. Eight justices heard the case, with David Josiah Brewer, a Republican appointee, recusing himself for reasons unstated. Tourgée's arrival "occasioned some interest and comment," according to the *Washington Post*, whose reporter overheard at least one member of the gallery predict that it would be "another fool's errand" for him.[64] Only Samuel F. Phillips joined him to argue their case. Though a draft of Tourgée's oral argument survives, the Court unfortunately did not keep transcripts of their proceedings in the nineteenth century—a profound loss, as a transcript would have illuminated how the justices responded to Tourgée's individual points and how he defended his arguments before the court's interrogation.[65] The Court was in possession of two written briefs submitted on Plessy's behalf; one signed by Tourgée and Walker, the other signed by Phillips and his legal partner, F.D. McKenney. The Tourgée-Walker brief was divided into two sections, Tourgée's, thirty-one pages, offering the most comprehensive and direct arguments against the Separate Car Act, and Walker's, sixteen pages, providing supplementary evidence. Phillips and McKenney's twenty-three-page brief developed several original points and strengthened Tourgée's arguments against anticipated objections by the Court. None of the participants in the oral arguments left behind a description of what occurred in the Supreme Court on April 13.

Tourgée's brief requires the utmost care in explication; its moments of rhetorical brilliance and incisive logic are seemingly marred by internal contradiction. As a lawyer trying to win a case, he used every favorable

In this photograph taken less than two weeks after the *Plessy*
decision was announced, Albion's physical ailments are evident
as he relaxes outdoors with Emma (left), General W.W. Blackmar,
and his wife, May 31, 1896. Courtesy of The Beinecke Rare Book
and Manuscript Library, Yale University.

argument at his disposal and adopted multifaceted legal strategy on the
theory that, as Tourgée put it to his co-counsel Walker, "it is better to
have too many points . . . than not enough."[66] His multi-pronged attack
reflected a keen awareness that the majority of the justices he sought
to persuade would be overwhelmingly hostile to his cause. On the one
hand, the brief contains a straightforward case that the act's only purpose
was to insult and discriminate against any citizen the state chooses to
deem "black" and thus deprive that citizen of his or her constitutional
rights protected by the Thirteenth and Fourteeenth Amendments. On
the other hand, it presents several alternative arguments through which
Tourgée attempted to manipulate the presumed conservative bias of the
Supreme Court. These latter arguments have often been misunderstood
by scholars who have read their meaning too literally. Those who have
recognized their strategic, and even ironic, content have been closer to
the mark.[67]

The most straightforward line of Tourgée's argument followed Radical
Republican constitutional principles. He asserted that the Reconstruction

Amendments had redefined the nature of United States citizenship. More than part of a program for protecting African American rights and restoring order in the South, the amendments had achieved a revolution in civic life by ousting the states "of *all control over citizenship.*" In his words, "the Fourteenth Amendment *creates* a *new* citizenship ... embracing new rights, privileges and immunities, derivable in a *new* manner, controlled by a *new* authority, having a *new* scope and extent, dependent on national authority for its existence and looking to national power for its preservation."[68] This statement, revisiting the themes of Ingersoll's 1883 speech, emphasized the radical results of the Civil War.

According to Tourgée, the Reconstruction Amendments also marked the constitutional inscription of the egalitarian principles of the Declaration of Independence. Taking a progressive view of history, he told the Supreme Court that a ruling against this broad construction of the amendments would be an anachronistic attempt to undo the results of the Civil War. Echoing Lincoln's "Gettysburg Address," which proposed that the Union fought so that the nation may rededicate itself to the principle that all men were created equal, he insisted that the Declaration of Independence expressed "the controlling idea of our [Governmental] institutions." The war had destroyed slavery and the theory of "state sovereignty," and the Court could not bring them back. The Fourteenth Amendment, he explained, was conceived:

> in strict accord with the Declaration of Independence, which is not a fable as some of our modern theorists would have us believe, but the all-embracing formula of personal rights on which our government is based and toward which it is tending with a power that neither legislation nor judicial construction can prevent.[69]

Like the Fugitive Slave Act and the *Dred Scott* decision, he suggested, an attempt to suppress these principles would be a dangerous and futile reaction against the march of human progress and democratic freedom.[70]

Proof of the law's discriminatory intent could be found in the provision of the Separate Car Act that provided for the "exemption" of nurses "attending to children of the other race" from being separated from their attendees on the railroad cars. This exemption belied the fact that there was no real concern over health or public safety, as the law purported, but was rather "for the gratification and recognition of the sentiment of white superiority and white supremacy."[71] In upholding the Separate Car Act, the Louisiana Supreme Court had ruled that racial segregation was a "reasonable use" of state police powers to secure the health and "moral welfare" of society. But, since only black nurses attended to children of the other race by local custom, and never the reverse, the clause in the law exempting nurses revealed the true purpose of the law. Tourgée asked, "if color breeds contagion in a railway coach," then why was the risk to public health and comfort not applicable to nurses? The answer was as plain as the law's intent: "The exemption of nurses shows that the real evil lies not in the color of the skin but in the relation the colored person sustains to the white. If he is a dependent it may be endured; if he is not, his presence is insufferable." The state intended to reduce those designated as "black" to the "condition of a subject race" and thus violated the spirit of the Reconstruction Amendments. "It is an act of discrimination pure and simple," he concluded, "it is not a matter of health or morals, but simply a matter intended to re-introduce the caste-ideal on which slavery rested." In driving home this argument, he concluded, "Justice is pictured blind and her daughter the Law, ought to at least be color-blind."[72]

In its spirit, Tourgée argued, the Separate Car Act violated the Thirteenth Amendment's prohibition of slavery and involuntary servitude. He reminded the Court that the legal definition of the term *slave*, under both U.S. and Louisiana antebellum law, was merely "a person without rights." Thus, the condition of being a slave was *not* the condition of being owned—in fact its *legal* definition made no reference to either property or ownership. The condition of slavery meant complete subjection to the "civil and political society" to which the slave belonged. Nothing more or less than a racial caste system, slavery held "the African in bondage to the whole white race as well as to his owner." By abolishing slavery, the Thirteenth Amendment, he concluded, prohibited more than the "incident of [individual] ownership"; it meant the permanent destruction of any such caste system.[73]

Cogent as these arguments may appear, they faced grave difficulties before the Court. Most of the precedents in regard to the scope of the Reconstruction Amendments, beginning with the *Slaughter-House Cases*, contradicted Tourgée's claims about its revolutionary effect on the nature of national citizenship. Rather than attempt to circumvent *Slaughter-House* and the precedents flowing out of it, Tourgée confronted them in a surprisingly blunt and condemnatory manner. Perhaps overreaching, he asked the court to undo all of the constitutional mischief *Slaughter-House* had initiated. More than anything else, Tourgée's excoriation of the *Slaughter-House* reasoning demonstrated his awareness that a straightforward attack faced serious obstacles.

In the *Slaughter-House Cases*, Justice Samuel Miller's majority opinion had established the controlling view that the Fourteenth Amendment's "one pervading purpose" had been to protect the rights of blacks from hostile legislation and *not* to broaden the traditional scope of U.S. citizenship because it found no words expressly stating this latter intention within the amendment itself.[74] Tourgée demolished this interpretation of the "original intention" of the Fourteenth Amendment in *Slaughter-House* by adopting a formalist critique of it. The "plain meaning" of the amendment, he argued, was clear from its language, which made no mention of race or color despite the Court's contention that its "one pervading purpose" was to protect the rights of blacks. The Court's reasoning was contradictory: whereas the *Slaughter-House* decision refused to infer that an expansion of federal power was implied in the Fourteenth Amendment because it was not expressly stated, it nonetheless inferred that the amendment's intended scope was restricted to the protection of blacks although no such motive was expressly stated or even implied in its wording. Tourgée wrote pointedly, "No man can deny that the language employed is of the broadest and most universal character. 'Every person,' 'any law,' 'any person' are the terms employed . . . the language used is not particular but universal." Tourgée made no effort to hide his outrage as he chastised the Court: "'All' can never be made to mean 'some,' nor 'every person' be properly construed to be only one class or race, until the laws of English speech are overthrown."[75]

While *Slaughter-House* restricted the scope of the Fourteenth Amendment, the *Cruikshank* decision all but nullified its application to most cases involving the violation of civil rights. *Cruikshank*, Tourgée told the Court, "proceeds upon the same, as we conceive, mistaken view, both of the character and effect of the XIVth Amendment." Elaborating on the restricted definition of national citizenship suggested by *Slaughter-House*, the Court had proceeded in *Cruikshank* to rule that the protection of all the "privileges and immunities" of state citizens from infringement by other citizens "rests alone with the State." As a result, it declared unconstitutional certain provisions of the Enforcement Act of 1870 because they overstepped the scope of federal power—of course, these provisions had been drafted by the Reconstruction Congress on the assumption that the Fourteenth Amendment had expanded federal protection of citizenship rights. Pointing to one precedent in his favor, *Strauder v. West Virginia* (1880), in which the Court stated that the Fourteenth Amendment "prohibited legislation prejudicial to any class of citizenship whether colored or not," Tourgée gambled by asking the Court to follow their own logic and overturn *Cruikshank* directly. "It is freely admitted that Cruikshank's case is squarely against us," he declared, but the *Cruikshank* doctrine simply "cannot stand" because it had been based on a "false hypothesis."[76]

Tourgée expressed utter contempt for the *Slaughter-House* and *Cruikshank* rulings that he considered a resurrection of the "States rights doctrine." Indeed, they meant that the Fourteenth Amendment had virtually no impact on the legal status quo. "If this construction be the correct one," he said of *Cruikshank*, then "the [14th] amendment is the absurdest piece of legislation ever written in a statute book." With repeated references to the issues of Southern secession and the "long and bloody war" against state sovereignty, he wondered what other purpose the Fourteenth Amendment could have meant to serve, if not to establish federal protection over the rights of its citizens. Tourgée's harsh language echoed that of Justice Field in his *Slaughter-House* dissent, in which he remarked that if the rights protected by the Fourteenth Amendment were truly intended to be restricted to a few esoteric areas of "national citizenship," then "it was a vain and idle enactment, which accomplished nothing and most unnecessarily excited Congress and the people on its passage."[77] If he succeeded in resurrecting Field's indignation of twenty-three years earlier, perhaps the senior justice would seize the opportunity to correct the past error.

Having laid out his Radical Republican constitutionalism in the most forthright manner possible, Tourgée developed a number of alternative arguments for the Court to consider. Even if the Court stood by its precedents and rejected his view of the revolutionary nature of the Reconstruction Amendments, the question still remained of whether racial segregation violated the Fourteenth Amendment's equal protection clause. None would claim that the amendment did not apply to state legislation. But how could he prevent the Court from using the logic of the *Roberts* case to rule that racial segregation was not a hostile and unreasonable distinction? The burden of Tourgée's position in the 1890s was to explain why race should *not* be a reasonable category for legislative discrimination, especially when accommodations were required to be kept equal.

By introducing a plaintiff of indeterminate race, Tourgée brought attention to the arbitrariness of racial classifications. In Homer Plessy, he asserted, "we have the case of a [seven-eighths white] man who believed he had a right to the privilege and advantage of being esteemed a white man." A man of Plessy's complexion, he pointed out, may not even know *himself* to which race he belongs and may believe that he belongs in the white car. "Who are white and who are colored? By what rule then shall any tribunal be guided in determining racial character?" There was no adequate instruction as to make the "officer of the railroad competent to decide the question of race." Tourgée asked the court, "Is [the law] not bound to set out the facts that constitute [his race to be] the wrong one?" Since the Separate Car Act did not and could not prove that Plessy was black, Tourgée reasoned: "The statement 'in a car to which he did not by race belong' is a conclusion, not a fact."[78]

Historians who have suggested that Tourgée's manipulation of Plessy's light-skinned complexion amounted to a defense of the privileged status of the "Creole elite" against the "penalties of color" have missed his point entirely.[79] He used the whiteness of Homer Plessy to probe the very logic of racial categories themselves. By way of argument, he attempted to place the burden of defining race on the Louisiana legislature by asking, *how does the law define race?* Pointing out that many individuals who were white in appearance were often considered black by social reputation, especially in Louisiana, he suggested that the law must provide a strict definition. On what criteria were the railroad conductors to decide to which race a person belonged when appearance was clearly not enough? "Race-intermixture has proceeded to such an extent," he observed, that it is often "impossible of ascertainment" even after "the most careful and deliberate weighing of evidence." "By what law? With what Justice?" then, could it be accomplished by "the casual scrutiny of a busy conductor"?[80]

Further emphasizing the social construction of racial definitions, James C. Walker's brief surveyed the various and contradictory definitions of race that existed from state to state throughout the nation. While most states lacked any definition of race at all, Michigan defined a "Negro" as a person of no less than one-fourth African ancestry, while in Georgia the proportion was one-eighth, and North Carolina it was one-sixteenth.[81] Thus Tourgée challenged lawmakers to prove that categories of race were more than the arbitrary rites of social customs, or to put it in contemporary terms, *social constructions.* "Race," Tourgée told the Supreme Court in his oral argument, "is a question which the law of Louisiana has not decided and which science is totally unable to solve." He pointed out that the state of Louisiana had followed no known definition of race:

> They are called "races" it is true, but the only racial distinctions recognized by the act are "white" and "colored." The statute does not use the ordinary scientific terms Caucasian, Mongolian, Indian, Negro, &c. . . . they reduce the whole human family into two grand divisions which [are given] the term "races," the white "race," and the "colored" race.

Once again, this suggested that the definitions were based entirely on prejudice, rather than hard science. He bitterly remarked: "It is a new ethnology but prejudice based on the lessons of slavery does not stop at trifles."[82]

Tourgée gambled a large portion of his argument on the perils of arbitrarily determining the race of passengers like Homer Plessy. In one sense, this was a dangerous argument that may have been doomed to backfire. This was especially true when Tourgée asked, "Where on earth should [Plessy] have gone? Will the court hold that a single drop of African blood is sufficient to color a whole ocean of Caucasian whiteness?"[83] Many advocates of segregation would have subscribed to the infamous "one-drop" rule—that any trace or reputation of color classified one as "colored"—and his attempt to question this logic might have served to aggravate believers in this doctrine. Recognizing this possibility, he made his argument double-edged. On one side, he attacked the racial categories in an egalitarian manner, claiming that the state had no right or competence "to label one citizen white and another colored."[84] However, he also thrust his argument in the opposite direction by simultaneously appealing to the threat to the privileges of whiteness posed by the law, and by pointing to the potential ill effects that public assessments of race might have for whites.

According to the Separate Car Act, neither the railroad conductor nor the railway company could be liable for damage if a passenger was expelled from the train for refusing to comply with the conductor's car assignment. Therefore, Tourgée argued, a white man assigned to the wrong car was conceivably "deprived of property" without the "due process of law" as guaranteed by the Fourteenth Amendment. In a passage that dripped with irony, Tourgée reminded the Court that whiteness was a valuable piece of property. "The most precious of all inheritances," he told the Court, "is the reputation of being white." It amounted to a badge of good character opening the doors to every social advancement and opportunity. On the other hand, he said, "The blight of color is the greatest misfortune that can befall a man or woman" in American society, and "probably most white persons if given a choice would prefer death to life in the United States *as colored persons.*"[85] Faulty assessment of passengers could have drastic social consequences: If a white person were to be mistakenly assigned into a colored car, Tourgée argued, that person should be able to sue for damages for having his reputation besmirched and having been deprived of the benefits of his whiteness. Building on a racist legal tradition that had implicitly treated whiteness as property, he made this claim explicit: "Belonging to the dominant . . . white race, is *property* in the same sense that a right of action or of inheritance is *property.*"[86] Thus, he challenged the court to strike down the Separate Car Act in order to protect both *property* and *whiteness.*

In another appeal to broad sentiment, Tourgée asserted that the Louisiana Law interfered with the sanctity of the family, invading the "natural domestic rights of the most sacred character." This claim invoked a tradition that harkened back to such mainstream antislavery novels as *Uncle Tom's Cabin* that highlighted slavery's violation of family bonds. On this issue, he presented two scenarios: "A man may be white and his wife colored" or a "wife may be white and her children colored."

The state, he insisted, should not have the right to separate a man from his wife or a mother from her daughter simply because the child was "of a darker tinge."[87] He pointed out that the law literally *required* the separation of families and deprived wives and children of their natural protectors in public conveyances.

In his brief to the court, Phillips also relied upon the sanctity of the family to make another unusual point. Phillips anticipated that the Court would uphold the Separate Car Act out of fear for the implications of its ruling on segregated schools—the most thoroughly defended segregated institution in the South. To allay its fears, he argued that an exception could be made for separate schools. In its effort to respect "the old plan of allowing parents to educate children as they choose," he argued, the government has greater power to discriminate and to conform to the "prevailing sentiment of the community upon this interesting and delicate subject [segregation] . . . and may therefore in many things well conform to the will of the natural parents." The government acts in a special role as educator: "in educating the young the government steps 'in loco parentis,'" that is, it acts in the role of parent. In the name of parental and family rights, Phillips concluded that "*separate cars* and *separate* schools, therefore, come under different orders of consideration. A conclusion as to one of these does not control determinations as to the other."[88]

In the context of the 1890s, the discussion of both property rights in whiteness and the sanctity of the family may be viewed as either very radical or very reactionary. It is doubtful that Tourgée was sincere in his assertion that whiteness should be considered property, but rather more likely that he intended to force the Court to consider the social meaning of whiteness, and also to suggest the unforeseen and embarrassing consequences that public assessments of race might have for whites. Moreover, in an era of near-hysteria over the dangers of miscegenation or racial amalgamation, Tourgée's brief is filled with casual references to mulattos and mixed-race families. One critic plausibly suggested that for Tourgée "the mulatto symbolizes America's legal and political commitment to color blindness" by personifying an integrated America.[89] The fear of racial amalgamation lurked behind the desire to segregate the races. Yet, the races had mixed for centuries; Homer Plessy himself was living testimony to this fact. On an almost subconscious level, Tourgée's brief repeatedly hammered home the reality that racial intermixture and intermarriage—the bugaboo of integration—was an accomplished fact that was benign, commonplace, and could not be stopped by segregation laws.

Finally, like the "tragic" mulatto of popular fiction, the light-skinned complexion of Homer Plessy—to all appearances a white man—eased the imaginative ability of the fair-skinned justices of the Supreme Court to put themselves in his place. The figure of the so-called tragic mulatto had been a staple of antislavery literature—including Tourgée's own novels—in part because it offered an instance in which race prejudice existed despite the fact that all the qualities that marked racial difference were absent.[90] Thus racism appeared in its most arbitrary light. In the end, the strongest argument against segregation, Tourgée believed, was rooted in radical individualism. His final appeal was not to conservative fears, legal technicalities, or even to the Constitution, but to the eternal moral principle of the Golden Rule—the higher law. Would the judges do unto others as they would have done to them?

As he concluded his argument to the Court, Tourgée asked the justices to consider the following hypothetical scenario: "Suppose a member of this court, nay suppose every member of it," he wrote, "should wake tomorrow with a black skin and curly hair—two controlling indications of race—and in traveling through that portion of the country where the 'Jim Crow Car' abounds, would be ordered into it by the conductor." He asked the justices to seriously consider how would they feel about this treatment, knowing that their outward appearance was not an accurate indication of the quality of their personhood. "It is easy to imagine what would be the result," Tourgée mused, "the indignation, the protests, the assertion of pure Caucasian ancestry. . . . What humiliation; what rage would then fill the judicial mind! How would the resources of language not be taxed in objurgation!" "Why would this sentiment prevail in your minds?" he asked rhetorically, "simply because you would then feel and know that such assortment of the citizens on the line of race was a discrimination intended to humiliate and degrade . . . an attempt to perpetuate the caste distinctions on which slavery rested."[91] This exercise depended on the justices accepting the following two premises: that race was a superficial physical attribute that told nothing of one's individual worth, and that black people were entitled to the same feelings of indignation when forced into segregated railroad cars as Supreme Court justices. Would a majority of the Court accept these premises? Would they treat others as they would themselves expect to be treated?

THE AFTERMATH

Tourgée returned from Washington in extremely low spirits. He never discussed, in any surviving documents, how the members of the Court responded to his oral presentation, but it seems they were distinctly unreceptive. Emma's terse and irregular diary entries in the days after the oral presentation, as they awaited the Court's decision, recorded the gloom at Thorheim. "Troubled about not hearing from Albion," she wrote ominously on Tuesday, April 14. Then:

> April 15. Albion came.
> April 16. Albion pretty tired from his trip.
> April 21. Most distressing, disheartening day. Went to club to get away from the depressing atmosphere . . . so heavy-hearted. Will no relief ever come?
> April 22. Nothing comes to lighten the gloom.
> May 4. Most blue and distressing day. Nothing seems to give any hope.
> May 7. Things look so disheartening!

When Albion returned to Washington on May 12 to give a lecture at the Colored Israel Methodist Church, and possibly await the announcement of the *Plessy* decision, Emma's only recorded comments upon his return was that he had not received "his pay" from the lecture. Her journal did not record their response to the Supreme Court's decision in *Plessy*.[92]

The Supreme Court's 7–1 ruling against *Plessy* came down on May 18, 1896. Many white Northern newspapers expressed surprise and outrage at it, though none gave it extensive coverage. The *Rochester Democrat and Chronicle* called it "A Strange Decision" and applauded Harlan's dissent. "Justice Harlan's vigorous dissent denouncing these laws as mischievous," it wrote, "comes very much nearer the sentiment of the American people upon that question than the decision of the majority does." The *New York Tribune* also called the decision "unfortunate to say the least," but it seemed prepared to accept the sad fact that the constitutionality of segregation had been settled at last. The *Springfield* [MA] *Republican* predicted that segregation laws would now "spread like measles" throughout the South and wondered, "did Southerners ever pause to indict the Almighty for allowing negroes to be born on the same earth as white men?"[93] The acquiescence and resignation of the Northern public at the legal triumph of segregation was clearly evident in the press, but it does not follow that the majority of Northerners necessarily endorsed the Court's *Plessy* decision—as is often presumed. Many lamented the constitutional sanction of the separate-but-equal doctrine that they felt stood in stark contrast to America's professed democratic principles.

If Tourgée had expected a point-by-point response to his legal assault, he must have been disappointed. Justice Henry Billings Brown's majority opinion, though complimenting the "learned counsel for the plaintiff," side-stepped most of Tourgée's arguments. The Massachusetts-born Brown followed Justice Lemuel Shaw's logic in *Roberts* by declaring that the statute implied "merely a legal distinction between the white and colored races" and not "the inferiority of either race." Implications of inferiority did not arise from "anything found in the act," Brown wrote, but rather arose only in the minds of "the colored race [who] chooses to put that construction upon it." Furthermore, Brown called Tourgée's bluff on the issue of property rights in whiteness by explicitly urging him to attempt such a suit in court. Declaring unconstitutional that part of the Separate Car Act that protected the railroad conductor from being liable for damages, Brown wrote: "If he [Plessy] be a white man and assigned to a colored coach, he may have his action for damages against the company for being deprived of his so called property." Brown suggested that the definition of race may be easily decided "under the laws of each State" or according to their traditions and customs. As to either the scientific or constitutional validity of such "traditions and customs" that were derived from antebellum slave codes, he made no comment.[94]

Though Brown did not revisit *Slaughter-House*'s definition of national versus state citizenship, he agreed that the Fourteenth Amendment carried certain "affirmative rights" of national citizenship. Nevertheless, the Court held that racial segregation was a "reasonable use" of state police powers so long as those accommodations provided remained substantially equal. Also, he dismissed any discussion of the Thirteenth Amendment, whose irrelevance he felt was "too clear for argument." Brown's opinion has been sharply criticized by some scholars, while others have defended it as a solid constitutional rationale that followed the precedents of the time.[95] It is interesting to note that, while Brown could have simply affirmed the decision with little comment, he chose to go on in an irritated fashion about the immutable nature of racial distinctions. Explaining that the legislation was "powerless to eradicate racial instincts or to abolish distinctions based solely upon physical distinctions," Brown claimed that Tourgée's argument "assumes that social prejudices may be overcome by legislation and that equal rights cannot be secured to the negro except by an enforced commingling of the races." In response to this "fallacy," he explained in a curious *non sequitur* that the Constitution cannot make the races equal or force citizens to treat each other equally (of course the law in question attempted nothing of the kind). Finally, his response to the "enforced commingling of the two races" that he implied had been proposed by Plessy's attorneys included what might have been a reference to Booker T. Washington's "Atlanta Compromise" address, in which he claimed that these terms were "unsatisfactory to either" race. The broad and memorable rhetoric of both the majority's opinion and Harlan's lone dissent were a reflection of the provocative character of Tourgée's vigorous attack on the law.

Harlan's dissent is in many ways a far less radical and less egalitarian document than Tourgée's brief. In his dissenting opinion, Harlan, of course, affirmed Tourgée's assertion of the color-blind ideal, stating that both the Thirteenth and Fourteenth Amendments prohibited "any public authority to know the race of those" whom it protects. He also unambiguously affirmed that the Fourteenth Amendment had revolutionized U.S. citizenship, and he berated the majority for relying on antebellum case law that dated from a time when the country had been "dominated by the institution of slavery." Most compellingly—in contrast to Justice Brown, who kept a conspicuous silence on the issue of the law's intent—Harlan frankly remarked that despite "the thin disguise" of equal accommodations "everyone knows that the statute in question had its origins in the purpose" of maintaining white supremacy. To support this contention, he followed Tourgée's suggestion by citing the clause allowing for the exemption of nurses.[96]

Yet, Harlan was not prepared to engage those arguments on behalf of Plessy that called into question the scientific basis of racial classifications themselves. In fact, he made absolutely clear that he regarded the white race as superior "in prestige, in achievements, in education, in wealth, and in power" and that he believed it would "continue to be [so] for all time." Harlan also felt it necessary to insist that social equality would not result merely from integrated public facilities. "Social equality," he wrote, "no more exists between two races when members of the same races sit by each other in a street car" than when they come into contact in any other ordinary function of civic life. He scoffed, in fact, at the idea that "the integrity of the white race may be corrupted, or that its supremacy be imperilled, by contact on public highways with black people." Thus while Justice Brown needlessly endorsed the notion of "racial instincts" to separate, Harlan gratuitously reassured whites that "amalgamation" would not result, nor white supremacy become "imperilled," by contact with blacks on public conveyances.[97]

Though Harlan has been justly remembered for his brave and powerful dissent, Tourgée's name has less often been associated with the *Plessy* case. This was not due to the lack of acknowledgment by his New Orleans clients afterward. When the case was finished, the Citizens' Committee spent sixty dollars of their remaining funds for a testimonial to "Judge Tourgée" while donating the balance, $160, to charity. In their final statement about the case to the public, the committee wrote, "We . . . still believe that we were right and our cause is sacred, when we are encouraged by the indomitable will and noble defence of the Hon. Albion W. Tourgée, and supported by the courageous dissenting opinion of Justice John Harlan." They told their followers, "the people should never forget these men, particularly Tourgée."[98]

The adverse decision by the Supreme Court decimated the New Orleans Citizens' Committee. Not only did they dissolve the committee—

abandoning its protest activities, which had expanded into areas such as church segregation, miscegenation laws, and jury box exclusion—but they discontinued the *Crusader*. The only black daily newspaper in the United States in 1896, the *Crusader* ended publication less than a year after *Plessy*. Rodolphe Desdunes explained the state of mind that led to the decision: "Seeing that the friends of justice were either dead or indifferent, [the editors] believed that the continuation of the *Crusader* would not only be fruitless but decidedly dangerous." Desdunes bitterly remarked that they determined "it was better to suffer in silence than to attract attention to [their] misfortune and weakness."[99] In the absence of the Citizens' Committee, segregation spread rapidly throughout New Orleans into nearly all areas of public life over the next decade, and a new generation of Creole leaders embracing Booker T. Washington's accommodationist philosophy replaced the men who led the Citizens' Committee. Indeed, the Creoles as a class would gain a reputation as the years passed as especially accommodating to segregation, while the militant stance of the Citizens' Committee would be largely forgotten, or sometimes even distorted, in historical memory.[100]

The *Plessy* decision marked the end of civil rights activism for both Tourgée and Martinet. Signs of disillusionment were increasingly evident in their letters as their movement continued to encounter obstacles and their hopes grew increasingly bleak. "'What have I to gain in fighting this battle?' Like you, I have asked myself this question a thousand times," Martinet wrote to Tourgée in 1892. "One is surrounded by so much petty jealousy & envy that it's quite disgusting." He insisted, "I want no political influence, no prestige, no office. Like you, I believe I do it because I am built that way."[101] Stung by the lack of support for their efforts, both men, at different times, expressed a desire to turn their talents and their energies toward more profitable pursuits. After terminating the *Crusader*, Martinet presumably did just that. After 1897, Martinet retreated into a quiet life as a physician in New Orleans, where he remained until his death in 1917.[102]

Tourgée too seemed to be losing faith in the strategy of agitation. In the thirteen months leading up to the *Plessy* hearing, he kept himself occupied by publishing a modest journal out of Buffalo with McGerald & Sons. *The Basis: A Journal of National Citizenship*, which began on March 20, 1895, was drastically less ambitious then what had been planned with *National Citizen*; it was, in essence, a family venture that struck a kind of compromise between attending to his family's needs and Tourgée's desire to carry on his civil rights work. Operating on a tiny budget, Albion and Aimée wrote nearly all of the thirty-two-page journal, which carried as regular columns Albion's "A Bystander's Notes" and

Aimée's "In A Lighter Vein." Remuneration was too slight to attract submissions by prominent names, but among the interesting contributions were works of fiction, poetry, and prose by unknown black authors. Although subscription forms for the NCRA (now renamed the National Citizens' League) were included in each issue, the pretense of serving as the organization's mouthpiece seemed hardly worth keeping up. Circulation never exceeded more than 1,200 subscribers, and despite Tourgée's best efforts to spread its reputation through word-of-mouth among African Americans, it barely lasted one year. *The Basis* was unceremoniously discontinued in April 1896, the same month that the *Plessy* case was argued.[103]

Tourgée's retirement from civil rights agitation and his self-censorship on race issues after *Plessy* suggest that he regarded the case as a terrible mistake. He had warned his clients of the severe consequences of an adverse decision, and afterward, he was haunted by the belief that it would cost a great deal of blood to overcome the precedent. One of the few comments he made regarding the decision came in a letter to the New Orleans *Leader* in 1899, in which he expressed his gratitude to the citizens of New Orleans for their testimonial. But his words of consolation must have provided very cold comfort. "Thank God, the supreme court of the United States is not omnipotent," he wrote:

> God has found a way to overrule the unholy decisions of this court against liberty and in favor of oppression. It required the blood of a million of men to blot out and reverse the specious infamy of the Dred Scott decision. What will it require to obliterate this last judicial crime by which it is sought to bind the colored citizen and cast him down again, helpless and irremediable under the oppression of a "white man's government?"[104]

The Fate of Color-Blind Citizenship

> Real individualism then is the obligation to act as a citizen.
> This has nothing to do with conformism or obedience to inter-
> ests outside the public good . . . [it] is not a particularly pleas-
> ant or easy style of life. It is not profitable, efficient, competitive
> or rewarded. It often consists of being persistently annoying to
> others as well as being stubborn and repetitive . . . criticism is
> perhaps the citizen's primary weapon in the exercise of her
> legitimacy.
>
> —John Ralston Saul, *The Unconscious Civilization*, 1995

LBION TOURGÉE'S DEVOTION to the cause of racial equality was
extraordinary. It was impressive not merely because of his unwavering faith in the principle itself but because of his willingness to
sacrifice so much to advance it. He did so as a matter of conscience.
Radical individualism, as I have termed it, was a demanding ethic that led
men and women of conscience to speak, write, and agitate for social justice often before the most hostile audiences or under the most adverse
and unrewarding circumstances. Critics and opponents of such radicals
always have been quick to look for psychological explanations for their
behavior. While undoubtedly psychological motives exist for all human
actions, I find little reason to look beyond those that Tourgée himself
repeatedly gave to explain his actions. His crusade for color-blind justice
did not arise from a mental disorder, such as the monomaniacal fixation
on African Americans that Joel Chandler Harris once accused him of possessing. His belief that racism was a dangerous and unjustified evil, born
of his firsthand experience as a witness to its grossest effects, was itself
enough to drive him to act.

"It has fallen to my lot to speak the truth very plainly to those whom
others flattered," Tourgée once explained:

Personally, it has probably been to my detriment; but I trust it has done some good. I may never derive advantage from it—I do not know that any man has a right to expect that duty will bring him advantage—but I think I have helped the cause of liberty and civilization which is the cause of God.[1]

Though, in its context, this passage might have been a rationalization for other motives, it summed up Tourgée's larger ethic quite well. Whatever underlying psychological motives drove him, he acted in accordance with a well-established political tradition. To do other than to speak the truth, as his conscience revealed it, would have been an act of moral cowardice and a betrayal of the higher law of God. His mode of political engagement, however, was of an earlier era, and he found that it was largely out of step with the 1890s.

As a point of comparison, Booker T. Washington's mode of political engagement was much more in tune with his times. Washington fought back against white patronage networks by forging one of his own. The so-called Tuskegee Machine, operated by Washington, who controlled an enormous amount of money as principal of the acclaimed Tuskegee Institute, disbursed financial support and jobs to those whom it favored. Seeking salvation through interest-group politics, Washington tried to enforce solidarity in the black community behind his leadership to better exert influence on the political and economic system. Like any patronage boss, he demanded loyalty and obedience to all within his sphere of influence. Outwardly, Washington presented a deferential, almost obsequious public image to whites, going so far as to tell racist "darky" jokes and to join in the ridicule of the "absurd" policies of Reconstruction that had given political power to ignorant field hands.[2] He did this, presumably, to achieve peace between the races in the South and to ingratiate himself to wealthy Northern philanthropists whom he believed were put at ease by this kind of talk. Privately, Washington used his power to advance black interests in business and politics, lobbying for appointments whenever possible and even funding legal challenges to disenfranchisement and segregation in secret. Though he probably imagined the eventual downfall of the white supremacist power structure from the damage inflicted by his unseen structural sabotage, Washington eventually lost influence by attempting to silence all of those African American leaders who resisted him.

Moreover, Washington subscribed to the liberal view of individuals as motivated by rational self-interest and calculated advantage. Believing that salvation awaited in the practice of a Horatio Algerian philosophy of economic uplift by one's own bootstraps, as it were, Washington was almost obsessed with material success. Never an enthusiast for civil rights organizations, he founded the National Negro Business League, believing that the acquisition of black wealth, above all, would bring about the end of racism. But Washington's own example was contradictory. He ridiculed the idea of higher education for blacks implemented during Reconstruction as impractical toward their material success, but his own power had been achieved as much through his mastery of oratory and his keen manipulation of dominant ideologies as by mere thrift and plodding hard labor. In his autobiography, in fact, he recalled that the art of debate and public speaking had been his favorite courses as a young student at the Hampton Institute—hardly the quintessential vocational training he showcased at Tuskegee. Despite his contradictions, Washington was ideologically committed to the interest-group politics and the underlying liberal individualism that dominated his times.[3]

Tourgée had resisted this kind of politics throughout his whole career. Time and again, he had attacked Republicans for dishonesty and cronyism, and he had nearly always practiced public speech that argued positions forthrightly with intent to persuade, not deceive. But, in the wake of his defeat in Plessy, even Tourgée seemed prepared to concede that his style of politics were no longer suited to the task before him. Bewildered and disheartened, he succumbed to the organizational ethic that had domi-nated the Republican Party—and the two-party system generally—for the past two decades. With his appeals to the public conscience having failed, there was nothing more to do but quit the field to allow Booker T. Washington to try to achieve by dissembling and subterfuge what had failed to be accomplished by direct and open democratic combat.

DISILLUSION AND DESPAIR

In the final phase of his career, Tourgée appeared a beaten man. After Plessy, he discontinued The Basis and turned his energy to campaigning for Republican presidential candidate William McKinley. In the summer of 1896 he composed a one-hundred-page pamphlet on the silver issue, War of the Standards, which received endorsement by the Republican National Committee. Uncharacteristically, he deferred to party leadership by expunging some objectionable language to conform to the RNC's specifications. Though not widely distributed during the campaign, a distilled version of the pamphlet was published in the North American Review.[4] Though his position was highly unorthodox—proposing such forward-looking measures as a centralized banking system and the inflation of the currency by expanding federal credit—his thorough unmasking of the flawed silver coinage solution made it a useful docu-ment for the Republicans.

Though he admired McKinley for having lent crucial support to his anti-lynching bill in Ohio in 1896, Tourgée had preferred Thomas B. Reed for the nomination, and he was not deluded into believing that a McKinley administration would initiate any new program for civil rights. McKinley, in fact, made a distinct effort to reach out to those Southern whites disaffected with the populist tone of Democrat William Jennings Bryan's campaign. Yet, the conservative Republican 1896 campaign, marked by a virtual absence of civil rights issues, did not elicit any public protest from Tourgée.

Just two years previously, Tourgée had seemed on the verge of abandoning the Republican Party. Outraged at the insistence of party leaders making high tariffs the centerpiece of the party platform, he briefly announced his candidacy for Congress in the 34th District of New York State as an Independent Republican in 1894. Declaring his campaign as a blow against the political "bosses" who "bought and sold" nominations, he rankled the Republican state party machine by calling for a return to the original principles of the party.[5] Longing for the time when Republicans were held together by ideas rather than by organizational discipline, he told a New York audience: "Take the impulse of justice, liberty, and equal right away from the Republican party and it ceases to be Republican—it is only the old Whig party all over again. . . . The Republican Party at its inception was simply purely an Anti-Slavery party. It had no other excuse for being and professed no other motive or purpose."[6] It had lost sight of its antislavery principles, without which was its raison d'être. After drawing public attention to the role of the state political machine, he withdrew his candidacy, confident that his point had been made.

Now, he faithfully subordinated his own views to the party's in hope of gaining his long-deserved reward: a political appointment. After McKinley's victory, Tourgée began his own campaign for a foreign consulship, a position traditionally reserved for men of literary distinction. No doubt recalling Tourgée's irregular candidacy of two years earlier, New York State Republican Party boss Thomas C. Platt, who disbursed patronage to men from his state, firmly opposed Tourgée.[7] Attempting to bypass Platt, Tourgée appealed directly to McKinley and mustered an impressive heap of personal and public support to boost his case. Twenty-one U.S. congressmen, including House Speaker Thomas B. Reed, several state governors, dozens of noted political and literary figures, and even Booker T. Washington, who was fast becoming the power broker of all-things-negro, contributed letters of testimonial. One of McKinley's closest confidants, Herman H. Kohlsaat, a part owner of the *Chicago Inter Ocean* and a man after whom Ferdinand Barnett and Ida B. Wells-Barnett would name her second son, strongly urged the new president to reward Tourgée for his many services to his country. Emma, who worked even harder than Albion to get the appointment, traveled alone to Washington, D.C., and extracted a personal pledge of support from McKinley himself at the White House. Still, all of this did not guarantee the appointment. Afterward, Speaker Reed, to Emma's dismay, discounted McKinley's pledge to her as "a fairy tale." Only when Platt finally relented did the appointment go through. After nearly three months of lobbying, the Tourgées received the news as a great relief, as did others, including Secretary of War Russell Alger, who had begun to feel harassed by "the constant importunities of the Judge and his wife."[8]

After accepting the position of consul to Bordeaux, France, Tourgée promised McKinley, gratuitously perhaps, that he would restrict the "free utterance of truth" that had been the hallmark of his career. "Questions might arise . . . in which it would be impossible for me to be in accord with your administration," Tourgée admitted, but he assured the president, "in such case, I [am] determined to make no utterance . . . unless it should be to my conscience a matter of supreme importance, and then only after resignation of my place."[9] It is possible that Republican Party leadership had made this pledge an explicit condition of his appointment, or that Emma offered it when she saw McKinley at the White House. The opportunity to silence Tourgée's troublesome dissenting voice may well have been enticing for the new president, who had been forced to succumb to public pressure on Tourgée's Anti-Lynching Bill in Ohio less than a year earlier and probably wished to avoid another confrontation on the divisive issue on the national stage. (To his chagrin, Ida B. Wells-Barnett would keep the pressure on, gaining a personal interview with him at the White House in 1898 and lobbying for a national Anti-Lynching Law.)[10]

Explaining his vow of public silence to McKinley, Tourgée expressed a profound sense of disillusionment with his fellow Americans. His desire for a foreign consulship arose from his feeling of disappointment, he confessed, "in the country which I have always loved with a passionate devotion not easy to explain even to myself." He accepted the consulship, he said, as an "escape" from the "utter hopelessness" he felt as he witnessed the worsening conditions for African Americans.[11] Though he spoke of disillusionment, his views had not fundamentally changed. While keeping to his promised public silence, he found it impossible to stifle his impulse to speak his mind to those in positions of power or influence. From his post in Bordeaux, he kept up a steady stream of letters—to McKinley, to his successor Theodore Roosevelt, and others—in which he vented his anger, lamented his mistakes, and sometimes even imagined ultimate victory.

A moment for despair came in 1898 when a race riot in Wilmington, North Carolina, broke out in which at least twenty-five blacks were killed by white supremacists in a raid against politically outspoken black leadership of the city that was meant to drive blacks out of politics completely. Lamenting for the "good seed" that he had helped to sow in North Carolina during Reconstruction, he confided to McKinley that this final triumph of disenfranchisement in the state left him "unable to advise in regard to the steps necessary or desirable to ameliorate the present condition." He went on to explain:

> For a time I believed that American Christianity and the inherent love of liberty and justice of the American people, would find a way to solve this problem. . . . There was a time when we had a conscience upon this subject; when the American people believed that Liberty and Justice were essential elements of republican freedom and prosperity. That time has passed away. The pulpit is silent; the press regards such manifestations as those in North and South Carolina, only with a sort of vague disfavor.[12]

Under these circumstances, he was glad to live in self-imposed exile where he would not be subject to the daily reminders of his disappointment in America. Living in France during the wave of anti-Semitism that accompanied the trial of Alfred Dreyfus, he found no escape from the spread of genocidal intolerance around the globe. In a grim premonition, he told McKinley, "I believe that the United States would just as readily approve the massacre of the colored race throughout her borders, as France would approve by the verdict of her masses, the slaughter of the Jews."[13]

In various letters from Bordeaux, Tourgée often mentioned another reason for his retirement from public protest and agitation. He had become convinced that the "race problem" was leading inevitably toward a violent convulsion. "[I have] ceased to write or speak upon the subject," he explained to one correspondent; not because "I do not consider it of prime importance but because I [do] not wish to be the one whose voice should loose the avalanche."[14] He had learned the power of backlash and was loath to provoke the counterrevolution any further. When Ferdinand Barnett wrote to Tourgée in 1900 inquiring about his prolonged public silence, he received a lengthy reply that predicted violence and warned of great sacrifices ahead for African Americans. "In my opinion, the condition of the American Negro will not improve until for years the world and God have heard his agonizing cry for justice — until the race has furnished martyrs by the thousands perhaps by the hundreds of thousands," he predicted in dire tones, "perhaps when the year two thousand dawns, the colored man in the United States will have regained the right of

person, civil and political."[15] These thoughts offered slight encouragement to Barnett, who continued to work alongside his wife within the radical tradition of protest and public agitation.

The onset of Jim Crow and the accelerated pace of Western imperialism throughout the world left him doubting the whole premise of "uplift"
and "civilization" on which his civil rights work had been founded. No
longer did he believe in the inherent righteousness of "Christian civilization" that he had always viewed as an agent of material prosperity, individual liberation, and social justice to the downtrodden of the globe. Of
his previous faith, he wrote in 1900, "Twenty one years ago [in *A Fool's
Errand*] I thought I knew the remedy . . . I sincerely believed at that time
that education and Christianity were infallible solvents." Experience,
however, had taught him that education and Christian principles had
done nothing to diminish white racism. He lamented to Theodore
Roosevelt: "[E]ducation does not eradicate prejudice, but intensifies it.
Christianity does not condemn or prevent injustice done to the weak by
the strong, but encourages and excuses it. Civilization has small regard for
justice, but the highest reverence for success and power."[16] He no longer
viewed these great ideals as effective agents of combating white prejudice.
Even the courageous military service of black soldiers in the Spanish-
American War, reminiscent of black service in the Civil War, had failed
to advance the cause of racial equality. "I had entertained the hope, perhaps a foolish one, that the bravery of the colored people as manifested in
the late war" would lead to the full integration of the military, he told
McKinley.[17] This was just another "foolish" notion.

For many whites, civilization had become a fixed and racialized ideal.
In abolitionist discourse, a generation earlier, the ideal of civilization had
been equated with moral progress, an open-ended goal that all human
beings could take part in achieving. As this concept became more associated with white supremacy, underpinned with biological determinacy, it
lost this openness. Historians have shown that African American leaders,
such as Du Bois and Wells-Barnett, continued to rely upon the ideal of civilization, but in ways that emphasized its flexibility and even refashioned
it in pluralist and multicultural directions.[18] As Tourgée became disaffected with the dominant culture, he was less apt to propose education
and cultural assimilation as the solution to racism. In 1893 in an essay he
wrote for the *Crusader*, he suggested a more pluralistic view of American
citizenship. "There is no reason why the Negro should not be as secure in
his individual rights in the United States as a Jew," he wrote, drawing a
comparison to one of the largest of the new immigrant groups pouring
into the country. "It is not at all a question of social relation, in the sense
of an enforced individual intercourse. It is quite possible[,] as our life

shows, for varying social currents to co-exist without any infraction on the rights of either . . . such foreign-born or alien-descended citizens stand on equal terms with all the others [in America]."[19] As civilization lost its luster, a nation of separate cultural identities, mutually respectful and tolerant of each other, seemed a fine alternative. For him, Christianity and civilization had served humanity historically as forces for liberty, justice, and humanitarian tolerance. Shorn of these purposes, perhaps these great social ideals had outlived their usefulness.

THE LIBERAL CO-OPTION OF COLOR-BLINDNESS

A ray of hope shone through the gloom in October of 1901. President Theodore Roosevelt, who had taken office only weeks beforehand, hosted Booker T. Washington for dinner at the White House. Although the main purpose of the dinner was to discuss patronage for blacks in his administration, their breaking bread together was interpreted in the Southern press as a deliberate act of "social equality" and a sign of Roosevelt's intent to undermine segregation. Tourgée received the news in Bordeaux with an almost euphoric wonderment. Instantly, he wrote to congratulate Roosevelt on his historic act. "It would be hard for me to give any idea of the emotions I have experienced in contemplating this momentous incident," he wrote. "To say that I have been thoroughly dazed is not too much. . . . I thank you—I congratulate you—I pity you . . . I am glad that I have lived to know that an American President is brave enough to ask a colored gentleman to his table. Whatever may hap[pen], it is a brave man's act, a true Christian's act which the world can never forget."[20]

Urging him to stand firm against the brutal criticism that was sure to follow, Tourgée hoped that Roosevelt would defend himself with a strong statement against white supremacy. He had known Roosevelt slightly in New York City. The two men once belonged to the Captain Rice Club, a small club formed in 1883 of twenty notable egalitarians that included such radicals as Edward Everett Hale, William Lloyd Garrison, Jr., and Henry George, Roosevelt's later mayoral campaign opponent. Nothing is known of the origin or purpose of the short-lived club, which dissolved soon after its formation, but Roosevelt must have struck Tourgée at the time as a young man of radical inclinations.[21] Now, he fantasized that the magnetic Roosevelt could lead a movement to revitalize the humanitarian values that he once attributed to civilization and Christianity and reclaim them from their complicity in racial oppression. He told him: "Whether you so intended or not, or whether you now desire or not, you have written your name large across the future in which a *new civilization* and a *new Christianity* lie hidden which shall establish for all time on earth the divine decree that, 'White is not always right.' "[22]

Tourgée was correct in estimating Roosevelt as a public figure of rare power and influence. He soon learned, however, that Roosevelt would not go down in history as a defender of the principle that "white is not always right." Roosevelt nevertheless sympathized with Tourgée's feelings and took time to write a thoughtful reply that affirmed a desire to champion Christian principles. "Your letter pleases and touches me," Roosevelt responded. Admitting that he had not anticipated sparking a controversy, he explained, "When I asked Booker T. Washington to dinner I did not devote very much thought to the matter one way or the other. I respect him greatly and believe in the work he has done . . . as things have turned out, I am very glad that I asked him, for the clamor aroused by the act makes me feel as if the act was necessary." Agreeing that racial prejudice was a despicable trait, he confided to Tourgée with evident pride, "[T]he very fact that I felt a moment's qualm on inviting him because of his color made me ashamed of myself and made me hasten to send the invitation." Overcoming some deep-lying personal prejudice, therefore, he affirmed in principle that Washington was due the same treatment a white man would receive in his place. But Roosevelt's articulation of this principle had disturbing undercurrents. Believing his attitudes in harmony with Tourgée's, he went on to candidly explain:

> I too have been at my wits end in dealing with the black man. . . . I have not been able to think out any solution of the terrible problem offered by the presence of the negro on this continent, but of one thing I am sure, and that is inasmuch as he is here and can neither be killed nor driven away, the only wise and honorable thing to do is *to treat each black man and each white man strictly on his merits as a man, giving him no more and no less than he shows himself worthy to have.* I say I am sure that this is the right solution.

His adoption of the principle of color-blind justice in this passage stands in jarring juxtaposition to his expression of regret that the negro "can neither be killed nor driven away." Though in Roosevelt's hyperbolic phraseology he often discussed eliminating problems by "shooting" or "exterminating" them, nevertheless his words indicate an overriding desire to make the problem—defined as the dealing with the "presence of the negro on this continent"—disappear quickly, not to solve it judiciously.[23]

The distance between Theodore Roosevelt's use of the principle of color-blind justice and Tourgée's own was indicative of yet another watershed in American race relations. The color-blind principle allowed Roosevelt to reduce the problem by individualizing his solution. He freely co-opted the language of *color-blindness*—treating each person according to their own individual merit—because it allowed him to appear as a champion of racial justice to himself, while at the same time ignoring the social and institutional structures that produced and perpetuated racial oppression. "I do not intend to offend the prejudices of anyone else," he explained to Tourgée, "but neither do I intend to allow their prejudice to make me false to my principles."[24] Color-blind treatment of one's fellows was a matter of private conscience, not a matter of public concern that might be required of others. Turning a blind eye to the systemic causes of racism, Roosevelt regarded racial discrimination rather as a matter of private moral choice. Unlike Tourgée, who wished to transform the culture that created a privileged caste of citizens based on their racial "whiteness," Roosevelt used the principle of color-blindness as a justification to ignore the larger problem altogether.[25] We do not know how Tourgée reacted to Roosevelt's letter, but his expressions of disillusionment returned swiftly afterward.

Had Tourgée read Roosevelt's 1905 speech, "Lincoln and the Race Problem," he would have been further dismayed. Delivered to the Republican Club of New York City, the speech further transformed radical principles by calling upon the legacy and example of Abraham Lincoln to justify a policy of noninterference with Southern racial issues. One of Roosevelt's most complete statements on the "race problem," he declared racism one of "the gravest problems before our people" and suggested, "our effort should be to secure to each man, whatever his color, equality of opportunity [and] equality of treatment before the law." But, he maintained that a principle of tolerance and equal treatment must extend to white Southerners as well. He declared:

> We of to-day, in dealing with all our fellow-citizens, white or colored, North or South should strive to show just the qualities that Lincoln showed —his steadfastness in striving after the right and his infinite patience and forbearance with those who saw that right less clearly than he did; his earnest endeavor to do what was best, and yet his readiness to accept the best that was practicable when the ideal best was unattainable; coupled with his refusal to make a bad situation worse by any ill-judged or ill-timed effort to make it better.[26]

Emphasizing Lincoln as a moderate who brokered compromise between extreme factions, he rejected both racism and radicalism in the same breath. His allusion to "ill-judged and ill-timed" efforts distinctly referred to Radical Republican attempts to use government power to protect equal citizenship in the South and perhaps even obliquely to more recent efforts to oppose segregation through civil rights agitation and litigation, such as in the *Plessy* case. Repudiating those efforts, Roosevelt counseled patience and urged that "all good Americans who dwell in the North must, because they are good Americans, feel the most earnest friendship for their fellow-countrymen who dwell in the South" and should remind themselves that "the attitude of the North toward the negro is far from what it should be."[27]

In the name of nationalism and sectional harmony, Roosevelt preached tolerance of Southern viewpoints—meaning, in effect, white supremacy—and made color-blindness a matter for one's own individual conscience. He eventually came to regard his dinner with Booker T. Washington as one of the few blunders of his first administration because it disrupted this sectional harmony. It was a mistake he never repeated afterwards—he and Washington continued to meet, but never shared another meal at the White House.[28] Roosevelt's views exemplified the stance of many progressive white Northerners who disapproved of most Jim Crow policies in theory yet felt little power or inclination to do anything about it. With Northern progressives openly acquiescent to Jim Crow and preaching tolerance for white Southerners, the path was cleared for the Southern white racial extremism to go national. There had never been a shortage of white supremacists in the North, of course, but the Northern audience for neo-Confederate views on the Civil War and Reconstruction was about to explode far beyond the old Copperhead crowd. The stage had been set, quite literally, for Thomas Dixon.

THE TRIUMPH OF THOMAS DIXON

As conservative mythology about Reconstruction solidified by degrees into historical facts, the acquiescence of the Northern public to segregation grew all the more complete. It "doesn't go," Tourgée's publisher informed him of a new edition of *A Fool's Errand* in 1894, adding helplessly, "I can't explain it . . . so cheap an edition of so famous a book ought to sell well."[29] Within a few years of this comment, a new genre of aggressive anti-Reconstruction novels appeared in the form of Thomas Nelson Page's *Red Rock* (1898), Joel Chandler Harris's *Gabriel Tolliver* (1902), and most of all, Thomas Dixon, Jr.'s *The Leopard's Spots* (1902) and *The Clansmen* (1905). Page and Harris were established writers of romantic stories in the Southern "plantation tradition," who turned from slavery times to the Civil War and Reconstruction for their subject matter.[30] Neither of them defended either the Confederacy or secession, they concentrated instead on the humiliations of so-called negro domination, the corruption of the plundering carpetbaggers, and the treachery of the opportunistic, poor white scalawags, which were painted in unforgettably villainous hues.

Thomas Dixon began his path to success as a carpetbagger in reverse. Born and raised in North Carolina, he left the state soon after graduating from Wake Forest in 1883, for awhile was in the Ph.D. program in history at Johns Hopkins, and then established himself as a Baptist preacher first in Boston and then in New York City. Dixon experienced his first taste of fame as a spellbinding preacher at the Twenty-third Street Baptist Church in New York, where he tested his favorite themes of nationalism, imperialist expansion, and white racial unity. Though considered by many vulgar and sensationalist, Dixon captured a large, enthusiastic following that included the powerful patronage of none other than John D. Rockefeller, the oil mogul to whom Emma had once turned in vain for salvation. Rockefeller enthusiastically pledged a half-million dollars for the construction of a massive, forty-story temple—and office building—in lower Manhattan to house Dixon's own nondenominational congregation, after a sectarian controversy caused the minister to leave his Baptist parish in 1896. As it turned out, popular resistance blocked the plan and Dixon's "People's Church" moved instead into the old Academy of Music building near Union Square. It was the only available building large enough to house his congregation.[31]

One night Dixon happened to attend a performance of *Uncle Tom's Cabin*, which he found so disturbing that he left the theater in a rage. Vowing to write the "true history" of the South, Dixon consciously strove to reach a Northern audience in the belief that he could use fiction to "reach and influence with [his] argument the minds of millions."[32] Significantly, rather than tackle the subject of slavery, Dixon turned instead to the history of the Civil War and Reconstruction and seemed to take aim at the works of Tourgée. Dixon had a particular interest in Tourgée, a towering local Reconstruction figure from his boyhood. As a student at Wake Forest, Dixon began an "animated correspondence" with Tourgée while he was editor of *Our Continent* and later received his "kindly advice" when he visited him in person at his New York offices to discuss his own aspirations for a literary career.[33] Following *A Fool's Errand* more closely in plot and style than *Uncle Tom's Cabin*, Dixon prefaced *The Leopard's Spots* by vouching for the historical truth of the contents within, insisting, "[T]he only serious liberty I have taken with history is to tone down the facts to make them credible in fiction." Claiming to have written it with "the utmost restraint," he insisted, "It will be a century yet before people outside the South can be made to believe a literal statement of the history of those times."[34]

As his preface indicated, Dixon presumed that his views would have many detractors in the North. The popularity of *The Leopard's Spots*, which sold over 100,000 copies in its first few months, must have surprised as well as pleased him.[35] Yet, acceptance of his views was far from universal. Dixon's own brother scorned his "hideous theology" and his father later said his books "bore down a little too hard on the Negro [who] wasn't to blame for Reconstruction."[36] Walter Hines Page, his publisher, defended himself against critics by stating that he believed "the surest way to overcome [Dixon's] point of view was to bring it into the light."[37] The controversy merely helped fuel the publicity that Dixon and his work received. Soon Dixon became virtually obsessed with proselytizing the North with his views of Reconstruction. Attempting to widen his public exposure, Dixon adopted his second novel, *The Clansmen*, to the stage where it became a national hit, with productions opening across the North and South. His play attracted the attention of the film director D.W. Griffith, who approached the author with his idea of adapting it to film. Griffith and Dixon would collaborate closely during the production of *The Clansmen*, which was retitled *The Birth of a Nation* soon after its release in 1915. The film would revolutionize cinema and become the most successful and profitable film ever made.[38]

Griffith intended for his film to be understood by audiences as authentic history. To bolster its credibility, scholarly citations were included in title frames, mostly from President Woodrow Wilson's *A History of the American People*. Wilson, an academic, had received his Ph.D. in history from Johns Hopkins, and it was there that he had met Dixon, with whom he remained on friendly terms. *The Birth of a Nation* therefore enjoyed the endorsement of the president of the United States, who held a private screening of it at the White House, where he famously deemed it all "so terribly true," a comment he later retracted under heavy criticism. The unprecedented realism Griffith achieved in many spectacular historical scenes, such as Lincoln's assassination, may have convinced audiences that they were witnessing history as it had occurred even without the president's endorsement. Performances in the film, on the other hand, in which white minstrel actors play African Americans cannot be described in any way as realistic even though they conform to long-held stereotypes about Southern slaves.[39]

Viewed by millions, *The Birth of a Nation* remained in theaters for more than a decade, sparking a modern revival of the long-defunct Ku Klux Klan. Historian Joel Williamson has written that Thomas Dixon "probably did more to shape the lives of modern Americans than have some Presidents."[40] While his impact is impossible to measure, Dixon certainly had a longer-lasting influence than Tourgée ever did. However, the radical Civil War as an ideological construct was not completely forgotten, even during Dixon's time of triumph. It lived on and continued to shape the public discourse about Reconstruction.

Evidence of Tourgée's own enduring influence can be found, in of all places, the film *The Birth of a Nation*. The only dissenting historical source cited in Griffith's scholarly screenplay belongs to him. Just before the Ku Klux Klan appears on the screen for the first time, Griffith's title frame reads: "The Ku Klux Klan, the organization that saved the South from the anarchy of black rule, but not without the shedding of more blood than at Gettysburg, according to Judge Tourgee of the carpet-baggers." At once boasting of the bloodshed and suggesting doubt about Tourgée's credibility, this passage illustrates how much Dixon remained in dialogue with Tourgée. The title frame alludes to a passage from *A Fool's Errand* in which Tourgée wrote:

> Ah! the wounded in this silent warfare were more thousands than those who groaned upon the slopes of Gettysburg! Dwellings and schools and churches burned! People driven from their homes, and dwelling in the woods and fields! The poor, the weak, the despised, maltreated and persecuted—by whom? Always the same intangible presence . . . it name[d] itself the "Invisible Empire."[41]

Griffith's heroic depiction of the Ku Klux Klan that follows the title frame—with charging, armed horsemen in flowing white sheets assaulting venal blacks and white "carpetbaggers"—does nothing to deny the level of violence, but portrays it as entirely justified vigilantism.

Adherents to alternative memories of Reconstruction did not keep silent upon the release of *The Birth of a Nation*. Organized protests and

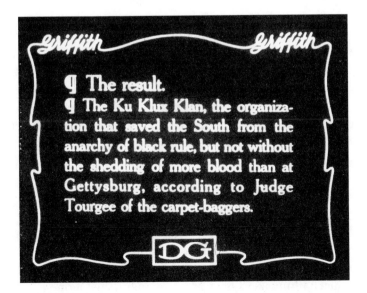

Title frame from the film *The Birth of a Nation* (1915).

spontaneous race riots followed the opening of the film in several cities. Bowing to public pressure, in the wake of the protests Hollywood censors forced Griffith to expunge two scenes, including one of whites castrating a black rapist.[42] W.E.B. Du Bois publicized the protests through the pages of *The Crisis*, the organ of the recently formed National Association for the Advancement of Colored People. "Like the book, 'The Clansmen,' on which it is founded," said one white NAACP member, "it is a gross perversion of a period of our history about which the people have been persistently lied to for a generation. Even the most eminent historians suppress the truth about it, in the interest, I suppose, of national harmony."[43]

A Ph.D. in history from Harvard University, Du Bois was well positioned to respond to the film's historical falsifications. A few years earlier, he had taken on academic historians who perpetuated the myths of Reconstruction in his paper "Reconstruction and Its Benefits," which was delivered in 1910 at the annual meeting of the American Historical Association in front of leading academic proponents of the conservative mythology, including Columbia University Professor William Dunning. In his remarks, Du Bois prominently used a long passage from Tourgée, taken from one of his "Bystander's Notes" columns, as testimony that described the relative honesty and the long-term beneficial reforms of the Reconstruction governments.[44]

Not until 1935 did Du Bois complete his magisterial vindication of Reconstruction in *Black Reconstruction in America*. The book tells the history of the Civil War and its aftermath as a conflict shaped by irony but ultimately led by revolutionaries who struggled to establish a truly interracial democracy—its original, more sweeping title, *Black Reconstruction of Democracy in America*, was modified by his editors. In the book, Du Bois singles out Tourgée as "the bravest of the carpetbaggers," and he gives due credit to other Radical Republicans who "reached the highest level of self-sacrificing statesmanship ever achieved in America" and who "laid down their lives on the altar of democracy and were eventually paid . . . by the widespread contempt of America."[45] Viewing the underlying conflict of the era as an ironic result of the oppression of labor, black and white, Du Bois saw in Reconstruction the stirrings of an empowered interracial working class whose incipient rise had been repressed by a renewed alliance between Northern capitalists and the Southern planter aristocracy that amounted to a "counter-revolution of property." As a work of history, it made the most thorough case for Reconstruction as a revolutionary event, thwarted by a cross-sectional counterrevolution, than had appeared before.

Others too sought to preserve a different history of Reconstruction. Pioneer black filmmaker Oscar Micheaux launched a one-man crusade in the 1920s to refute Griffith's *The Birth of a Nation* in films marketed for black audiences. Both Micheaux's *Within Our Gates* (1920) and *Symbol of the Unconquered* (1920) deal more accurately with the injustice and brutality of the Ku Klux Klan than Griffith's film. Desiring more historical material, Micheaux turned to the works of Charles Chesnutt, with whom he struck up a correspondence, and subsequently he adopted two of Chesnutt's works to film. As he completed work on Chesnutt's *The House Behind the Cedars* (1924), Micheaux announced that his next film would be an adaptation of Tourgée's *A Fool's Errand*. What became of this production is uncertain. Actor Lorenzo Tucker, who was hired to star in it, recalled that *A Fool's Errand* was filmed on a very tight budget and finished in 1926, but when Micheaux failed to pay the film processor, the processing company confiscated the film and sold it to a South American distributor. Thus, it was never seen in the United States. Nevertheless, the radical memory of Reconstruction, though driven underground, remained alive and awaiting recovery.[46]

THE LEGACY OF RADICAL INDIVIDUALISM

Characteristically, Tourgée did not find the peace and tranquility one might have hoped for in Bordeaux's picturesque surroundings. Always the impatient reformer, he irked the local businessmen with his strict enforcement of customs practices, including traditionally evaded inspection of agricultural and livestock exports, and he confounded the locals when he openly advocated diversification of the economy to prevent overreliance on grape-growing and wineries. The teetotaler's sympathies were out of accord with the local culture. Cynics might find it fitting that Tourgée, who spent the bulk of his career trying to convince Americans to give up racism, should end it trying to convince the French to give up wine. But, he was never content to accept things as they were, especially when he felt custom and tradition stood in the way of moral progress.[47]

Tourgée found a little time to write in Bordeaux. He resumed publication of "A Bystander's Notes" in the *Inter Ocean* for a final run that lasted from November 1896 to October 1898. Though he managed to avoid criticizing the McKinley administration, Tourgée felt no obligation to hold his tongue on the controversial treason charge against the Jewish military officer Alfred Dreyfus that had stirred up an outburst of anti-Semitism in France. His criticism of the French court's handling of the case in an installment of "A Bystander's Notes" caused him to be censured by his superiors in Washington for his undiplomatic "breach of discipline," showing that he had not lost his power to provoke. Further, he published one last collection of notable short stories, fittingly entitled *The Man Who*

Tourgée in Bordeaux, ca. 1900. Courtesy of the Chautauqua County
Historical Society, Westfield, NY.

Outlived Himself (1898), that contained some suggestively autobiographical elements. The title story deals with a Civil War veteran, ruined by
a bad business investment, whose emotionally overwrought condition
induces amnesia that happily blots out the memory of his personal
"shame," but it also wipes out his memory of his beloved wife and talented
daughter. Psychologically deeper than much of his fiction, the tale concludes with the veteran reconnecting with his wife and daughter after
many years but without ever regaining the memory of his former life.
Century Magazine had declined to publish it because the editors considered it too "painful," despite favorable readers' reports.[48]

A return of Tourgée's back ailments confined him to bed for nearly five
months in 1900, after which his health never fully recovered. As his activities at the consulate slowed, his writing and letters home became infrequent. An operation on his hip in 1904 excavated a piece of shrapnel that

Tourgée claimed as a souvenir from Perryville. Less than a year later, he died on May 21, 1905, from a case of acute uremia, which was reported by the consulate to be a complication from his Bull Run injuries. If true, he became a belated casualty of the Civil War. A respectful memorial service was held in Bordeaux, but Emma had his remains cremated and shipped home to Mayville, where she planned a more elaborate burial service. Her plans would dovetail with those of a new civil rights organization, founded that summer in Buffalo, New York, that soon called the nation's attention to the loss of Albion Tourgée.

The Niagara Movement, whose founding members included W.E.B. Du Bois, William Monroe Trotter, and Harry C. Smith, along with twenty-six other black men, attempted to reignite the tradition of protest and agitation that had dimmed in the decade since Booker T. Washington's 1895 Atlanta Compromise speech. Without openly breaking with Washington, they adopted a militant "Declaration of Principles" that refused to capitulate to segregation and called for the "abolition of all caste distinctions based simply on race or color." The founders also resolved to hold memorial services on Thanksgiving Day in honor of three "Friends of Freedom": Frederick Douglass, William Lloyd Garrison, and Albion Tourgée.[49] Trotter did not wait until Thanksgiving but during July presided over a mass meeting in honor of "Judge Tourgée" in Boston. The eulogist, who praised Tourgée as one never corrupted by "money or other influence," made headlines when he took the opportunity to directly challenge Booker T. Washington, calling him a "a time-serving sycophant" who had sold his "birthright for the pottage of [his] race's shame."[50]

A group of Tourgée's old allies associated with the Niagara Movement took the initiative to propose a special memorial service for him in Mayville, which they arranged with Emma to closely coincide with their national day of honor on Thanksgiving.[51] On November 14, 1905, the town of Mayville, New York, closed all businesses as hundreds gathered to pay their final respects to Albion Tourgée. More than thirty African Americans arrived from many parts of the country to take part in the ceremony at the Mayville Methodist Episcopal Church. Among the main eulogists were Charles Chesnutt and Ida B. Wells-Barnett; present for the service were Ferdinand Barnett and Harry C. Smith. To the dismay of some audience members, Booker T. Washington, who had been expected, sent his regrets by telegram, stating simply, "My race owes much to the courage and helpful work of Judge Tourgée, which we shall not forget."[52]

The remarks of Ida B. Wells-Barnett are preserved in a printed memorial that she read on the occasion, delivered as a representative of the Illinois Division of the Niagara Movement and the Appomattox Club of Chicago. She stirringly captured the militant spirit and humanitarian philosophy of Tourgée, the man to whom she liked to refer to simply as "The Bystander." "His voice is silenced and his forceful pen fails—an incalculable loss to our race and nation," she intoned. Describing his life's work as a tireless effort "to so arouse the conscience of the country that justice should know no race, color or creed," she believed his example would "encourage his earnest co-workers to persevere in their self-sacrificing endeavor, even though, at times, success is uncertain and defeat seems sure." She concluded by praying for more "great minds" to be as filled with a sense of eternal justice as his was:

> May the inspiration of his noble life be as "bread cast upon the waters" returning after many days to bless the nation by bringing to the service of the oppressor and oppressed, other great minds whose aim shall be to so strengthen the "Golden Rule" that it will not waiver or fail in its measurement of justice to the "brother in black."[53]

Echoing Wells-Barnett, Emma said that her husband's work could be summed up simply in "his idea of Justice—justice to all men, no matter what their color or previous condition, because they were men."[54]

Activists such as Wells-Barnett and her fellow Niagara members wished to reinvigorate the tradition of protest that Tourgée had exemplified. By 1910, the Niagara Movement would be absorbed by the interracial National Association for the Advancement of Colored People (NAACP), which would eventually topple the constitutional rationale for Jim Crow by persuading the U.S. Supreme Court to overturn its ruling in *Plessy v. Ferguson* in the landmark case of *Brown v. Board of Education* (1954). Thus, an unbroken line to final victory can be detected, stretching from the memorials for Tourgée in 1905, and the parallel founding of a new civil rights movement that took inspiration from his life, to the pronouncement of the Warren Court that racial segregation is "inherently unequal" and that "any language in *Plessy v. Ferguson* contrary to this finding is rejected."[55]

In reality, the path to *Brown* was far from straight, as ideas about race and citizenship continued to develop and change along the way. In fact, the most prominent rationale against *Plessy* offered by Justice Warren in the *Brown* decision was based on social scientific evidence of the 1950s, now discredited, which hypothesized that segregation causes an inferiority complex in black children. Tourgée had argued nothing of the sort—and nowhere in the *Brown* case does one find the kind of ringing egalitarian language and probing of racial logic found in Tourgée's *Plessy* brief.[56]

Since the First World War, religiously based political arguments have usually been mobilized on the side of conservative causes, not radical ones. The radical individualist tradition has persisted—thrived even—in our political culture in various guises and modified forms. But in the wake of the *Brown* decision, it would re-emerge as one of the primary discourses of the Civil Rights Movement. Though many streams of intellectual and political thought combined in support of racial equality at that time, the man whose message first predominated the movement, Martin Luther King, Jr., embodied the radical individualist tradition more fully than anyone had since Tourgée's time. King's success among white middle-class Northerners perhaps owed much to his ability to revive a discourse that had deep-lying roots in American political culture.

Steeped in the social gospel tradition, King couched his civil rights protest in terms of conquering one's enemies with "Christian love" and appealing to the Christian conscience of whites as the path toward overcoming racism. In the name of conscience, he urged the breaking of unjust laws—laws he defined as ones out of harmony with "the moral law or the law of God"—and he exercised his right to speak out against all forms of injustice, including the War in Vietnam, even at great personal cost to himself. His "I Have A Dream" speech, upheld as one of the finest expressions of the color-blind ideal, was full of religious overtones. He spoke of the universal brotherhood of "all God's children" and his dream to one day live in a nation where his children "will not be judged by the color of their skin but by the content of their character." Reasserting the religious principle of human oneness, King revived the radical message of the abolitionist movement that had once provided the ideological justification for those constitutional amendments whose promises King asked America to finally fulfill. Like all great movements in history, the meaning and legacy of the Civil Rights Movement, and of Martin Luther King in particular, has been claimed by many competing interests and continues to be fought over by those who look to the past as a guide to the present.[57]

It has been the purpose of this book to reexamine a political tradition that has been often distorted and misunderstood. The life and thought of Albion Tourgée illuminates the tradition of radical individualism out of whence he came. Through his struggles it is possible to assess the fate of that tradition in the late nineteenth century as the political culture moved away from its intellectual premises. Viewing the history of this period through the lens of Tourgée's career, the primary forces that undermined the nation's commitment to Reconstruction's higher racial egalitarian principles become evident. These include new forms of biological and deterministic notions of the self that became fashionable among Northern intellectuals, the success of white conservative propaganda in fashioning public perception, and subsequent historical memory about Reconstruction, the hostility of the Supreme Court toward black civil rights, and the co-option of color-blindness as a laissez-faire rationale to justify government inaction against racism. Each of these obstacles would have to be overcome in time before the promises of Reconstruction could be fully realized. Whether that process has been completed is still a matter of public debate.

It has not been the purpose of this book to argue that the radical individualist tradition of protest and agitation is the best way, or the only way, to bring about a more democratic society. Clearly, there were times when Tourgée's cause would have been better served had he acted less provocatively, approached his opponents with more tact, compromised with his allies who had similar goals, or even accepted a strategic retreat to renew the fight on a better day. Tourgée often acknowledged this himself, although he was more apt to caution others to compromise or to avoid provoking backlash than to prevent himself from doing so. Nevertheless, men and women who have felt it their moral duty to speak their conscience about injustice, however they define it, have been essential in American history to keep democracy vibrant. Without such individuals, one wonders whether democracy as an ideal would have survived our history at all.

Tourgée was an important figure for his lifelong adherence to the politics of conscience (until the *Plessy* defeat), for his powerful formulations of the color-blind principle, and for his struggle to maintain his radical principles despite the changing circumstances of the late nineteenth century. His story reminds us that there have been traditions of racial egalitarianism in American history that have shaped our understanding of citizenship, and concepts of the self, in ways not yet fully appreciated. It is important to remember, and to argue about, the meaning and legacy of these traditions and of the radicals like Tourgée who made them. I have tried to present an accurate account of his life and ideas, within their historical context, that cuts through the mythology and misrepresentation of his times. I leave it to others to decide whether this story helps to clarify or correct the mythologies and misrepresentations of our own times.

Acknowledgments

I would like to thank the following institutions for providing me with crucial financial support and access to scholarly resources that allowed me to finish my manuscript during the academic year 2005–2006: the National Endowment for the Humanities, for awarding me a long-term fellowship; the Newberry Library, for the Lloyd Lewis Fellowship in American History; the Henry E. Huntington Library for the Andrew W. Mellon Short-term Fellowship; the Gilder Lehrman Center for the Study of Slavery, Resistance, and Abolition, Yale University, for a three-month postdoctoral fellowship; and the Wagner College Board of Trustees, for the Maureen Robinson Fellowship.

I greatly appreciate the assistance I received from research staff and librarians of many institutions, in particular the entire research staff at the Newberry and Huntington Libraries; Ellen Schwanekamp and Barbara Wills-Czolowski, of the Chautauqua Historical Society, Westfield, New York; Rebecca Hankins, of the Amistad Research Center, New Orleans; Leon C. Miller, of the Special Collections and Manuscripts Department, Tulane University; Lester Sullivan, of the Xavier University Library, New Orleans; and Stephen Catlett at the Greensboro Historical Museum. In addition, I thank the research assistants of the Southern Historical Collection and the North Carolina Collection, at the Wilson Library, University of North Carolina; the William R. Perkins Library, Duke University; the Beinecke Rare Book and Manuscript Library and the Sterling Memorial Library, Yale University; the Manuscripts Division of the Library of Congress; the National Archives; the Patterson Library, Westfield, New York; the Mayville Library, Mayville, New York; the Western Reserve Historical Society; the Schomburg Center for Research in Black Culture; the Henry and Albert Berg Collection, New York Public Library; the New York Historical Society; the Rutherford B. Hayes Presidential Center; the Massachusetts Historical Society; the American Antiquarian Society; the Connecticut Historical Society; the Historical Society of Pennsylvania; the Buffalo and Erie County Public Library; the Chicago Historical Society; the Indiana Historical Society; Rockefeller Family Archives; the Rush Rhees Library, University of Rochester; the Pierpont Morgan Library; the Gilder Lehrman Collection; the Houghton Library, Harvard University; Milton S. Eisenhower Library, Johns Hopkins; Princeton University Library; Alderman Library, University of Virginia; John Hay Library, Brown University; Lee Library, Brigham Young University; Friends Historical Library, Swarthmore College; University of California at Los Angeles Library; University of Iowa Library; Cornell University Library; University of Chicago Library; Kent State University Library; Colby College Library; and Drew University Library.

I am grateful to John Boles and the *Journal of Southern History* for allowing me to reprint portions of my article "Race, Color Blindness and the Democratic Public: Albion W. Tourgée's Radical Principles in *Plessy v. Ferguson*," in chapters 8 and 9 of this work.

I express my heartfelt thanks to Naurice Frank Woods for sharing his privately owned materials with me as well as his knowledge and speculations regarding the life of his great-great-grandmother Adaline Patillo. Thank you also to Dean H. Keller, Bonnie Tidd Miller, and Debbie Kelly for sharing their personal materials and knowledge about Albion W. Tourgée.

This book began as my dissertation at New York University, where I was fortunate to receive guidance and direction from a model adviser, Thomas Bender. Tom fostered a spirit of collective academic endeavor among his many advisees, bringing us together for regular seminar meetings, discussions, and dinners, while challenging us to reach a high standard of scholarship through our readings and discussions of each other's work. I thank Tom for the unsurpassed intellectual experience I had in graduate school and for his support of my work and me personally in ways too numerous to recount. Without him, this book simply would not exist.

Others at NYU and the University of California at Riverside who provided advice, criticism, inspiration, and friendship that made this book what it is include Martha Hodes, Walter Johnson, Robin D.G. Kelley, Scott Martin, Roger Ransom, Sharon V. Salinger, Kenneth Silverman, Stewart Stehlin, Sterling Stuckey, John Baick, Dan Bender, Erin Clune, Andrew Darien, Betsy Esch, Saverio Giovacchini, Bill Johnson, David Kinkela, Michael LaCombe, Mark Ladov, Michael Lerner, Neil Mahr, Molly McGarry, Stephen Mihm, Jasmine Mir, Kevin Murphy, Deborah Paes

De Barros, David Quigley, Amy Richter, Greg Robinson, Andrew Schroeder, Carlton Smith, Traci Tullis, and Rebecca Welch.

In the process of revising this book for publication, I received helpful feedback and criticism from many people whom I wish to thank. I am grateful especially to George Rappapport, who read and extensively commented on the entire manuscript *pro bono*, and to John David Smith and an anonymous reviewer, who read and commented on the manuscript for Oxford University Press. My editors at Oxford, Peter Ginna, Furaha Norton, Susan Ferber, and Joellyn Ausanka, have offered valuable suggestions and criticism. Barbara B. Heyman was an outstanding copy editor. Special thanks go to individuals at Wagner College: Anne Schotter, Jean Halley, Sarah Donovan, and other participants in the 2004–2005 Scholarship Circle as well as the students from my fall 2004 course "Research & Analysis." Others who have given much appreciated advice and encouragement on this project include: Shawn Alexander, David Blight, Jim Epstein, Betsy Erkkila, Leon Fink, Jim Grossman, Carolyn Karcher, Laura Matthew, Tony Pollock, Dana Schaffer, Joan Wallach Scott, and Tom Thurston.

I owe a deep debt of gratitude to President Richard Guarasci and Provost Devorah Lieberman of Wagner College for supporting my work on this book and granting me released time so that I could complete it. To all of my friends and colleagues at Wagner who have been tremendously supportive, and especially to Steve Snow and Lori Weintrob, I thank you.

My parents, Emory and Georgia, have been unwavering in their confidence and faith in my abilities throughout the many ups and downs of bringing this project to fruition. My siblings, Scott, Matt, Connie, and Laura, too, have always been quick with words of advice and encouragement, and they have kept me working hard for fear of falling short of their expectations. I thank Richard and Barbara Lutz for their support and for never once questioning the sacrifices that I have asked of their daughter and grandsons so that I could accept fellowships at distant libraries to finish the manuscript. I am grateful to Denise Hobrack, whose boundless devotion to my children made my separation from my family much easier to endure for all of us during the past nine months.

Finally, my wife, Kimberly, has shared in my passion to make this book live up to its promise and has sacrificed a great deal so that I could put forth my best effort to that end. I cannot begin to describe the extent to which her love, support, encouragement, companionship, collaboration, and hard work made this book possible. I never felt that a single page of the manuscript was complete until it had her approval. My two small children, Zachary and Nicholas, have given little thought to the book, but have done much to make it better. I treasure every moment with them, and they inspire me to always do better so that they can be as proud of me as I am of them.

Abbreviations

ARC	Amistad Research Center, New Orleans
AWT	Albion Winegar Tourgée
AWTP	Albion W. Tourgée Papers, Chautauqua County Historical Society, Westfield, NY
AV	Alderman Library, University of Virginia, Manuscripts Department
BEPL	Buffalo and Erie County Public Library, Rare Book Room, Buffalo, NY
BH	Benjamin Harrison Papers, Library of Congress, Washington, DC
BL	Beinecke Rare Book and Manuscript Library, Yale University
DU	Duke University, William R. Perkins Library, Durham, NC
EKT	Emma (Lodoilska) Kilborn Tourgée
FDP	Frederick Douglass Papers, Library of Congress
FLS	Friends Historical Library, Swarthmore College
FU	Fisk University Library, Nashville, TN
HL	Henry E. Huntington Library, San Marino, CA
IHS	Indiana Historical Society, Indianapolis
KSU	Kent State University Libraries, Special Collections and Archives, Kent, OH
JG	James A. Garfield Papers, Library of Congress
LC	Library of Congress, Washington, DC
NARA	National Archives and Records Administration, Washington, DC, and College Park, MD
NYHS	New York Historical Society, New York City
NYPL	New York Public Library, New York City
PL	Patterson Library, Westfield, NY
RBH	Rutherford B. Hayes Presidential Center, Fremont, OH
RFA	Rockefeller Family Archives, Sleepy Hollow, NY
SCBC	Schomburg Center for Research in Black Culture, New York Public Library

SCO	Surrogate's Court Office, Mayville, NY
SMLY	Sterling Memorial Library, Yale University
TR	Theodore Roosevelt Papers, Library of Congress
TU	Tulane University Library, Special Collections, New Orleans
UC	University of Chicago, Special Collections
UI	University of Iowa Libraries, Manuscripts Department
UNC	University of North Carolina at Chapel Hill, Wilson Library
UR	University of Rochester, Rush Rhees Library, Rare Books and Special Collections
USG	Ulysses S. Grant Papers, Library of Congress
WM	William McKinley Papers, Library of Congress
WRHS	Western Reserve Historical Society, Cleveland
XU	Xavier University Archives, New Orleans

Notes

Introduction: Albion Tourgée and Color-Blind Citizenship

1. Albion W. Tourgée, *A Fool's Errand. By One of the Fools* (New York: Fords, Howard & Hulbert, 1879). Although the main character of *A Fool's Errand* was only partly autobiographical, Tourgée often spoke of himself as "the Fool" of his famous book. See, for example, AWT to Anna Julia Cooper, June 1890, #5690, AWTP. First epigraph, clipping, "Lincoln Number Two: Is Judge Tourgee," *Indianapolis World,* January 30, 1893, #6692, AWTP; second epigraph quoted from Albion W. Tourgée, *Is Liberty Worth Preserving?* (Chicago: Inter-Ocean, 1892), 12, Daniel A.P. Murray Pamphlet Collection, LC.

2. Frederick L. Hoffman, "Vital Statistics of the Negro," *The Arena* 5 (April 1892):531; also, Hoffman quoted in Charles A. Lofgren, *The Plessy Case: A Legal-Historical Interpretation* (New York: Oxford University Press, 1987), 106; and in Brook Thomas, ed., *Plessy v. Ferguson, A Brief History with Documents* (New York: Bedford Books, 1997), 77.

3. [My emphasis]. "A Tourgee Disciple," clipping from unnamed Indianapolis newspaper, April 1, 1892, #6195, AWTP.

4. "Where are the Patriots?" *Chicago Times*, March 31, 1892, #6154, AWTP.

5. Monomania was a favorite epithet to hurl at abolitionists and antislavery reformers going back at least to the 1830s. It was a form of insanity that was characterized by obsession with a particular issue. Harris is quoted from the *Atlanta Constitution*, April 23, 1890. See also Tourgée, "A Bystander's Notes," *Chicago Daily Inter Ocean*, May 10, 1890, 4. On monomania, see John Stauffer, *The Black Hearts of Men: Radical Abolitionists and the Transformation of Race* (Cambridge: Harvard University Press, 2002), 43–44.

6. George Fredrickson has called Tourgée "the North's leading exponent of racial egalitarianism" and deemed his *An Appeal to Caesar* "the most profound discussion of the American racial situation to appear in the 1880s" in *The Black Image in the White Mind: The Debate on Afro-American Character and Destiny, 1817–1914* (Middletown, CT: Wesleyan University Press, 1971), 242–43. Similar estimations of him were made by contemporaries, including Ida B. Wells, in *Crusade for Justice:*

The Autobiography of Ida B. Wells, ed. Alfreda M. Duster (Chicago: University of Chicago Press, 1970), 120–21, 156; and Anna Julia Cooper, *A Voice from the South* (Xenia, OH: Aldine, 1892), 188.

7. AWT to J.C. Walker, March 1892, #6073; *Plessy v. Ferguson*, draft of oral arguments, A.W. Tourgee, #6472, AWTP.

8. Albion W. Tourgée, *An Appeal to Caesar* (New York: Fords, Howard & Hulbert, 1884), 357.

9. Albion W. Tourgée, "Brief of Plaintiff in Error," in *Landmark Briefs and Arguments of the Supreme Court of the United States: Constitutional Law*, ed. Philip B. Kurland and Gerhard Casper, vol. 13 (Washington, D.C.: University Publications of America, 1975), 19.

10. *Plessy v. Ferguson*, 163 U.S. 537 (1896), at 559.

11. An eccentric progressive Southerner and former slaveholder, Harlan has been described by a recent biographer as a "judicial enigma." Tinsley E. Yarbrough, *Judicial Enigma: The First Justice Harlan* (New York, 1995). On the elusive search for Harlan's original intention in using the phrase, see Liva Baker, "John Marshall Harlan I and a Color Blind Constitution: The Frankfurter-Harlan II Conversations," *Journal of Supreme Court History*, I (1992): 27–37. Also, Linda Przybyszewski, *The Republic According to John Marshall Harlan* (Chapel Hill: University of North Carolina Press, 1999).

12. Amy Elizabeth Ansell, *New Right, New Racism: Race and Reaction in the United States and Britain* (New York: New York University Press, 1997); Leslie G. Carr, *"Color-Blind" Racism* (Thousand Oaks, CA: Sage Publications, 1997); Eduardo Bonilla-Silva, "Color-Blind Racism: Toward an Analysis of White Racial Ideology," in *White Supremacy and Racism in the Post-Civil Rights Era* (Boulder: Lynne Rienner, 2001).

13. Albion W. Tourgée, "A Bystander's Notes," *Chicago Daily Inter Ocean*, June 10, 1893, 4.

14. [His emphasis]. Tourgée, "Brief of Plaintiff in Error," 8.

15. For the legal history of the property argument, see J. Allen Douglas, "The 'Most Valuable Sort of Property': Constructing White Identity in American Law, 1880–1940," *San Diego Law Review* 40 (2003): 881–946. For critiques of color-blindness from leading Critical Race Theorists, see Kimberle Williams Crenshaw, "Color Blindness, History, and the Law," in *The House that Race Built*, ed. Wahneema H. Lubiano (New York: Pantheon, 1997); Derrick A. Bell, "Color-Blind Constitutionalism: A Rediscovered Rationale," in *Race, Racism, and American Law*, 4th ed.; ed. Derrick A. Bell, et al. (Gaithersburg, MD: Aspen Law & Business, 2000); Neil Gotanda, "A Critique of 'Our Constitution Is Color-Blind'," in *Critical Race Theory: The Cutting Edge*, 2nd ed.; ed. Richard Delgado (Philadelphia: Temple University Press, 1999). Other probing critiques of racial color-blindness can be found in Anthony Appiah and Amy Gutman, *Color Conscious: The Political Morality of Race* (Princeton: Princeton University Press, 1996); Patricia J. Williams, *Seeing a Color-Blind Future: The Paradox of Race* (New York: Noonday Press, 1998); Michael K. Brown, et al., *Whitewashing Race: The Myth of a Color-Blind Society* (Berkeley: University of California Press, 2003); Peggy Pascoe, "Miscegenation Law, Court Cases, and Ideologies of 'Race' in Twentieth-Century America," *Journal of American History* 83 (June 1996): 44–69.

16. This book does not provide a comprehensive biography of Tourgée but examines his life as it relates to the history of color-blind citizenship and radical individualism. By far the most successful biography of him is Otto H. Olsen, *Carpetbagger's Crusade: The Life of Albion Winegar Tourgée* (Baltimore: Johns

Hopkins University Press, 1965), which is especially rich in its detailed contextualized analysis of Tourgée's North Carolina years. Tourgée's Reconstruction years also get extensive treatment in Richard Nelson Current, *Those Terrible Carpetbaggers: A Reinterpretation* (New York: Oxford University Press, 1988) and Deborah Patrice Hamlin, "'Friend of Freedom': Albion Winegar Tourgee and Reconstruction in North Carolina" (Ph.D. diss., Duke University, 2004). Earlier, much less successful biographies include Theodore Gross, *Albion W. Tourgée* (New York: Twayne Publishers, 1963) and Roy F. Dibble, *Albion W. Tourgée* (New York: Lemcke & Buechner, 1921). The most important, shorter treatments of Tourgée include: George M. Fredrickson, "The Travail of a Radical Republican: Albion W. Tourgée and Reconstruction," in *The Arrogance of Race: Historical Perspectives on Slavery, Racism, and Social Inequality* (Middletown, CT: Wesleyan University Press, 1988), 94–106; Edmund Wilson, "Novelists of the Post-war South," in *Patriotic Gore: Studies in the Literature of the American Civil War* (New York: W.W. Norton, 1962), 529–48; Russell B. Nye, "Judge Tourgée and Reconstruction," *Ohio State Archaeological and Historical Quarterly* 50 (1941): 101–14; George J. Becker, "Albion W. Tourgée: Pioneer in Social Criticism," *American Literature* 19 (March 1947): 59–72.

17. See Paul Goodman, *Of One Blood: Abolitionism and the Origins of Racial Equality* (Berkeley: University of California Press, 1998). However, some abolitionists struggled with their commitment to racial equality. See, for example, Lawrence Friedman, *Gregarious Saints: Self and Community in American Abolitionism, 1830–1870* (New York: Cambridge University Press, 1982), 160–95.

18. William Lloyd Garrison, *Thoughts on African Colonization: Or an impartial Exhibition of the Doctrines, Principles, and Purposes of the American Colonization Society* (Boston: Garrison and Knapp, 1832), 145.

19. Of course, without the concept of race there is no concept of racial equality. Because theories of race were not fully articulated until the mid-1700s and only began to achieve popularity in the United States in the early 1800s, the egalitarian responses to them do not become prominent until the 1830s. Interestingly, most of the early racial egalitarian responses do not challenge the objective category of race itself. For the origins and growth of the concept of race, see Winthrop Jordan, *White Over Black: American Attitudes Toward the Negro, 1550–1812* (Chapel Hill: University of North Carolina Press, 1968); Thomas Gosset, *Race: The History of An Idea in America*, New Edition (New York: Oxford University Press, 1997); Fredrickson, *Black Image*.

20. Douglas M. Strong, *Perfectionist Politics: Abolitionism and the Religious Tensions of American Democracy* (Syracuse, NY: Syracuse University Press, 1999); Straughton Lynd emphasizes the influence of Quakerism on the abolitionists' individualist creed in *Intellectual Origins of American Radicalism* (New York: Pantheon, 1968), 100–129; see John Ashworth's insightful discussion of abolitionism, individualism, and the family in *Slavery, Capitalism, and Politics in the Antebellum Republic*, vol. 1, *Commerce and Compromise, 1820–1850* (New York: Cambridge University Press, 1995), 168–91. Another important perspective on individualism in abolitionism can be found in Stauffer, *Black Hearts of Men*, 1–7, 16–17. For the classic discussion of anarchism in abolitionist thought, see Lewis Perry, *Radical Abolitionism: Anarchy and the Government of God in Antislavery Thought* (Knoxville: University of Tennessee Press, 1973).

21. [Her emphasis]. E.D.E.N. Southworth, *The Deserted Wife* (Philadelphia: T.B. Peterson, 1855), 229. Quoted in Susan K. Harris, "'But is it any good?': Evaluating Nineteenth-Century American Women's Fiction," *American Literature* 6 (March 1991): 55.

22. For the abolitionists' argument for tolerance, see David A.J. Richards, *Conscience and the Constitution: History, Theory, and Law of the Reconstruction Amendments* (Princeton: Princeton University Press, 1993).

23. Albion W. Tourgée, "Christian Citizenship," *The Golden Rule* 7 (August, 1892). Tourgée most fully articulated his theory of citizenship in Albion W. Tourgée, *Letters to a King* (New York: Phillips and Hunt, 1888).

24. Wendell Phillips, "William Lloyd Garrison," quoted in James Brewer Stewart, *Wendell Phillips: Liberty's Hero* (Baton Rouge: Louisiana State University Press, 1986), 318.

25. Tourgée, *Is Liberty Worth Preserving?*, 18–19.

26. My definition of individualism follows in the path of political scientists who have identified a number of competing traditions in American liberal thought. See, for instance, Barry Alan Shain, *The Myth of American Individualism: The Protestant Origins of American Political Thought* (Princeton: Princeton University Press, 1994); Rogers M. Smith, "Beyond Tocqueville, Myrdal, and Hartz: The Multiple Traditions in America," *American Political Science Review* 87 (September 1993): 549–65; and Rogers M. Smith, *Civic Ideals: Conflicting Ideals of Citizenship in U.S. History* (New Haven: Yale University Press, 1997); Richard O. Curry and Lawrence B. Goodheart, eds., *American Chameleon: Individualism in Trans-National Context* (Kent, OH: Kent State University Press, 1991).

27. Alexis de Tocqueville, *Democracy in America*, ed. J.P. Mayer; trans. George Lawrence (Garden City, NY: Doubleday, 1969), 506–7. Orig. published 1840.

28. Important books on this cultural shift include, George M. Fredrickson, *The Inner Civil War: Northern Intellectuals and the Crisis of the Union* (New York: Harper & Row, 1965); T.J. Jackson Lears, *No Place of Grace: Antimodernism and the Transformation of American Culture, 1880–1920* (New York: Pantheon, 1981); Julie Reuben, *The Making of the Modern University: Intellectual Transformation and the Marginalization of Morality* (Chicago: University of Chicago Press, 1996); Louis Menand, *The Metaphysical Club: A Story of Ideas in America* (New York: Farrar, Straus and Giroux, 2001).

29. Senator John T. Morgan, "Shall Negro Minorities Rule?" *The Forum* 6 (February 1890): 588.

30. John W. Burgess, *Reconstruction and the Constitution* (New York: Charles Scribners and Sons, 1902), 133. On the racist underpinnings of Reconstruction historiography at this time, see W.E.B. Du Bois, *Black Reconstruction in America, 1860–1880* (New York: Harcourt, Brace, ca. 1935), 718–19.

31. On the political and ideological dimensions of the struggle over the memory of the Civil War, see Alice Fahs and Joan Waugh, eds., *The Memory of the Civil War in American Culture* (Chapel Hill: University of North Carolina Press, 2004); David W. Blight, *Race and Reunion: The Civil War in American Memory* (Cambridge: Harvard University Press, 2001); David W. Blight, *Beyond the Battlefield: Race, Memory, and the American Civil War* (Amherst: University of Massachusetts Press, 2002); Nina Silber, *The Romance of Reunion: Northerners and the South, 1865–1900* (Chapel Hill: University of North Carolina Press, 1993); Michael Kammen, *Mystic Chords of Memory: The Transformation of Tradition in American Culture* (New York: Vintage, 1991), 109–31; Paul Buck, *The Road to Reunion, 1865–1900* (Boston: Little, Brown, 1937).

32. Hundreds of letters that he received in the 1880s and 1890s, from blacks and whites alike, will be discussed in more detail later. John S. Crum to AWT, Aug. 1, 1892, #6434; B.J. Dyer to AWT, May 29, 1892, #6283, AWTP.

33. Du Bois quoted Tourgée prominently in his 1910 paper at the American Historical Association Annual Meeting that was the original germ of his book. See

W.E.B. Du Bois, "Reconstruction and Its Benefits," *American Historical Review* 15 (July 1910): 796; and *Black Reconstruction in America*, 621.

34. On the Niagara Movement's honoring of Tourgée, see "Our Monthly Review," *The Voice of the Negro* 3 (January 1906): 19; "Our Monthly Review," *The Voice of the Negro* 3 (July 1906): 455.

Chapter 1: Judge Tourgée and the Radical Civil War

1. AWT to E.H. Johnson, May 15, 1902, 1, #9691, AWTP; epigraph quoted from W.E.B. Du Bois, *Black Reconstruction in America, 1860–1880* (New York: Harcourt, Brace, ca. 1935), 83.

2. Thomas Dixon, Jr., *The Leopard's Spots: A Romance of the White Man's Burden, 1865–1900* (New York: Doubleday, Page, 1902), see "Historical Note" on unnumbered page prior to title page; AWT to E.H. Johnson, May 15, 1902, 1, #9691, AWTP.

3. Thomas Dixon, Jr., to AWT, Feb. 25, 1888, #3368, AWTP.

4. When Dixon published an article on the Ku Klux Klan that was full of factual misinformation about the recently deceased Tourgée, Emma Tourgée demanded that he publicly correct his mistakes. Dixon, showing his disdain for factual accuracy, dismissed her complaints as "mere womanly quibbles." See EKT to Thomas Dixon, Jr., February 24, 1906, #9966; Thomas Dixon, Jr., to EKT, March 4, 1906, #9982, AWTP; Thomas Dixon, "The Story of Ku Klux Klan: Some of Its Leaders, Living and Dead," *Metropolitan Magazine* 22 (September 1905), 657–69.

5. E.H. Johnson to AWT, May 1, 1902, #9690, AWTP.

6. Dixon, *The Leopard's Spots*, 387. The sexual hysteria that infused the politics of Reconstruction in the South are detailed in Martha Hodes, *White Women, Black Men: Illicit Sex in the Nineteenth-Century South* (New Haven: Yale University Press, 1997); Leon F. Litwack, *Trouble in Mind: Black Southerners in the Age of Jim Crow* (New York: Alfred A. Knopf, 1998).

7. Dixon, *The Leopard's Spots*, 114–15.

8. AWT to E.H. Johnson, May 15, 1902, 1, #9691, AWTP.

9. Prof. E.H. Johnson, " 'The Leopard's Spots' and 'The Fool's Errand'," *The Watchman*, April 24, 1902, clipping, #9690, AWTP; similarly, the review of Dixon's *The Clansmen*, in *New York Times Book Review*, three years later claimed of its likeness to *A Fool's Errand*, "Their only essential difference is in their estimate of the black man's character and behavior. Undiscriminating condemnation of 'The Clansmen' condemns 'A Fool's Errand.'" Stephanson Browne, "The Clansmen," *New York Times Book Review*, February 11, 1905; E.H. Johnson happily embraced the term *mugwump* to describe his own politics in E.H. Johnson to AWT, August, 19, 1887, #2797, AWTP.

10. AWT to E.H. Johnson, May 15, 1902, 2, 5, 31, 35, #9691, AWTP.

11. Ibid., 4–5.

12. Ibid., 10, 11.

13. Ibid., 5–6.

14. Ibid., 3–5, 34. AWTP; Otto H. Olsen, *Carpetbagger's Crusade: The Life of Albion Winegar Tourgee* (Baltimore: Johns Hopkins University Press, 1965), 338.

15. AWT to E.H. Johnson, May 15, 1902, 35, #9691, AWTP.

16. Michael Rogin, " 'The Sword Became a Flashing Vision': D.W. Griffith's *The Birth of a Nation*," in Robert Land, ed., *The Birth of a Nation: D.W. Griffith,*

Director (New Brunswick, NJ: Rutgers University Press, 1994), 276–86; Thomas Dixon, Jr., "Southern Horizons: The Autobiography of Thomas Dixon. A Critical Edition," Karen M. Crowe, ed. (Ph.D. diss., New York University, 1982).

17. [My emphasis]. *Rochester Herald*, May 23, 1905. *Chicago Inter Ocean*, May[?] 1905, clippings, #9907, AWTP.

18. *Brooklyn Daily Eagle*, May 22, 1905, clipping, item #9907, AWTP.

19. Andrew Joyner, "The Real Hero of 'A Fool's Errand.' Albion Tourgee's Life in North Carolina: A Brave and True Man," *Raleigh Daily News and Observer*, May 28, 1905; Joyner's article was also reprinted as "Judge Albion W. Tourgee, Stormy Petrel of Stirring Period of Reconstruction," *Atlanta Constitution*, May 29, 1905.

20. Ibid.

21. Frank Nash, "Albion Winegar Tourgee," in *Biographical History of North Carolina: From Colonial Times to the Present*, ed. Samuel Ashe (Greensboro, NC: Charles L. Van Noppen, 1906); 443–45.

22. *Brooklyn Daily Eagle*, May 22, 1905, clipping, item #9907, AWTP.

23. Nothing was more indicative of Washington's capitulation to white supremacy than his utter repudiation of Reconstruction in "Chapter V. The Reconstruction Period," *Up From Slavery: An Autobiography* (New York: Doubleday, 1901). On white reformers and race, see Leslie H. Fishel, Jr., "The 'Negro Question' at Mohonk: Microcosm, Mirage, and Message," *New York History* (July 1993): 277–314.

24. The historiographical controversy is usually described as a divide between the "revisionists," who emphasize the fundamentally revolutionary nature of Reconstruction, and the "post-revisionists," who insist upon its relative conservatism. Eric Foner provides the definitive revisionist statement in *Reconstruction, 1863–1877: America's Unfinished Revolution* (New York: Harper & Row, 1988). Amy Dru Stanley underplays the importance of radicalism and asserts the conservative ideal of "contract" as the paradigm for Reconstruction in *From Bondage to Contract: Wage Labor, Marriage, and the Market in the Age of Slave Emancipation* (New York: Cambridge University Press, 1998). For classic works of the "post-revisionist" school see Herman Belz, *Abraham Lincoln, Constitutionalism, and Equal Rights in the Civil War Era* (New York: Fordham University Press, 1998); and Michael Les Benedict, *A Compromise of Principle: Congressional Republicans and Reconstruction, 1863–1869* (New York, 1974).

25. Du Bois, *Black Reconstruction*, 319–20.

26. *Reconstruction*, illustrated by Horatio Bateman, engraved by J.T. Giles (New York: Printed by Francis Ratellier, 1867), HL and NYHS; H. Bateman, *Explanation of Bateman's National Picture of Reconstruction, Together with the Declaration of Independence and the Constitution of the United States* (New York: Blackwell, Printer, 45 Cortlandt Street, 1867), quotations taken from unnumbered pages [1], [3], front matter, NYHS; for a brief analysis of Bateman's illustration, see Berbard F. Reilly, *American Political Prints, 1766–1876: A Catalogue of the Collections in the Library of Congress* (Boston: G.K. Hall, 1991), 573; Bateman eventually published a full-length historical reference book that told the history of the United States through biographies of all of the men appearing in his illustration. Horatio Bateman, *Biographies of Two Hundred and Fifty Distinguished Men*, 1st ed., vol. 1 (New York: John T. Giles, 1871).

27. [His emphasis]. Explanation of Bateman's National Picture, 2.

28. [His emphasis]. Ibid, 2 and unnumbered front matter [1].

29. [His emphasis]. Ibid, 2.

30. [His emphasis]. Ibid.

31. Ibid.

32. Daniel T. Rodgers pointed out two decades ago that "The higher law deserves more than its current footnote status in the history of antislavery thought," in Daniel T. Rodgers, *Contested Truths: Keywords in American Politics since Independence* (Cambridge: Harvard University Press, 1987), 135. Few studies of abolitionism have followed up on Rodgers's call. Two exceptions are Albert J. Von Frank, *The Trials of Anthony Burns: Freedom and Slavery in Emerson's Boston.* (Cambridge: Harvard University Press, 1998); and Greg Crane, *Race, Citizenship, and the Law in American Literature* (Cambridge: Cambridge University Press, 2002).

33. Charles Sumner, "Equality before the Law: Unconstitutionality of Separate Schools in Massachusetts" in George F. Hoar, ed., *Charles Sumner: His Complete Works*, vol. 2 (Boston: Lee and Shepard, 1900), 99–100.

34. Anne-Marie Taylor, *Young Charles Sumner and the Legacy of the American Enlightenment, 1811–1851* (Amherst: University of Massachusetts Press, 2001).

35. Eric Foner's discussion of Radical Republicanism, for instance, says nothing about the religious dimensions of their philosophy in *Reconstruction*, 228–39. One exception to this trend is Victor B. Howard, *Religion and the Radical Republican Movement, 1860–1870* (Lexington: University Press of Kentucky, 1990). Lincoln's Second Inaugural Address and Julia Ward Howe's "Battle Hymn of the Republic" are two famous instances of the war being imbued with a religious and antislavery meaning.

36. Foner, *Reconstruction*, 512–34; William Gillette, *Retreat from Reconstruction, 1869–1879* (Baton Rouge: Louisiana State University Press, 1979).

37. Andrew Johnson quoted in Du Bois, *Black Reconstruction*, 283.

38. Schenk quoted in Paul Moreno, "Racial Classifications and Reconstruction Legislation," *Journal of Southern History* 61 (May 1995): 274–76. On Andrew Johnson's attacks on the Civil Rights and Freedmen's Bureau Bills, see Foner, *Reconstruction*, 243–51.

39. Phillips, quoted in Kull, *Color-Blind Constitution*, 62–63. See also Richard Kluger, *Simple Justice: The History of Brown v. Board of Education and Black America's Struggle for Equality* (New York, 1975), 625–36; William E. Nelson, *The Fourteenth Amendment: From Political Principle to Judicial Doctrine* (Cambridge: Harvard University Press, 1988).

40. *Greensboro Patriot*, September 2, 1869.

41. *Testimony Taken by the Joint Select Committee to Inquire into the Condition of Affairs in the Late Insurrectionary States: North Carolina* (Washington, D.C.: Government Printing Office, 1872), 335.

42. AWT to D.W. Hodgin, March 21, 1868, #1239–57, AWTP.

43. "Can Any Good Thing Come Out of Radicalism?" clipping in Tourgée scrapbook with items of 1873, #2428, AWTP.

44. First quotation, scrapbook item, #2428, AWTP; second quotation from *Greensboro Patriot* quoted in Olsen, *Carpetbagger's Crusade*, 146; third quotation from James McCleery to AWT, May 24, 1869, #1472–78, AWTP.

45. AWT to Editor, January 28, 1870, *North Carolina Standard*, North Carolina Collection, UNC.

46. Ibid.

47. AWT to EKT, June 9, 1869, #1131 AWTP.

48. Nash, "Albion Winegar Tourgee," 444–45; Olsen, *Carpetbagger's Crusade*, 150–55; Current, *Those Terrible Carpetbaggers*, 201–2.

49. A white Southerner, Strayhorn also mentioned interestingly in this letter, "I enjoyed your books immensely, only that sometimes 'between the lines' I would be living over again that sad, sad past it so truly painted; and no one who lived with you

through those dark days of 1869–70, when to be Republican was to be outlawed from society and sometimes from existence itself, can ever revisit those days without extreme sadness." Ike Strayhorn to AWT, June 22, 1887, #2742, AWTP; Olsen, *Carpetbagger's Crusade*, 152.

50. "Many Persons" to AWT, no date [1872], #1574; another threatening note written in a similar style with similar complaints came from "Many Citizens" to AWT, March 23, 1872, #1613, AWTP.

51. *Greensboro Patriot, Extra*, August 1, 1870, North Carolina Collection, UNC.

52. Tourgée irritated Judge Caldwell of the North Carolina Supreme Court with his repeated petitions on this matter; see Judge Caldwell to AWT, Sept., 16, 1873, #1702, AWTP; Current, *Those Terrible Carpetbaggers*, 202; Olsen, *Carpetbagger's Crusade*, 187.

53. Olsen, *Carpetbagger's Crusade*, 152; Ike R. Strayhorn to Tourgee, June 22, 1887; AWT to EKT, May 16, 1869, #1110, AWTP.

54. AWT to unknown, 1870, #1475–46, AWTP.

55. For a dim view of the education of freedpeople, see Saidiya Hartman, *Scenes of Subjection: Terror, Slavery, and Self-Making in Nineteenth-Century America* (New York: Oxford University Press, 1997); works that discuss the mixture of conservatism and egalitarianism in the education of freedpeople include: Robert C. Morris, *Reading, 'Riting, and Reconstruction: The Education of Freedmen in the South, 1861–1870* (Chicago: University of Chicago Press, 1981); Joe M. Richardson, *Christian Reconstruction: The American Missionary Association and Southern Blacks, 1861–1890* (Athens: University of Georgia Press, 1986); Foner, *Reconstruction*, 96–102; Ronald Butchart, *Northern Schools, Southern Blacks, and Reconstruction: Education, 1862–1875* (Westport, CT: Greenwood Press, 1980); a work that focuses on the antiracist strains of the Yankee schoolmarm's ideology is Jacqueline Jones, *Soldiers of Light and Love: Northern Teachers and Georgia Blacks, 1865–1873* (Chapel Hill: UNC Press, 1980).

56. First quotation, Albion W. Tourgée, *An Appeal to Caesar* (New York: Fords, Howard, & Hulbert, 1884), 365; second quotation, Albion W. Tourgée, *Is Liberty Worth Preserving?* (Chicago: Inter Ocean, 1892), 15, Daniel A.P. Murray Pamphlet Collection, LC.

57. Testimonial for Albion W. Tourgée's lecture series, #2101, AWTP.

58. "The Ben Adhemite Era," Speech, 1876–7[?], Item #2115, AWTP. It is ironic that the poem that inspired Tourgée's lecture on Christian democratic ethics, James Leigh Hunt's "Abou Ben Adhem" (1838), was about a mystic Muslim saint. In Hunt's poem, Ben Adhem wins God's love by choosing to love his fellow men rather than professing his love for God. Tourgée was so influenced by the poem that he chose his own epitaph from it. When Ben Adhem is told in the poem that he is not counted among those who love God, he replies, "I pray thee then, write me as one who loves his fellow men." These words appear on Tourgée's gravestone monument in the public cemetery of Mayville, New York.

59. "A Lady Lawyer," *Current Thought*, Chicago, IL, (Feb. 1878), and Tourgée to Miss Ellen A. Martin, July 6, 1886, #2523, AWTP; Kelley Harris, "Tabitha Anne Holton: First in North Carolina, First in the South," Women's Legal History Biography Project, Robert Crown Law Library, Stanford Law School, 2002, 16–20. Website: www.law.stanford.edu/library/wlhbp/profiles/HoltonTabitha.html

60. *Current Thought*; Tourgée to Miss Ellen A. Martin, July 6, 1886, #2523, AWTP; Kelley Harris, "Tabitha Anne Holton," 26–28.

61. "A Lady Lawyer," *Current Thought* (Feb. 1878), clipping with AWT to Miss Ellen A. Martin, July 6, 1886, #2523, AWTP.

62. AWT to E.H. Johnson, May 15, 1902, 36–37, #9691, AWTP.

Chapter 2: The Making of a Radical Individualist in Ohio's Western Reserve

1. Albion W. Tourgée, *A Memorial of Frederick Douglass from the City of Boston* (Boston: Printed by the order of the City Council, 1896), SCBC; "Revere the Man: Frederick Douglass Lives in the Memory. . . . Eulogy Delivered by Hon. Albion W Tourgée," *Boston Herald*, Dec. 21, 1895; first epigraph quoted from Henry David Thoreau, "Resistance to Civil Government," in *The American Intellectual Tradition: A Sourcebook*, vol. 1, *1630–1865*, 4th ed., David A. Hollinger and Charles Capper, eds. (New York: University Press, 2001), 405, 409; second epigraph quoted from *The Complete Essays and Other Writings of Ralph Waldo Emerson*, Brooks Atkinson, ed. (New York: Random House, 1940), 148.

2. Tourgée, *A Memorial*, 32.

3. For instance, William Lloyd Garrison's son introduced Tourgée to one Boston audience in April 1894, "Duty and Destiny," #7635. For more comparisons of Tourgée with Garrison, see W.E. Turner to AWT, June 8, 1892, #6214; Alexander S. Jackson to AWT, Nov. 13, 1891, #5788, AWTP.

4. Challenging the traditional version of Truth's speech, Nell Painter has suggested that the hostility of the crowd may have been exaggerated in later retellings, Nell Painter, *Sojourner Truth: A Life, A Symbol* (New York: W.W. Norton, 1996); 121–31, 164–69; Tourgée, *A Memorial*, 30.

5. Tourgée, *A Memorial*, 30–31.

6. Ibid.

7. William Lloyd Garrison recounts how he and Frederick Douglass were heckled, threatened, and pelted with rotten eggs in Western Pennsylvania as late as 1847. William E. Cain, ed., *William Lloyd Garrison and the Fight against Slavery: Selections from The Liberator* (New York: St. Martin's, 1995), 118–20.

8. "Frederick Douglass—Western Reserve College," *Frederick Douglass's Paper*, August 4, 1854, UR.

9. *Frederick Douglass's Paper*, August 11, 1854, UR.

10. Parker Pillsbury, *Acts of the Antislavery Apostles* (Rochester, NY: Clague, Wegman, Schlicht, 1883; Reprint, New York: Negro Universities Press, 1969).

11. The audience Tourgée addressed, according to the *Boston Herald*, was, in fact, predominantly black. Nevertheless, Tourgée's speech was clearly written with the expectation that he would be addressing an audience of largely white, former abolitionists. It is indicative of the cultural climate of the 1890s, perhaps, that so few whites attended the ceremony. *Herald*, December 21, 1895.

12. Tourgée, *A Memorial*, 36, 53.

13. Tourgée, *A Memorial*, 52–53, 61.

14. Alfred Mathews, *Ohio and Her Western Reserve* (New York: D. Appleton, 1902), xix; Harlan Hatcher, *The Western Reserve* (New York: Bobbs-Merrill, 1949), 14–15.

15. Douglass Hurt, *The Ohio Frontier: Crucible of the Old Northwest, 1720–1830* (Bloomington: Indiana University Press, 1996), 287; Traci A Hodgson, "Egalitarian Transformations: Gender, Religious Culture and Family Government on the Western Reserve of Ohio, 1800–1820" (Ph.D. diss., Boston University, 1997), 141–48; Nathan O. Hatch, *The Democratization of American Christianity* (New Haven: Yale University Press, 1989).

16. Eric Foner, *Free Soil, Free Labor, Free Men: The Ideology of the Republican Party before the Civil War* (New York: Oxford University Press, 1970), 108–9.

17. Albion W. Tourgée, "Nellie Wade Colfax and the Western Reserve," manuscript draft, 1868, #966, AWTP.

18. Hatcher, *The Western Reserve*, 285–89.

19. Albion's father, Valentine, Jr., lived from Oct. 21, 1813, to April 26, 1889. Tourgée's grandfather, Valentine Tourjee [Tourgée], Sr., lived from Feb. 14, 1773, to Aug. 5, 1850. Rebekah Tourjee [Tourgée], his grandmother, lived from Jan. 10, 1773, to Oct. 16, 1870. Both died in the Western Reserve, having followed their sons in the West sometime later, #9735, AWTP.

20. Valentine Tourgée to "Sister" [Sophronia Winegar?], May 19, 1856, #35, AWTP.

21. Roy Dibble, *Albion W. Tourgée* (New York, Lemcke & Buechner, 1921), 1–4.

22. Otto H. Olsen, *Carpetbagger's Crusade: The Life of Albion Winegar Tourgée* (Baltimore: Johns Hopkins University Press, 1965), 2.

23. Louisa Tourgée to Jacob Winegar, Oct. 6, 1841, #16, AWTP. John Brown, grandson of Valentine Sr., and Rebekah Tourgée, born June 15, 1816, died Aug. 13, 1840; and Cyrus Williams Tourjee [Tourgée], born Aug. 21, 1800, died Oct. 4, 1840, #9735, AWTP.

24. Valentine Tourgée to "Sister" [Sophronia Winegar?], May 15, 1843, #26, AWTP.

25. Olsen, *Crusade*, 3.

26. Valentine Tourgee to "Sister" [Sophronia Winegar?], June 4, 1848, #32, AWTP.

27. Quoted words from Hurt, *Ohio Frontier*, 287; Dibble, *Tourgée*, 15.

28. Valentine Tourgée to Sophronia Winegar, Sept. 19, 1847, #31, AWTP.

29. Dibble, *Tourgée*, 15.

30. Ibid.

31. Jacob Winegar to Valentine Tourgée, April 14, 1852, KSU.

32. Dibble, *Tourgée*, 14–15; Albion W. Tourgée, *An Outing with the Queen of Hearts* (Cambridge: John Wilson, 1894), 1–20.

33. AWT to Valentine Tourgée, April 14, May 7, 8, 1852, KSU.

34. Valentine Tourgée to "Sister" [Sophronia Winegar?], May 15, 1843, #26, AWT to EKT, August 14, 1859, #83, AWTP.

35. Dibble, *Tourgée*, 19.

36. Jacob Winegar and AWT to Valentine Tourgee, April 14, May 7, 8, 1852, from Lee, Mass. KSU.

37. Valentine Tourgée to "Sister" [Sophronia Winegar?], May 19, 1856, #35, AWTP.

38. AWT, "To the people of Kingsville and Vicinity," clipping, #8902, AWTP.

39. Ibid.

40. AWT to EKT, May 29, 1860, #126, AWTP.

41. In particular, Ashtabula County has been called "the political Gibraltar of Western abolitionists," Mathews, *Ohio*, 175, 180.

42. AWT to EKT, Feb. 4, 1860, #139, AWTP.

43. AWT to M. Coleman, Esq., February 4, 1868, #765, AWTP.

44. AWT to EKT, Nov. 4, 1860, #215, AWTP.

45. Albion W. Tourgée, *Hot Plowshares: A Novel* (New York: Fords, Howard, & Hulbert, 1882), 297–98.

46. "Preface" to Tourgée, *Hot Plowshares*, pages unnumbered.

47. Tourgée, *Hot Plowshares*, 70, 74.

48. Stephen E. Maizlish, *The Triumph of Sectionalism: The Transformation of Ohio Politics, 1844–1856* (Kent, OH: Kent State University Press, 1983), xii.

49. Frank U. Quillin, 1913; Reprint, *The Color Line in Ohio: A History of Race Prejudice in a Typical Northern State* (New York: Negro Universities Press, 1969), 22–24.

50. Douglas M. Strong, *Perfectionist Politics: Abolitionism and the Religious Tensions of American Democracy* (Syracuse, NY: Syracuse University Press, 1999), 35–37; Stanley M. Elkins, *Slavery: A Problem in American Institutional and Intellectual Life* (Chicago: University of Chicago Press, 1959), 181–83.

51. *Cleveland Leader*, Sept. 10, 1858, quoted in Cochran, 119.

52. Strong, *Perfectionist Politics*, 35–37; Hodgson, "Egalitarian Transformations," 261–64.

53. Paul Finkleman has shown that substantial gains against racial discrimination were being made in the north on the eve of the Civil War. Finkleman, "Rehearsal for Reconstruction: Antebellum Origins of the Fourteenth Amendment," in *The Facts of Reconstruction: Essays in Honor of John Hope Franklin*, ed. Eric Anderson and Alfred A. Moss, Jr. (Baton Rouge: Louisiana State University Press, 1991), 2, 22; Finkleman's work challenges Leon Litwack's 1961 claim that "change did not seem imminent" in Northern race relations during the antebellum period. Litwack, *North of Slavery: The Negro in the Free States, 1790–1860* (Chicago: University of Chicago Press, 1961), 279.

54. James Brewer Stewart, *Joshua R. Giddings and the Tactics of Radical Politics* (Cleveland: Case Western Reserve University Press, 1970); Hans Trefousse, *Benjamin Franklin Wade: Radical Republican from Ohio* (New York: Alfred A. Knopf, 1963).

55. "Nellie Wade Colfax and the Western Reserve," 1868, #966, AWTP.

56. See Peter Walker, *Moral Choices: Memory, Desire, and Imagination in Nineteenth-Century American Abolition* (Baton Rouge: Louisiana State University Press, 1978).

57. Tourgée, *Hot Plowshares*, 69.

58. Rodney D. Olsen, *Dancing in Chains: The Youth of William Dean Howells* (New York: New York University Press, 1991), 68–71.

59. Albion W. Tourgée, *The Story of a Thousand: Being a History of the Service of the 105th Ohio Volunteer Infantry, in the War for the Union from August 21, 1862 to June 6, 1865* (Buffalo, NY: S. McGerald, 1896), 31; for an excellent discussion of conscience and abolitionism, see John Ashworth, *Slavery, Capitalism, and Politics in the Antebellum Republic*, vol. 1, *Commerce and Compromise, 1820–1850* (Cambridge: Cambridge University Press, 1995), 168–91.

60. Trefousse, *Wade*, 36–37.

61. Vincent Harding, *There Is a River: The Black Struggle for Freedom in America* (New York: Harcourt Brace, 1981), 154–71.

62. See Foner, 109; David A. Gerber, *Black Ohio and the Color Line, 1860–1915* (Urbana: University of Illinois Press, 1976), 12–13; Eugene H. Rosenboom, *The History of the State of Ohio*, vol. 4, *The Civil War Era, 1850–1873* (Columbus: Ohio State Archaeological and Historical Society, 1944).

63. David S. Reynolds, *John Brown, Abolitionist: The Man Who Killed Slavery, Sparked the Civil War, and Seeded Civil Rights* (New York: Alfred A. Knopf, 2005), 60–61.

64. Tourgée, *Story of a Thousand*, 31; William C. Cochran, *Publication No. 101: The Western Reserve and the Fugitive Slave Law: A Prelude to Civil War* (Cleveland: Western Reserve Historical Society, 1920), 118–20.

65. *Ashtabula Weekly Telegraph*, July 15, 1854, WRHS.

66. Tourgée, *Story of a Thousand*, 34.

67. Cochran, 128–29; Nat Brandt, *The Town That Started the Civil War* (Syracuse, NY: Syracuse University Press, 1990).

68. *Cleveland Leader*, Sept. 10, 1858, quoted in Cochran, *Western* Reserve, 119.

69. Warren Gutherie, "The Oberlin–Wellington Rescue Case, 1859," in *Antislavery and Disunion, 1858–1861*, ed. J. Jeffrey Aver (New York: Harper and Row, 1963), 87.

70. Ibid. On Chase, see Mark S. Weiner, *Black Trials: Citizenship from the Beginnings of Slavery to the End of Caste* (New York: Vintage Books, 2004), 142–52.

71. Quoted in Cochran, *Western Reserve*, 146.

72. Quoted in Brandt, *The Town*, 154–55.

73. *Cleveland Leader*, Oct. 29, 1858 [emphasis in original], quoted in Cochran, *Western Reserve*, 134.

74. Ibid.

75. Cochran, *Western Reserve*, 141.

76. Gutherie, "Oberlin—Wellington," 91; Cochran, *Western Reserve*, 148.

77. Quoted in Brandt, *The Town*, 205.

78. Quoted in Cochran, *Western Reserve*, 174.

79. *Ashtabula Weekly Telegraph*, April 30, 1859, WRHS.

80. William Cooper Howells, "To the Voters of Ashtabula County," *Ashtabula Sentinel*, Sept. 19, 1861, WRHS.

81. Quoted in Cochran, *Western Reserve*, 179.

82. Quoted from Reynolds, *John Brown*, 354.

83. See "Salmon P. Chase: the Constitution and the Slave Power," chap. 3, in Foner, *Free Soil, Free Labor, Free Men*, 73–102.

84. Albion W. Tourgée, "Brief of Plaintiff in Error," in Philip B. Kurland and Gerhard Casper, eds., *Landmark Briefs and Arguments of the Supreme Court of the United States: Constitutional Law*, vol. 13 (Arlington, VA: University Publications, 1975), 12, 34–35.

85. AWT to EKT, May 8, 1859, #73, AWTP.

86. Ibid. His emphasis.

87. AWT to EKT, June 9, 1859, #74, AWTP.

88. Ashworth, *Slavery, Capitalism*, 181–85.

89. Quoted from Kenneth S. Lynn, *William Dean Howells: An American Life* (New York: Harcourt Brace Jovanovich, 1971), 68. Howells was born in Ohio in 1837 and spent most of his childhood in Ashtabula County.

90. Olsen, *Carpetbagger's Crusade*, 7; AWT to EKT, Jan. 15, 1860, #133, AWTP.

91. Olsen, *Carpetbagger's Crusade*, 6–7; Dibble, *Tourgée*, 16–17.

92. EKT to AWT, March 1, 1858, #45, AWTP.

93. Ibid., and EKT to AWT, March 31, 1858, #46, EKT to AWT, Oct. 29, 1858, #51, AWTP.

94. EKT to AWT, March 1, 1858, #45, EKT to AWT, Oct. 18, 1859, #104, AWTP.

95. Ned Kilbourne to EKT, Jan. 31, 1859, #54, AWTP.

96. EKT to AWT, March 1859, #56; EKT to AWT, August 24, 1859, #86, AWTP.

97. His emphasis. AWT to EKT, March 8, 1859, #57, AWTP.

98. EKT to AWT, March 1859, #56, AWTP.

99. EKT to AWT, August 24, 1859, #86, AWTP. For a conflicting interpretation of Emma's and Albion's relationship, see Ruth Currie McDaniel, "Courtship and Marriage in the Nineteenth Century: Albion and Emma Tourgée, a Case Study," *North Carolina Historical Review* 61 (July 1984): 287–88.

100. EKT to AWT, Oct. 18, 1859, #104, AWTP.

101. [Her emphasis]. EKT to AWT, April 4, 1861, #266, AWTP.

102. William Leach, *True Love and Perfect Union: The Feminist Reform of Sex and Society* (New York: Basic Books, Inc., 1980); Chris Dixon, *Perfecting the Family: Antislavery Marriages in Nineteenth-Century America* (Amherst: University of Massachusetts Press, 1997).

103. [His emphases]. AWT to EKT, Nov. 12, 1859, #114, AWTP.

104. AWT to EKT, Aug., 1859, #87, 1859, AWTP.

105. EKT to AWT, Sept. 14, 1859, #97, EKT to AWT, Jan. 4, 1861 #239, AWTP.

106. AWT to EKT, Sept. 24, 1859, #97, AWTP.

107. He made this reasoning clear somewhat later, AWT to EKT, Jan. 15, 1860, #133, AWTP.

108. AWT to EKT, May 11, 1859, #73, AWTP.

109. AWT to EKT, June 9, 1959, #74, AWTP.

110. AWT to EKT, Aug. 7 1859, #81, AWT to EKT, Nov. 26, 1859, #129, AWTP; a few amusing stories of Tourgée's financial hardships, and his attempts to overcome them, while at Rochester can be found in "One of the Foolish: Some Anecdotes about Albion W. Tourgee: Friend of the Negro . . ." Undated newspaper clipping, Alumni File, UR.

111. Paul Johnson, *A Shopkeeper's Millennium: Society and Revival in Rochester, New York, 1815–1837* (New York: Hill and Wang, 1978).

112. AWT to EKT, April 15, 1860, #160, AWTP.

113. AWT to EKT, Feb. 4, 1860, #139, AWTP.

114. AWT to EKT, Oct. 2, 1859, #99, AWTP.

115. AWT to EKT, July 25, 1859, #80, AWTP.

116. AWT to EKT, Feb. 19, 1860, #146, March 18, 1860, #156, AWTP.

117. AWT to EKT, Oct. 2, 1859, #99, AWTP.

118. AWT to EKT, Feb. 4, 1860, #139, AWT to EKT, Oct. 28, 1860, #212, AWTP.

119. EKT to AWT, Oct. 6, 1860, #206, AWTP.

120. Ned Kilbourne to EKT, Jan. 1, 1860, #129, AWTP.

121. AWT to EKT, Feb. 4, 1860, #139, AWTP.

122. AWT to EKT, Oct. 14, 1860, #209, AWTP; Albion W. Tourgée, "As a Public Man," in *Martin B. Anderson, LL.D.: A Biography*, ed. A. Kendrick (Philadelphia: American Baptist Pub., 1895), 286–87, UR.

123. Rosenboom, *History of Ohio*, 181.

124. AWT to EKT, Nov. 4, 1860, #216, AWTP.

125. AWT to "Sister Mille," Sept. 26, 1860, #205, AWTP.

126. AWT to EKT, March 3, 1861, #260, AWTP.

Chapter 3: Citizen-Soldier: Manhood and the Meaning of Liberty

1. AWT to EKT, Nov. 30, 1860, #225, AWT to EKT, Dec. 15, 1860, #231, AWTP; first epigraph, John William De Forest, *Miss Ravenel's Conversion From Secession to Loyalty* (1867; reprint, New York: Rinehart, 1955), 50; second epigraph, AWT to "Brothers of the Union," January ?, 1863, #454, AWTP.

2. AWT to EKT, Dec. 15, 1860, #221, AWTP.

3. AWT to EKT, April 22, 1861, #272, AWTP.

4. Martin B. Anderson, "The Issues of the Civil War," in William C. Morey, ed., *Papers and Addresses of Martin B. Anderson* (Philadelphia: American Baptist Pub., 1895), 137–38, UR.

5. AWT to EKT, April 22, 1861, #272, AWTP; on the effect of Anderson's speech, see Tourgée's chapter "As A Public Man," in A. Kendrick, *Martin B. Anderson, LL.D.: A Biography* (Philadelphia: American Baptist Pub., 1895), 287–88, UR.

6. Quoted in James McPherson, *The Struggle for Equality: Abolitionists and the Negro in the Civil War and Reconstruction* (Princeton: Princeton University Press, 1964), 48.

7. Ibid., 55–56.

8. Tourgée, "As A Public Man," 283, UR.

9. Anderson, 130–31, 134.

10. Ibid., 133, 136.

11. Tourgée, "As A Public Man," 277–78, 283. Tourgée also said of Anderson's nationalism, "The same tendencies made him love a strong people and despise a weak one. As he counted it the first duty of man to be strong that he might achieve, he regarded it as the prime essential of nationality to be powerful. He gloried in the strength of England, and was intensely interested in the unification of Germany," 281–82.

12. Anderson was a prime example of the patrician type of social conservative who, as George Fredrickson has argued, feared the anti-institutionalism of the 1850s and perceived the Civil War as the tragic consequence of it. Fredrickson, *The Inner Civil War: Northern Intellectuals and the Crisis of the Union* (New York: Harper and Row, 1965), 23–35.

13. Tourgée, "As A Public Man," 277.

14. On the prominence of appeals to manliness and duty, see Reid Mitchell, "Soldiering, Manhood, and Coming of Age: A Northern Volunteer," and David W. Blight, "No Desperate Hero: Manhood and Freedom in a Union Soldier's Experience," in Catherine Clinton and Nina Silber, eds., *Divided Houses: Gender and the Civil War* (New York: Oxford University Press, 1992).

15. AWT to EKT, April 22, 1861, #272, AWTP.

16. The *Conneaut Reporter*, April 18, 1861, WRHS.

17. Nellie to AWT, April 24, 1861, #270, AWTP; EKT to AWT, April 21, 1861, #271, AWTP.

18. EKT to AWT, April 24, [1861]. This letter is misdated by Emma as "1860," and although it is filed with the letters of 1860, the envelope is dated "April 24/61," #162, AWTP.

19. AWT to EKT, April 25, 1861, # 275; AWT to EKT, May 19, 1861, #281, AWTP.

20. EKT to AWT, April 25, 1861, #274, AWTP.

21. Ibid.

22. Compiled Military Records, 27th New York Volunteers, NARA.

23. Charles Bryant Fairchild, *History of the 27th Regiment N.Y.* (Binghamton, NY, 1883), 10–14.

24. AWT to EKT, July 23, 1861, #295, AWTP.

25. AWT to EKT, July 23, 1861, #295, AWTP. Also see the vivid description of Bull Run in "The Sergeant's Story," chap. 4, Tourgée, *Figs and Thistles: A Romance of the Western Reserve* (New York: Fords, Howard, & Hulbert, 1879).

26. AWT to Valentine Tourgée, published as "Kingsville Boys at Bull Run," *Conneaut Reporter*, Aug. 8, 1861, WRHS.

27. AWT to EKT, July 23, 1861, #295, AWTP.

28. Ibid.

29. Fairchild, *27th Regiment*, 14.

30. E.P. Gould, 2nd Serg., Co. E, 27th Reg., affidavits, Nov. 23, 1861; Feb. 11, 1862. Albion W. Tourgée, Pension File, Records of the Veterans Administration, NARA.

31. Ibid.

32. *Figs and Thistles*, 274.

33. The 27th lost a total of one hundred and thirty men at Bull Run: twenty-seven men were killed and forty-four were wounded. Fairchild, *27th Regiment*, 14–18.

34. "Kingsville Boys at Bull Run," *Conneaut Reporter*, Aug. 8, 1861, WRHS; AWT to EKT, July 23, 1861, #295, AWTP.

35. AWT to EKT, July 23, 1861, #295, AWTP; "Kingsville Boys at Bull Run," *Conneaut Reporter*, Aug. 8, 1861, WRHS.

36. Certificate of Disability for Discharge, Albion W. Tourgée, Compiled Military Records, NARA.

37. Elizabeth Everitt to EKT [September 1862], #438; AWT to Mr and Mrs. K., Aug. 23, 1861, #308; AWT to EKT, Oct. 17, 1861, #328, AWTP.

38. AWT to Mr. and Mrs. K, August 23, 1861, #308, AWTP.

39. The situation led to a reconciliation between father and son. Though Albion did not enjoy living at home, his hostility was directed primarily at his stepmother, Rowena, during this time. If I "have a wife one half as contemptible as my father's," he told Emma, "I do believe I should be guilty of murder or suicide." He swore Rowena would never be allowed to visit their house after their marriage. AWT to EKT, Sept. 25, 1861, #317, AWTP.

40. AWT to EKT, April 27, 1861, #276, AWTP.

41. Angie Kilbourne to AWT, Aug. 17, 1861, #303, AWTP.

42. AWT to Mr and Mrs. K, Aug. 23, 1861, #308, AWTP.

43. AWT to EKT, Oct. 17, 1861, #328, AWTP.

44. AWT to EKT, May 14, 1862, #399, AWTP.

45. AWT to EKT, Jan. 18, 1862, #359, AWTP.

46. AWT to EKT, May 4, 1862, #396, AWTP; AWT to EKT, May 14, 1862, #399, AWTP.

47. EKT to AWT, Jan. 9, 1862, #357, AWTP.

48. AWT to EKT, May 27, 1862, #403, AWTP.

49. Edmund Wilson, *Patriotic Gore: Studies in the Literature of the American Civil War* (New York: W.W. Norton, 1962), 537.

50. On the ideal Northern soldier, see Gerald F. Linderman, *Embattled Courage: The Experience of Combat in the American Civil War* (New York: Free Press, 1987), 83–85. John W. De Forest's 1867 novel about the Civil War, *Miss Ravenel's Conversion From Secession to Loyalty*, provided perhaps the finest illustration of the difference between Northern and Southern concepts of manhood. The contrast between North and South are represented by Lillie Ravenel's rival suitors— the aristocratic Virginian, Colonel Carter, and the high-minded New Englander, Captain Colburne. While Carter's dashing heroism is undermined by his dissolute and indulgent private life, Colburne's quiet dedication to duty and unflinching moral nature ultimately wins both the war and Lillie's heart. Colburne is described as possessing "patience," "fortitude," "resolute self-reliance," "incorruptible honor," and "more physical and intellectual vigor than is merely necessary to exist [but will enable him to] succeed in the duties of life," De Forest, 484.

51. AWT to EKT, Jan. 5, 1862, #356, AWTP.

52. EKT to AWT, Jan. 9, 1862, #357, AWTP.

53. Albion W. Tourgée, Pension File, Records of the Veterans Administration, NARA.

54. Ibid.

55. Roy F. Dibble, *Albion W. Tourgée* (New York: Lemcke & Buechner, 1921), 24.

56. AWT to EKT, July 14, 1862, #410, AWTP.

57. Albion W. Tourgée, Pension File, Records of the Veterans Administration, NARA.

58. EKT to AWT, August 6, 1862, #419, AWTP.

59. AWT to M. Coleman, Esq. Feb. 4, 1868, #765, AWTP.

60. Tourgée personally recruited forty men for the 105th Ohio after being commissioned as an officer on July 11, 1862. See notarized affidavit, #611, AWTP. Albion W. Tourgée, *The Story of a Thousand: Being a History of the Service of the 105th Ohio Volunteer Infantry, in the War for the Union from August 21, 1862 to June 6, 1865* (Buffalo, NY: S. McGerald & Son, 1896), 168.

61. AWT to M.L. Maynard, Feb. 1893, #6641, AWTP.

62. Tourgée, *The Story of a Thousand*, 12–13. His depiction of the 105th as an "abolition regiment" with antislavery motivations was supported by his comrades who praised its historical accuracy and even-handedness. None complained that he exaggerated or distorted their political ideals. See, for instance, Henry H. Cummings to AWT, Feb. 17, 1894, #7620 AWTP.

63. Hans L. Trefousse, *Benjamin Franklin Wade: Radical Republican from Ohio* (New York: Twayne, 1963), 147.

64. *Cincinnati Daily Times*, Dec. 17, 1860, WRHS.

65. Albion W. Tourgée, *The Veteran and His Pipe* (Chicago: Inter Ocean, 1886), 26.

66. In fact, more than one-third of the 105th deserted or were captured or incapacitated during what the men came to call the "hell march." At one point, during the long march, Tourgée—whose legs had not recovered from a year of inactivity—collapsed on the road and was left behind. Fortunately for him, he was picked up by the quartermaster of another company and driven much of the way in a buggy. AWT to EKT, [Sept. 3], 1862 [misdated "Aug. 3"], #426, AWTP.

67. Tourgée, *The Story of a Thousand*, 88–92.

68. Ibid., 107.

69. Ibid., 106. Also, Whitelaw Reid. *Ohio in the War: Her Statesmen, Her Generals, and Soldiers*, vol. 2, *The History of Her Regiments, and Other Military Organizations* (Cincinnati: Moore, Wilstach & Baldwin, 1868), 565–71.

70. AWT to EKT, Nov. 23, 1862, #446, AWTP.

71. AWT to "Brothers of the Union," Jan. 1?, 1863, #454, AWTP.

72. Ibid.

73. Because Tourgée copied it over in his own hand, this poem has been misidentified as his by both Otto Olsen and Richard Current. See, Olsen 29–30, and Current, 52. Current compounded this mistake by commenting in regard to it: "[Tourgée] expressed his own emotion (though not necessarily his comrades') in the following verse. . . ." Tourgée clearly identifies the poem as Kee's in *Story of A Thousand*, 168–69. The poem can be found at #11133 and #11147 in the AWTP.

74. Lines, by Clement [AWT pseudonym], April 17, 1862, #980, AWTP; also see #11117, AWTP.

75. Diary fragment, dated Tuesday, June 13, 1863, #980, AWTP.

76. Albion Tourgée, *An Appeal to Caesar* (New York: Fords, Howard and Hulbert, 1884), 214. Tourgée, *The Story of a Thousand*, 72–73.

77. This particular diary entry was edited in a misleading fashion by Dean Keller in Keller, ed., "A Civil War Diary of Albion W. Tourgée," *Ohio History*, vol. 74 (spring 1965): 107. Keller mistakenly inserted the word *not* into the text, which unfortunately reverses the meaning of the sentence so that it reads: "I have [not] heard worse things than I have listened to there today." The original document reads as quoted above in Tourgée diary, Sunday, June 7, 1863, #577, AWTP.

78. Tourgée diary, Saturday, Oct. 24, 1863, #577, AWTP.

79. Mussey, quoted in Joseph T. Glatthaar, *Forged in Battle: The Civil War Alliance of Black Soldiers and White Officers* (New York: Free Press, 1991), 38–39.

80. Glatthaar, *Forged in Battle*, x, 53. The records of the Bureau of Colored Troops show that they received Tourgée's application; however, his file is not among the thousands still held at the National Archives. His lost application file may explain why he never received an examination hearing or an appointment. Applications for Commissions in the Colored Units, Record Group 94, NARA.

81. Tourgée diary, June 22–23, 1863, #577, AWTP.

82. Captain Canfield was not executed by the Confederates. Elizabeth Everitt to EKT, Feb. 22, 1863, #460, AWTP; Tourgée, *The Story of a Thousand.*

83. Tourgée diary, Monday, June 22, 1863, #577, AWTP.

84. George M. Fredrickson, *The Inner Civil War: Northern Intellectuals and the Crisis of the Union* (New York: Harper & Row, 1965). Louis Menand has argued that the Civil War "swept away almost the whole intellectual culture of the North," especially in respect to radical individualism. See *The Metaphysical Club: A Story of Ideas in America* (New York: Farrar, Straus and Giroux, 2001), x.

85. Fredrickson, 130–50. James McPherson challenges part of Fredrickson's thesis in *For Cause and Comrades: Why Men Fought in the Civil War* (New York: Oxford University Press, 1997). Based on a prodigious reading of soldiers' letters, McPherson writes: "They [Civil War soldiers] came from a society that prized individualism, self-reliance, and freedom from coercive authority. The army broke down some of this individualism, or tried to, but could never turn these volunteer soldiers into automatons," 61.

86. Daniel Aaron, *The Unwritten War: American Writers and the Civil War* (New York: Alfred A. Knopf, 1973), 195.

87. Tourgée, *The Story of a Thousand*, 31, 43.

88. Newspaper clipping, #2540, AWTP.

89. Fairchild, *History of the 27th Regiment*, 3–4. Long afterward Tourgée continued to fume over the food situation, blaming the adulterated food for the "strong showing of intestinal disease among" veterans of the war in *The Story of a Thousand*, 99.

90. Tourgée, *The Story of a Thousand*, 44.

91. Tourgée diary, June 10, 1863, #577, AWTP; Tourgée, *The Story of a Thousand*, 43.

92. O.L. Marsh to AWT, March 12, 1887, #2583, AWTP.

93. Scapegoated in the opinion of his men, Captain Canfield was dismissed from the service for his role as commanding officer of the foraging expedition on Jan. 21, 1863, that led to the capture of himself and more than one hundred men, including Tourgée. See Tourgée's comments in *The Story of a Thousand*, 179–83.

94. Tourgée diary. May 31–June 3, 1863, #577, AWT to Lieut. Col. Goddard, June 2, 1863, #475, AWTP; Cummings Diary, May 31–June 3, 1863, WRHS.

95. AWT to Valentine, July 18, 1863, #510, AWTP; AWT to EKT, June 21, 1863, #489, AWTP; Tourgée diary, June 11–18, 1863, #577, AWTP; Rochester Notebook, #980, AWTP.

96. Henry Cummings Diary, June 28, 1863, WRHS.

97. Tourgée, *Story of a Thousand*, 168–69; also, items #11133 and #11147, AWTP.

98. Cummings diary, July 1, 1863, WRHS.

99. AWT to Valentine Tourgée, July 8, 1863, #501, AWTP.

100. AWT to EKT, Aug. 6, 1863, #527, AWTP.

101. AWT to Valentine Tourgée, July 8, 1863, #501, AWTP.

102. Cummings diary, July 1, 1863, WRHS.

103. Tourgée, *Story of a Thousand*, 355. For a description of Sherman's march that supports Tourgée's characterization, see Charles Royster, *The Destructive War: William Tecumseh Sherman, Stonewall Jackson, and the Americans* (New York: Random House, 1991), 3–33, especially.

104. Cummings diary, Nov. 16, 1864, WRHS.

105. Cummings diary, Aug. 21, 1864, WRHS. While Gerald F. Linderman argues that disillusionment was a widespread phenomenon late in the war, James M. McPherson counters this argument in *For Cause and Comrades.*

106. AWT to James F. Morrison, Esq., Nov. 14, 1894. Reprinted in Jason Fradenburgh, *In Memoriam. Henery Harrison Cummings* (Charlotte J. Cummings. Oil City, PA: Derrick, 1913). WRHS.

107. R.M. Tuttle to AWT, Jan. 30, 1864, #591, AWTP.

108. AWT to EKT, May 6, 1863, #467, AWTP.

109. Albion W. Tourgée, Pension File, Affidavit of Joseph R. Warner, Records of the Veterans Administration, NARA.

110. Albion W. Tourgée, Pension File, Records of the Veterans Administration, NARA.

111. AWT to EKT, Sept. 29, 1863, #556, AWTP; AWT to Valentine Tourgee, Dec. 6, 1863 #587, AWTP; AWT to EKT, May 30, 1863, #473, AWTP.

112. EKT to AWT, Nov. 24, 1863, #583, AWTP.

113. AWT to Lieut. Col. Goddard, Dec. 1, 1863, #586, AWTP; AWT to Valentine Tourgée, Dec. 6, 1863. #587, AWTP. Albion W. Tourgée, Compiled Military Records, 105th Ohio Volunteers, Adjutant General's Office, NARA.

114. No reference to this event can be found in his Civil War diary. Dean H. Keller also believes that this later claim by Tourgée was probably an embellishment of the Canfield incident, "Civil War Diary," 100–101. Deborah Patrice Hamlin credits the story, though without a specific citation in " 'Friend of Freedom': Albion Winegar Tourgée and Reconstruction in North Carolina" (Ph.D. diss., Duke University, 2004), 35.

115. He makes this claim, for instance, in Albion W. Tourgée, "A Bystander's Notes," *Daily Inter Ocean* (Chicago), July 7, 1888.

116. AWT to Valentine Tourgee, April 14, May 7, 8, 1852, KSU; AWT to EKT, April 27, 1861, #276, AWTP; Olsen, 58.

117. In the immediate aftermath of Perryville, Tourgée reported not being shot in letters to Emma and others, but later he would claim to have a piece of shrapnel in his hip from the battle. The truth is difficult to determine, since he was not always forthright in describing his injuries to Emma during the war and doctors did remove shrapnel from his hip more than forty years later. Elizabeth Everitt to EKT, Nov. 4, 1862, #441; AWT to EKT, Nov. 17, 1862, #445, AWTP; Richard Current, *Those Terrible Carpetbaggers*, 403.

118. AWT to EKT, Nov. 17, 1862, #445, AWTP.

119. Tourgée, *A Fool's Errand*, 20.

120. Woodrow Wilson, "An Address at the Gettysburg Battlefield, July 4, 1913," in Thomas J. Brown, *The Public Art of Civil War Commemoration: A Brief History with Documents* (New York: Bedford/St. Martin's, 2004), 21 [my emphasis].

121. David W. Blight, *Race and Reunion: The Civil War in American Memory* (Cambridge, MN: Belknap/Harvard University Press, 2001), 208–10.

122. [His emphasis]. Albion W. Tourgée, *An Appeal to Caesar* (New York: Fords, Howard & Hulbert, 1884), 44–45.

Chapter 4: A Radical Yankee in the Reconstruction South

1. Auguste Laugel, *The United States during the War* (New York, 1866; reprint, ed. Allan Nevins, Bloomington, 1961), 159; first epigraph, from "The Mission of the War," in *Frederick Douglass, Selected Speeches and Writings*, ed. Phillip Foner, abridged and adapted by Yuval Taylor (Chicago: Chicago Review Press, 1999), 562; second epigraph, Albion W. Tourgée, *To the Voters of Guilford* [County, North Carolina]. Broadside. October 21, 1867, AWTP.

2. A.W. Tourgée, "Root, Hog or Die," clipping, 1878[?], #10845, AWTP.

3. Saidiya Hartman most fully makes the case for the "resubordination of the emancipated" by Northern missionaries in *Scenes of Subjection: Terror, Slavery, and Self-Making in Nineteenth-Century America* (New York: Oxford University Press, 1997), 116. Amy Dru Stanley underplays the importance of radicalism in *From Bondage to Contract: Wage Labor, Marriage, and the Market in the Age of Slave Emancipation* (New York: Cambridge University Press, 1998), ix–xiii. Other recent works minimizing the egalitarianism of the radicals are Heather Cox Richardson, *The Death of Reconstruction: Race, Labor, and Politics in the Post–Civil War North, 1865–1901* (Cambridge: Harvard University Press, 2001); and Laura F. Edwards, *Gendered Strife and Confusion: The Political Culture of Reconstruction* (Urbana: University of Illinois Press, 1997).

4. Albion W. Tourgée, *An Appeal to Caesar* (New York: Fords, Howard & Hulbert, 1884), 57–58.

5. AWT to EKT, March 9, 1861, #262, AWTP.

6. EKT to AWT, July 27, 1865, #618, AWTP.

7. Albion Tourgée, "Preface" to *A Royal Gentleman* (New York: Fords, Howard, & Hulbert, 1881), iii.

8. Tourgée maintained that the letters and news articles that he included in *A Fool's Errand* were genuine, although the originals no longer exist. The character of the former college President Rev. Enos Martin was a thinly disguised representation of University of Rochester President Martin B. Anderson. Albion W. Tourgée, *A Fool's Errand. By One of the Fools* (New York: Fords, Howard & Hulbert, 1879), 27.

9. Otto H. Olsen, *Carpetbagger's Crusade: The Life of Albion Winegar Tourgee* (Baltimore: Johns Hopkins University Press, 1965), 45.

10. W.W. Holden to AWT, June 16, 1865, #614, AWTP; Horace W. Raper, *William W. Holden: North Carolina's Political Enigma* (Chapel Hill: UNC Press, 1985), 46–65. William C. Harris, *William Woods Holden: Firebrand of North Carolina Politics* (Baton Rouge: Louisiana State University Press, 1987).

11. Jeffrey J. Crow, "Thomas Settle, Jr., Reconstruction, and the Memory of the Civil War," *Journal of Southern History* 62 (November 1996): 696; Richard Current, *Those Terrible Carpetbaggers: A Reinterpretation* (New York: Oxford University Press, 1988), 51. Tourgée quoted from in a fragment of a letter or diary entry dated "Greensboro, NC, April 6, 1866," #980, AWTP.

12. According to Richard Current, most Northern carpetbaggers immigrating into the state chose to settle in the coastal regions. *Those Terrible Carpetbaggers*, 47–51.

13. AWT to EKT, July 20, 1865, #414, AWTP. This letter is mistakenly filed with those of July 1862.

14. AWT to EKT, July 22, 1865, #616, AWTP.

15. Seneca Coon, born Dec. 22, 1836, graduated from Rochester in 1861 and changed the spelling of his last name to Kuhn upon entering the South. Reuben True Pettengill, born Jan. 2, 1840, graduated from Rochester in 1862, alumni file, UR.

16. Emma's older sister Angie continued to teach in Erie but owned property in Greensboro and would make extended visits there. Angie Kilbourne to EKT, Sept. 23, 1866, #656, AWTP.

17. Current, *Those Terrible Carpetbaggers*, 52–54; Olsen, *Carpetbagger's Crusade*, 27–33.

18. This quote comes from a letter home from "Metta," who is the fictional counterpart of Emma in Tourgée, *A Fool's Errand*, 55.

19. Report to General O.O. Howard quoted in Olsen, *Carpetbagger's Crusade*, 32–33; Freedmen's Bureau agent quoted in J. T. Trowbridge, *The South: A Tour of Its Battle-Fields and Ruined Cities* (Hartford, Conn., 1866), 581–82.

20. Tourgée's role in founding the school is mentioned in the memoir of William George Mattan, a Quaker. Memoir, William George Mattan Papers, DU.

21. Albion W. Tourgee to F.A. Fiske, December 2, 1867, Bureau Records, Educational Division, North Carolina, letters received. Records of the Bureau of Refugees, Freedmen, Abandoned Lands, NARA; "Minutes of the Instruction Committee of the Friends Freedmen's Association, 1864–67," December 1, 1865; Friends Freedmen's Association Records, FLS; Morris, *Reading, 'Riting, and Reconstruction*, 57, 265; EKT to AWT, Jan. 14, 1867, #759, AWTP.

22. Tourgée is credited with originating the Loyal Leagues in J.G. de Roulhac Hamilton, *Reconstruction in North Carolina* (New York: Longmans, Green, 1914), 336. In *A Fool's Errand*, he describes being invited to join the league by black allies, which is probably more accurate. Tourgée, *A Fool's Errand*, 113–27.

23. "The Douglass Dynasty," clipping, Nov. 19, 1877, Scrapbook of Gov. Daniel L. Russell, North Carolina Collection, UNC.

24. Roberta Sue Anderson, *North Carolina Faces the Freedmen: Race Relations During Presidential Reconstruction, 1865–1867* (Durham, NC: Duke University Press, 1985), 44–51.

25. This league formed in Wilmington in October, 1865. Quoted in Alexander, 29.

26. *Greensboro Patriot*, August 24, Sept. 14, 1866; *Raleigh Standard*, Sept. 4, 1866, North Carolina Collection, UNC.

27. Current, *Those Terrible Carpetbaggers*, 54.

28. Ibid., 54–59.

29. AWT to EKT, August 31, 1866, #644; AWT to EKT, Sept. 16, 1866, #651, AWTP.

30. Though Tourgée perceived strong support for black rights among the non-border state delegates, Eric Foner has argued to the contrary that the delegates supported the Fourteenth Amendment largely *in spite* of its support for equal rights. Because the amendment excluded ex-Confederates from political office, he argues, loyal Southerners had a strong personal interest in its passage. Foner, *Reconstruction*, 268–71.

31. This description and quote is taken from the account given in the *New York Herald*, Sept. 8, 1866, 1.

32. AWT to EKT, Sept. 16, 1866, #651, AWTP.

33. Current, *Those Terrible Carpetbaggers*, 56.

34. AWT to Emma, Sept. 6, 1866, #650, AWTP.

35. Untitled speech, #686, with papers of Oct. 1866, AWTP.

36. Current, *Those Terrible Carpetbaggers*, 54–59.

37. *New York Herald*, September 8, 1866, 1.

38. Jonathan Worth to A.M. Tomilson, Sept. 13, 1866; Jonathan Worth to Nereus Mendenhall, Oct. 1, 1866, in *The Correspondence of Jonathan Worth*, vol. 2, ed. J.G. de Roulhac Hamilton (Raleigh, NC: Edward & Broughton, 1909), 780, 808–9.

39. Jonathan Worth to Nereus Mendenhall, Sept. 10, 1866, and Jonathan Worth to John A. Gilmer, *Correspondence*, 772–77.

40. Historians have largely dismissed Tourgée's story as an invention. One reason for this, perhaps, is that historian Theodore Gross mistakenly quoted Tourgée's statement from the *New York Herald* as having claimed that this incident occurred "in Guilford County," in Theodore L. Gross, "The Fool's Errand of Albion W. Tourgée,"

Phylon 24 (1963): 243. In fact, Tourgée made no mention of Guilford County in relation to the incident as reported by the *Herald* (or elsewhere). Tourgée later confirmed the story with his source—a Greensboro Quaker. A note among Tourgée's legal papers indicates that he heard the man's story about witnessing fifteen dead black men taken from a South Carolina river near the end of the war just a few days before leaving for Philadelphia, and he provides the place he heard it and the name of two witnesses to the statement. "Note on Slanders," #10959, AWTP. By 1884, the story had grown so, Conservatives were claiming that Tourgée had told the convention of "1500 murdered negroes taken from one pond." See John H. Wheeler, *Reminiscences and Memoirs of North Carolina and Eminent North Carolinians* (Columbus, OH: Columbus Printing Works, 1884), 111–12.

41. Jonathan Worth to Rufus Y. McAdden, Sept. 23, 1866, *Correspondence*, 793.

42. Anonymous to AWT, Sept. 19, 1866, #659, AWTP.

43. "The friend of all Loyal people" to EKT, Oct. 16, 1866, #669, AWTP.

44. Anonymous to AWT, Sept. 24, 1866, #657, AWTP.

45. EKT to AWT, Oct. 7, 1866, #665, AWTP.

46. EKT to AWT, Oct. 7, 1866, #665, AWTP.

47. AWT to Major W. Worth, May 24, 1867, #724, AWTP.

48. D. Hodgin to Benjamin Sherwood Hendrick, Oct. 20, 1866, Benjamin Sherwood Hendrick Papers, DU.

49. Lease between Albion Tourgée, Seneca Kuhn, and Cyrus P. Mendenhall. Amended in December 1866 with terms of settlement described. #676, AWTP; E.B. French, Auditor, to AWT, June 25, 1867, #734, AWTP.

50. Seneca Coon to EKT, April 1860[?], #165, AWTP; Jobez? Coon to AWT, March 28, 1867, #709, AWTP.

51. Foner, *Reconstruction*, 137–38.

52. "Carpet Baggers," *Greensboro Patriot*, Feb. 11, 1869, North Carolina Collection, UNC.

53. AWT to Nathan Hill, June 7, 1867, Nathan Hill Papers, DU.

54. Angie Kilbourne to EKT, June 21, 1867, #733, AWTP.

55. The plan already had the support of Thaddeus Stevens and others in Congress. Current, *Those Terrible Carpetbaggers*, 65–66.

56. This phrase is taken from a Tourgée speech made roughly two months earlier. #686, with papers of Oct. 1866, AWTP.

57. Otto H. Olsen, "North Carolina: An Incongruous Presence," in Otto H. Olsen, ed., *Reconstruction and Redemption in the South* (Baton Rouge: Louisiana State University Press, 1980), 164.

58. Paul D. Escott, *Many Excellent People: Power and Privilege in North Carolina, 1850–1900* (Chapel Hill: University of North Carolina Press, 1985), 145.

59. For instance, W.W. Holden was born an illegitimate child, in extreme poverty, in rural Hillsborough, and he began his career as a printer's apprentice before working his way up to become the editor of Raleigh's *North Carolina Standard*. Hinton Helper was born the son of a yeoman farmer in Rowan County, and he worked as a store clerk in Salisbury before heading West during the California Gold Rush. Harris, *Holden*. Olsen, "North Carolina: An Incongruous Presence," 157–58.

60. Albion W. Tourgée, *To the Voters of Guilford*, broadside, Oct. 21, 1867, #746, AWTP.

61. Olsen, "North Carolina," 157–58.

62. R.M. Pearson to William Scott, July 1, 1868, William Lafayette Scott Papers, DU.

63. Joel Ashworth to Nathan Hill, April 15, 1867, Nathan Hill Papers, DU.

64. Speech delivered in Rockingham, March? 1867. In this oft-quoted speech, Settle also proclaimed: "It has been very fashionable to denounce Yankees and ridicule Yankee notions. I tell you Yankees and Yankee notions are just what we want in this country. We want their capital to build factories, and work shops and railroad . . . we want their intelligence, their energy and enterprise to operate those factories and to teach us how to do it. . . . We should all teach our children to love the whole Union, to celebrate the Fourth of July with the Yankee." Thomas Settle Papers, Southern Historical Collection, UNC.

65. Samuel F. Phillips to unknown, July 18, 1878, #2221, AWTP. This testimonial continued on: "His [Tourgée's] radical views of society have seemed to me to be the very medicine required for the Conservative community in which I have seen him." See also James McCleery to AWT, May 24, 1869, #1472–78, AWTP, in which a friend reported overhearing Conservative lawyers privately praising him, especially one named Phillips.

66. Samuel F. Phillips to AWT, May 12, 1873, #1670, AWTP.

67. AWT to Rutherford B. Hayes, March 7, 1877, RBH. Tourgée also recommended Phillips a second time in 1880 and perhaps subsequent times as well. AWT to Rutherford B. Hayes, Dec. 8, 1880, RBH.

68. *Union Register*, Jan. 3, 25, 1867, North Carolina Collection, UNC.

69. AWT to D.W. Hodgin, April 4, 1868, #1239–64, AWTP.

70. Tourgée, *A Fool's Errand*, 66.

71. *New York Tribune*, April 4, 1881, 5.

72. Robert Dick to Benjamin Sherwood Hendrick, May 30, 1867, Benjamin Sherwood Hendrick Papers, DU. Testimonial for Albion W. Tourgée's upcoming lecture series, #2101, AWTP.

73. AWT to EKT, Sept. 18, 1875, #1845, AWTP.

74. In this instance, the *Patriot* accused Tourgée of unequal justice in his courtroom regarding his ten-year sentence for a white teenager who pleaded guilty to murder as compared to a "colored boy" who was found not guilty of murder—by a jury of mostly Conservatives, Tourgée pointed out. AWT to Editor of the *Greensboro Patriot*, Sept. 6, 1869, #1196, AWTP.

75. AWT to Editor of the *Greensboro Patriot*, Sept. 14, 1866, North Carolina Collection, UNC.

76. "Grant and Wilson. The Republican Mass Meeting in Dansville! Stirring Speech by Judge Tourgee of North Carolina," clipping, #2428, AWTP.

77. "Horrible Blasphemy," *Southern Home*, clipping, #2428, AWTP.

78. David Schenck Journal, V, 84–85, David Schenck Papers, Southern Historical Collection, UNC; Olsen, *Carpetbagger's Crusade*, 69.

79. Jonathan Worth to B.G. Worth, Dec. 26, 1867, *Correspondence*, 1094.

80. Jonathan Worth to B.G. Worth, Dec. 26 1867; and Jonathan Worth to William Clark, Oct. 26, 1867, *Correspondence*, 1063, 1094.

81. United States Senate, *Testimony Taken by the Joint Select Committee to Inquire into the Condition of Affairs in the Late Insurrectionary States: North Carolina* (Washington: Government Printing Office, 1872), 385.

82. Ibid., 385. Despite their sometimes paramilitary appearance, the leagues were nonviolent and their activities were confined to political rallies where patriotic songs were sung, speeches delivered, and new members ritualistically initiated into the "secrets" of the order. See Tourgée, *A Fool's Errand*, 126–27.

83. Greensboro *Times* editorial of 1868, quoted in Current, *Those Terrible Carpetbaggers*, 108.

84. AWT to Martin B. Anderson, May 25, 1870, Martin B. Anderson Papers, UR.

85. Olsen quoted from *Carpetbagger's Crusade*, 83. See also Austin Marcus Drumm, "The Union League in the Carolinas" (Ph.D. diss., UNC, 1955).

86. Tourgée at one point publicly offered a reward of $1,000 for anyone who could substantiate the penitentiary story. He remarked that many of his friends in Ohio had been "sucked as dry of reminiscences as a squeezed lemon" by Conservative detectives sent to dig for skeletons. AWT to Editor, *Greensboro Patriot*, Sept. 14, 1866, "Albion W. Tourgee," *University Monthly*, vol. 1 (December 1882): 125–26, North Carolina Collection, UNC. Various newspaper clippings, #2428, AWTP.

87. Olsen, *Carpetbagger's Crusade*, 66.

88. Current, *Those Terrible Carpetbaggers*, 65.

89. *Raleigh Standard*, March 26, 1867; B.F. Wade to Union Executive Committee, April 1, 1867, #712, AWTP.

Chapter 5: The Unfinished Revolution

1. A draft of this Feb. 21, 1868, speech can be found at #801, AWTP. For the views of the Conservative minority to which he was responding, see *Journal of the Constitutional Convention of the State of North Carolina, at its Session 1868* (Raleigh: Joseph W. Holden, Convention Printer, 1868), 235–38. HL. Epigraph quoted from "Reconstruction: Hon. Thaddeus Stevens on the Great Topic of the Hour. An Address Delivered to the Citizens of Lancaster, Sept. 6, 1865," *New York Times*, Sept. 10, 1865.

2. Speech, #801, AWTP.

3. Ibid.

4. James M. McPherson, *The Struggle for Equality: Abolitionists and the Negro in the Civil War and Reconstruction* (Princeton: Princeton University Press, 1964), 417–32.

5. Speech, #801, AWTP.

6. Ibid.

7. Ibid. Though Tourgée's precise whereabouts on April 12, 1864, cannot be verified, it seems highly unlikely that he could have witnessed the massacre at Fort Pillow, which occurred several months after he left the military. He never again made reference to witnessing the Fort Pillow massacre. Also, Tourgée's claim that he had believed "the Negro akin to the brute" before the war seems exaggerated. I believe, it would have been more correct, if less dramatic, for him to have stated that before the war his opinion on the issue of racial equality was undecided.

8. Ibid.

9. Richard Hume, "Carpetbaggers In the Reconstruction South: A Group Portrait of Outside Whites In the 'Black and Tan' Constitutional Conventions," *Journal of American History* 64 (September 1977), 315.

10. *Raleigh North Carolinian*, Feb. 11 and 12, 1868; quoted in Karin L. Zipf, "'The Whites Shall Rule the Land or Die': Gender, Race, and Class in North Carolina Reconstruction Politics," *Journal of Southern History* 65 (August 1999), 514–16.

11. *Constitution of the State of North-Carolina, Together with the Ordinances and Resolutions of the Constitutional Convention, Assembled in the City of Raleigh, January 14, 1868* (Raleigh: Joseph W. Holden, Convention Printer, 1868): 3; Article I, Section I. HL.

12. AWT to Francis H. Rawley, Sept. 1893, #7370, AWTP.

13. *Raleigh Standard*, Feb. 25, 1868. Quoted in Otto Olsen, *Carpetbagger's Crusade: The Life of Albion Winegar Tourgee* (Baltimore: Johns Hopkins University Press, 1965), 104.

14. *Raleigh North Carolinian*, Feb. 11, 1868, and *Wilmington Daily Journal*, March 25, 1868. Quoted in Zipf, " 'Whites Shall Rule'," 514, 529.

15. *Raleigh Sentinel* and *Wilmington Daily Journal*, quoted in Zipf, " 'Whites Shall Rule'," 519–20.

16. Zipf, " 'Whites Shall Rule'," 513.

17. W. B. Rodman to David Miller Carter, March 7, 11, 1868. David Miller Carter Collection, Southern Historical Collection, UNC. On the centrality of sexual language and white fears about race-mixing during Reconstruction, see Martha Hodes, *White Women, Black Men: Illicit Sex in the Nineteenth-Century South* (New Haven: Yale University Press, 1997), 147–75.

18. *Constitution of the State of North-Carolina*, 122. Black U.S. congressmen were also lukewarm on racial integration of schools. See Ward M. McAfee, *Religion, Race, and Reconstruction: The Public School Crusade of the 1870s* (Albany: State University of New York, 1998), 112.

19. *Journal of the Constitutional Convention*, 343.

20. Howard Rabinowitz, "From Exclusion to Segregation: Southern Race Relations, 1865–1890," in *Race, Ethnicity, and Urbanization: Selected Essays* (Columbia: University of Missouri Press, 1994), 137–63.

21. *Constitution of the State of North-Carolina*, 6. Article I, Section 27.

22. *Journal of the Constitutional Convention*, 487.

23. Quotations from Albion W. Tourgée, *Bricks Without Straw: A Novel* (New York: Fords, Howard & Hulbert, 1880), 508–9, and Albion W. Tourgée, *The Invisible Empire* (New York: Fords, Howard & Hulbert, 1880. Reprint, ed. Otto Olsen (Baton Rouge: Louisiana State University Press, 1989), 118–9.

24. First quote, *Invisible Empire*, 118–9; second quote, *Bricks Without Straw*, 508–9.

25. Olsen, *Carpetbagger's Crusade*, 99–100.

26. "A Plan for the Organization of the Judiciary Department, Proposed by A.W. Tourgée," #798, AWTP; *Constitution of the State of North-Carolina*, 18–19; Article IV, Section 1–3; *Journal of the Constitutional Convention*, 258–59.

27. Olsen, *Carpetbagger's Crusade*, 99–100; *Journal of the Constitutional Convention*, 180–84, 258–59.

28. AWT to William J. Allison, ed. *Friends Review*, May 2, 1870, #1492–147, AWTP.

29. *Constitution of the State of North-Carolina*, 36. Article 11, Section 2.

30. Tourgée was especially sensitive to poor prison conditions because of his own experience in the dreadful Confederate war prisons. Pressing for legislative action, he wrote in exasperation to an ally in the State Assembly at one point: "I have had to fight almost to get stoves put up in our jails and now the Courts in some counties refuse or neglect to furnish fuel. . . . It is horrible! damnable! Think of Dec. 22, 23, & 24 of last month and then of these poor devils, half clad and in a room as exposed as our jails are, without fire! . . . Oh hell! It is enough to sicken one with the whole bipeded creation! . . . For God's sake do induce the legislature to do one decent, manly, Christian act!" AWT to W. Welker, Jan. 7, 1871, #1575–206. See also Levi T. Scofield to AWT, May 27, 1869, #1472–86; and Levi T. Scofield to AWT, Sept. 16, 1869, #1472–118, AWTP.

31. Olsen, *Carpetbagger's Crusade*, 107–8.

32. Ibid., 110–11; Richard Current, *Those Terrible Carpetbaggers: A Reinterpretation* (New York: Oxford University Press, 1988), 105–6.

33. [My emphasis]. *Constitution of the State of North-Carolina*, 6. Article 1, Section 26.

34. AWT to EKT, March 12, 1868, #783, AWTP; Current, *Terrible Carpetbaggers*, 106.

35. *Willington Morning Star*, March 25, 1868, quoted in Olsen, *Carpetbagger's Crusade*, 120–21, and Sara Ann Trott, "Old Tourgée: The Villain as Hero," *Greensboro Daily News*, December 15, 1963, quoting Rufus Weaver, North Carolina Collection, UNC.

36. "Albion W. Tourgee," *University Monthly* 1 (Dec. 1882), 125–26. North Carolina Collection. UNC.

37. Thomas H. Tate, quoted in C. Alphonso Smith, *O. Henry, Biography* (New York: Doubleday, Page, 1916), 67.

38. Tourgée uncovered two plots against him through court testimony. AWT to EKT, March 20, #1612, AWTP. According to oral tradition, the Ku Klux Klan had picked out the very limb on which he was to be hung before being talked out of the plot by two of its members who feared consequences. "Greensboro Tolerantly Regards Memory of Albion Winegar Tourgee, Once Hated Carpetbagger Judge," *Sunday Greensboro Record*, Nov. 8, 1925, North Carolina Clipping File, Biography. North Carolina Collection. UNC.

39. R.E. Park, "Extracts from Newspapers Showing the Disorders of Reconstruction, Collected by Dr. R.E. Park," *Journal of Negro History* 7 (July 1922), 304.

40. AWT to EKT, Jan. 13, 1873, #1653, AWTP.

41. "Judge Tourgee and his Wife," clipping from *Cincinnati Commercial*, 1880? North Carolina Clipping file, Biography, North Carolina Collection, UNC.

42. Reference to Emma's hair turning white is repeated in many sources, but with some factual variation. " 'The Continent' Judge Albion Tourgee's Failure on the Threshold of Success," *Philadelphia Press*, ca. 1884, clipping, #2540, AWTP. See also, Lea Leonard Carr to EKT Piechl, Librarian, Patterson Library, July 10, 1950, Tourgée Collection, Patterson Library, Westfield, New York; AWT to Martin B. Anderson, May 25, 1870, Anderson Papers, UR.

43. AWT to EKT, Jan. 25, 1873, #1658, AWTP.

44. *University Monthly*, 125–26; "Albion W. Tourgée," Records of the Veterans Administration, NARA.

45. AWT to Angie Kilborn, Sept. 5, 1870, #1575–130, AWTP.

46. Deborah Patrice Hamlin, " 'Friend of Freedom': Albion Winegar Tourgée and Reconstruction in North Carolina" (Ph.D. diss., Duke University, 2004), 137.

47. Thomas H. Tate quoted in Smith, *O. Henry, Biography*, 67.

48. Allen W. Trelease, "John Walter Stephens," in William S. Powell, *Dictionary of North Carolina Biography*, Vol. 5 (Chapel Hill: University of North Carolina Press, 1994), 439–40. Some of the slanders against Stephens are repeated in Hamilton, *Reconstruction*, 473–74.

49. Park, "Disorders of Reconstruction," 302.

50. Tourgée refutes the slanders against Stephens in an untitled legal document, #1861, AWTP; Park, "Disorders of Reconstruction," 302–3.

51. Hamilton, *Reconstruction*, 366.

52. Allen Johnson, "A Magical Mystery Tour into Family, History, Heritage, and Color," *Greensboro News and Record*, Feb. 20, 2000.

53. There is not enough evidence to tell whether Adaline's mother, Louisa, was employed as the Tourgée's cook or merely cooked some meals on her own volition. Her role in their home may have been unclear to the Tourgées themselves, as Albion's undated letter to Emma suggests: "The idea that Louisa should propose to

dictate as to who should be in the house and whether we should have a greater or less family is too absurd. I am afraid she got the idea that she was to have the complete swing of those premises while she saw fit to live there whether we liked it or not." AWT to EKT, no date, but kept with letters of 1875, #1879, AWTP.

54. Two letters indicate that they were trying to conceive a child in the spring of 1869: AWT to EKT, Jan. 13, 1869, #999; AWT to EKT, March 18, 1869, #1072, AWTP; vague references to the death of the Tourgées' first child appear in later newspaper accounts, such as the *Springfield Republic*, Sept. 3, 1881, which records "another daughter, a young lady" having died "some years since." Clipping, #4329, AWTP.

55. N. Frank Woods of Greensboro, the great-grandson of Adaline Patillo Woods, kindly shared information from family documents and oral tradition. Postcard to Hampton Institute from Addie P. Woods, July 13, 1897, copy provided to me by Frank Woods. On Woods's own research into Adaline, see Johnson, "Magical Mystery Tour," and N. Frank Woods, "Heritage," *Our State North Carolina* 67 (March 2000), 40–43.

56. Raleigh *Sentinel*, April 20, 1869.

57. AWT to EKT, May 14, 1869, #1108, AWTP. Richard Current asserts that "Emma began to wonder a bit about her husband's interest in the girl" based on Tourgée's reference to her "romantic suppositions." Whether Tourgée's use of the ambiguous word *romantic* was meant to imply that Emma had accused him of an illicit interest in Adaline is questionable. Current supports this speculation by suggesting that Tourgée's first novel, *'Toinette*, was inspired by his adoption of Adaline and his fantasies about her. In *'Toinette*, a bright and attractive, light-skinned slave girl is transformed into a refined, educated lady as an "experiment" by her young master, Geoffrey. Geoffrey eventually falls in love with his creation when she reaches maturity and makes her his concubine. But Geoffrey is an unsympathetic character who bears no biographical resemblance to Tourgée and is duly punished by the author for his despicable behavior. Also, Tourgée began writing *'Toinette* in 1868, which well preceded his adoption of Adaline. The suggestion that he was addressing his own fantasies regarding Adaline therefore seems tenuous at best. Current, *Those Terrible Carpetbaggers*, 196–97.

58. Addie Patillo to EKT and AWT, July 18, 1875, #1822, AWTP. Although Albion usually called her "Ada," Adaline always signed her name "Addie."

59. Addie Patillo to EKT, Oct. 27, 1893, #7425, AWTP; see also, "Greensboro Tolerantly Regards Memory of Albion Winegar Tourgee, Once Hated Carpetbagger Judge," *Sunday Greensboro Record*, Nov. 8, 1925, North Carolina clipping file, Biography, North Carolina Collection, UNC.

60. "Greensboro Tolerantly Regards Memory."

61. AWT to EKT, Dec. 12, 1878, #2265, AWTP. In *A Fool's Errand*, Emma's fictional counterpart, "Metta," is depicted in "almost hysterical fright" when attending an African American church service for the first time. Though she is later emotionally moved by the experience, it is hard to imagine Metta actually joining such a church. See Tourgée, *A Fool's Errand* (New York: Fords, Howard & Hulbert, 1879), 102–4.

62. EKT to AWT, Dec. 18, 1875, #1877, AWTP; AWT to Aimée Tourgée, Feb. 1, 1890, #4418, AWTP.

63. Quoted in Current, *Those Terrible Carpetbaggers*, 210.

64. Adaline Patillo to EKT and AWT, July 18, 1875, #1822, AWTP.

65. AWT to EKT, Jan. 5, 1873, #1649, AWTP.

66. AWT to EKT, Dec. 12, 1878, #2265, AWTP.

67. AWT to EKT, Sept. 13, 1878, #2230, AWTP.

68. Manuscript, "The Slave's Wages," Jan. 1, 1870, delivered in Greensboro. #1718, AWTP.

69. Ibid.

70. Ibid.

71. Ibid.

72. *Greensboro Patriot*, quoted in Olsen, *Carpetbagger's Crusade,* 178.

73. Southern paternalism was in many ways the slaveholders' version of the American revolutionary ideology of Republicanism. See Stephanie McCurry, "The Two Faces of Republicanism: Gender and Proslavery Politics in Antebellum South Carolina," *Journal of American History* 68 (March 1992): 1245–64.

74. Works on the education of freedmen that discuss the mixture of Conservatism and egalitarianism among Northern missionaries include Morris, *Reading, 'Riting, Reconstruction*; Joe M. Richardson, *Christian Reconstruction: The American Missionary Association and Southern Blacks, 1861–1890* (Athens: University of Georgia Press, 1986); Foner, *Reconstruction,* 96–102; Ronald Butchart, *Northern Schools, Southern Blacks, and Reconstruction: Education, 1862–1875* (Westport, CT: Greenwood Press, 1980). A work that focuses on the antiracist strains of the Yankee schoolmarm's ideology is Jacqueline Jones, *Soldiers of Light and Love: Northern Teachers and Georgia Blacks, 1865–1873* (Chapel Hill: University of North Carolina Press, 1980).

75. For useful overviews of black political thought, see Wilson Jeremiah Moses, *Creative Conflict in African American Thought: Frederick Douglass, Alexander Crummell, Booker T. Washington, W.E.B. Du Bois, and Marcus Garvey* (Cambridge: Cambridge University Press, 2004), and Kevin Gaines, *Uplifting the Race: Black Leadership, Politics, and Culture in the Twentieth Century* (Chapel Hill: University of North Carolina Press, 1996). For a more controversial view, see Tunde Adeleke, *UnAfrican Americans: Nineteenth-Century Black Nationalism and the Civilizing Mission* (Lexington: University Press of Kentucky, 1998).

76. AWT to Mr. Armstrong, Freedmen's Bureau, 1867, #11028, AWTP; AWT to Nathan Hill, July 17, 1867, Nathan Hill Papers, DU.

77. Tourgée, *To The Voters of Guilford*, Oct. 21, 1867, #746, AWTP.

78. Harmon Unthank to EKT, September 27, 1887, #2932, AWTP; Stafford Allen Warner, *Yardley Warner: The Freedman's Friend: His Life and Times* (Didcot, Great Britain: The Wessex Press, 1957).

79. AWT to Mr. Armstrong, Freedmen's Bureau, 1867, #11028, AWTP; AWT to Nathan Hill, July 17, 1867, Nathan Hill Papers, DU.

80. Ibid.

81. AWT to Nixon, Jan. 9, 1871, #1575–197, AWTP.

82. Hamlin, " 'Friend of Freedom'," 184–85; Olsen, 177.

83. AWT to Martin B. Anderson, Dec., 1873, #1716, AWTP; Hamlin, " 'Friend of Freedom'," 184.

84. AWT to Martin B. Anderson, Dec., 1873, #1716, AWTP. Tourgée's novella *Mamelon* discusses the Wood Handle Company with fictive embellishment, including an attempted suicide by the main character when the business fails. Albion W. Tourgée, *John Eax and Mamelon: or, The South without the Shadow* (New York: Fords, Howard & Hulbert, 1882).

85. *Greensboro North State*, Aug. 28, 1879, quoted in the *New York Times*, Sept. 3, 1879.

86. See "Real Friends" and "Going Back on Their Friends," *Greensboro Patriot*, July 29, 1869. A Republican newspaper responded to Bur Mendenhall, the freedman quoted in the *Patriot*, by calling him a known drunkard who would say anything for

money. See "Sop on his Taters," *Register*, Aug. 4, 1869, North Carolina Collection, UNC.

87. AWT to J. E. O'Hara, Aug. 4, 1876, #2200, AWTP.

88. AWT to J. E. O'Hara, Aug. 12, 1876, #2200, AWTP.

89. O'Hara would go on to be elected to the United States Congress twice in 1882 and 1884, but he was defeated for a third term. Born in New York, he moved to North Carolina during Reconstruction, where he served as a clerk to the 1868 Constitutional Convention and a delegate to the 1875 Convention. Admitted to the bar in 1873, he maintained a law practice in North Carolina until his death on September 15, 1905. George W. Reid, "Four in Black: North Carolina's Black Congressmen, 1874–1901," *Journal of Negro History* 64 (Summer 1979): 229–43.

90. Addie Patillo to EKT and AWT, July 18, 1875, #1822, AWTP.

91. Addie Patillo to AWT, letter fragment, 1875?, #10964, AWTP.

92. Ibid.

93. *Raleigh Sentinel*, April 20, 1869.

94. [Her emphasis]. Addie Patillo to AWT, letter fragment, 1875? #10964, AWTP.

95. [My emphasis]. Addie Patillo to EKT and AWT, July 18, 1875, #1822, AWTP.

96. Addie P. Woods to Miss Sherman, January 3, 1921. Copy of letter provided to the author by Frank Woods of Greensboro.

97. Evelyn Brooks Higginbotham, *Righteous Discontent: The Women's Movement in the Black Baptist Church, 1880–1920* (Cambridge: Cambridge University Press, 1993), 192.

98. "Greensboro Tolerantly Regards Memory."

99. Mary Patillo Moore to EKT, Feb. 23, 1895, #8313, AWTP; Addie Pattillo Woods to EKT, March 12, 1895, #8383, AWTP.

100. Tourgée, *Bricks Without Straw*, 165.

101. Ibid., 217–18.

102. Morris, *Reading, 'Riting, and Reconstruction*, 57.

103. Tourgée, *Bricks Without Straw*, 169–170.

104. Ibid.

105. Ibid., 171–75.

106. Ibid.

107. Ibid., 443–45.

108. Ibid., 446.

109. Foner, *Reconstruction*, 440–41.

110. Union League Certificate, Wyatt Outlaw Papers, Southern Historical Collection, UNC; AWT to U.S. Grant, Dec. 28, 1871, HL; Carole Watterson Troxler, "'To look more closely at the man': Wyatt Outlaw, a Nexus of National, Local, and Personal History," *North Carolina Historical Review* 77 (2000): 403–33.

111. Quote from Green B. Raum, *The Existing Conflict between Republican Government and Southern Oligarchy* (Washington, D.C.: Charles Green, 1884), 7.

112. Wm. S. Ball to AWT, June 8, 1870, #1472–130, AWTP.

113. AWT to Martin B. Anderson, May 25, 1870, Anderson Papers, UR.

114. AWT to J.C. Abbott, May 24, 1870, in *New York Tribune*, Aug. 3, 1870. Also, this letter has been reprinted in T.H. Breen, *The Power of Words: Documents in American History*, vol. 2 (New York: HarperCollins, 1996), 17–20.

115. Ibid.

116. Senator John Pool remarked to Abbott of the letter, "It is a most important and terrible disclosure. I think the country should see it." After being copied and circulating widely among politicians, it was published in the *New York Tribune* in August. Quoted in Current, *Those Terrible Carpetbaggers*, 205.

117. Ibid.

118. AWT to U.S. Grant, June 12, 1871, USG; AWT to U.S. Grant, Dec. 28, 1871, HL.

119. Among these threats came an ominous one from the men representing the Bar of Guildford. AWT to Ralph Gurell, C.P. Mendenhall, L.M. Scott, Aug. 16, 1870, #1575–97, AWTP; AWT to Joe Warner, Sept. 5, 1870, #1575, AWTP.

120. The *Tribune* quoted Tourgée as citing "twelve murders, 9 rapes, 14 arsons, 7 mutilations," along with "Four thousand or 5000" break-ins. The mention of "14 arsons" appears to be a simple error of transcription of Tourgée's "11 arsons" (not 4, as he later thought), while the last statistic seems to oddly contradict Tourgée's own citing, in the first paragraph of the letter, of "1,000" total outrages committed, and later "seven hundred or 800 persons" having been beaten or maltreated as a result of the break-ins. *New York Daily Tribune*, Aug. 3, 1870; Tourgée's letter to Martin B. Anderson written on the next day provides an interesting comparison with the letter of April 24 to Abbott. In it, Tourgée estimates a total of 800 Ku Klux Klan incidents with "12 murders, 9 rapes, 11 arsons, 6 men castrated, and any number of houses broken open and men and women dragged from their beds and beaten or otherwise cruelly outraged," AWT to Martin B. Anderson, May 25, 1870, Anderson Papers, UR; Current, *Those Terrible Carpetbaggers*, 206–7.

121. "Where Our Troubles Come From," *Greensboro Patriot*, Aug. 11, 1870, North Carolina Collection, UNC.

122. J. R. Warner to AWT, June 20, 1870, #1492–139, AWTP.

123. J. Dunceson (?), from Erie, to AWT, May 30, 1870, #1492, AWTP.

124. AWT to Thomas Settle, Aug. 20, 1870, #1575–116, AWTP.

125. AWT to unknown, August? 1870, #1575–83, AWTP.

126. AWT to Thomas Settle, August 20, 1870, #1575–116, AWTP.

127. Current, *Those Terrible Carpetbaggers*, 208–9.

128. AWT to W.W. Holden, May 11, 1869, #1472–96, AWTP.

129. Allan Rutherford to AWT, Aug. 27, 1870, #1492–161, AWTP; on Tourgée's opinion of Holden, see AWT to unknown, August? 1870, #1575–83, AWTP.

130. AWT to EKT, Sept. 7, 1875, #1840, AWTP. Olsen, *Carpetbagger's Crusade*, 204–6; Current, *Those Terrible Carpetbaggers*, 288–89; Hugh Talmage Lefler and Albert Ray Newsom, *A History of the State of North Carolina*, 3rd ed. (Chapel Hill: University of North Carolina Press, 1973), 499–500.

131. AWT to E.B. Taylor, May 3, 1875, #1807, AWTP; AWT to EKT, April 13, 1879, #2315, AWTP.

Chapter 6: The Politics of Remembering Reconstruction

1. C. Vann Woodward, *The Strange Career of Jim Crow*, 3rd ed. (New York: Oxford University Press, 1974); C. Vann Woodward, *Origins of the New South*, 1877–1913 (Baton Rouge: Louisiana University Press, 1951); Edward L. Ayers, *The Promise of the New South: Life after Reconstruction* (New York: Oxford University Press, 1992), 300–304; first epigraph, Gunnar Myrdal, *An American Dilemma*, vol. 1, *The Negro Problem and Modern Democracy* (1944, reprint, New Brunswick, NJ: Transaction Publishers, 1996), 446–48; second epigraph, Albion W. Tourgée, *A Fool's Errand. By One of the Fools* (New York: Fords, Howard, & Hulbert, 1879), 180.

2. Greeley quoted in Richard Current, *Those Terrible Carpetbaggers: A Reinterpretation* (New York: Oxford University Press, 1988), 261–62.

3. [Greeley's emphasis]. Ibid.

4. Eric Foner, *Reconstruction*, 497–511; Greeley quoted on 503.

5. Jeffrey J. Crow, "Thomas Settle, Jr., Reconstruction, and the Memory of the Civil War," *Journal of Southern History* 62 (Nov. 1996): 689–726.

6. "Hayes attacked. Wendell Phillips Calls the President to account," clipping, in scrapbook of Gov. Daniel L. Russell, North Carolina Collection, UNC. Rayford Logan, *The Betrayal of the Negro: From Rutherford B. Hayes to Woodrow Wilson*, new, enlarged ed. (New York: Collier Books, 1965), 31; originally published as *The Negro in American Life and Thought: The Nadir, 1877–1901* (1954).

7. AWT to Martin B. Anderson, April 24, 1877, Anderson Papers, UR.

8. [His emphasis]. AWT to Dr. Sumberland, April 15, 1877, #2176, AWTP.

9. [His emphasis]. AWT to Dr. Sumberland, April 15, 1877, #2176, AWTP. Most historians agree that Hayes did not view the "let-alone" policy as an abandonment of African Americans at all, but rather as a "new departure" in dealing with the South that would calm the tide of reaction and stop the violence by allowing carpetbagger governments to collapse in favor of home rule. Though a gradualist, Hayes remained an active supporter of black advancement and black education until the end of his life. Brooks D. Simpson, *The Reconstruction Presidents* (Lawrence: University Press of Kansas, 1998), 199–228; Logan, *Betrayal of the Negro*, 23–47.

10. AWT to James C. Young, Aug. 24, 1903, #9722, AWTP.

11. Ibid.

12. Quotations taken from the *Greensboro North State*, July 25, 1878. Quoted Olsen, *Carpetbagger's Crusade*, 212.

13. Olsen, *Carpetbagger's Crusade*, 212–13.

14. See AWT to EKT, Aug. 19, 1878, #2224; AWT to EKT, Nov. 12, 1878, #2251 AWTP.

15. AWT to EKT, Oct. 5, 1878, #2236 AWTP; AWT to EKT, Oct. 6, 1878, #2237, AWTP.

16. AWT to EKT, Nov. 6, 1878, #2248, AWTP.

17. AWT to EKT, Jan. 5, 1879, #2279, AWTP.

18. AWT to EKT, Dec. 22, 1878, #2269, AWTP; Current, *Terrible Carpetbaggers*, 372.

19. AWT to EKT, Dec. 29, 1878, #2272, AWTP.

20. *New York Tribune*, Dec. 3, 1879. See excerpted reviews in front matter, Albion W. Tourgée, *A Fool's Errand By One of the Fools; The Famous Romance of American History. New, Enlarged, and Illustrated Edition* . . . (New York: Fords, Howard, & Hulbert, 1880).

21. Ibid., see excerpt from the *Chicago Tribune* review.

22. Ibid., see excerpted reviews from *Salem Gazette, Concord Monitor*.

23. Regarding the Union League Club "testimonial to Judge Tourgée," see Whitelaw Reid to C.H. Blair, March 29, 1881, #2403, AWTP.

24. Emma K. Tourgée, "Memories of the Campaign of 1880," Oct. 1908, newspaper clipping in scrapbook, #10532, AWTP; Dibble, *Tourgée*, 68–69.

25. "Mrs. Stowe's Seventieth Birthday," *Washington Post*, June 15, 1882, 1; "The Stowe Garden Party," *Christian Union* 25 (June 22, 1882), 564.

26. Troy (New York) Whig, in Tourgée, *A Fool's Errand . . . New, Enlarged, and Illustrated Edition*, front matter.

27. Review of *A Fool's Errand*, in *The Nation* 38 (1879), 444.

28. Elizabeth L.R. Comstock to L.R., Aug. 21, 1880, in Elizabeth L. Comstock, *Life and Letters of Elizabeth Comstock*, ed. Catherine Hare (Philadelphia: John C. Winston, 1895), 384; John Emery Bryant to Mrs. Bryant, Feb. 1, 1880, John Emery Bryant Papers, DU.

29. *Raleigh Observer*, in Tourgée, *A Fool's Errand . . . New, Enlarged, and Illustrated Edition*, front matter.

30. Tourgée, *A Fool's Errand*, 6–7.

31. AWT to Unknown, Feb. 1893, #6688, AWTP; Tourgée, *A Fool's Errand*, 205–31.

32. Tourgée, *A Fool's Errand*, 22–28.

33. Ibid., 133.

34. Ibid., 132.

35. Ibid., 171.

36. AWT to Charles Martindale, March 30, 1880, IHS.

37. [His emphasis]. Tourgée, *A Fool's Errand*, 140.

38. Ibid., 167.

39. Ibid., 141.

40. Ibid., 148.

41. Tourgée quoted in the *New York Tribune*, Sept. 3, 1879.

42. Albion W. Tourgée, *The Invisible Empire* (New York: Fords, Howard, and Hulbert, 1880; reprint, Baton Rouge: Louisiana State University Press, 1989), 141.

43. Tourgée, *A Fool's Errand*, 387.

44. Ibid., 388–89.

45. Ibid., 388–89.

46. Ibid., 133, 171.

47. Ibid., 180.

48. Ibid., 171.

49. Ibid., 255.

50. Ibid., 137.

51. *Buffalo News* and *New York Tribune*, in "Press Notices," *A Fool's Errand By One of the Fools . . . New Edition*, front matter.

52. *Harper's Magazine* 60 (February 1880), 471. *Christian Union*, *Philadelphia Times*, and *Erie* (Pennsylvania) *Dispatch*, in "Press Notices," *A Fool's Errand By One of the Fools . . . New Edition*, front matter.

53. "Recent American Fiction," *Atlantic Monthly* (Sept. 1880): 424.

54. A. J. Emerson, "A Carpetbagger's View of the Ku Klux Klan," *Confederate Veteran* 24 (1916): 308–10. SMLY.

55. Cornelia P. Spencer to Charles Spencer, March 3, 1880, Cornelia Phillips Spencer Papers, Southern Historical Society, UNC.

56. Sallie Holley to Elizabeth Smith Miller, July 13, 1880, in *A Life For Liberty: Antislavery and Other Letters of Sallie Holley*, ed. John White Chadwick (New York: G.P. Putnam's Sons, 1899), 292. As Everett Carter has pointed out, Tourgée's "tricky tone" has perpetuated some confusion about his politics, most particularly in Wilson's *Patriotic Gore*. Wilson badly misreads the irony of some passages in *A Fool's Errand* that praise the Ku Klux Klan for its "wonderful" defiance of the government. Everett Carter, "Edmund Wilson Refights the Civil War: The Revision of Albion Tourgée's Novels," *American Literary Realism, 1870–1910* 29 (Winter, 1997): 68–75.

57. "Our Southern Letter. The Scene of the 'Fool's Errand,'" clipping, #4329, AWTP.

58. Ibid.

59. "A Chatty Letter," Luther Benson to the *Indianapolis Sentinel*, 1881? Clipping, #4329, AWTP.

60. *Evening Post and News* (Louisville, KY), March 1880, clipping, item #4329, AWTP.

61. Though Tourgée had borrowed money from Milton S. Littlefield and George W. Swepson—who would later be convicted of bribing Republican legislators in Florida and North Carolina—he attempted to repay it as a legitimate loan, and he never lent his political support toward any of their railroad schemes. William Lawrence Royall, *A Reply to "A Fool's Errand, By One of the Fools"* (New York: E.J. Hale, 1880); and "About Carpetbaggers," *New York Tribune*, Jan. 31, 1881. One Conservative remarked that Royall's attempt to discredit Tourgée was a "failure . . . about on a par with the like attempted by the author of 'Monon Ou.'" "Albion W. Tourgee," *University Monthly*, vol. 1 (Dec. 1882): 125–26, UNC-NCC.

62. Quoted from excerpt on title page of *The State* (Richmond, VA). Several similar excerpts are included inside the front cover. N. J. Floyd, *Thorns in the Flesh. A Voice of Vindication from the South in Answer to "A Fool's Errand" and Other Slanders* (Lynchburg, VA: J.P. Bell, 1884).

63. Books that supported Tourgée's views include Harriet N. Goff, *Other Fools and Their Doings or Life Among the Freedmen by One Who Has Seen It* (New York: J. S. Ogilivie, 1880), which relates several fictionalized anecdotes regarding Southern white violence against blacks; and [John Patterson Green], *Recollections of the Inhabitants, Localities, Superstitions and Kuklux Outrages of the Carolinas. By a "Carpetbagger" Who Was Born and Lived There* (Cleveland, 1880), NYHS.

64. Floyd, *Thorns*, 20.

65. Ibid., 458–60.

66. Of blacks, Floyd writes: "Let it be known, to the honor of the negro race, that no such outrages were perpetrated by them until after the close of the war, and the Puritan 'philanthropists' had assumed the task of attending to their moral training, and instructing them concerning their social and religious duties." Ibid., 561.

67. Ibid., 46.

68. James S. Pike, *The Prostrate State: South Carolina Under Negro Government* (New York: Loring and Mussey, 1935) [Originally New York, 1873]. For an examination of Pike's questionable research and strong anti-black prejudices, see Robert Franklin Durden, *James Shepherd Pike: Republicanism and the American Negro, 1850–1882* (Durham, NC: Duke University Press, 1957), 194–219.

69. "Albion W. Tourgee," *University Monthly*, vol. 1 (December 1882): 125–26, North Carolina Collection, UNC.

70. [His emphasis]. Tourgée, *The Invisible Empire*, 25.

71. AWT to E.S. Parker, editor of *Wilmington Journal*, May 24, 1875, clipping, #2428, AWTP.

72. Ward M. McAfee, "Reconstruction Revisited: The Republican Public Education Crusade of the 1870s" *Civil War History* 42 (June 1996): 136. See also Ward M. McAfee, *Religion, Race, and Reconstruction: The Public School Crusade of the 1870s* (Albany: State University of New York, 1998).

73. AWT to Grant, Jan., 1870, published in Tourgée, *An Appeal to Caesar*, 409–10.

74. William Scott to Alexander Gates and the "Colored men" of Salem, June 6, 1870, William Lafayette Scott Papers, DU.

75. See Henry Wilson, "The New Departure of the Republican Party," *Atlantic Monthly* 27 (Jan. 1871): 114–20.

76. AWT to Martin B. Anderson, May 11, 1874, #1739, AWTP.

77. Ibid.

78. Ward McAfee, agreeing with Tourgée, emphasizes the role of Sumner's Bill in provoking the 1874 backlash. *Religion, Race, and Reconstruction*, 125–73. William Gillette also views Sumner's Bill as the paramount issue in the campaign that drove

white Southerners from the Republican Party. See William Gillette, *Retreat from Reconstruction, 1869–1879* (Baton Rouge: Louisiana State University Press, 1979), 202–58.

79. AWT to Martin B. Anderson, May 11, 1874, #1739, AWTP.

80. As a result, even in its final form, which made no mention of schools, the Civil Rights Act of 1875 never had a discernable impact on the South. Un-enforced while on the books, the U.S. Supreme Court struck it down as unconstitutional within eight years of its existence in the *Civil Rights Cases* (1883). Never more than a dead letter for its "beneficent purposes," as Tourgée had predicted, its "evil influences" were vivid and active indeed.

81. Nell Painter, *Exodusters: Black Migration to Kansas after Reconstruction* (W.W. Norton, 1876), 234–55.

82. [My emphasis]. Hayes's speech in Youngstown, Ohio, quoted in the *Evening News*, Sept. 18, 1879. See Stanley P. Hirshon, *Farewell to the Bloody Shirt: Northern Republicans and the Southern Negro, 1877–1893* (Chicago: Quadrangle Books, 1962), 59.

83. Grant spoke of the defeat of the Ku Klux Klan "as so admirably told by Judge Tourgée in his 'Fool's Errand.'" Speech delivered in Warren, Ohio, Sept. 28, 1880. He later declared, "We are all carpetbaggers—nothing else. . . . What has been the effect of the carpetbag government in the Northwest? Let us hope that after this election that carpetbaggers may go freely into the South, build up their waste places, make them happy and rich, [and] introduce schools," in *Gems of the Campaign of 1800 By Generals Grant and Garfield*, ed. George P. Edgar (Jersey City, NJ: Issued by the Lincoln Association, 1881), 16, 22. SMLY.

84. AWT to James A. Garfield, Aug. 16, 1880, JG; Albion W. Tourgée, "Garfield and the Astrologer," *Atlanta Constitution*, Oct. 4, 1896; Hirshon, *Farewell to the Bloody Shirt*, 87.

85. Asa Lamb? to James A. Garfield, Sept. 18, 1880, JG; R.N. Baker to M. Micals, Sept. 30, 1880, #2381, AWTP.

86. Tourgée, quoted from a speech at the Union League of Philadelphia delivered soon after the campaign, 1881, #2414, AWTP.

87. *Garfield and Arthur Campaign Song Book* (Washington, DC: Republican congressional committee, 1880), 9, 24, NYHS.

88. [His emphasis]. Asa Lamb? to James A. Garfield, Sept. 18, 1880, JG.

89. AWT to James A. Garfield, Dec. 14, 1880, JG.

90. AWT to James A. Garfield, Dec. 14, 1880, JG. See also, AWT to James Garfield, Dec. 1880, #2389, AWTP.

91. Albion W. Tourgée, "Aaron's Rod in Politics," *North American Review* 132 (Feb. 1881): 151–53.

92. Coincidentally, Tourgée's novel *Figs and Thistles: A Romance of the Western Reserve*—about a young man's rise from obscurity on the Western Reserve to become a Brigadier General and Congressman—bore enough resemblance to Garfield's life that some readers believed it was a fictionalized campaign biography. AWT to Joshua N. Steed, April 30, 1888. Tourgée, Miscellaneous Letters, Southern Historical Collection, UNC. On Garfield's early life, see Hendrik Booraem V, *The Road to Respectability: James A. Garfield and His World, 1844–1852* (Lewisburg, PA: Bucknell University Press, 1988).

93. Garfield, quoted in Simpson, *Reconstruction Presidents*, 216.

94. Garfield, quoted in Hirshon, *Farewell to the Bloody Shirt*, 88.

95. Hinsdale to Garfield, Jan. 4 and 8, 1881; Garfield to Hinsdale, Dec. 30, 1880. In Mary L. Hinsdale, ed., *Garfield-Hinsdale Letters: Correspondence between James Abram Garfield and Burke Aaron Hinsdale* (Ann Arbor: University of Michigan Press, 1949), 469, 473, 478.

96. [My emphasis]. "Inaugural Address," in Burke A. Hinsdale, ed., *The Works of James A. Garfield*, vol. 2 (Boston: James R. Osgood, 1883), 790. According to Rayford Logan, more blacks than whites attended Garfield's Inaugural Ball because of the widespread perception that he was truly committed to their interests. Logan, *Betrayal of the* Negro, 53–54.

97. AWT to James A. Garfield, March 4, 1881, JG.

98. "Suggesting a Cabinet: Whom the People Name as Advisors to President-Elect Garfield," *New York Times*, Dec. 4, 1880; "Notes from Washington," *Washington Post*, April 8, 1881; "The Substance of It," *Washington Post*, May 11, 1881.

99. AWT to James A. Garfield, March 5, 1881, JG.

100. AWT to James A. Garfield, March 22, 1881; AWT to James A. Garfield, May 30, 1881, JG.

101. AWT to Theodore Roosevelt, Oct. 21, 1901, TR.

102. Logan, *The Betrayal of the Negro*, 57.

103. Hinsdale quoted in Hirshon, *Farewell to the Bloody Shirt*, 94; McAfee, "1870s Pubic Education Crusade," 151.

Chapter 7: Radical Individualism in the Gilded Age

1. Tourgée, *A Veteran and His Pipe* (Chicago and New York: Belford, Clarke, 1886), 15, 23; first epigraph, Albion W. AWT, *Murvale Eastman: Christian Socialist* (New York: Fords, Howard & Hulbert, 1889), iv–v.; second epigraph, William Graham Sumner, "Sociology," *Princeton Review* 2 (Dec. 1881): 311, 321.

2. Tourgee, *A Veteran and His Pipe*, 23, 25.

3. On the debate over pensions, see Stuart McConnell, *Glorious Contentment: The Grand Army of the Republic, 1865–1900* (Chapel Hill: University of North Carolina Press, 1992), 153–65.

4. Tourgée, *A Veteran and His Pipe*, 24.

5. Ibid., 19, 24.

6. Stanley P. Hirshon, *Farewell to the Bloody Shirt: Northern Republicans and the Southern Negro, 1877–1893* (Chicago: Quadrangle Books, 1962), 126–42.

7. Nancy Cohen, *The Reconstruction of American Liberalism, 1865–1914* (Chapel Hill: University of North Carolina Press, 2002), 1–19, 61–85; also, Foner, *Reconstruction*, 488–99; Hirshon, *Farewell to the Bloody Shirt*, 126–42; George M. Fredrickson, *The Inner Civil War: Northern Intellectuals and the Crisis of the Union* (New York: Harper & Row, 1965), 194–96; Mark Wahlgren Summers, *Rum, Romanism & Rebellion: The Making of a President, 1884* (Chapel Hill: University of North Carolina Press, 2000), 23–26.

8. Cohen, *Reconstruction of American Liberalism*, see chap. 2 especially.

9. Tourgée, *Letters to a King*, 238.

10. Cohen, *Reconstruction of American Liberalism*, 11; on mugwumps, see Hirshon, *Farewell to the Bloody Shirt*, 126–42.

11. Tourgée, *Letters to a King*, 238.

12. Hirshon, *Farewell to the Bloody Shirt*, 127; Rayford Logan, *Betrayal of the Negro: From Rutherford B. Hayes to Woodrow Wilson*, new and enlarged ed. (New York: Collier Books, 1965), 50.

13. Summers, *Rum, Romanism & Rebellion*, 41, 43.

14. See Allen W. Trelease, *White Terror: The Ku Klux Klan Conspiracy and Southern Reconstruction* (New York: Harper and Row, 1971), 294.

15. The *Globe* provided this definition in response to a reader's inquiry about the origin and meaning of the "unrefined and most despicable phrase, 'bloody shirt'

which the press and especially the independent element thereof, are flinging about so 'promiscuous-like.'" See, "The Bloody Shirt," *Boston Globe*, Sept. 4, 1875.

16. Tourgée, "Aaron's Rod in Politics," *North American Review* 132 (Feb. 1881), 139–62.

17. Hoar's speech reprinted in the *Springfield Daily Republican*, July 1, 1885; quoted in Hirshon, *Farewell to the Bloody Shirt*, 133.

18. AWT to Editor, *New York Sun*, 1880[?], #2387, AWTP.

19. Albion Tourgée, *An Appeal to Caesar* (New York: Fords, Howard & Hulbert, 1884), 9–20.

20. Fredrickson quoted from *The Black Image in the White Mind: The Debate on Afro-American Character and Destiny, 1817–1914* (Middletown, CT: Wesleyan University Press, 1971), 242–43.

21. One reviewer points out that the 1870 census was very incomplete in regard to its statistics for Southern blacks. This may account for the apparent sharp rise in the black population in 1880. See *New York Examiner*, Jan. 15, 1885. Review of *An Appeal to Caesar*, clipping, #2540, AWTP.

22. Tourgée, *An Appeal to Caesar*, 104–5, 363.

23. Ibid., 357.

24. Ibid., 362.

25. Ibid., 357–59.

26. Ibid., 281.

27. See collection of review clippings, #2457, AWTP.

28. Review of "An Appeal to Caesar," *Saturday Review*, Dec. 20, 1884, #2540, AWTP.

29. "Tourgée's Appeal," *New York Commercial Advertiser*, Oct. 20, 1884, clipping, #2540, AWTP.

30. Ibid.

31. Ibid.

32. Ibid.

33. Ibid.

34. Ibid.

35. Ibid.

36. "The Lifting Up of the Negro," *The Nation* (Nov. 27, 1884), 462–63.

37. Ibid.

38. EKT to Roberts Bros., March 30, 1887, #2510, AWTP.

39. "Judge Tourgee's Home," *The Dispatch*, Aug. 16, 1883, clipping #2539, AWTP.

40. "The Continent: Judge Albion Tourgee's Failure on the Threshold of Success," *Philadelphia Press*, undated clipping [1884?], #2340, AWTP; Frank Luther Mott, *A History of American Magazines, 1865–1885*, vol. 3 (Cambridge: Harvard University Press, 1948), 558.

41. EKT to Mr. Moot, June 17, 1905, #97722 AWTP.

42. Mott, *American Magazines*, 42.

43. Quoted in EKT's Diary, May 17, 1882, #9906, AWTP.

44. "The Fate of the Continent," *The Literary World or A Monthly Review of the Current Literature* (Sept. 1844): 15; Mott, *A History*, 558–59. The first advertisements appeared in March, 1882.

45. Quoted in Roy F. Dibble, *Albion W. Tourgée* (New York: Lemke and Buechner, 1921), 90.

46. Frank Leslie, "Mrs. Frank Leslie and *The Continent*," *The Critic: A Literary Weekly* (Sept. 1884), 37.

47. AWT to Emily Sartain, March 28, 1886, Tourgée Miscellaneous Letters, UI.
48. AWT to B.A. Barlow, Esq., Feb. 7, 1890, #4473, AWTP.
49. Otto H. Olsen, *Carpetbagger's Crusade: The Life of Albion Winegar Tourgée* (Baltimore: Johns Hopkins University Press, 1965), 266–67.
50. Tourgée, Eulogy for Angie Kilbourne, May 8, 1897, #9351, AWTP.
51. Tourgée, *Queen of Hearts*, 61–63.
52. Emma's Diary, April 9, 1885, #9906, AWTP.
53. Emma's Diary, #9906, AWTP; Olsen, *Carpetbagger's Crusade*, 265–71.
54. Emma's Diary, 1885–1889, #9906, AWTP; Tourgée, *An Outing with the Queen of Hearts* (New York: Merril & Baker, 1894), 1–3.
55. AWT to Emily Sartain, March 28, 1886, UI; AWT to Emily Sartain, May 24, 1886, KSU.
56. Aimée Tourgée, *The Culwin Luck Stone*, #10896, AWTP: Aimée Tourgée. Last Will and Testament, Surrogate's Court Office, Mayville, New York; "Aimee Tourgee Dead: Daughter of Famous Judge Stricken with Heart Disease," *Syracuse Herald*, April 20, 1909.
57. Aimée Tourgée to AWT, Jan. 30, 1890, #4401, AWTP.
58. AWT to Aimée Tourgée, Feb. 1, 1890, #4418, AWTP.
59. These were, respectively, *Bricks Without Straw* (1880); *A Royal Gentleman* (1881); *Hot Plowshares* (1883); *Button's Inn* (1887); *Black Ice* (1888); *'89, or the Grand Master's Secret* (1888); *Murvale Eastman: Christian Socialist* (1890); *Pactolus Prime, or the White Christ* (1890); *Zouri's Christmas* (1881); *John Eax* (1882); *Mamelon: or, the South without the Shadow* (1882); *With Gauge and Swallow, Attorneys* (1889); *An Appeal to Caesar* (1884); *A Man of Destiny* (1885); *A Veteran and His Pipe* (1886); and *Letters to A King* (1888).
60. J. R. Howard to Emma, March 15, 1893, #6746, AWTP.
61. Emma's disdain for realism is discussed in Tourgée, *Queen of Hearts*, 54–58. Tourgée praises Cooper's style in "A Bystander's Notes," *Chicago Inter Ocean*, Sept. 28, 1889, 4.
62. Eric J. Sundquist, "Realism and Regionalism," in *Columbia Literary History of the United States*, ed. Emory Elliott (New York: Columbia University Press, 1988), 511; other Tourgée enthusiasts include George J. Becker, in "Albion W. Tourgée: Pioneer in Social Criticism," *American Literature* 19 (March 1947), 70; and Edmund Wilson, who hailed *A Fool's Errand* as an "historical classic" for its effective realistic qualities in *Patriotic Gore: Studies in the Literature of the American Civil War* (New York: W.W. Norton, 1962), 536.
63. *Our Continent* 4 (Aug. 15, 1883), 219; Aug. 22, 1883, 252; Sept. 26, 411. Tourgée's criticism of Howells becomes personal, focusing particularly on his effeminacy, in "A Tide-Watcher's Thoughts," May 30; and June 14, 26, 1889, #3833, AWTP.
64. David Shi, *Facing Facts: Realism in American Thought and Culture* (New York: Oxford University Press, 1995), 103–4.
65. Shi, *Facing Facts*, 123.
66. *Our Continent* 3 (Jan. 6, 1883): 732.
67. Tourgée, *Queen of Hearts*, 44–45, 69–70. See also, Albion W. Tourgée, "The Claim of Realism," *The North American Review* 148 (March 1889), 386–88.
68. AWT to S. S. McClure, May, 1894, #7748, AWTP.
69. *A Fool's Errand*, 101–3.
70. *Bricks Without Straw*, 26.
71. *Bricks Without Straw*, 206–8.
72. "Poll Tax Song," clipping from *Anti-Slavery Standard*, 1867, #2428, AWTP.

73. For a useful overview of black folk music, see Lawrence Levine, *Black Culture and Black Consciousness: Afro-American Folk Thought From Slavery to Freedom* (New York: Oxford University Press, 1977), 190–297.

74. *Our Continent*, Dec. 20, 1882, Jan. 3, 1883.

75. AWT to George Washington Cable, Jan. 12, 1885, TU. Arlin Turner, *George W. Cable: A Biography* (Durham: Duke University Press, 1956), 132.

76. AWT to General O. O. Howard, March [?] 1893, #7621, AWTP.

77. AWT, *Hot Plowshares*, 464–65.

78. *Our Continent* 2 (1883), 571.

79. Review of *Hot Plowshares* in *The Nation* (June 25, 1883), clipping, item #2539, AWTP. Another indication of its poor reception came from the former head of the Freedmen's Bureau, General O. O. Howard, who asked Tourgée permission for his son to write a parody of *Hot Plowshares* for the purpose, he said, of protesting the "liquor traffic." AWT to General O. O. Howard, March, 1893, #7621, AWTP.

80. Blight, *Race and Reunion*, 174–81.

81. In its final form, *John March, Southerner* would receive poor reviews in the leading mugwump journals *Atlantic Monthly* and *The Nation*. Gilder quoted in Turner, *Cable*, 293; Wilson, *Patriotic Gore*, 583–87. Although he was critical of Tourgée's literary talents and a political mugwump, Gilder was no realist. His aesthetic standards remained "prim and prissy," according to Thomas Bender in *New York Intellect: A History of Intellectual Life in New York City, From 1750 to the Beginning of Our Own Time* (Baltimore: Johns Hopkins University Press, 1987), 214–15.

82. On Crane's aesthetic, see David Halliburton, *The Color of the Sky: A Study of Stephen Crane* (Cambridge: Cambridge University Press, 1989); Shi, *Facing Fact*, 223–30. Donna Gerstenberger, " 'The Open Boat': Additional Perspective," *Modern Fiction Studies* 17 (Winter, 1971–1972): 557–61.

83. Harold Frederic, *New York Times*, Jan. 12, 1896, 22. Interestingly, Frederic would publish his own work of realism the following year, *The Damnation of Theron Ware*, which belittled the moral absolutism of middle-class America that Tourgée embraced.

84. AWT, *An Outing*, 70.

85. Nina Silber, *The Romance of Reunion: Northerners and the South, 1865–1900* (Chapel Hill: University of North Carolina Press, 1993), 94–96. 116; on the culture of reconciliation, see also Buck, 215–16; Diffley, 54–79; and Lyde Cullen Sizer, "Still Waiting: Intermarriage in White Women's Civil War Novels," in Martha Hodes, ed., *Sex, Love, Race: Crossing Boundaries in North American History* (New York: NYU Press, 1999).

86. Tourgée, "The South as a Field for Fiction," *The Forum* 4 (Dec. 1888): 405.

87. Ibid., 409.

88. Ibid, 408–9, 411.

89. Anna Julia Cooper, *A Voice from the South* (1892; Reprint, New York: Negro Universities Press, 1969), 188–91, 201; Sterling Brown, *The Negro in American Fiction* (Washington, DC: Associates in Negro Folk Education, 1937); and Hugh Gloster, *Negro Voices in American Fiction* (Chapel Hill: University of North Carolina Press 1948).

90. Chesnutt's journal, March 16, 1880, *The Journals of Charles W. Chesnutt*, ed. Richard H. Broadhead (Durham: Duke University Press, 1993), 124–26. In later speeches and essays, Chesnutt often mentioned Tourgée's novels as an inspiration. For instance, see his 1929 speech, "The Negro in Present Day Fiction," in *Charles W. Chesnutt: Essays and Speeches*, ed. Joseph R. McElrath, Jr., et al. (Stanford

University Press, 1999), 516. On Tourgée's literary influence on Chesnutt, see Richard O. Lewis, "Romanticism in the Fiction of Charles W. Chesnutt: The Influence of Dickens, Scott, Tourgée, and Douglass," in *College Language Association* 26 (Dec. 1982): 145–71; Peter Jerome Caccavari, "Reconstructions of Race and Culture in America: Violence and Knowledge in works by Albion Tourgée, Charles Chesnutt, and Thomas Dixon, Jr." (Ph.D. diss., Rutgers University, 1993).

91. Chesnutt, May 29, 1880, *Journal*, 139. Chesnutt went on to elaborate on his "high, holy purpose," stating: "The object of my writings would be not so much the elevation of the colored people as the elevation of the whites."

92. AWT to Charles W. Chesnutt, Dec. 8, 1888, Charles Chesnutt Papers, FU. Quoted in Frances Richardson Keller, *An American Crusade: The Life of Charles Waddel Chesnutt* (Provo, UT: Brigham Young University Press, 1978), 120–21.

93. Charles W. Chesnutt to AWT, April 18, 1893, #6875, AWTP.

94. Charles W. Chesnutt to Houghton Mifflin & Co., Oct. 26, 1901, Charles Chesnutt Papers, FU.

95. AWT, *Letters*, 77.

96. Ibid., 237–38.

97. Ibid., 72–74.

98. AWT, "A Bystander's Notes," *Chicago Daily Inter Ocean*, Oct. 12, 1889.

99. Ibid., June 2, 1888.

100. Ely, quoted in Charles Howard Hopkins, *The Rise of the Social Gospel in American Protestantism, 1865–1915* (New Haven: Yale University Press, 1940), 94. Richard T. Ely, *The Labor Movement in America* (New York: Thomas Crowell, 1886). See also, Henry F. May, *Protestant Churches and Industrial America* (New York: Harper & Brothers, 1949); Susan Curtis, *A Consuming Faith: The Social Gospel and Modern American Culture* (Baltimore: Johns Hopkins University Press, 1991).

101. AWT, "A Bystander's Notes," *Chicago Daily Inter Ocean*, Jan. 25, 1890.

102. AWT, *Eighty-Nine*, 394–98.

103. AWT, *Pactolus Prime*, 17.

104. Charles Chesnutt to George Washington Cable, June 13, 1890, Cable Collection, TU. Quoted in Keller, *American Crusade*, 122; Helen M. Chesnutt, *Charles Waddell Chesnutt* (Chapel Hill: University of North Carolina Press, 1952), 58–59.

105. AWT to T. Thomas Fortune, Feb. 1893, #6703, AWTP.

106. Emma's diary, Sept. 17, 1889, #9906, AWTP.

107. Entry for Wednesday, June 15, 1890, in Charles Richard Williams, ed., *The Diaries and Letters of Rutherford B. Hayes*, vol. 4, 1881–1893 (Columbus, OH, 1925), 579.

108. *Atlanta Constitution*, quoted in Marguerite Ealy and Stanford E. Marovitz, "Albion Winegar Tourgée (1838–1905)," *American Literary Realism, 1870–1910* (Winter 1975), 64–65.

109. George J. Becker, "Albion W. Tourgée: Pioneer in Social Criticism," *American Literature* 19 (March 1947): 59. Even Theodore Gross, whose 1963 assessment of Tourgée was mostly scathing about the quality of his fiction, acknowledged that it "contains some of Tourgée's finest writing and demonstrates how impressive he can be when he deals with a social or political issue that is of deep personal concern to him." Theodore Gross, *Albion W. Tourgée* (New York: Twayne, 1963), 131; Constance Shepard to AWT, July 14, 1893, AWTP.

110. Tourgée, *Murvale Eastman*, 28, 43.

111. Ibid., 121–24.

112. Tourgée describes the Church of the Golden Lilies as bordering on a plot of land known as the "Flat-iron tract," and facing a private, gated park called "Garden

Square." St. George's, J. P. Morgan's parish, faced a private, gated park—Stuyvesant Square Park—within what is known today as the Flatiron district. On Morgan's role at St. George's, see Jean Strouse, *Morgan: American Financier* (New York: Random House, 1999), 218–22.

113. Tourgée, *Murvale Eastman*, 385.

114. Ibid., 236.

115. Ibid, 519–21.

116. Ibid., "Preface," v–vi.

117. Ibid., 121.

118. AWT to Prof. Frank W. Rathurn, Oct. 24, 1892, #6445, AWTP.

119. AWT to Bishop John H. Vincent, 1891[?], #5898, AWTP.

120. Quoted from preface, *Murvale Eastman*, iv–v.

Chapter 8: Beginning the Civil Rights Movement

1. AWT to Rev. John H. Frazer, Feb. 27, 1885, Jenkins Autograph Collection, FLS; first epigraph, Harry C. Smith, quoted from the *Cleveland Gazette*, Nov. 21, 1891; second epigraph, Ida B. Wells to Tourgée, Feb. 22, 1893, #6645, AWTP; Louis A. Martinet to AWT, May 30, 1893, #6998, AWTP.

2. These were "A Veteran and His Pipe," April 25–Sept. 19, 1885; "Letters to a Mugwump," Sept. 26–Dec. 12, 1885; "A Child of Luck," March 20–Dec. 4, 1886.

3. William H. Busbey to AWT, Nov. 17, 1893, #7501, AWTP.

4. William H. Busbey to EKT, August 13, 1894, #7969, AWTP. Originally called the *Chicago Republican* in 1872, the *Inter Ocean* would later become the *Herald*, and then the *Herald-Examiner*. Its motto is quoted in Mott, *American Journalism*, 463. See also Olsen, *Carpet Bagger's Crusade*, 277.

5. Albion W. Tourgée, "A Bystander's Notes," *Inter Ocean*, April 28, May 5, 1888.

6. William H. Busbey to AWT, Nov. 17, 1893, #7501, AWTP; Tourgée responded to the *Inter Ocean's* disclaimers regarding his comments on the tariff in "A Bystander's Notes," April 28, 1888.

7. "A Bystander's Notes," July 7, 14, August 4, 1888; AWT to Benjamin Harrison, no date, 1888, BH.

8. AWT to Benjamin Harrison, Oct. 12, 1888, BH; Tourgée explained later about the RNC attempt to muzzle him, AWT to Benjamin Harrison, Sept. 25, 1891, BH.

9. AWT to Benjamin Harrison, July 25, 1888, BH.

10. "A Bystander's Notes," Dec., 22, 1888; Jan. 5, Feb. 9, 1889.

11. "A Bystander's Notes," Jan. 19, 1889. On White Cap incidents, see *Cleveland Gazette*, July 28, Dec. 8, 1888, Dec. 17, 1892.

12. "A Bystander's Notes," March 23, 1889.

13. "A Bystander's Notes," Nov. 30, 1894.

14. "A Bystander's Notes," March 8, 1890.

15. "The Inter-Ocean in Mississippi," by T. Cotton, newspaper clipping, May 5, 1892, #6211, AWTP. See Otto H. Olsen, "Albion W. Tourgée and Negro Militants of the 1890's: A Documentary Selection," *Science and Society* 28 (1964), 183–207.

16. First quotation, C.J. Taggart to AWT, April 21, 1892; second quotation, Jane Evans and Minnie Evans Dec. 17, 1891; third quotation, Walter H. Griffin, "sons of liberty," June 7, 1892; fourth quotation, Dudley Stuard to AWT, Aug. 15, 1892. All NCRA responses are filed under #7416, AWTP; also reprinted in Olsen, *Science and Society*, 185. Stuard's release was subsequently obtained.

17. Alexander S. Jackson to AWT, Nov. 13, 1891, #5788; Geo. E. Taylor to AWT, July 17, 1892, #6412, AWTP.

18. A. L. Bailey to AWT, March 16, 1893, #6753, AWTP.

19. "A Bystander's Notes," March 8, 1890.

20. AWT to McKinley, reprinted in the *Cleveland Gazette*, March 3, 1894. Discussed in David Gerber, "Lynching and Law and Order: Origin and Passage of the Ohio Anti-Lynching Law of 1896," *Ohio History* 83 (1974): 44–45.

21. Gerber, "Lynching and Law," 46–49.

22. These were South Carolina, Kentucky, Illinois, Minnesota, Nebraska, New Jersey, Pennsylvania, West Virginia, and Wisconsin. Gerber, "Lynching and Law," 49.

23. "Ohio's Anti-Lynching Law," *Washington Post*, June 7, 1897.

24. H. C. Smith to Emma, Oct. 12, 1908, #10527, AWTP; the occurrence of lynching in Ohio declined from five incidents during 1890 to 1900 to two incidents during 1900 to 1910. See David Gerber, "Lynching and Law," 43–48, 50.

25. Carolyn L. Karcher, "The White 'Bystander' and the Black Journalist 'Abroad': Albion W. Tourgée and Ida B. Wells as Allies Against Lynching," *Prospects: An Annual of American Cultural Studies* 29 (2005): 91–92.

26. Ida B. Wells to AWT, July 2, 1892, #6374, AWTP.

27. Although he did not take her case, Tourgée remained involved in it, as evinced by F. L. Barnett's letter remarking: "My partner and I fell under many obligations to you for your helpful advice" on her lawsuit. F. L. Barnett to AWT, Feb. 23, 1893, #6646; Ida B. Wells to AWT, Feb. 22, 1893 #6645; AWT to Ida B. Wells, Feb. 1893, #6687. AWTP. Ida B. Wells, *Crusade for Justice: The Autobiography of Ida B. Wells*, ed. Alfreda M. Duster (Chicago, 1970), 120–21, 156.

28. Frances Willard to AWT, Dec. 21, 1894, #8217; Ida B. Wells to AWT, Nov. 27, 1894, #8202, AWTP; "A Bystander's Notes," Nov. 24, 1892; Karcher, *Prospects*, 106.

29. Ida B. Wells to AWT, July 1, 1893, #7093, AWTP; see also F. J. Loudin to AWT, March 13, 1893, #6740; AWT to F.J. Loudin, March ?, 1893, #6810, AWTP.

30. Printed open letter by Catherine Impey to the "Society for the Recognition of the Brotherhood of Man," Feb. 12, 1895, #8277, AWTP.

31. Wells, *Autobiography*, 82, 85.

32. A facsimile of this photograph and its inscription can be found in Ida B. Wells et al., eds., *The Reason Why the Colored American Is Not in the World's Columbian Exposition, 1893*, ed. Robert W. Rydell (Chicago, 1893; Reprint, Urbana and Chicago, 1999); see Wells, *Crusade for Justice*, 138–39; "Ida B. Wells," *Atlanta Constitution*, July 29, 1894; Carolyn L. Karcher, "Ida B. Wells and her allies against lynching: A transnational perspective," *Comparative American Studies* 3, no. 2 (2005): 131–51.

33. AWT to W.P. Nixon, July 15, 1893, #3174, AWTP.

34. [My emphasis]. Wells, *Autobiography*, 151.

35. Catherine Impey to AWT, Sept. 23, 1894, #8044, AWTP; for a previous invitation to Britain, see Catherine Impey to AWT, June 24, 1893, #7069, AWTP.

36. Quoted in "A Bystander's Notes," unpublished, this installment was rejected by the *Inter Ocean* editors for discussing matters they deemed too inflammatory, July 8, 1892, #6386, AWTP.

37. "A Bystander's Notes," July 13, 1889; "Another South Hater," clipping from the *Alabama Mountain Eagle*, 1893[?], #6994, AWTP.

38. William W. Bates to AWT, May 20, 1893, #6973, AWTP.

39. AWT to Benjamin Harrison, April 12, 16, and May 2, 1890, HP; Olsen, *Carpetbagger's Crusade*, 303–5; Rayford Logan, *The Betrayal of the Negro: From Rutherford B. Hayes to Woodrow Wilson*, new, enlarged ed. (New York: Collier Books, 1965), 62–87. Originally published in 1954 as *The Negro in American Life and Thought: The Nadir, 1877–1901*.

40. Harrison Kelley to EKT, May 15, #4729, 1890, AWTP.

41. "The Blair Bill and Judge Tourgee's Plan," *Republican Champion* (Newport, NH), clipping, #2450, 1884, AWTP.

42. [His emphasis]. Tourgée's discussion of his testimony on the Blair Bill is quoted from Albion W. Tourgée, "The Negro's View of the Race Problem," in Barrows, *First Mohonk Conference*, 114.

43. See printed pamphlet on H.R. 4980, "Support of Common Schools . . . Mr. Joseph D. Taylor, from the Committee on Education, submitted the following as the Views of the Minority," #2446, AWTP.

44. AWT to unknown, 1890, #4406, AWTP; Daniel W. Crofts, "The Black Response to the Blair Education Bill," *Journal of Southern History* 37 (Feb., 1971): 52–53.

45. Joseph C. Price is quoted from the Afro-American League debate on the Blair Bill at their 1890 Convention in Chicago. He was responding to T. Thomas Fortune and Harry C. Smith, who expressed strong reservations that echoed Tourgée's. Quoted in Crofts, "The Black Response," 57–58; he afterwards told Tourgée the same thing privately, J.C. Price to AWT, March 18, 1890, #4586, AWTP.

46. AWT to J.C. Price, 1892, #11043, AWTP; Thomas Adams Upchurch, *Legislating Racism: The Billion Dollar Congress and the Birth of Jim Crow* (Lexington, KY: University Press of Kentucky, 2004), 46–65.

47. Brook Thomas suggests Tourgée's influence on the Blair Bill was responsible for the failure of Congress to pass any bill supporting education. Thomas, ed. *Plessy v. Ferguson: A Brief History with Documents* (Boston, 1997), 4. Crofts suggests that Republican defectors, far from taking a radical position, agreed with Ohio Senator John Sherman, who explained his vote by saying, "conditions have changed since I voted for the [Blair] bill a few years ago. The South is now prosperous and is making fair and reasonable efforts to educate its illiterates," "Black Response," 60.

48. These included, "Our Semi-citizens," *Frank Leslie's Illustrated Weekly* 69 (Sept. 28, 1889), 122–23; "Shall We Re-barbarize the Negro?," *The Congregationalist* 41 (Dec. 5, 1889), 411; "Shall White Minorities Rule?" *The Forum* 7 (April, 1889); "The American Negro: What Are His Rights and What Must Be Done to Secure Them?," *New York Tribune*, Feb. 16, 1890; "The Right to Vote," *The Forum* 9 (March 1890), 78–92.

49. John Tyler Morgan, "Shall Negro Majorities Rule?" *The Forum* 6 (February 1889): 595.

50. "Shall White Minorities Rule?" *The Forum* 7 (April, 1889), 144, 152, 154.

51. Ibid.

52. In the wake of the Blair Bill's defeat, T. Thomas Fortune, who would later ally with Washington, urged, "Let the race pull itself together. What others will not do for us we must do for ourselves," quoted in Croft, "The Black Response," 59.

53. Leslie H. Fishel, Jr., "The 'Negro Question' at Mohonk: Microcosm, Mirage, and Message," *New York History* (July 1993): 277–314. Ralph Luker, *The Social Gospel in Black and White: American Racial Reform, 1885–1912* (Chapel Hill: University of North Carolina Press, 1991), 26–27. Also see Eric Foner, *Reconstruction: America's Unfinished Revolution, 1863–1877* (New York, 1988), 605–6.

54. Tourgée's emphasis removed. Tourgée, "The Negro's View of the Race Problem," in *First Mohonk Conference on the Negro Question. Held at Lake Mohonk, Ulster County New York, June 4, 5, 6,* ed. Isabel C. Barrows (New York, 1969), 24–25, 108–10; Entry for Friday, June 6, 1890 in Rutherford B. Hayes, *Diaries and Letters of Rutherford B. Hayes,* vol. 4, ed. Charles R. Williams (New York, 1971), 579.

55. "Judge Tourgee's Splendid Speech," *The Republican*, clipping #8251, AWTP.

56. Luker, *Social Gospel*, 28; AWT to Bishop Turner, Nov. 7, 1893, #7471, AWTP.

57. James Bryce, "Thoughts on the Negro Problem," *North American Review* 143 (1891): 549, 654.

58. Buck, *Road to Reunion*, 27–81; Upchurch, *Legislating* Racism, 66–166.

59. Logan, *The Betrayal of the Negro*, 62.

60. Eli C. Freeman to AWT, Aug. 4, 1890, #4872, AWTP. Tourgée's response (now lost) was probably published in the *New Orleans Crusader*, but that installment of the newspaper has not been found. Freeman, a twenty-eight-year-old graduate of Straight University in New Orleans, apologized to Tourgée for publishing it without his permission. Eli C. Freeman to AWT, Aug. 26, 1890, #4895, AWTP.

61. Eli C. Freeman to AWT, Aug. 4, 1890, #4872, AWTP; Eli C. Freeman to AWT, Aug. 26, 1890; #4895, AWTP; Charles A. Lofgren, *The* Plessy *Case: A Legal-Historical Interpretation* (New York: Oxford University Press, 1987), 28–32.

62. *Report of Proceedings for the Annulment of Act 111 of 1890 By the Citizens' Committee of New Orleans, La.* 2, folder 13, box 1, Charles Rousseve Papers, ARC; Joseph Logsdon and Caryn Cossé Bell, "The Americanization of Black New Orleans 1850–1900," *Creole New Orleans: Race and Americanization*, ed. Arnold R. Hirsch and Joseph Logsdon (Baton Rouge: Louisiana State University Press, 1992), 256–57; Martinet quoted in C. Vann Woodward, "The Birth of Jim Crow," *American Heritage* 15 (April 1964): 53.

63. See Desdunes's commentary on Martinet in *Our People and Our History*, 146–47.

64. Citizens' Committee of New Orleans, *Report of Proceedings for the Annulment of Act 111*, vol. 2, Charles Rousseve Papers, box 1, folder 13, ARC.

65. *United States v. Cruikshank*, 92 U.S. 542 (1876); *Civil Rights Cases*, 109 U.S. 3 (1883).

66. The New Orleans *Crusader*, July 4, Aug. 15, 189, clippings, Charles Rousseve Papers, folders 8, 20, box 1, ARC.

67. Louis A. Martinet to AWT, Oct. 5, 1891, #5760, AWTP.

68. Lofgren, *The* Plessy *Case*, 28–31.

69. *The Daily Crusader*, May 10, 1890, clipping in the Rousseve Papers, folder 15, ARC.

70. Martinet to Tourgée, Oct. 5, 1891, #5760, AWTP.

71. Ibid.

72. The enrollment form would be included at the bottom of all subsequent installments of "A Bystander's Notes." "A Bystander's Notes," Oct. 17, 1891.

73. Colored Citizens of New Orleans to AWT, Nov. 16, 1891, #5791, AWTP.

74. John [Le Leavent?] to AWT, Nov. 15, 1891, #5790, AWTP.

75. Mrs. Nettie S. Chapin, National Headquarters of the Ladies of the Grand Army of the Republic, to AWT, May 9, 1892, #6222; AWTP; Olsen, *Carpetbaggers Crusade*, 313.

76. AWT to "Madame" [Florence A. Lewis] with letters of June, 1892, #6297, AWTP.

77. Albion Tourgée, *Is Liberty Worth Preserving?* (Chicago: Inter Ocean, 1892), 25, Daniel A. Murray Pamphlet Collection, LC.

78. AWT to unknown, Nov. 1891, item #5813, William Penn Nixon to AWT, March 21, 1892, #6133, AWTP; Albion W. Tourgée, *Headquarters: National Citizens' Rights Association* (Broadside) Oct., 15, 1893. F.J. Cooke Papers, DU; Olsen, *Carpetbagger's Crusade*, 294–96, 325.

79. *Is Liberty Worth Preserving?* 17, 19, 25.

80. AWT to Thomas B. Reed, undated [1892], #6500, AWTP.

81. AWT to unknown, 1892? #5999, AWTP.

82. AWT to Bishop Turner, Oct. 1893, #7433; AWT to Thomas B. Reed, un-dated [1892], #6500, AWTP; see also AWT to unknown, no dates, [1892?] #5999, #6009, and #6025, AWTP; AWT to Capt. R.H. Pratt, March 3, 1892, BL.

83. AWT to unknown, no date, [1892?], #6025, AWTP.

84. AWT to W.E. Turner, 1892, #6366, AWTP.

85. George Washington Cable to AWT, Dec. 19, 1891, #5862, AWTP.

86. AWT to unknown, Jan. [1892?] #5999; Mrs. Nettie S. Chapin to AWT, May 9, 1892, #6222, AWTP.

87. AWT to unknown, no date, [1892?], #6025, AWTP.

88. AWT to Hon. Phillip C. Garret, [July, 1892?], item #6439, AWTP.

89. Ibid.

90. Catherine Impey to EKT and AWT, June 24, 1893, #7068, AWTP.

91. Wells, *Autobiography*, 104–5.

92. AWT to T. Thomas Fortune, July 1893, #7179, AWTP. Fortune initially passed Mrs. Mayo's letter on to Tourgée, as Mayo instructed him to do, with non-committal comments about it. Tourgée thus responded to Fortune, who he indirectly criticized for spreading the rumor. T. Thomas Fortune to AWT, July 9, 1893, #7112; and T. Thomas Fortune to AWT, July 15, 1893, #7129, AWTP; on Douglass's reluctance to assist Wells after she sided with Impey, see Ida B. Wells to Frederick Douglass, April 6, 1894. From Manchester, Eng. Ida B. Wells Papers, box 10, folder 6, UC.

93. Patricia Schechter, *Ida B. Wells and American Reform, 1880–1930* (Chapel Hill: University of North Carolina Press, 2001), 109.

94. Tourgée, "A Bystander's Notes," Oct. 26, 1894.

95. *Headquarters. National Citizen's Rights Association.* Broadside. Included with AWT to Flavius Josephus Cook, Oct. 15, 1893, F.J. Cook Papers, DU.

96. Regarding Wells's fund-raising activities, see T.B. Morton, the president of the Afro-American League, to AWT, July 7, 1894, #7874, AWTP.

97. Charles Chesnutt to Tourgée, Nov. 21, 1893, reprinted in *"To Be An Author": Letters of Charles W. Chesnutt, 1889–1905*, ed. Joseph R. McElrath, Jr., and Robert C. Leitz, III (Princeton: Princeton University Press, 1997), 79.

98. Charles Chesnutt to Tourgée, Nov. 27, 1893, in *"To Be An Author,"* 79.

99. Mrs. H. Davis to Benjamin Harrison, corrected and forwarded by AWT, March 16–17, 1892, BH.

100. Benjamin Harrison to Mrs. H. Davis, April 1, 1892, HP.

101. AWT to Benjamin Harrison, April 12, 1892, HP.

102. AWT to Prof. Jenks, May 26, 1892, #6273, AWTP.

103. AWT, "The Negro in the United States." Draft of speech for the African branch of the Ethnological Congress of the World's Fair, 1893, #7618, AWTP.

104. Susan B. Anthony to AWT, June 22, 1892, #6339, AWTP. Also *Programme of the Suffrage Congress. Commencing August 7, 1893 in the Memorial Art Palace, Michigan Ave and Adams Street, Chicago,* #7222, AWTP. Mildred I. Thompson, *Ida B. Wells-Barnett: An Exploratory Study of An American Black Woman, 1893–1930* (Brooklyn, NY: Carlson, 1990), 47.

105. Wells, *Autobiography*, 120–22; Linda O. McMurry, *To Keep the Waters Troubled: The Life of Ida B. Wells* (New York: Oxford University Press, 1998), 267.

Chapter 9: The Rejection of Color-Blind Citizenship: *Plessy v. Ferguson*

1. "Shall White Minorities Rule?" *The Forum*, 7 (April 1889): 146–47. First quo-tation, *Plessy v. Ferguson*, 163 U.S. 537 (1896), at 544; second quotation, AWT to Louis A. Martinet, Oct. 31, 1893, #7438, AWTP.

2. *The Civil Rights Cases*, 109 U.S. (1883), 25.

3. Booker T. Washington was, of course, the exemplar of this tradition. Despite his behind-the-scenes subversion of Jim Crow, Washington's public face of accommodation presented a serious obstacle to agitators like Tourgée, Wells, and later Du Bois. See W. Fitzhugh Brundage, *Booker T. Washington and Black Progress: Up From Slavery 100 Years Later* (Gainesville: University Press of Florida, 2003).

4. Historians who have made this critique include, Kevin K. Gaines, *Uplifting the Race: Black Leadership, Politics, and Culture in the Twentieth Century* (Chapel Hill, 1996), 29; and David W. Bishop, "*Plessy v. Ferguson*: A Reinterpretation," *Journal of Negro History* 62 (April 1977): 127; Harvey Fireside, *Separate and Unequal: Homer Plessy and the Supreme Court Decision that Legalized Racism* (New York: Carroll & Graf, 2004), 120–21.

5. [His emphasis]. Tourgée Brief, 29.

6. Draft of Tourgée's oral argument, #6472, AWTP.

7. Louis A Martinet to AWT, Oct. 5, 1891, #5760, AWTP; the gender of the litigant played an important part in other challenges to segregation law in which black women were denied access to the ladies car. See Barbara Y. Welke, "When All the Women Were White and All the Blacks Were Men: Gender, Class, Race and the Road to *Plessy*, 1855–1914," *Law and History Review* 13 (fall 1995): 262–316.

8. AWT to J.C. Walker, March 11, 1892, #6101; AWT to J.C. Walker, March, 1892, #7063, AWTP.

9. "Jim Crow is Dead," *Crusader*, July 1892, XU, quoted in Keith Weldon Medley, *We As Freemen: Plessy v. Ferguson* (Gretna, LA: Pelican, 2003), 157.

10. Martinet to AWT, July 4, 1892, #6377, AWTP; Medley, *We as Freemen*, 13–14, 32, 140–49; John R. Howard, *The Shifting Wind: The Supreme Court and Civil Rights from Reconstruction to Brown* (Albany: SUNY Press, 1999), 143–44.

11. Cheryl I. Harris, "Whiteness as Property," *Harvard Law Review* 106 (1993), 1747, footnote 179. Harris cites as her source Jack Greenberg, *Litigation for Social Change: Methods, Limits, and Role in Democracy* (New York: Association of the Bar of the City of New York, 1974), 14. Greenberg cites only Martinet's letter of Dec. 7, 1891, discussed below, which he refers to more accurately as evidence of "a bit of organizational and personal disagreement which seems to appear with more than ordinary frequency in cases seeking to advance principles." Keith Medley, whose *We as Freemen* digs more deeply into the social history of the Citizens' Committee movement in New Orleans than any other historical study, has found no evidence of conflict in the black community over the *Plessy* or *Desdunes* cases.

12. Also, Eric Sundquist has interpreted Martinet's advice to Tourgée about the complications arising from using a light-skinned woman as the plaintiff as "opposition" to the idea of using any mixed-race person. In my view, Martinet was not expressing an objection at all but merely discussing the difficulties in carrying out his request. Eric Sundquist, *To Wake the Nations: Race and the Making of American Literature* (Cambridge: Harvard University Press, 1993), 234. Other scholars whose work has reinforced this view include C. Vann Woodward, *American Counterpoint: Slavery and Racism in the North-South Dialogue* (Boston: Little, Brown, 1971), 224; Bishop, "*Plessy v. Ferguson*: A Reinterpretation," 127; and Gaines, *Uplifting the Race*, 29.

13. Louis A Martinet to AWT, Dec. 7, 1891, #5837, AWTP.

14. Eli C. Freeman to AWT, Aug. 4, 1890, #4872, AWTP.

15. Louis A. Martinet to AWT, Dec. 28, 1891, #5877, AWTP.

16. Kull, *Color-Blind Constitution*, 42, 47. See also, Harlan Phillips, "The Roberts Case: Source of the 'Separate But Equal Doctrine,'" *American Historical Review* 56 (1951): 510–18; Charles Lofgren, *The Plessy Case: A Legal-Historical Interpretation* (New York: Oxford University Press, 1987), 179–80.

17. Wendell Phillips's proposed amendment, quoted in Kull, *Color-Blind Constitution*, 62–63. See also Richard Kluger, *Simple Justice: The History of Brown v. Board of Education and Black America's Struggle for Equality* (New York: Alfred A. Knopf, 1976), 625–36; William E. Nelson, *The Fourteenth Amendment: From Political Principle to Judicial Doctrine* (Cambridge, 1988).

18. *Slaughter-House Cases,* 83 U.S. (16 Wall) 36 (1873); for evidence that the Thirteenth Amendment had been intended by its framers to prohibit racial discrimination of all kinds, see Alexander Tsesis, *The Thirteenth Amendment and American Freedom: A Legal History* (New York: New York University Press, 2002).

19. *U.S. v. Cruikshank,* 92 U.S. 542 (1876); *Civil Rights Cases,* 109 U.S. 3 (1883).

20. Brook Thomas, *Plessy v. Ferguson: A Brief History with Documents* (New York: Bedford Books, 1997), 24.

21. Albion W. Tourgée, *With Gauge and Swallow, Attorneys* (Philadelphia: J.B. Lippincott, 1890), 3.

22. Samuel F. Phillips to AWT, April 4, 1878, #2213; Samuel F. Phillips to AWT, Sept. 9, 1889, #4003, AWTP.

23. Ingersoll's speech was reprinted in Bishop Henry M. Turner, ed., *The Black Man's Doom. The Two Barbarous and Cruel Decisions of the United States Supreme Court . . .* (Philadelphia, 1896), 55, 58, SCBC.

24. Turner, *Black Man's Doom,* 55.

25. An extraordinary figure, Ingersoll was widely regarded to be the finest orator of his age, in an age of great orators. Best known for his outspoken agnosticism, and his fondness for "bloody shirt" speeches during Republican campaigns, he mirrored Tourgée's adherence to radical individualism in his politics and ideology. David D. Anderson, *Robert Ingersoll* (New York: Twayne, 1972), 2–3, 70–76, 92–93. Martinet to Tourgée, Oct. 5, 1891, #5760, AWTP; Bishop Turner published a pamphlet in 1893 of responses to the *Civil Rights Cases* that included Ingersoll's 1883 speech. He told Tourgée: "Things are growing worse all the time and the only two men in the United States who are saying anything that amounts to notice are you and Robert Ingersoll"; Bishop H.M. Turner to AWT, Nov. 2, 1893, #7454, AWTP.

26. Lofgren, *The Plessy Case*, 28–44, 57–60; Thomas, *Plessy v. Ferguson,* 5, "*Plessy v. Ferguson,*" Docket book, United States Supreme Court Records, NARA.

27. [His emphasis]. AWT to Louis A. Martinet, Oct. 31, 1893, #7438, AWTP.

28. Thomas, *Plessy v. Ferguson,* 180, 184–85.

29. AWT to Louis A. Martinet, Oct. 31, 1893, #7438, AWTP.

30. This quote comes from another letter of the same month in which he repeated many of these sentiments, see AWT to Bishop Turner, Oct. 1893, #7433, AWTP.

31. "Mrs. Tourgée Goes to Prison," *Washington Post,* Sept. 6, 1890. See also, "The Case of Mrs. Tourgée," *New York Times,* Sept. 2, 1890.

32. EKT to J.D. Rockefeller, RG1 (JOR), Series C3 (Office Correspondence), box 46, folder 349, Rockefeller Family Archives, Sleepy Hollow, NY. Also quoted in Scott Sandage, *Born Losers: A History of Failure in America* (Cambridge: Harvard University Press, 2005).

33. Ibid.

34. Ibid.

35. EKT's diary, Nov. 7, 1893, #9906, AWTP.

36. AWT to Bishop Henry McNeal Turner, Nov. 7, 1893, #7471, AWTP.

37. *Philadelphia Times,* June 18, 1892, clipping, #8251, AWTP.

38. Douglass's belief that no good could come of the challenge may have reflected a common misperception that the *Civil Rights Cases* of 1883 had already established the constitutionality of segregation laws. P.B.S. Pinchback promised to help but failed to deliver. Louis A. Martinet to AWT, July 4, 1892, #6377, AWTP.

39. Douglass quoted from William S. McFeely, *Frederick Douglass* (New York: W.W. Norton, 1991), 362.

40. AWT to Frederick Douglass, June 8, 1892, FDP.

41. AWT to "Madame" [Florence A. Lewis] with letters of June 1892, item #6297, AWTP.

42. Florence A Lewis to AWT, Dec. 2, 1891, #5816, AWTP.

43. Thomas W. Griffin to AWT, May 1, 1894, #7664, AWTP.

44. AWT to Louis A. Martinet, 1892, #6473, AWTP. Emma Lou Thornbrough, "The National Afro-American League, 1887–1908," *Journal of Southern History* 27 (Nov. 1961): 500–501.

45. Hazel Carby, *Reconstructing Womanhood: The Emergence of the Afro-American Novelist* (New York: Oxford University Press, 1987), 3–19; Schechter, *Ida B. Wells-Barnett*, 128–32; Alexander, "'We know our rights and have the courage to defend them': The Spirit of Agitation in an Age of Accommodation, 1883–1909" (Ph.D. diss., University of Massachusetts, Amherst, 2004), 36–37.

46. AWT to Joseph C. Price, [1890], #11043, AWTP; Alexander, "*We Know Our Rights*," 89–90. The incident was reported as follows, "This proposition [to accept Tourgée's letter] was opposed by several delegates on the grounds that Judge Tourgee was not an Afro-American, and that it was time for the Negroes to show they could get along without the help of white men. Prof. J.C. Price of [North Carolina] declared that Tourgee had written for the good of the Negro and knew more about the Negro question than many of the colored men themselves. He favored the adoption of good suggestions, no matter from where they came," "To Relieve the Whites: Afro-Americans Petition Congress," *Chicago Daily Tribune*, Jan. 17, 1890.

47. T. Thomas Fortune to AWT, Nov. 16, 1893, #7499, AWTP; Alexander, "'We know our rights,'" 98.

48. T. Thomas Fortune to AWT, Nov. 23, 1893, #7533, AWTP.

49. AWT to T. Thomas Fortune, Nov. 20, 1893, #7510, AWTP.

50. Ibid.

51. The origin of his distrust likely began with Fortune's controversial flirtation with the Democratic Party in 1886–1888, which rankled a great many loyal Republicans. In 1890, Tourgée warned League President Joseph C. Price about Fortune, including this harsh assessment: "Fortune, who is simply a restless, self-seeking, ambitious demagogue, will unquestionably foster [factionalism]. Do not allow him to speak for you and whenever occasion offers, withdraw yourself as much as positively as you can with all gentleness, from the area of his influence. He lacks the one essential of serious and successful manhood—sincerity . . . his idea of heaven is to be the focus of attention and he would see his race at the devil if it would make the world talk about him." AWT to J.C. Price, Jan. [?], 1890, #11043, AWTP; Emma Lou Thornbrough, *T. Thomas Fortune, Militant Journalist* (Chicago: University of Chicago Press, 1972), 86–95.

52. AWT to unknown, Aug. 1894, #8234, AWTP.

53. AWT to "Gentlemen," Aug. 1894, #8235, AWTP.

54. *Headquarters: National Citizens' Rights Association.* Broadside. Oct. 13, 1893, F.J. Cook Papers, DU.

55. From the "Atlanta Exposition Address," quoted in W. Fitzhugh Brundage, ed., *Up from Slavery By Booker T. Washington with Related Documents* (New York: Bedford/St. Martin's, 2003), 142–45. [Original edition, New York: Doubleday, Page, 1901.]

56. Martinet to AWT, July 4, 1892, #6377, AWTP.

57. Louis A. Martinet to AWT, May 30, 1893, #6998, AWTP.

58. Albion W. Tourgée, "Duty and Destiny," delivered April 16, 1894, #7635, AWTP.

59. Thornbrough, *T. Thomas Fortune*, 118–19, 161–71.

60. For more on this eulogy, see chapter 2. Albion W. Tourgée, *A Memorial of Frederick Douglass from the City of Boston* (Boston: Printed by the Order of the City Council, 1896), 62, 66.

61. N.E. Mansion, "Citizens' Committee," *Crusader*, February 14, 1895, clipping, Rousserve Papers, folder 28, ARC.

62. [My emphasis]. It is unknown whether Tourgée's letter to the Supreme Court Clerk played any role in preventing the case from being argued until he arrived. AWT to James H. McKinney, Esq., Clerk Supreme Court, United States Supreme Court, Appellate Case Files, NARA; Lofgren, *The Plessy Case*, 150–51.

63. Lofgren, *The Plessy Case*, 151.

64. *Washington Post*, April 14, 1896. Also quoted in Thomas, *Plessy v. Ferguson*, 127.

65. Tourgée oral argument, #6472. Some of this text is quoted in "Another Fool's Errand," *Washington Post* April 14, 1896, by a reporter who witnessed the actual presentation.

66. AWT to James C. Walker with letters of 1892, #6502, AWTP.

67. Scholars who have misread Tourgée's arguments on "whiteness as property" include: Woodward, *American Counterpoint*, 224; Bishop, "*Plessy v. Ferguson*: A Reinterpretation," 127; and Gaines, *Uplifting the Race*, 29. An interesting discussion comparing Tourgée's ironic strategy to Swift's "A Modest Proposal" can be found in Marcia Beth Bordman, *Dear Old Golden Rule Days: A Study in the Rhetoric of Separate-But-Equal in* Roberts *v.* City of Boston (1849), Plessy *v.* Ferguson (1896), *and* Brown *v.* Board of Education (1954) (Ph.D. diss., University of Maryland, 1993), 41–72.

68. [His emphasis]. Tourgée Brief 12–13.

69. Ibid., 12, 34–35.

70. Ibid., 34.

71. Ibid., 9, 17, 26.

72. Ibid., 19, 26.

73. Ibid., 14, 32.

74. *Slaughter-House Cases*, 83 U.S. (16 Wall) 36, (1873); *Plessy v. Ferguson*, 163 U.S. 537 (1896), at 542–43.

75. Tourgée Brief, 19–20. Section I of the Fourteenth Amendment reads: "*All* persons born or naturalized in the United States and subject to the jurisdiction thereof, are Citizens of the United States and of the State in which they shall reside. No State shall make or enforce *any* law which shall abridge the privileges and immunities of citizens of the United States. Nor shall *any* State deprive *any* citizen of life, liberty or property without due process of law, nor deny *any* person within its jurisdiction, the equal protection of the laws" [my emphasis]. Quoted from Tourgée Brief, 7.

76. *Strauder* held that a West Virginia law excluding blacks from serving on juries violated the Fourteenth Amendment. *Strauder v. West Virginia*, 100 U.S. 303 (1880). *Strauder* opinion quoted in Howard, *The Shifting Wind*, 146. On *Cruikshank*, see Eric Foner, *Reconstruction: America's Unfinished Revolution* (New York: Harper & Row, 1988), 530–31.

77. Tourgée Brief, 21–22, 26. Justice Field's dissent in *Slaughter-House* quoted in Foner, *Reconstruction*, 529.

78. Tourgée Brief, 5, 11, 24; oral argument, #6472, AWTP.

79. C. Vann Woodward's extremely influential reading of the case suggested that "this was not a defense of the colored man against discrimination by whites, but a defense of the 'nearly' white man against the penalties of color." Woodward, *"Plessy v. Ferguson*: The Birth of Jim Crow," *American Heritage* 15 (April 1964): 101; Woodward, *American Counterpoint*, 224; Luker follows Woodward's interpretation in *Social Gospel in Black and White*, 87.

80. Tourgée Brief, 10–11.

81. Lofgren, *Plessy Case*, 153–54.

82. Oral argument, #6472, AWTP.

83. Tourgée Brief, 31.

84. Ibid., 29.

85. [His emphasis]. Oral argument, #6472, AWTP; Tourgée Brief, 9.

86. [His emphasis]. Tourgée Brief, 8.

87. Ibid., 10.

88. S.F. Phillips and F.D. McKenney, "Brief of Plaintiff in Error," in *Landmark Briefs and Arguments of the Supreme Court of the United States: Constitutional Law* 13, ed. Philip B. Kurland and Gerhard Casper (Arlington, 1975), 11.

89. Bordman, *Dear Old Golden Rule Days*, 61.

90. See, for instance, Werner Sollors, *Neither Black Nor White Yet Both: Thematic Explorations of Interracial Literature* (Cambridge: Harvard University Press, 1999).

91. Tourgée brief, 35–36.

92. See also May 14, 1896, Emma's diary, #9906, AWTP.

93. *Rochester (N.Y.) Democrat and Chronicle*, May 20, 1896; *New York Tribune*, May 18, 1896; *Springfield Republican*, May 20, 1896. Quoted in Otto Olsen, ed., *The Thin Disguise: Plessy v. Ferguson, A Documentary Selection* (New York: Humanities Press, 1967), 124–32.

94. In his opinion, Brown appears to accept the argument of the state of Louisiana that Tourgée's points regarding Plessy's indeterminate race were irrelevant because information regarding Plessy's racial identity had not been properly introduced as evidence into the record during the original case. Tourgée's decision *not* to introduce into evidence whether or not Plessy was "colored" was probably an attempt to force Louisiana to bear the burden of defining Plessy's race. *Plessy v. Ferguson*, 163 U.S. 537 (1896), at 549 and 552.

95. Charles Lofgren, in *The Plessy Case*, argues that shortcomings of Brown's opinion are not necessarily of constitutional doctrine, in which his decision had a reasonable grounding, but in his flawed presentation with its excessive obiter dicta. Robert Harris, on the other hand, has memorably called Brown's opinion "a compound of bad logic, bad history, bad sociology, and bad constitutional law." Put more simply by Judge A. Leon Higginbotham, Jr., it was "a case wrongly decided." Higginbotham, *Shades of Freedom: Racial Politics and Presumptions of the American Legal Process* (New York: Oxford University Press, 1996), 108–18. Harris quoted in Sundquist, *To Wake the Nations*, 237.

96. Harlan's dissent reprinted in Olsen, *The Thin Disguise*, 117–18, 120.

97. Ibid., 117–19.

98. *Report of Proceedings for the Annulment of Act 111 of 1890 By the Citizens' Committee of New Orleans, La.*, 7–8, folder 13, box 1, Rousseve Papers (Amistad Research Center, New Orleans); Desdunes, *Our People and Our History*, 141–42.

99. Desdunes, *Our People and Our History*, 147.

100. The memory of the Citizens' Committee would live on, however, and in 1957 black civil rights leaders in New Orleans would create the new Citizens'

Committee paying explicit homage to Desdunes and Martinet. Lodson and Bell, "The Americanization of Black New Orleans," 258–60; Hirsch, 285.

101. Louis A. Martinet to AWT, July 4, 1892, #6377, AWTP.

102. Facts about Martinet's life are sparse: he was born on Dec. 28, 1849, and died June 7, 1917, but his public activism certainly ended with the *Crusader*. Quote from Louis A. Martinet to AWT, May 30, 1893, item #6998, AWTP.

103. Dean H. Keller, "Albion W. Tourgee as Editor of the Basis," *Niagara Frontier* 12 (spring 1965), 24–28; AWT to William McComber, Feb. 25, 18954, Rare Book Room, BEPL; Olsen, *Carpetbagger's Crusade*, 333–34.

104. *Tourgée to New Orleans Leader, quoted in* Cleveland *Gazette*, Feb., 25, 1899; Interestingly, when Tourgée recounted the history of the *Plessy* case in "A Bystander's Notes," he failed to mention the personal role he played in it; see Tourgée, "A Bystander's Notes," *Inter Ocean*, May 26, 1897.

Chapter 10: The Fate of Color-Blind Citizenship

1. Albion Tourgée to J.C. Price, [1890], #11043, AWTP. Epigraph quoted from John Ralston Saul, *The Unconscious Civilization* (New York: Free Press, 1995), 88, 164–65.

2. See his comments in chapter 5, "The Reconstruction Period," in *Up From Slavery*, in W. Fitzhugh Brundage, ed., *Booker T. Washington and Black Progress: Up From Slavery 100 Years Later* (Gainesville: University Press of Florida, 2003), 76–82

3. Washington, *Up From Slavery*, 71–75.

4. Albion W. Tourgée, "The Best Currency," *North American Review* 163 (October 1896), 416–27; Albion Tourgée, *War of the Standards, Coin and Credit versus Coin without Credit* (New York: G. P. Putnam's Sons, 1896).

5. Albion W. Tourgée, *To the People of the 34th Congressional District*, broadside, 1894, #7631, AWTP.

6. Speech, New York 34th District, "The Republican Party," 1894, #8247, AWTP. Perhaps Tourgée's fullest statement on his view that, among Republicans, loyalty to principle had been trumped by loyalty to party was "Nominations and Principles: Judge Tourgee Corrects An Erroneous Impression," clipping dated April 24, 1894, #7644, AWTP.

7. Tourgée reviews his history with Platt in AWT to Thomas C. Platt, Feb. 4, 1897, #9218, AWTP.

8. Booker T. Washington, "To whom it may concern," Feb. 22, 1897; Russell Alger to Sherman, April 30, 1897; H.H. Kohlsaat to Mrs. Tourgée, Feb. 27, 1897; Thomas C. Platt to William McKinley, May 1, 1897. Several petitions arrived also, including ones from the North Carolina State Assembly, the Pennsylvania and New Jersey State Legislatures, and from the citizens of Chicago, Illinois; Mayville, New York; Pensacola, Florida; and Osborne, Kansas. Consular Recommendations, State Department, NARA; Olsen, *Carpetbagger's Crusade*, 337–38; John Addison Porter to Thomas C. Platt, May 4, 1897, WMP; Wells, *Autobiography*, xxiii.

9. AWT to William McKinley, Aug. 18, 1900, WM.

10. Ida B. Wells, *Crusade for Justice: The Autobiography of Ida B. Wells*, Alfreda M. Duster, ed. (Chicago: University of Chicago Press, 1970), 253.

11. AWT to William McKinley, Nov. 23, 1898, WM.

12. Ibid.

13. Ibid.

14. AWT to E.H. Johnson, May 15, 1902, #9691, AWTP.

15. AWT to F.L. Barnett, Aug. 6, 1900, #9665, AWTP.

16. AWT to Theodore Roosevelt, Oct. 21, 1901, TR.

17. AWT to William McKinley, Nov. 23, 1898, WM.

18. On Wells, see Gail Bederman, *Manliness and Civilization: A Cultural History of Gender and Race in the United States, 1880–1917* (Chicago: University of Chicago Press, 1996); on other leaders, see Wilson J. Moses, *Creative Conflict in African American Thought: Frederick Douglass, Alexander Crummell, Booker T. Washington, W.E.B. Du Bois, and Marcus Garvey* (Cambridge: Cambridge University Press, 2004).

19. Albion W. Tourgée, "Does Injustice Pay?" in *The Violation of a Constitutional Right. Published by Authority of the Citizen's Committee*, ed. L.A. Martinet (New Orleans: The Crusader Print, August, 1893), 19–24, Charles Rousseve Papers, box 1, folder 12 A, ARC.

20. [My emphasis]. AWT to Theodore Roosevelt, Oct. 21, 1901, TR.

21. Evidence of this club comes from a mysterious slip of paper auctioned on www.historyforsale.com. Dated ca. 1883, the document reads: "We the subscribers hereby organize ourselves into a society to be called by the name of 'The Captain Rice Club' to meet annually on the evening of the last Tuesday of August." It is signed by James S. Baker, J. Osborne Baker, Noah Brooks, James N. Wilder, Theodore Roosevelt, Edward Everett Hale, William Lloyd Garrison, Henry George, Edgar Fawcett, Hezekiah Butterworth, Justin Huntley McCarthy, John James Ingalls, George Parsons Lathrop, Austin Dobson, Sir Walter Besant, Sidney Howard Gay, Albion Winegar Tourgée, Morton Q. Thaxter, Thomas D. Hinkley, and George Easton. Copy in possession of author.

22. [My emphasis]. AWT to Theodore Roosevelt, Oct. 21, 1901, RP.

23. Theodore Roosevelt to AWT, Nov. 8, 1901, RP; in discussing this passage, Eric Rauchway argues that Roosevelt spoke in similar terms about all social problem groups. In Roosevelt's rhetoric, he states, "troublesome people deserved nothing as much as a good shooting." Eric Rauchway, *Murdering McKinley: The Making of Theodore Roosevelt's America* (New York: Hill and Wang, 2003), 35–36.

24. Theodore Roosevelt to AWT, Nov. 8, 1901, RP.

25. Seth Scheiner, "Theodore Roosevelt and the Negro, 1901–1908," *Journal of Negro History* 47 (July 1962): 169–82; Thomas Dyer, *Theodore Roosevelt and the Idea of Race* (Baton Rouge: Louisiana State University Press, 1980).

26. Theodore Roosevelt, "Lincoln and the Race Problem," delivered to the Republican Club of New York City, Feb. 13, 1905. Published as a special introductory article in *Complete Works of Abraham Lincoln*, vol. 2, ed. John G. Nicolay and John Hay (New York: Lamb Publishing, 1905), v–xiv.

27. Ibid.

28. Scheiner, "Roosevelt and the Negro," 172; Joel Williamson, *The Crucible of Race: Black-White Relations in the American South since Emancipation* (New York: Oxford University Press, 1984), 351–54.

29. Frank Bell to AWT, June 21, 1894, #7821, AWTP.

30. Paul Buck, *The Road to Reunion, 1865–1900* (Boston: Little, Brown, 1937), 201–4.

31. Raymond Cook, *Thomas Dixon* (New York: Twayne, 1974), 40–51.

32. Thomas Dixon, Jr., "Southern Horizons: The Autobiography of Thomas Dixon. A Critical Edition," Karen M. Crowe, ed. (Ph.D. diss., New York University, 1982).

33. Thomas Dixon, Jr., to AWT, Feb. 25, 1888, #3368, AWTP. In this letter Dixon makes reference to "animated correspondence" they had when Tourgée was

editor of *The Continent*. Unfortunately most of Tourgée's correspondence from that time was lost.

34. Dixon, *The Leopard's Spots*, "Historical Note," unnumbered pages prior to title page.

35. Williamson, *Crucible of Race*, 158.

36. Williamson, *Crucible of Race*, 174.

37. Peter Jerome Caccavari, "Reconstructions of Race and Culture in America: Violence and Knowledge in Works by Albion Tourgée, Charles Chesnutt, and Thomas Dixon, Jr." (Ph.D. diss., Rutgers University, 1993), 256.

38. Robert Land, ed., *The Birth of a Nation: D.W. Griffith, Director* (New Brunswick, NJ: Rutgers University Press, 1994).

39. Ibid.

40. Williamson, *Crucible of Race*, 40.

41. Land, *Birth of a Nation*, 114; Griffith probably chose this passage because it was quoted by James Ford Rhodes in his celebrated *History of the United States from the Compromise of 1850 to the Final Restoration of Home Rule in 1877*, VI (New York: Macmillan, 1906), 307. Rhodes, in a footnote, impeaches the credibility of his own use of the quotation, calling it "the most fictitious part of this fiction" while still using it to illustrate the history of the Klan in his text. The same ambivalence carries over into Griffith's use of it in the film. Also see Tourgée, *A Fool's Errand*, 252.

42. Michael Rogin, "'The Sword Became a Flashing Vision': D.W. Griffith's *The Birth of a Nation*" in Land, *Birth of a Nation*, 276–86.

43. Albert E. Pillsbury, quoted in "The Birth of a Nation," *The Crisis* 10 (June, 1915), 69.

44. Du Bois quotes Tourgée's words from the *Chicago Inter Ocean*. See W.E.B. Du Bois, "Reconstruction and Its Benefits," *American Historical Review* 15 (July 1910): 796.

45. David Levering Lewis, "Introduction," *Black Reconstruction in America, 1860–1880* (New York: Free Press, 1998, org. 1935), ix, 186, 621.

46. Earl James Young, Jr., *The Life and Work of Oscar Micheaux: Pioneer Black Author and Filmmaker, 1884–1951* (San Francisco: KMT Publications, 2003), 88, 121, 205–6.

47. Olsen, *Carpetbagger's Crusade*, 335–44.

48. Albion W. Tourgée, *The Man Who Outlived Himself* (New York: Fords, Howard, and Hubert, 1898); Olsen, *Carpetbagger's Crusade*, 341; R.U. Johnson, associate editor, *Century Magazine*, to J.R. Howard, Nov. 7, 1896.

49. "The Growth of the Niagara Movement," *Voice of the Negro* 3 (Jan. 1906): 19–20. Olsen, *Carpetbagger's Crusade*, 352.

50. "Honor His Name: Negroes Speak of the Late Judge Tourgee. Rev. Mr. Berle's Reference to Booker T. Washington," *Boston Globe*, July 31, 1905. Similarly, the eulogist at Tourgée's memorial in Washington, DC, used the opportunity to attack Booker T. Washington, "Honor Garrison and Tourgee," *Washington Post*, Dec. 1, 1905.

51. David Levering Lewis, *W.E.B. Du Bois: Biography of a Race, 1868–1919* (New York: Henry Holt, 1993), 321–24.

52. "Last Rites Over Judge Tourgee: Ashes of the Famous Defender of the Negro Buried in Mayville, His Home," clipping, newspaper unknown, Nov. 15, 1905, #9907, AWTP. Booker T. Washington quoted in Olsen, *Carpetbagger's Crusade*, 350.

53. "In Memoriam. Tributes of Respect by Colored Citizens of Chicago to the Memory of Judge Albion W. Tourgee . . . Presented on the occasion of the funeral obsequies at Mayville, New York, November 14, A.D. 1905, by Mrs. Ida B. Wells Barnett," pamphlet, #9838, AWTP.

54. EKT to Charles L. Van Noppen, n.d., AWTP.

55. *Brown v. Board of Education* 347 U.S. 483 (1954).

56. Ibid.

57. For insightful discussions of King's debated place in American civil rights traditions, see Nikhil Pal Singh, *Black Is a Country: Race and the Unfinished Struggle for Democracy* (Cambridge: Harvard University Press, 2004), 1–14; and Michael Eric Dyson, *I May Not Get There with You: The True Martin Luther King, Jr.* (New York: Free Press, 2000).

Index

Note: Page numbers in italics refer to illustrations.